a century of genocide

UTOPIAS OF RACE AND NATION

■ ■ ■ ■

Eric D. Weitz

D0068664

PRINCETON UNIVERSITY PRESS

Princeton and Oxford

LIBRARY OF CONGRESS CATALOGING-IN-PUBLICATION DATA
Weitz, Eric D.
A century of genocide : utopias of race and nation / Eric D. Weitz.
p. cm.
Includes bibliographical references and index.
ISBN 0-691-00913-9 (alk. paper)
1. Genocide — History — 20th century — Case studies. I. Title.

HV6322.7 .W45 2003
364.15'1'0904 — dc21   2002030264

British Library Cataloging-in-Publication Data is available

a century of genocide

contents

Abbreviations vii

An Armenian Prelude 1

introduction
Genocides in the Twentieth Century 8

chapter one
Race and Nation: An Intellectual History 16

chapter two
Nation, Race, and State Socialism:
The Soviet Union under Lenin and Stalin 53

chapter three
The Primacy of Race: Nazi Germany 102

chapter four
Racial Communism:
Cambodia under the Khmer Rouge 144

chapter five
National Communism:
Serbia and the Bosnian War 190

Conclusion 236

Notes 255

Bibliography 311

Acknowledgments 339

Index 343

abbreviations

AfRGB	*Archiv für Rassen- und Gesellschafts-Biologie*
Cheka	Extraordinary Commission to Combat Counterrevolution and Sabotage
CPK	Communist Party of Kampuchea
DK	Democratic Kampuchea
EC	European Community
FVC	Fortunoff Video Collection (Sterling Memorial Library, Yale University)
ICTY	International Criminal Tribunal for the Former Yugoslavia
IMF	International Monetary Fund
JNA	Yugoslav People's Army
KWI	Kaiser Wilhelm Institute
LCY	League of Communists of Yugoslavia
MK	*Mein Kampf*
NATO	North Atlantic Treaty Organization
NDH	Independent State of Croatia
NEP	New Economic Policy
NKVD	People's Commissariat of Internal Affairs (Soviet secret police)
NSDAP	National Socialist German Workers Party (or Nazi Party)
RHA	Racial-Hygienic and Heredity Research Center
SPS	Socialist Party of Serbia
UN	United Nations
UNPROFOR	United Nations Protection Force
USSR	Union of Soviet Socialist Republics

An Armenian Prelude

Johannes Lepsius was a German missionary with decades of experience in the Ottoman Empire. In 1916, in the middle of World War I, he wrote a confidential report that circulated within the ministries in Berlin. Despite its top secret billing, the report quickly became known outside government circles. "The oldest people of Christianity," Lepsius wrote, "is in danger of being annihilated."[1] Some months earlier, the American consul in Aleppo, Syria, J. B. Jackson, had written to his superior, Henry Morgenthau, American ambassador in Istanbul (Constantinople), describing fearsome scenes:

> Men and boys have been deported from their homes in great numbers and disappeared en route, and later on the women and children have been made to follow. For some time stories have been prevalent from travelers arriving from the interior of the killing of the males, of the great numbers of bodies along the roadsides, and the floating in the Euphrates river; of the delivery to the Kurds by the gendarmes accompanying the convoys of women and children . . . of unthinkable outrages committed by gendarmes and Kurds, and even the killing of many of the victims. At first these stories were not given much credence, but as many of the refugees are now arriving in Aleppo, no doubt longer remains of the truth of the matter.[2]

The issue, Jackson noted, "is nothing less than the extermination of the Armenian race."[3]

Lepsius and Jackson were describing a genocide. The word did not yet exist, but both of them knew that they were witnessing something even worse than the pogromlike violence that had occurred earlier against Armenians. What they could not know, of course, was that the genocide of Armenians, one of the first of the twentieth century, displayed so many of the characteristics that would be replicated at other times and in other places around the globe, including Nazi Germany, Stalin's Soviet Union, Cambodia under the Khmer Rouge, and the former Yugoslavia, the four cases explored in detail in this book.[4] As in the genocides that would follow, the forced deportations and direct killings of Armenians were so widespread and systematic that they could have been organized only by a state with a clearly defined goal—to eliminate entirely a particular population that it viewed as a threat to its grand political ambitions. In each of these cases, a regime, partly out of desperation, partly because of utopian visions, seized the opportunity presented by war and severe internal crisis to transform dramatically the very composition of the population within its domain. To accomplish its goals, it relied on the security organs of the state but also mobilized broad segments of the population, which became complicit in the killings.

But modern genocides do not happen just because a particular regime wills them into existence. They are the result of political decisions executed at moments of crisis, but they are also embedded in complex historical processes, notably, the emergence in the modern world of race and nation as the primary categories of political and social organization. The Ottoman Empire—to return to the specific example—was once a vital, dynamic power. At its height in the sixteenth and seventeenth centuries, the Ottoman dynasty ruled a vast expanse of territory in Asia, the Middle East, and Europe. As with most early modern empires, never for a moment did its rulers think that all of their subjects had to possess the same religion or nationality. The empire was, by definition, multireligious and multinational. True, Christians and Jews were subordinated to Muslims, but they were also protected, and their communities were granted extensive autonomy. But by World War I, the Ottoman Empire had been battered for at least a century by encroachments of its Christian subjects in Europe, many of whom had won autonomy or outright independence; by internal disarray and corruption; and by competition from the new dynamic nation-states of Europe, whose powers rested upon the great wealth produced by industrial economies, colonial empires abroad, and complex but rational and efficient government bureaucracies.

From the 1830s onward, the Ottoman Empire had undergone various reform efforts, none of which had succeeded. In 1908 officers associated with the Committee for Union and Progress overthrew the dynasty that had ruled the empire for six centuries. Like the sultans before them, the Young Turk rulers of the late Ottoman Empire were groping for a formula that would help them revive the glory of the past in the vastly altered modern world of European hegemony. They sought various ways to restructure the empire, and among the programs on the palette of possibilities was nationalism. They also admired the prowess of the German military, whose officers, beginning in the late nineteenth century, helped train the soldiers of the Ottoman Empire. Among Westerners, Germans came to have privileged access to the Ottoman rulers, especially following the Young Turk revolution in 1908.

After the failure of the various reform efforts, nationalism seemed to be one of the formulas that might enable the Young Turks to create a new, vital empire, one that could unite Turkic peoples from Europe to Asia Minor to Central Asia. From their imagined view of modern Germany and modern France, the Young Turks understood nationalism as a key to the creation of a strong, powerful state that would be able to harness and mobilize the energies of the united people—for warfare to protect the integrity of the territory, for development to build the economy and culture and thereby create a lively, dynamic society that would be at least the equal of those of western Europe.

By World War I, Turkey was an empire in the throes of becoming a nation-state. In the conception of its rulers, the new state would be populated by an exclusive, homogeneous, Turkish population. That process immediately threatened the myriad of non-Turkic peoples in the empire, and no population was so endangered as the Armenians. Armenians were, after all, a people with a long history and culture, a powerful sense of their identity as descendants of the members of the first state to adopt Christianity (in 301). Like many minorities, they occupied important positions in the economy and professions, even though the vast majority of Armenians were peasants. Through the nineteenth century the Ottomans had endured the successful revolts of other Christian groups, including Greeks, Serbs, and Bulgars. With the backing of more powerful European states, these people had pushed the Ottomans nearly completely out of Europe. Since the 1870s, some Armenians had become politically active, shedding the subject people's mentality that had led them, for centuries, to pursue improvements in their conditions by appeals to the sultan. No less than the Young Turks, they came into contact with European ideas and movements—not via military advisers and diplomats, however, but in schools established by European and American missionaries and by travels to Paris and London and other European capitals. Impressed with the vigor and possibilities of nineteenth-century developments, they began to demand greater autonomy and political rights within the empire.

Ottoman rulers viewed the political activism of some Armenians as a serious security danger, especially in light of the shrinkage of Ottoman rule in Europe from the 1820s onward. Moreover, the Armenians' historic homeland stood right in the middle of an imagined pan-Turkish state. For Ottomans considering the road to Turkish nationalism, Armenians came to be seen as the great threat. Already in the 1890s massacres had erupted with the connivance of the authorities and had resulted in the killing of hundreds of thousands of Armenians. While horrific and tragic, these were still largely traditional forms of violence, much like pogroms against Jews in the Russian Empire, though on a vastly greater scale.

The Ottoman Empire's entrance into World War I raised the stakes dramatically. Germany pledged to its Ottoman ally that the empire would remain intact—even extend further at the expense of Russia—and that the coffers of Germany's powerful state and economy would be opened to it. On the basis of these promises and of its fear of further Russian intrusions, the Ottoman Empire joined the hostilities in November 1914. In the Balkan Wars that had immediately preceded the outbreak of the Great War, the Ottoman Empire had lost more territory and peoples in Europe, a blow whose impact can hardly be underestimated. Now the first total war in history—and the Ottomans entered the hostilities when the war's revolutionary character should have been clear—meant for the Young Turk rulers either heady success, the reconstitution of a Greater Turkish state, or utter catastrophe. The beginnings were not auspicious, with some disastrous military encounters. Increasingly, the rulers began searching for internal enemies—in total war, internal security was as vital as the army's defenses. Armenians, with cross-border ties to conationals in the Russian Empire, quickly became a target. More important—and as with so many other cases of genocide in the twentieth century—war provided the Young Turks with the opportunity to refashion drastically the very character of the population. The emergency circumstances of wartime and the heightened fears all meant that the rulers felt liberated to carry out extreme measures that they would not dare venture in peacetime. War provided the cover, but war also provided the great opportunity. If it all worked out, the Young Turks would rule a vastly expanded territory that would be purged of its "alien" populations, the Armenians chief among them.

The procedures began quickly after the empire's entrance into World War I. In February 1915 an order went out for the disarming of all Armenians. Since thousands of Armenian men were serving in the Ottoman army, this meant that they had to be forced out of the regular ranks, their weaponry taken from them, their status reduced to that of laborers. Groups of them were often summarily shot. Civilians also had their weapons taken from them. Then the government began deporting entire civilian populations. It issued the first order of deportation on 8 April 1915, and more extensive ones followed the next month. Typically, Ottoman officials separated men from women and children. Large numbers of men were executed outright, while the women and children were sent out on the long march from their homelands across the desert to Iraq and Syria. The only food and water they had was what they could carry, and sometimes even that was stolen from them. On the marches the columns were set upon by marauding bands, and the gendarmes accompanying the Armenians often joined in the depredations. Many thousands succumbed to starvation and beatings; others were summarily killed. The Young Turks also targeted leaders of the Armenian community. On the evening of 23/24 April 1915, in Istanbul, they rounded up scores of Armenian intellectuals, politicians, educators, and priests, who were deported inland and then executed. Similar measures were taken against notables in localities all over Armenia.[5] Churches were destroyed, names of villages and streets changed. As with the other genocides that would follow, the perpetrators sought to eliminate not just the presence of a people but their past as well.[6]

All over Armenia, the pattern described by Lepsius and Jackson prevailed—entire villages given an hour to gather what they could, then sent on the road, families often separated, small children left behind in the chaos. Armenians endured burnings with hot iron and continual beatings. Men and woman had their hair and nails ripped out. Countless thousands of women and girls were raped. By the time the columns of desperate refugees reached Aleppo, Baghdad, and other safe havens, half their members had been killed directly or had succumbed to the exactions they suffered, and the survivors were mostly women and small children.[7] Probably around a million Armenians out of a population of approximately 2.1 million were killed, a devastatingly large proportion of the population.[8]

If the experience of extreme deprivation and death was chaotic—no one in the columns of refugees knew when they might be set upon; survival was usually a matter of chance—there was most definitely an overall structure to the events. From the extensive reports, Lepsius concluded, correctly, that

[t]he deportations were ordered and carried out by the central government in Constantinople. Such extensive measures covering such

a vast area cannot have had any kind of accidental and uncontrollable origins.[9]

The Young Turk rulers had indeed ordered the deportations and had them organized by the Interior and War Ministries, which they commanded directly.[10] Alongside their regular troops and gendarmes, Ottoman military and civilian officials then mobilized into action extra forces, like Kurdish bands and the local party organizations of the Committee of Union and Progress. According to Morgenthau, minister of war Enver Pasha reacted with indignation when Morgenthau tactfully suggested that the violence against Armenians had not been ordered by the government, and that its subordinates had taken matters into their own hands. "We have this country absolutely under control," Enver told him. "I have no desire to shift the blame on to our underlings and I am entirely willing to accept the responsibility myself for everything that has taken place. The Cabinet itself has ordered the deportations."[11] To be sure, higher officials did not control every aspect of the events. Commanders and officials on the ground had a great deal of leeway in the implementation of orders. In the chaos that typically accompanies the extreme events of mass deportations and mass killings, all sorts of people—local residents, criminal bands, tribal groups— joined in to rob and beat those identified as "alien" elements and to steal their belongings and property. In the vast majority of towns and villages, officials made no effort to control the crowds. In this manner, the Young Turks fostered a broad-scale mobilization of segments of the Turkish population. They made genocide a popular event, though certainly some Turks protected their Armenian neighbors, and many of those who survived the desert crossing found refuge among other Muslims.[12]

To the Ottoman rulers, political repression of the Armenians no longer sufficed. A population marked, in this case, by its religion and nationality—one that, despite instances of violence, had largely coexisted with a dominant group—suddenly became targeted as the supreme danger. The very existence of the people constituted the threat, and, as individuals and as a group, they had to be eliminated by either forced deportations or mass killings, the borders between the two extreme policies never sharp and clear. Episodes of intercommunal violence like riots, pogroms, even warfare are tragic events that can result in substantial losses of life. But in the twentieth century, only states have the capacity to formulate and implement policies on the vast, systematic scale that modern genocide entails. Like the late Ottoman Empire, states engaged in genocides will mobilize and unleash their bureaucrats, armies, and loyal citizenry to carry out extreme acts of violence, which may appear random at the moment they occur. But as we shall see in more detail in the subsequent chapters, the violence overall is organized and has political intent — to eliminate physically one or more groups of people from the realm that the state controls.

■ ■ ■ ■

Genocides in the Twentieth Century

Genocides have occurred since the earliest recorded history, from the Israelite destruction of numerous communities in Canaan, depicted in the Book of Joshua, to the Roman annihilation of Carthage and its population. But beginning with the Armenians, genocides have become more extensive, more systematic, and more thorough. They represent a lethal, depressing culmination of the large-scale violence that so marked the twentieth century. Genocides stand at the center of our contemporary cultural crisis. They challenge our hopes for peaceful, tolerant coexistence among diverse peoples; they raise the deepest fears that the modern world we inhabit is not a site of continual improvement in the human condition but the very cause of more intense, seemingly unstoppable violence against civilian populations. In this book I try to provide a historical account for the escalation of genocides in the twentieth century by examining in detail four cases: Nazi Germany, the Soviet Union under Lenin and Stalin, especially the ethnic and national purges initiated by Stalin, Cambodia under the Khmer Rouge, and the former Yugoslavia. Each of the cases has its particularities, but together they also display some notably common features, especially in relation to the historical origins and the practices of genocide.

The word "genocide" is a much contested and overused term. Sometimes it is uttered with thoughtless abandon, and I hope, through the study of these four cases, to bring clarity to a word and a history heavily laden with the emotions of memory and politics. The word was invented in the 1940s by the international jurist Raphael Lemkin, who struggled to find a way to define the novelty of Nazi atrocities against Jews. But Lemkin also knew that there were precedents, notably in the late Ottoman Empire's genocide of Armenians. He hit on the Greek word *genos*, meaning a people or nation, and the Latin suffix of *-cide*, for murder. The United Nations codified the meaning of the term by adopting on 9 December 1948 the Convention on the Prevention and Punishment of the Crime of Genocide, commonly known as the Genocide Convention. By one recent count, the Convention has been accepted by 142 countries.[1]

Nearly everyone who considers the definition finds it insufficient for one reason or another.[2] It manages to be at one and the same time both too broad and too narrow. The Convention defines as genocide the intent to destroy "in whole or in part" a population defined by race, nationality, religion, or ethnicity. The Convention specifically does not include groups defined by their political orientation or class background. In the negotiations in the 1940s, the Soviet Union and its allies forced the exclusion of these categories for fear that its policies toward the peasantry and political opponents could be considered genocide. On the basis of the existing definition, for example, the regime in Indonesia could not be accused of genocide for the roughly 500,000 people it killed in 1965 because they were purportedly communists. The charge of genocide would be operative only if it could be shown that they were killed *because* of their Chinese ethnicity (as was true of so many of the victims). Similarly, if the Khmer Rouge were to come before an international tribunal, the indictment of genocide could be leveled only because of their treatment of Vietnamese, Muslims, and other minorities in Cambodia, but not for the vast repressions carried out against Khmer city dwellers and the educated elite. While the exclusion of populations defined by class and politics makes for too narrow a definition, the adoption of the qualifying term "in part" opens up a whole range of cases for consideration, including, for example, that of Native Americans.

For all of the difficulties surrounding the definition of genocide contained in the Convention, intentionality is clearly a critical criterion. For genocide to occur, there needs to be demonstrable intent to destroy "in whole or in part" particular population groups. This is a central point that distinguishes genocides from the civilian casualties that may occur in wartime, from pogroms, from massacres, from forced deportations — even if the number of victims is massive, and although any one of these actions may subsequently evolve into a genocide. By the criterion of intentionality, the atomic bombings of Hiroshima and Nagasaki were by no means genocides, however horrific the events, because the United States intended military victory over Imperial Japan, not the destruction of the Japanese people as such. One might also argue — though with much less certainty, I believe — that in its campaigns against Native Americans, the United States sought rather "typical," age-old territorial conquests achieved by warfare, not the physical annihilation of the Native American population.

Clearly, "intention" is not always easy to define. Since in most instances direct orders to commit genocide are rarely given, the case, both legal and historical, has to be built from the evidence of actions on the ground and often circumstantial links in the chain of command between those who occupy positions of power and those who carry out the actual killings. Despite some looseness in the wording that enables still looser readings, the Convention focuses on the *physical* destruction of defined population groups, not what is sometimes called cultural genocide or ethnocide (such as the forced assimilation of a group by preventing the use of its language). Nor does the Convention's definition encompass what we now call ethnic cleansing, the forced removal but not the killing of a population, although admittedly the line between genocide and ethnic cleansing can be quite indistinct. In fact, the initial General Assembly resolution of 1946 and the signed Convention of 1948 significantly narrowed Lemkin's original formulations, which had encompassed ethnocide and ethnic cleansing.[3]

Through its focus on intentionality, the fate of defined population groups, and physical annihilation, the Genocide Convention, despite its weaknesses, provides us with a fruitful working definition that can guide the study of past regimes and events. It is the definition I abide by in this book, though with perhaps a more restrictive interpretation than others might employ.[4]

In choosing the four cases for this study, I have been driven by concerns both substantive and personal in nature. To write about genocides in the twentieth century means grappling, of necessity, with the two very large and powerful dictatorial systems of twentieth-century Europe, Nazi Germany and the Stalinist Soviet Union. They happen to be, as well, the histories with which I am most familiar. But in writing a comparative study that moves closer to our contemporary world, I wanted also to trace the influences that these systems exercised, sometimes only indirectly, upon subsequent cases. The book is set up not only as the side-by-side examination of four parallel cases, but also as an exploration of the internal linkages among them. I do not argue that the Soviet Union and Nazi Germany learned from one another, although they were certainly highly attentive to one another's policies. They did, though, emerge out of a partly common historical background, notably World War I and the culture of violence that it spawned. And both systems had far-reaching reverberations that echoed well beyond their own life spans. Communism's influence extended out from the Soviet Union to the far reaches of Southeast Asia and the Balkans. As we shall see in the subsequent chapters, Soviet policies of the 1930s and 1940s had very direct bearing on the practices of the Khmer Rouge regime and of Yugoslavia even in its late stage of dissolution. Cambodia was of course spared Nazi influence, but Germany's occupation of the South Slav lands and its establishment of a puppet fascist state in Croatia in World War II played a significant role some fifty years later in the unraveling of Yugoslavia in the 1980s and 1990s. All the major actors in the Yugoslav crisis constantly referenced that history and mobilized its memory for their particular nationalist goals.

Another factor governed my choice of cases. A number of broad, general studies of genocides exist, and they have been important resources for me.[5] Many more detailed studies of individual cases have been written, and I have learned a great deal from these as well. Yet historians (as I am) tend to be averse to the large-scale generalizations or even lawmaking to which many social scientists are prone. Historians favor the detailed study of a particular place and time; they seek to render the nuance that comes with knowledge of language and culture as well as empirical facts, and to be open to the indeterminacy of events. At the same time, that deep immersion in the history of a particular people makes it difficult to move beyond individual cases, beyond the national frame that structures not only modern politics but the training of modern historians as well. I have sought in this book to tread a middle ground, to write a comparative study that tries to be faithful to the historian's propensity for detail, nuance, and contingency, but that also goes beyond an individual case to examine how, in the modern world, political models, not only capital and commodities, move in a global space.[6]

Each of these cases continues to generate high-intensity politics and emotions, and my treatment of them comparatively will no doubt arouse the ire of some. The issue is perhaps most raw in relation to the Holocaust because it occupies such a prominent role in contemporary culture, and because prior efforts to deal with it comparatively have so often been mendacious. Prominent scholars like Ernst Nolte in Germany as well as neofascist activists have sought to diminish the crimes of Nazi Germany by comparing them to other cases or by arguing that the Third Reich "merely" copied practices pioneered in the Soviet Union or elsewhere.[7] Needless to say, I completely reject that approach. But I also think that we should not allow our historical perspectives to be narrowed because comparisons have been done poorly or for notorious political purposes. The Holocaust was an atrocity of monumental proportions and the greatest tragedy in Jewish history. Like all historical events, it had its particular dimensions. The Nazis' industrial-style killing of Jews, rooted in Germany's highly developed bureaucratic and military culture, was and is unprecedented. But the Holocaust was not "unique" if by that term we mean an event that is incomparable and completely irreplicable. "Uniqueness" is a metaphysical or theological term. For historians, it can only have the mundane meaning that every event is specific to a time and place. Historians compare all the time, most often implicitly; indeed, the only way one could even sustain an argument of uniqueness is by comparison. If we insist on the incomparability of the Holocaust, we place it outside of history.[8] Instead, I work in this book in an explicitly comparative manner. The obvious, underlying premise is that many states, not just Nazi Germany, have organized the systematic killing of populations defined along national or racial lines. We can learn at least as much by looking at some of these tragic events together, exploring their similarities and differences, their historical links to one another, as by studying each case individually.

Similarities *and differences*. Each case of genocide has its particularities, and among the four that I explore in detail, I distinguish two "genocidal regimes," Nazi Germany and Democratic Kampuchea. My intent here is in no way to relativize or diminish the tragedies suffered by various populations, but, again, to bring some analytical clarity to a topic that is so emotionally and politically charged. Historically all sorts of regimes have perpetrated genocides. From the fifteenth to the nineteenth centuries European settlers acting under the aegis of liberal states annihilated indigenous populations in Australia and North America. In the first decade of the twentieth century a semiliberal German state committed the genocide of the Herero in Southwest Africa. As I will argue in chapter 2, the Soviet deportations of Chechens and Crimean Tatars were carried out in circumstances designed to lead to substantial death rates, so these events can also be characterized as genocides under the terms of the UN Convention. But in none of these cases did genocide come to constitute the nearly exclusive, central motor of the systems. A panoply of policies and concerns — economic development, social welfare, military security — played equal or even more important roles. Nazi Germany and Democratic Kampuchea, in contrast, unleashed such a vortex of violence that at some point in their existence, the actual physical annihilation of defined population groups moved to the very core of state policies, and all the normal aspects of governance retreated to the shadows. While genocides have not been uncommon, regimes on the order of these two have, thankfully, been less typical.

In writing this study, I have violated one of the historian's cardinal rules: to work only on areas where he or she knows the language of the people and has access to the primary sources. I have ventured far from my core areas of knowledge but felt that the last two of my selections — Cambodia and the former Yugoslavia — were at least partly justified by my familiarity with the history of twentieth-century communism. Yet I did not feel free to roam just anywhere, and readers will note that I do not deal with another very large and virtually undisputed case of genocide, that of Rwanda. There I felt that my lack of knowledge of African histories and cultures was too great, that its story should be left to those with much more substantial expertise. Moreover, while Rwanda was certainly shaped by Western colonialism, it lies outside the realm of Nazi and Soviet influence, a key factor that influenced my decision to explore the histories of Yugoslavia and Cambodia.

Of all the cases with which I deal, the literature on Nazi Germany and the Holocaust is the most voluminous. Histories, sociological studies, memoirs, philosophical ruminations — the literature is so vast that it is now beyond the grasp of any individual. As mentioned, it is also the case in which resistance to comparative analysis has been the greatest. Part of my impulse in writing this book has been my frustration, as a historian of Germany, with the constrictions of the national frame in German history and in Holocaust studies. But in some ways, this book is also an attempt to apply the insights gleaned from decades of scholarship on Nazi Germany and the Holocaust to other cases around the globe. In particular, my emphasis in this book on the dual character of genocides, their organization by states but also their enactment with high levels of popular participation, comes out of the vibrant discussions in the German field.

The tragic events in Cambodia and Yugoslavia painfully exposed as chimeras two hopes that were already rather forlorn: that the revelation of Nazi atrocities would forever stand as an obstacle to the reprise of such crimes in other places and at other times, and that the collapse of communism would lead necessarily to more prosperous and liberated lives in postcommunist societies. Clearly, something deeper has been at work than Russian or German particularities or even the many crises of Europe in the first half of the twentieth century. Those deeper currents, in my view, have to do with the very categories of race and nation, those inventions that define the modern world so thoroughly that we can barely imagine our histories and our contemporary lives without them. While there is no unmediated, direct connection between these categories and genocide — many national and racial systems are "merely" discriminatory rather than murderous, and in each of the cases, many other historical factors have to be taken into account — they lie at the heart of the genocides of the twentieth century, which is why I begin this book with an intellectual history of race and nation.

In none of the cases discussed in this book was genocide predetermined or inevitable, not even in Nazi Germany. In the chapters that follow, I try to delineate the various elements that, together, led to the unfolding of genocides. The chapters on Nazi Germany, the Stalinist Soviet Union, Cambodia under the Khmer Rouge, and the former Yugoslavia are structured similarly. Each begins with a section titled "Power and Utopia," which is about the ideological orientation of the movements and regimes in question. In each case, the leaders were animated by powerful visions of the future and sought to create utopia in the here and now. The transformations they sought to implement were so substantial that I characterize all four regimes as revolutionary. The leaders viewed the state as the key agency in the creation of the future society and sought to build states that would exercise total control over society. Though profound differences existed in the contours of the future each intended to create, each imagined a society bereft of difference and marked by a homogeneous population of one sort or another. Hence all the regimes discussed in this book obsessively divided and classified the populations under their domains. They went to great lengths to define the legal criteria of identities and then to place individuals in their "proper" class, national, and racial slots, the subject of the second section of each chapter, "Categorizing the Population."

The genocides discussed in each of the chapters did not emerge suddenly, and they were not the only forms of killing that the regimes implemented. Generally the genocides emerged after particular groups had already been subject to discrimination and exclusion, and the population at large had been barraged with incessant propaganda about their nefarious characteristics. Political and class opponents had also been repressed and killed, and preparations had begun for more extensive population purges. The third section of each chapter details these critical historical processes that formed the essential background to genocide. But these harsh and brutal policies did not quite constitute genocides.

Only at moments of extreme societal crisis—often self-generated—of immense internal upheaval and war, of great opportunities but also dread dangers, did the regimes initiate the most extreme form of population politics. The fourth section, "The Ultimate Purge," analyzes how each regime "tipped over" from pursuing discrimination and partial killings to perpetrating the more systematic and deadly policies of genocide.

These genocides were all the result of state policies. But genocides in the twentieth century became so extensive and systematic because the regimes engaged massive social projects that mobilized people for all sorts of activities, from the construction of dams to massive demonstrations to population purges.[9] The literal reshaping of the population could not simply be decreed and could not happen overnight; it had to be created by the hard work of thousands and thousands of people, whether obtained through force, begrudging compliance, enthusiastic support, or the innumerable forms in between. In the penultimate section of each of the chapters, "Rituals of Population Purges," I use eyewitness accounts, trial testimonies, memoirs, interviews, and poems and novels to explore how large numbers of people became active participants in the brutalities of genocide.

These four cases of genocide that I explore in detail are not the only ones that have occurred in the twentieth century. A variety of authoritarian regimes, sometimes acting with the tacit or direct support of the great powers, have also perpetrated genocides. But the four I have chosen have been some of the most important ones. The commonalities I have found among them may not apply to every single case of genocide; other historical factors may come into play in other situations. But I would venture that the combination of factors I delineate—ideologies of race and nation, revolutionary regimes with vast utopian ambitions, moments of crisis generated by war and domestic upheaval—might, in some form, serve as guides to other cases and warning signs for the future.

one

Race and Nation:
An Intellectual History

On 10 December 1948, the United Nations General Assembly approved the Universal Declaration of Human Rights. It was a great achievement that extended and deepened the venerable democratic principles espoused by the American and French Revolutions. The approval had come after months of difficult negotiations spearheaded by Eleanor Roosevelt. But the delegates apparently had very few disputes when it came to defining the categories that constitute the human population. After stating in the lead article that "[a]ll human beings are born free and equal in dignity and rights," Article 2 of the document went on to declare, "Everyone is entitled to all the rights and freedoms set forth in this Declaration, without distinction of any kind, such as race, colour, sex, language, religion, political or other opinion, national or social origin, property, birth or other status." Article 16 declared that everyone has a right to a nationality. Article 26 mandated that everyone has the right to education, which should "promote understanding, tolerance and friendship among all nations, racial or religious groups."[1]

How is it that the categories of "race" and "nation" appeared so self-evident, so natural to the delegates, that they required no further definition and hardly any negotiations about their meanings?[2]

Just a few years later, in 1955, and just a short walk from the UN building, the Museum of Modern Art (MOMA) displayed in its galleries *The Family of Man.* It would become the most famous photographic exhibition of the twentieth century. After its initial five-month run in New York City, *The Family of Man* toured the world for eight years. It appeared in thirty-seven countries on six continents and was seen by over nine million people. The exhibition catalog has been published in scores of languages and remains a popular item to this day. The brainchild of Edward Steichen, the famed photographer and onetime director of the Department of Photography at MOMA, the exhibition contained

503 photographs, which he had culled from over ten thousand images that had been submitted by amateurs and professionals from around the world. In Steichen's words, the exhibit "was conceived as a mirror of the universal elements and emotions in the everydayness of life — as a mirror of the essential oneness of mankind throughout the world."[3] Yet the power of the still image is such that the stunning photographs seem also to capture a certain timeless, unchanging quality of the people on display, as if they were the very embodiment of the distinct nations and races that make up the "essential oneness" of the human family. A small caption identifies the country of each photograph, fixing the notion of distinct nations in the mind of the viewer.

The Family of Man is a testament to the ideas of peace and human rights espoused by the UN in its Universal Declaration of Human Rights. Yet how is it that *The Family of Man* also assumed the division of humanity into races and nations with a certain fixed and timeless quality to them? And how is it that the categories that could be celebrated as representing the wonderful diversity of humanity were the very same categories through which states organized the most extreme violations of human rights, namely, genocides?

The categories race and nation are not, in fact, self-evident; they are not natural, timeless ways of understanding human difference and of organizing political and social systems. The word "race" dates only from the late fourteenth century and is of either Latin or Arabic derivation; its usage first became prevalent in the sixteenth century.[4] "Nation," rooted in the Latin *natio*, is a word with a much longer but also very diverse lineage. Like the Greek *ethnos* and *genos*, it simply meant a group of people, and writers from the ancient to the early modern world used it to describe all sorts of collectives: a kinship group, people with similar customs, the subjects of a particular state, or those with a common social function like students or even bonded laborers. Well into the Middle Ages, "nation" was often used pejoratively to refer to foreigners.[5] But in the modern period, the term has undergone such a profound transformation by becoming tightly bound to politics — to the form of the nation-state — that it has only a limited and restricted association with its earlier meanings.

Race and nation, far from timeless concepts, represent modern ways of understanding and organizing human difference. Ancient chroniclers were, of course, well aware of the great diversity of human life. Through the encounter with others, they sought to define better the particularity — and the higher moral and cultural standing — of their own people.[6] They often wrote and acted with enormous condescension and venom toward those outside their own group. In his *Histories*, written in the fifth century B.C.E., the historian Herodotus marked out the chasm that lay between the civilized Greeks and their barbarian neighbors by depicting, for example, the brutal customs of the Scythians, who lived as nomads and decorated their horses with the scalps of their victims.[7] In the Hebrew Bible, the Israelites' status as a chosen people gives them license utterly to destroy their opponents. After the walls of Jericho collapsed, the Israelites under Joshua's command "devoted to destruction by the edge of the sword all in the city, both men and women, young and old, oxen, sheep, and donkeys. . . . They burned down the city, and everything in it."[8] And so it goes with the other cities Joshua conquered—the Israelites "destroy" or "slaughter" everyone and everything in their path.[9] They humiliate rival kings by hanging their dead bodies for a day before unceremoniously dumping them into caves or covering them with rocks.[10]

But for all their intense hostilities toward outsiders, the Greeks and the Israelites did not think in terms of race, of fixed and immutable characteristics of a people, or of nation in its modern political sense. Neither Herodotus nor the anonymous authors of the Hebrew Bible ever imagined that in the lived world, all people of a particular group had to be politically unified with their own state. In the Bible's recounting, it took centuries of Jewish existence before the Israelites got a king and a state, and God himself was disappointed at their desire for political organization.[11] For a chosen people, the only true covenant was with God. The unified Kingdom of Israel lasted less than one hundred years, and the prophets who followed its division called not so much for the restoration of the political unity of the people as for their adherence to God's law. As for the Greeks, their political world was one of many city-states, with no sense that Greeks could or should live all together within a single political system. They warred against one another as much as they came together in alliances against external enemies like the Persians. When Alexander created a Hellenistic Empire in the fourth century B.C.E., it was, like all premodern empires, a vast multiethnic creation, and its rulers never imagined that all the subjects had to be of the same ethnicity or religion.

Nor was membership in a particular group completely closed and defined only by lineage, as the proponents of modern race thinking argued. To be sure, in the Bible the Lord's covenant is granted to a specific group, the children of Israel. But membership in the chosen people lay open to whoever accepted the covenant and Yahweh's commandments; it was not restricted to those who could claim, however fancifully, "blood" descent from the patriarchs. The Hebrew Bible recounts many instances of conversion and many allies, including those of quite different physical appearance from the Israelites. Kush (Ethiopia), a powerful nation, is counted among the friends of the Lord, Nubians among those who will eventually join in the covenant. In Psalms, Ethiopians are included "among those who know me," and God "records" and "registers" them—that is, he enters them in the book of life as faithful worshipers.[12] Individual Kushites play honored roles as a wife of Moses, a messenger to David, and an intercessor for Jeremiah.[13]

Christianity and Islam were even more open to those beyond the original community of believers, since both asserted the universal stature of their religions without identifying any particular people as chosen. Christians defined themselves from the outset as a community of salvation in Christ's body, not an ethnic, national, or racial group. As Saint Paul wrote to the Colossians: "In that renewal there is no longer Greek and Jew, circumcised and uncircumcised, barbarian, Scythian, slave and free; but Christ is all and in all!"[14] The great expansion of Islam resulted at least in part from its openness to all those who accepted Allah as the sole and indivisible God and Muhammad as his messenger.

Greeks considered themselves the most elevated people of all because they emphasized reason without excluding the passions, holding the two in appropriate balance. They generally used an environmental—not a "blood" or, in modern terms, racial—theory to explain the differences among people. Climate and terrain made some people fierce, others gentle, some wise, others savage, gave some a penchant for reason, others for the senses.[15] When people migrated from their area of origin, they, or at least their descendants, would adapt to the temperaments that prevailed in their adopted homeland. Herodotus related that when the Scythian traveler Anacharsis returned home after travels in Greece, he was killed because he had adopted Greek ways, and a similar fate awaited the Scythian king Syclas when his followers found him celebrating the rites of Dionysus.[16] Herodotus also described 240,000 Egyptian troops, left at guard posts unrelieved for three years, who decided to go over to the Ethiopians. "The result of their living there was that the Ethiopians learned Egyptian manners and became more civilized."[17] Culture and customs could be adopted or abandoned, they were not "natural" to the physical body, and nothing prevented the intermixing of groups. "Barbarian" was not a racial but a political and cultural concept, a term of contempt for those who had not mastered reason and rhetoric.[18]

Medieval Europeans often depicted outsiders in the most vile terms, as shown by even a cursory reading of the Church's condemnations of heretics and its tracts against Muslims and Jews. In the twelfth century, for example, Christian theologians condemned the heretic Henry of Le Mans by describing him as an animal, a "ravening wolf in sheep's clothing" and a "malicious fox" who moved about stealthily and deceptively. They also charged Henry with an assortment of sexual transgressions, from patronizing prostitutes to adultery to homosexuality. The "potent poison" of his speech supposedly "penetrated . . . the inner organs" of his listeners.[19] From the medieval *Song of Roland* to Luther's sermon about the Turks, Europeans depicted Muslims in similar fashion and associated dark skin with sin and apostasy.[20] The fervent language, which made beasts out of humans and awakened the deepest sexual anxieties, was not terribly different from the way North American slaveholders depicted Africans and Nazis described Jews.

Some scholars profess to see these medieval European expressions as evidence for the emergence of a "persecuting society" that then developed in a linear fashion to the modern world.[21] But overall the evidence for the medieval world is too mixed, the ruptures of the modern world too great, to permit any claim of continual development from medieval attitudes to modern race thinking and nationalism. Despite all its grotesque characterizations of "the other," the medieval Church held to its theological view that all people could be saved; it even welcomed Ethiopian Christians who made their way to Italy in the early fifteenth century. And only the barest glimmers of the modern nation-state are evident in the medieval period.[22]

To locate the birth of modern conceptions of race and nation, we need to turn to the eighteenth century, when Europeans developed new ways of understanding difference and invented new forms of politics. The intellectual and political leaps of this century did not emerge suddenly. They were rooted in nearly three centuries of overseas travel and conquest, which revealed a world far more diverse than anything Europeans had previously imagined. In association with New World discoveries, they also established more cohesive and assertive states and, perhaps most fatefully, colonial societies in which the benighted status of slavery became associated, for the first time in human history, with people of one and only one skin color. But before we explore the historical emergence of race and nation, some definitions are in order.

RACE, NATION, ETHNICITY

Race and nation represent ways of classifying difference. The two categories have never been hermetically sealed off from one another; rather, the lines between them are fluid and permeable. Nonetheless, for the sake of analytical clarity, it is important to disentangle them and to define the characteristics of each form of identity.[23] And they have to be defined in relation to a still more general term, "ethnicity."

The members of an ethnic group typically share a sense of commonality based on a myth of common origins (descent from Abraham in the case of the Israelites, from Hellen in later Greek accounts), a common language, and common customs. Ethnicity is the most open and permeable form of identity. Whatever the myth of common origins, outsiders are usually able to assimilate into the ethnic group by marriage and acculturation. Ethnic groups develop into nations when they become politicized and strive to create, or have created for them, a political order—the nation-state—whose institutions are seen to conform in some way to their ethnic identity, and whose boundaries are, ideally, contiguous with the group's territoriality.[24] In terms of acceptance of outsiders, nationality oscillates from fairly open to tightly closed forms. In the modern world, the states in which citizenship definitions are based upon political rights tend to be the most open (the United States, France); those that define citizenship by ethnicity tend to be the most closed (Germany, Romania).

Race is the hardest and most exclusive form of identity.[25] Race is present when a defined population group is seen to have particular characteristics that are indelible, immutable, and transgenerational.[26] Race is fate; there is no escape from the characteristics that are said to be carried by every single member of the group, bar none. Races can "degenerate" if they become "defiled"; they can go on to still greater accomplishments if they become "pure." But the essential characteristics of each race are seen as immutable, and they are borne "in the blood" by every individual member of that race. While racial distinctions have most often been based on phenotype, race is not essentially about skin color but about the assignment of indelible traits to particular groups. Hence ethnic groups, nationalities, and even social classes can be "racialized" in particular historical moments and places.[27]

Unlike ethnicity, race always entails a hierarchical construction of difference. Racial movements and states understand their creation and defense of a racial order as the great historical task of making the political and social world conform to the reality of nature, with its fixed system of domination and subordination. While ethnicity is often self-defined — and this was Max Weber's classic, subjectivist definition of an ethnic group — racial categorizations are most often assigned to a group by an outside power, usually a state, though over time, the group may then develop its own racial consciousness.[28] Ethnicity or nationality by no means always or necessarily takes on racialized forms, but the possibilities are certainly present, all too easily present when modern states seek to limit the pool of citizens and strive actively to shape the very composition of society. Moreover, while biology provided the pseudo-scientific underpinnings for race thinking in its heyday, roughly 1850 to 1945, race can also have a cultural basis. As the French theorist Étienne Balibar writes: "[B]iological or genetic naturalism is not the only means of naturalizing human behaviour and social affinities. . . . [C]ulture can also function like a nature, and it can in particular function as a way of locking individuals and groups a priori into a genealogy, into a determination that is immutable and intangible in origin. . . . [This perspective] naturalizes not racial belonging but racial conduct."[29]

While ethnicity has existed since time immemorial, race and nation emerged together historically in the Western world from around 1700 onward.

NEW WORLDS AND NEW IDEAS

Slavery was a standard and accepted institution of human societies until the nineteenth century. But slavery in the Americas expanded so forcefully and became such a central element of New World societies because it was intrinsically bound up with the rise of a global system of commercial capitalism.[30] By the eighteenth century, the colonial powers had made slavery a condition only of Africans and their descendants, a historically unprecedented development in which the debased condition of slavery became linked to people of only one skin color. The origins of "racial slavery" are much debated by scholars, some of whom see its emergence as the result of long-standing and deep-seated European prejudices against blacks and the concomitant cultural prohibitions on enslaving whites and Native Americans; others assert that traders and plantation owners simply found it more economical to enslave Africans.[31] Even if one accepts the former explanation, in the eighteenth century "mere" prejudice gave way to a far more comprehensive way of articulating and legislating human difference, a perspective that would also underpin many of the genocides of the twentieth century. Race thinking, formulated in the complex interactions among Europeans, Native Americans, and Africans, established a fixed hierarchy of difference rooted in the body. Race locked Africans into a position of eternal inferiority and also explained the middle ranking of Native Americans and the superior position of Europeans on the racial scale.

Race was made as European thinkers pondered the meaning of slavery and the world of great diversity. It was also made in colonial societies, in the interactions "on the ground" of Europeans, Native Americans, and Africans. The many sexual relations and even marriages across these lines and the "mulatto" progeny that resulted confounded clear lines of difference and became the flashpoints for establishing far more rigid boundaries designed carefully to demarcate groups from one another.[32] By attempting to place people in fixed categories, colonial legislation and social practices contributed decisively to the making of race. In the British colonies the matrilineal organization of Native American societies and the relative power — economic, social, sexual — that Indian women possessed seemed a direct threat to the more fervently patriarchal organization of English social life.[33] Many settlers feared that their European-derived religion and culture would dissipate in the unstable conditions of the colonies. In the early years of colonization, many of the settlers had expected Indian women to become assimilated into British colonial society by adopting British mores. They even expected Indian women to change physically; over time, through their relations with white men, their skin tones would "blanch," which would also signify transformed inner beings.

But in the course of the eighteenth century, ideas of fixed differences rooted in the body took hold as British settlers expanded their hold on the land. European men who engaged in long-term relationships with Indians or Africans were increasingly seen as endangering the entire colony.[34] A series of laws in the British colonies, starting with Virginia in 1691, banned marriages between white colonists and blacks or Indians and, in many cases, mulattoes as well. Additional laws, as in North Carolina, slapped supplemental taxes on those who had intermarried prior to the legal ban on such unions. The virulent language of the laws reflected a new level of racialization, and the tones would reverberate into the twentieth century (as we shall see in subsequent chapters). The intent of the new legislation was to prevent the "abominable Mixture and spurious Issue" that resulted from mixed unions.[35] As Kirsten Fischer writes:

> Laws against intermarriage helped define racial boundaries and contributed to the meaning of "race" itself. The expanding scope of the prohibition, which went from banning an "Indyan" spouse to outlawing marriage to someone with even one nonwhite grandparent, made race seem like a physically real and transferable substance, as if some essential "Indianness" coursed through blood lines in diminishing strength with every generation of added "whiteness." Only after three generations would such a mixture be so diluted as not to pose a significant threat of pollution to "white" blood. Marriage laws naturalized the idea that race inhered in the body as something substantive that was passed on to others.[36]

Older environmental and cultural understandings of difference — the kind of understanding that ancient Greeks and Hebrews had articulated — were overthrown with this newer conception that difference was rooted in the body itself and constituted a definable essence, for good or bad. This fatal move had to do with the colonists' perceived need to articulate their differences from — and superiority to — the Native Americans they conquered and the Africans they enslaved. The higher moral and cultural status of Europeans was now seen to inhere in their very bodies, the lowly status of Indians and, especially, Africans in their darker-skinned bodies. In response, Native Americans also began to transform their traditional understandings of difference into racialized ones, as did, ultimately, Africans and their descendants.[37] Racialization attempted to establish clear lines of difference among the three groups but also entailed a homogenizing process within each population.[38]

In this setting, "virtue" and "honor," especially of white women, became synonymous with monoracial sex and marriage. A whole set of limitations on slaves — their inability to control the status of their own children, restrictions on their movements, prohibitions on their carrying firearms and engaging in trade — further demarcated them from Europeans and Indians and solidified a racial caste system in the British colonies.[39] But perhaps more than anything else, the violence exercised against Africans defined the new reality of race and demonstrated, despite the continued existence of free black communities, the association of slavery and blackness. Over the course of the eighteenth century, the colonies regulated and limited the violence that could be exerted against white servants. In contrast, whites could enact virtually boundless violence against slaves. Since the atrocities were often visible on the bodies of slaves in the form of amputations or brandings, they served further to codify racial conceptions that rooted difference in the collective body of each group. Sexual violence — the liberties slaveowners took with their female slaves, the legal right slaveowners had to castrate male slaves who ventured to challenge their subordinate status — only intensified this trend. Rape and castration signified the ultimate physical and psychological power of the master, the utter dehumanization of his victims, but also his underlying, quaking fear.[40] As Fischer writes, "the divergence in legally acceptable forms of violence reinforced the idea that the bodies of African Americans were innately different and inherently 'black.' Violence was a social practice, another performance of race, that transformed official categories of race into a physical relationship."[41]

In the modern world, then, the "social death" of slavery, the complete dehumanization of slaves, became, for the first time, congruent with a population seen to possess a particular skin color. Slaves in previous societies had been subject to all sorts of bodily exactions and tortures, had been disparaged and denigrated. But few slaves in complex civilizations had been so completely demeaned as those in the New World. As David Brion Davis writes, "In no ancient society was the distinction between slave and freeman so sharply drawn as in America."[42] If slavery, by the eighteenth century, had made an essentially homogenous "black" race out of Africans of highly diverse ethnicities, it had also turned Europeans and Indians into races, since any individual categorization has to be part of a relational system.

In close connection with the creation of racial slavery, Europeans after 1500 strove to make sense of a world they now knew was much larger and much more variegated than they had ever imagined, and of a Christendom shattered by the Reformation into many competing groups. The effort to understand this new, exciting, and troubling world unfolded in both political and scientific realms, fields of endeavor that were, in any case, not so sharply distinguished as in our own day.

According to Hannah Arendt in her classic work, *The Origins of Totalitarianism*, Thomas Hobbes was the theorist who first broke radically with the received understandings of politics that had dominated ancient and Western society for nearly two millennia.[43] By positing that humankind existed naturally in a state of war and all individuals sought to pursue their egotistical interests, Hobbes destroyed the classical political check on race thinking and nationalism, the nonracial, nonnational distinction between virtue (or faith) and barbarism (or sin). Moreover, Hobbes contributed to the general secularization of European thought, a development that breached two powerful tenets of Christian thinking that, previously, had also served as a defense against race thinking. In Christian dogma, all human beings are imperfect; every individual embodies both sinful and divine characteristics. As Christian teachings weakened, an opening was created for a Manichaean perspective, one that "externalized evil."[44] Dangerous, sinful traits could be cast in toto onto other population groups, leaving—depending on the proclivities of the writer—Aryans or Nordics, English, French, or Germans, pristine and divine, the embodiment of strength, goodness, and achievement. As the body of Christ waned as the symbol of community, the racialized body, radically segregated by skin color, arose to take its place. This new symbol was rooted in the Christian spiritualization of the body but eliminated "the Christological element."[45] To the extent that the human body is, in Christian theology, ephemeral, it can never be seen as the ultimate determinant or symbol of moral or political value. But when secularization broke through that limit, the body was set free to become a symbol of a different sort: the racialized body now became the outer marker of inner worth, or of inner damnation.

The French philosopher Jean Bodin expressed such a perspective by arguing that human characteristics derive from nature, and the inner being is evident in outer, bodily forms. Men are formed not in politics but in nature.[46] Such an interpretation commingled easily with John Locke's emphasis on observation and Montesquieu's division of the human species into immutable groupings based on geography and climate. Unsurprisingly, Montesquieu praised the inhabitants of the north, the well-governed English and Scandinavians who had created liberty from its origins in the Germanic tribes. But Africans, he wrote, were beyond the pale: "It is hardly to be believed that God, who is a wise Being, should place a soul, especially a good soul, in such a black ugly body. It is so natural to look upon colour as the criterion of human nature." In these two brief sentences, Montesquieu made four significant moves in the direction of race thinking. He gave eternal characteristics to human groups based on skin color; argued that physiognomy, outward appearance, expresses inner being; made one group, Africans, incapable of ever joining the circle of the elect; and "naturalized" skin color as a marker—"it is so *natural*," he wrote. Hence the correct political order had to reflect particular racial properties.[47]

But a fully developed theory of race required a new science of human-kind. This is what anthropology, an Enlightenment invention, provided. Enlightenment thinkers fervently sought to redefine the place of human-kind in nature. Their critique of Christianity had undermined the primacy of religious dogma, setting human beings adrift in a sea of uncertainty. They had to be reanchored, and a desanctified, presumably scientific "nature" provided the weight.[48] Moreover, travel accounts from Persia, India, the South Sea Islands, and the west coast of Africa came to constitute a veritable genre in the eighteenth century, the stories of strange and exotic places and peoples very popular with an increasingly literate public. The great variety of cultures, languages, and appearances had to be explained. Religion, philosophy, and science, anthropology preeminently, all joined the fray.

Through their penchant for careful observation, scientists had already begun to categorize the natural elements of the universe. The Swedish botanist Carolus Linnaeus in the eighteenth century rigorously, even maniacally, classified all sorts of plants, establishing a methodology and a general scientific attitude about the virtues of classification that prevail to the present day. Soon after Linnaeus, geologists began to classify rocks and started to understand how to read prehistory through sedimentary layers. From the determination to categorize all flora and fauna in the world it was but a short step to categorizing human beings in a similarly rigorous, supposedly scientific manner.

Linnaeus himself had made some rough categorizations of the human species. He identified the European as "ingenious," the Asian as "melancholy," and the African as "crafty, lazy, careless."[49] Other writers, less scientifically minded than Linnaeus, popularized the concept of race in historical and class terms. The comte de Boulainvilliers defended the French nobility as a unified caste descended by blood from one of the Germanic tribes, the "Francs." They had conquered the "Gaules," whose descendants now were the commoners of the realm, the myriad elements of the Third Estate. The two classes of France were not united under the banner of king or nation; they were distinct entities, divided by blood descent, and their only contact entailed the conquest and rule of the one over the other.[50]

But the key figure in the emergence of the new discipline of anthropology was Johann Friedrich Blumenbach (1752–1840), whose *On the Natural Variety of Mankind* insisted on both the unity of the human species and the diversity within it, a diversity that could be accounted for only through rigorous scientific observation.[51] His "epoch-making catalogue of human races," in Peter Gay's words, included just five, each assigned to its own region of the globe — Caucasian, Mongolian, Ethiopian, American, and Malay.[52] For the next two hundred years, just about down to the present day, scientists would dispute the number and types, but not the effort to define and categorize races. Blumenbach's own collection of skeletons, the raw material of his scientific researches, would be rivaled only by the anthropologists of the nineteenth century who began to collect skulls and measure the cranium as a way of determining race-linked intelligence.[53]

At the same time that Enlightenment thinkers pondered the diverse origins of humankind and located difference in the body, another strain of Enlightenment thought radically postulated equality among men. This is, of course, the Enlightenment that figured so prominently in the language of the American Declaration of Independence and the French Declaration of the Rights of Man and Citizen.

By creating republics, the American and French revolutionaries made the nation the critical locus of political rights. In so doing, they dramatically altered the received understanding of "nation." No longer was the term reserved for the aristocracy or other legally defined groups. Instead, the American and French revolutionaries fused the concepts of nation and people, as reflected in the stirring words that begin both the Declaration of Independence and the Declaration of the Rights of Man and Citizen. Both the Americans and the French understood their movements as world-historical in significance, as expressed in the many metaphors of illumination that accompanied their efforts — the beacon, the shining light, the city on the hill bathed in sunlight. More practically, the French, by conquering the continent, carried the idea of the nation all across Europe. As Eric Hobsbawm writes about the impact of the French Revolution on the meaning of the nation: "Whatever else a nation was, the element of citizenship and mass participation or choice was never absent from it. . . . The equation nation = state = people . . . also implied a multiplicity of nation-states so constituted."[54]

Yet from the outset the meaning of the nation was laden with tension. As numerous feminist scholars have argued, the concept of equality was in fact highly gendered. The French Revolution opened up possibilities for imagining gender equality, as in Olympia de Gouges's Declaration of the Rights of Woman, penned just a few years after the Declaration of the Rights of Man and Citizen. Yet none of the revolutionaries was willing to go so far as to institute the equality of the sexes in law. In fact, as Joan Landes has argued, the French Revolution invested the concept of citizenship with qualities deemed to inhere only in men, like rationality and eloquence, and thereby inscribed a much more rigid division of the sexes that presumed the subordination of women.[55] Furthermore, citizenship was also limited to men of property. In important ways, the unpropertied were placed in a category with women, both considered dependents and therefore incapable of acquiring the independence and rationality upon which a republic had to rest.

Most important for the topic of this book, both revolutions articulated the nation not only in terms of gendered citizenship, but also as an ethnic and racial community. To be sure, the linkage of political rights with the sovereignty of the nation marked an enormous advance in democratic practices. The principles of both revolutions continue to resonate around the globe. Yet both revolutions oscillated between understandings of the nation as a political community bound by citizenship and as an ethnic or racial community bound by language and descent.[56] Slaves were denied any rights by the framers of the American Constitution. The reason for this blatant violation of the Enlightenment universalism that underlay the hallowed principles of democracy and the self-creation of a political community had to be located in the body, in the supposedly deficient racial constitution of African-descended populations. Thomas Jefferson, slaveowner and Enlightenment thinker, wrestled with this problem his entire life, giving it various turns. Ultimately, his understanding of the irreducible and incommensurable difference between black and white led the author of the Declaration of Independence to articulate a racial definition of the nation in conjunction with his radical republicanism.[57] In *The Federalist Papers*, John Jay articulated well the veil of deception composed of race when he wrote that "Providence has been pleased to give this one connected country to one united people — a people descended from the same ancestors, speaking the same language, professing the same religion, attached to the same principles of government, very similar in their manners and customs."[58] For Jay as for so many others, the nation was constituted not just in the political terms of republican citizenship but in terms of race as well, a tendency that burgeoned in the succeeding decades.[59]

The French revolutionaries, under pressure from slave revolts in the Caribbean, ultimately granted equality to free people of color and then abolished slavery. But in the long, tortuous discussions on these issues, many revolutionaries advocated an identity for France that was explicitly white and European.[60] Caribbean mulattoes and their supporters in the National Assembly and Convention defended the claim for equality precisely on the ground that the mulattoes were of partly white ancestry. On a less severe note, the attempt to impose linguistic uniformity on a heterogeneous population was also articulated in ethnic and racial terms, since those who resisted standard French came to be seen as "foreign." For the French revolutionaries, the nation was never only a political community, the realization of the Rousseauian myth of the social contract.

Indeed, William H. Sewell, Jr., has shown how the abbé Sieyes, the paragon of republicanism, the author of *What Is the Third Estate?* adopted a virulent racialized language that mitigated the political constitution of the nation that his pamphlet so fervently promoted.[61] Sieyes inverted the racial ideology that had developed over the course of the eighteenth century in defense of aristocratic privilege. He endowed commoners with all the noble (and inheritable) traits, the aristocracy with all the nefarious (and inheritable) traits. In defining who precisely could be a member of the nation, Sieyes deployed two key ideas—social utility and biological health—that we shall see deployed in each of the subsequent cases of genocide. Social utility became, perhaps, the most ubiquitous language of modernity, one used by liberals, socialists, communists, fascists, and nationalists generally, often with a racial tenor. To Sieyes, the members of the aristocracy could never be members of the nation because they performed no socially useful acts. They did not *produce* but lived a life of leisure off the labors of others. The nobility, he claimed, "is not part of our society at all; it may be a burden for the nation, but it cannot be a part of it."[62] The nobility was even dangerous to the health of the nation. The nobility constitutes a "horrible parasite eating the living flesh of an unfortunate man"; nobles are "vegetable parasites which can only live on the sap of the plants that they impoverish and blight."[63] Were nobles to be included, the social body of the nation would be completely sapped of its vitality. Sieyes writes:

> Do not ask what is the appropriate place for a privileged class in the social order. It is like deciding on the appropriate place in the body of a sick man for a malignant tumor that torments him and drains his strength. It must be *neutralized*. The health and the order of the organs must be restored, so as to prevent the formation of noxious combinations that vitiate the essential principles of life itself.[64]

This was a language that would reverberate through the decades as race thinking became ever more prevalent in the West, ever more firmly grounded through the proliferation of the nation-state and the rise of the biological sciences.

This "slippage" from the nation as a political community to the nation as a racial community became more prevalent when culture, not political rights, was made the defining element in the formation of the nation — an intellectual move accomplished largely by German theorists. Certainly, it is easy to understand why intellectuals in central Europe, devoid of a nation-state, claimed to find the nation in language, culture, and race, while the French, who had something akin to a single state going back centuries, could formulate a political concept of the nation. Johann Gottlieb Fichte and Johann Gottfried von Herder, two of the key figures in the formulation of a cultural concept of the nation, pursued problems set out by Immanuel Kant but focused more clearly on the relation of the individual to the collective. As an individual "grew into" freedom (in a Kantian sense), moved from the childhood of ignorance and bondage to the adulthood of self-knowledge and freedom, so the political form of the nation-state grew from — and remained organically linked to — the original manifestations of being in language and culture. And if, as Kant argued, there were preexisting mental categories like time and space that made possible the individual's journey of self-discovery, similarly the preexisting categories of human society were nations or races, timeless, eternal entities that underpinned the journey to collective self-consciousness and self-rule. Freedom is the self-determining nation, and, as Fichte also argued, consists of the individual's recognizing his indivisible connection to the totality. To reach the stage of autonomy and freedom that was its grand destiny, the nation, like the individual, had to struggle; it needed a severe countenance, an aesthetic temperament designed to conquer freedom as one climbs a mountain.[65]

Neither Kant nor Herder nor Fichte ever denied the essential unity of the human species, and Herder specifically rejected the terminology of race.[66] But the problem that preoccupied them, the more telling reality, was the diversity of human beings, a diversity rooted in nature, in God's creation, expressed first in language, then culture, then in political guise through the state. Herder and Fichte wrote about people and nations. But by defining a people as a closed community whose ties to one another were primordial — based in language and culture — the concepts they developed and the language they deployed slid easily into racial categories. Ernst Moritz Arndt, for example, claimed in 1815: "The Germans have not been bastardized by foreign peoples. They have not become mulatto. . . . The fortunate Germans are a genuine [*ursprüng-liches*] people."[67] With these kinds of comments, Arndt and others of his contemporaries virtually dissolved the distinction between nation and race, a process we shall see at work in the genocides of the twentieth century.

FROM ROMANTICISM TO RACE SCIENCE

By the turn into the nineteenth century in the West, race and nation had become established, though not necessarily predominant, ways of understanding human difference. New World slavery and more cohesive states; the writings of Hobbes, Linnaeus, and Blumenbach; the eruptions of the great revolutions of the late eighteenth century—all these trends contributed to the creation of new systems of classification that placed people in the categories of race and nation. Yet religion, village, and empire still framed the lives of so many people and, in various places, they coexisted—sometimes easily, sometimes not—with the more modern forms of race and nation. But over the course of the nineteenth century, new political and intellectual developments would make race and nation, along with gender, the most prevalent and powerful forms of articulating the differences among people and of organizing political and social systems.

In the early nineteenth century, those who provided a cultural definition of the nation also helped create the aesthetic style of romanticism. The romantic hero, noble or demonic, imposed his will on the canvas, the battlefield, or the state. But the romantic hero of the early nineteenth century, triumphing over all adversity, was not an isolated individual. He drew his powers and his creativity from the nation as people. Without that wellspring, he was nothing, a weak being adrift in a void. Like Kant's self-articulating individual becoming the self-articulating nation, so race thinking and nationalism absorbed the romantic notion of heroic creativity, of intense struggle, of a life of heightened feelings and grand achievements, a life that disparages the mundane. And the romantic hero as symbol of the race or nation was evident in physicality, the powerful presence of a muscular masculinity engaged in battle, politics, or the arts, or, occasionally, the fertile mother of the nation. He was Goethe's creative genius, Byron's Napoleon, Géricault's hussar, and Delacroix's defeated but still heroic Greek fighters at Chios. Romantics venerated the outer, male body as the sign of inner worth and, often, as the symbol for an entire people increasingly understood in a racialized fashion.[68]

The romantic hero, transferred from the individual to the collective, was also given a history in the first half of the nineteenth century.[69] These were histories of conquest and of freedom, of liberties enshrined in Germanic judicial practices and land tenure of old, of freeborn Englishmen, of valiant peasants. The lead actors in the script varied with the location of the scriptwriter: they were Saxons or Franks, Celts or Lombards. Invariably, they represented freedom and greatness; they were "organic," attached to the soil rather than to the mechanistic, degenerate city. Giving flesh and bones to Herder's theories, the authors identified original languages as the true expression of the *Volk* — literally a "people," but often written or spoken with mystical connotations. Out of histories of language, landholding, and governance emerged such constructions as "Anglo-Saxons" or "Semites" as distinctive racial types. In an often mystical fashion, race, transmitted through blood descent, remained organically entwined with land and language, which gave to each group its particular characteristics. In these accounts, the state was the ultimate expression of the racial characteristics of the *Volk*, almost an epiphenomenon built atop language, culture, and soil.

The search in the eighteenth and nineteenth centuries for the histories of peoples ran parallel with the search for the origins of the species. In fact, the term "ethnology" was coined in 1839 to describe this combined enterprise of the natural and human sciences.[70] While philologists studied languages and philosophers and historians pored over legal codes, naturalists examined skeletons, animal and human, anatomists exhumed corpses, and geologists explored sedimentary layers. The Aryan myth emerged in the context of this search for biological and historical origins, the positing of human races, and the romantic inclination toward the heroic and the exotic. Like many myths, it carried grains of truth, in this case, in the philological investigations that identified Indo-European languages as having common roots in Sanskrit. Friedrich Schlegel in 1808 drew many of the diverse elements together in his *Concerning the Language and Wisdom of the Indians*. The roots of classical Mediterranean culture, and its northern European successor, were located in the Indian subcontinent, from where the noble Aryans with their "organic" language, one uniquely suited to higher thoughts and aesthetic beauty, had migrated. In this mythology, the northern forests beckoned the Aryans as Ithaca awaited Odysseus, and they left behind a debased, darker skinned people. Language thus expressed inner being; in a sense, language was not learned but transmitted by blood descent. From its beginnings in linguistic studies, the Aryan myth would prove long-lasting, inspiring even Nazi quests to Tibet in search of Aryan origins.

Amid this fervent search for the origins and histories of humankind, two key figures loom at midcentury, one a towering presence even today, the other long forgotten except by scholars. Charles Darwin published in 1859 *The Origin of Species*, and the theory of evolution he postulated, with shattering effects, remains the most profound and forceful explanation for the development of humankind. The comte Arthur de Gobineau published from 1853 to 1855 his *Essay on the Inequality of the Human Races*. Not much read by contemporaries, it was rediscovered toward the end of the century. Gobineau's *Essay*, the first fully developed theory of race, was a brazen pronouncement that, like Marx and Engels's *Communist Manifesto*, published just a few years before, provided an anthropology and a history of the human species.

Gobineau was born on Bastille Day, the anniversary of the revolution he so despised, in 1816. His family background was bourgeois and noble, his career as journalist and government official mediocre. His horror at the perceived decline of France, its ruin by revolution, its supposed domination by hordes of middling and low-level bankers, tradesmen, and bureaucrats, was the common stuff of conservative thinking at the time. Gobineau's powerful intellectual invention was to explain this decline, indeed, to explain all of history, by the category of race. Gobineau brought together the strands of thinking of the preceding centuries that had hesitantly, incompletely, begun to explain human society in terms of race.

For Gobineau, the human species was divided into discrete races, each with defined intellectual and moral traits. After pages of verbose ramblings, he finally delivered to his readers his grand theory: "[T]he racial question overshadows all other problems of history, . . . it holds the key to them all, and . . . the inequality of the races from whose fusion a people is formed is enough to explain the whole course of its destiny."[71] In Gobineau's view, races were by definition unequal, and the qualities of each, physiological and moral, were permanent, immutable, and inescapable. Moreover, all civilizations decline, and the source of the decline is race mixing.[72]

For all the historical knowledge it revealed, Gobineau's *Essay* descended to a compendium of the most common prejudices. He identified just three races, black, yellow, and white, in ascending order.[73] Like all race theorists, Gobineau considered fine outer appearance a symbol of inner nobility. Charlemagne's "tall and nobly proportioned figure," the "intelligent regularity of Napoleon's features," and, strangest of all, "the imposing majesty that exhales from the royal countenance of Louis XIV" — these rather startling examples of beauty were the signs of the glory of the French race.[74] People not of white (or perhaps French) blood may come close to, but will most certainly never attain, true beauty. "As these races recede from the white type," he wrote, "their features and limbs become incorrect in form; they acquire defects of proportion which, in the races that are completely foreign to us, end by producing an extreme ugliness."[75] This inequality in beauty is "rational, logical, permanent and indestructible" — that is, it is based on racial inequality.[76] The same is true for strength, courage, intellect, and morality.

The *Essay on the Inequality of the Human Races* demonstrates just how easy was the slippage between race and nation. It is often unclear whether Gobineau is writing about Europeans, white people, or, quite simply, the French. In this regard, his book was firmly in keeping with the common tendency of his day to use interchangeably the terms "English race" and "English nation" or with the ambiguities that were always present at the invocation of the German *Volk*, a term that simply means people but could connote the citizenry of a democratic polity, the members of the German cultural nation, or a group bound by kindred descent that stamped indelible characteristics upon its members.

Gobineau saw society threatened by race mixing and looked for a "race of princes," the Aryans, to defend society, history itself, from the mob. But his work conveyed predominantly a tone of profound despair. Gobineau could see only race mixing and degeneration on the horizon, a world full of mediocrity, in which nations will constitute "human herds," mournfully somnolent, "benumbed in their nullity."[77]

And that is the extent of Gobineau's profundity. A thinker on the scale of his contemporaries Marx and Darwin he was not. A stylist worthy of his sometime mentor, Alexis de Tocqueville, he was not. But a synthesizer with one inventive thought he was, and he would be dutifully recognized by his successors as the first to perceive the profound "truth" of race as the dominant, indeed exclusive, factor in the shaping of humankind.[78]

Darwin's contribution to our ways of understanding is so monumental that it almost defies description. In the initial version of *The Origin of Species* he did not use two of the most memorable locutions with which he is associated, "evolution" and "survival of the fittest." His supporters often took his ideas down paths he was loath to follow. In particular, his entire system of thought demonstrated the mutability of species, a position often at variance with the advocates of race. Yet many of his formulations, especially in his later work *The Descent of Man* (1871), proved very congenial to race theorists, some of whom would claim—with at least some legitimacy—to be his intellectual descendants.[79]

Darwin, first of all, provided an explanation for the development of the species. All the varied attempts since the eighteenth century to give to humankind a natural rather than a sacred past had faltered or been incomplete. Now, at long last, humanity had found its compelling historian. But the story had not necessarily reached its culmination. Upon reading Darwin, people found it possible to envisage a further progression of human development. The French Revolution envisaged perfectibility through politics; Darwin posited advance through adaptation, and Darwinians would come to imagine purification through purges, an engineered process of weeding out unwanted traits and peoples to achieve a healthier, more accomplished race.

Moreover, Darwin's depiction of the process of human development as a struggle among various species in a harsh environment provided a scientific explanation for what many people considered a natural, eternal condition of human life. From a struggle among species it was but a simple step to argue that human society was characterized by struggle among races, who operated in a harsh world of scarce resources. The analogical argument between the natural and social worlds had a firm, scientific grounding: just as the species progressed through competition, so did human society. One's own group had to be ever vigilant, ever ready to engage the fight, whether for territory, markets, or sea-lanes.

Finally, the great popularization of Darwin's theory rested to a considerable degree on its lawlike character. He had uncovered the hidden workings of nature, which, to many of his supporters, meant that he could also explain the social world. Every subsequent race theorist would base his claims, whether "scientific" or "mystical," on the nature that Darwin had depicted in *The Origin of Species*—whether or not they had read the work. Profound thinkers like Herbert Spencer and street-corner ideologues alike were drawn to the theory of natural selection because Darwin had articulated it as a simple but very powerful law. From that original law all sorts of subsidiary laws followed. For

Spencer, the author of "survival of the fittest" and, arguably, Social Darwinism, these were, very importantly, laws of competition by which a "purifying process [eliminated] . . . the sickly, the malformed, and the least fleet or powerful."[80] State policies to protect the weak interfered with the laws of nature, an interference that would wreak social and political havoc and destroy the possibilities of continued progress. Those who occupied the lower rungs were there because they deserved to be. They were deficient intellectually, often morally as well. Such categorizations applied to the working classes and the poor, as well as to the "lesser" races, who required the direction and tutelage of white Europeans.

Darwin and Gobineau were brilliant synthesizers, both of whom gathered together various strands of thought from the previous centuries and, with intellectual leaps, recast them into radically new systems. Darwin, clearly the more brilliant of the two, drew from Linnaeus's system of categorization, Blumenbach's anthropology, Charles Lyell's geological discoveries, and, of course, his own incisive observations, especially on his famed journey to the Galapagos Islands. For the first time science offered a compelling explanation for the diversity and movement of the natural world. Darwin provided the "science" that many race thinkers adopted to make their case in a century enamored of progress and technology.

Gobineau's pessimism might alone have consigned his book to obscurity, so out of tone was it with the mid-nineteenth-century belief in progress. Gobineau's tract is one long lament about race mixing as the source of the decline of civilization. He projected his own aristocratic frustrations onto the world. But by the turn into the twentieth century, his concern with decadence had many adherents. Gobineau needed, however, a more optimistic reading, one that turned his fundamental invention, race, not only into an epitaph, but also into a clarion call for action.

This Houston Stewart Chamberlain provided. English by birth, German by choice, he became an intimate of Richard Wagner's circle and then the composer's son-in-law. Like Gobineau's *Essay*, Chamberlain's *Foundations of the Nineteenth Century*, published in 1899, is a fundamental text of racist thought.[81] Chamberlain, less concerned with the science of race, postulated a mystical "race-soul" possessed only by Germans, a constituent component of their blood. This race-soul made Germans moral, spiritual, and creative, the signs of a special "German Christianity." In Chamberlain's hands, even Jesus became an Aryan hero. History was made, though, by the inhabitants of northern Europe.[82] Teutons were the ones who developed great ideas, produced magnificent art, created civilization. The Italians of the Renaissance were either Teutons or were saturated with Teutonic blood, whether Lombard, Gothic, or Frankish.[83] "[B]ut for the Teuton," Chamberlain wrote, "everlasting night would have settled upon the world." Only the birth of the Teuton has made possible the revival of Hellenistic and Roman culture.[84] With all the bombast and megalomania typical of race theorists, Chamberlain claimed that "true history, the history which still controls the rhythm of our hearts and circulates in our veins, inspiring us to new hope and new creation, begins at the moment when the Teuton with his masterful hand lays his grip upon the legacy of antiquity."[85]

The consciousness of being a member of a pure race endows a man, the Teuton in particular, with extraordinary powers. A man of "pure origins" who is also gifted will tower above those who muddle around in the swamp of race chaos. From the purity of race he absorbs the life force that gives him the ability to achieve greatness in every field of endeavor — war, art, politics, science.[86] Chamberlain disparaged the tendency to make Jews scapegoats for all problems and claimed that Jewish influence was much exaggerated. Yet he also described Jews as materialistic, immoral, and conniving, the very antithesis of Greco-Roman greatness embodied in the modern Teuton.[87] "The Indo-European, moved by ideal motives, opened the gates in friendship; the Jew rushed in like an enemy, stormed all positions and planted the flag of his, to us, alien nature."[88] Yet the Jews were also a model, because they alone had maintained the purity of their blood and therefore possess "physiognomy and character."[89] The Jews, in short, had proven the race principle.[90]

Chamberlain's mystical Aryan hero aroused the suspicions of those who were determined to found race thinking as a science. Chamberlain's verbose writing, grand historical claims, and absurd assertions were the very antithesis of the scientific spirit. Scientific race thinkers looked to Darwin, Chamberlain to Wagner and his medieval Teutonic heroes. Indeed, Chamberlain's writing had something of the epic quality of a Wagnerian composition, though without any of the opera's grace and melody. Yet the science and the mysticism of race could also coexist quite easily.

In an era replete with memorable phrases and fluent coinages — survival of the fittest, blood and iron, cross of gold — the British statistician Francis Galton invented, in 1881, "eugenics." The word is not much used today—the Nazis made it a term of opprobrium. Yet in the last two decades of the nineteenth century and on into the twentieth, it was bandied about with ease in lecture halls and parliaments, newspaper columns and scientific journals. Learned societies were founded to promote eugenics, mass organizations to popularize it. The term denotes selective breeding for favored characteristics, and the breeding out of those traits deemed dangerous. Scientists discussed the possibilities with the cool tones appropriate to their disciplines in the austere pages of journals like the *Archiv für Rassen- und Gesellschafts-Biologie* (Journal for racial and social biology), in seminars and laboratories at the Francis Galton Laboratory for National Eugenics, in lectures to the British Eugenics Education Society and the German Racial Hygiene Society, all of them founded between 1904 and 1907. Just beneath their cool veneer lay a rough-hewn hysteria, the fear that the poor and ignorant were breeding at fantastic rates, while the "better" classes practiced family limitation. The gene pool (admittedly, a term invented later) would be swamped by deleterious traits, leading to the decline of the race. In yet another memorable phrase, Theodore Roosevelt mused aloud about the dangers of "race suicide." With eugenics, race thinking reached an apex of sorts, a merger of anthropology, Darwinism, and medicine—a fateful collusion termed by the Germans "racial and social biology."

Eugenicist thinking developed out of the great advance of biological and medical knowledge from the 1850s down to World War I.[91] Scientists made enormous strides in identifying the basic mechanisms of the human body. They discovered cell division, leading to the recognition of the cell as the basic organic unit of life, and isolated bacteria that caused virulent diseases, resulting in the triumph of the germ theory of disease.[92] The first real therapies for such scourges as typhoid and diphtheria quickly followed (though tuberculosis proved more difficult), as did extensive public health measures to clean up water supplies, remove waste, and reduce overcrowding. Such advances contributed to a growing belief that science reigned supreme, and that society, a sick patient if there ever was one, needed the careful attention of the physician or scientist, who had it in his powers to cure the ills. From government ministers to socialist reformers, people increasingly thought of society as analogous to the body and the race: as a biological organism, whose health needed constant attention, whose vitality was continually in danger of being sapped by killer bacteria borne by the weaker members and by those of completely alien races.[93]

Karl Pearson, the leading British eugenicist after Galton, was a tireless campaigner for the cause. He was convinced that science alone provided the prescriptions that would forestall rampant degeneration and prepare the path for still greater progress of the race. The world that Pearson depicted was a fearful place. The unhealthy, the indigent, the lesser races bred at will, while the "better" elements, the strong, industrious, and intelligent, limited family size or dissipated their "stock" in endless luxuries and unhealthy liaisons. The weak, sickly, and degenerate threatened to swamp the healthy. Pearson's world was also a combative place, its history defined by virile, masculine contests among the races for domination. The contest could be military; it was also scientific, cultural, and economic. Only by expunging the "lesser races" could the better races thrive: it was their right, indeed, their destiny, to dominate those beneath them. And if, in some fit of feminine sentimentality, the better races chose to renounce the struggle, to pursue a path of peace, they would inevitably degenerate. "The biological factors," Pearson wrote, "are dominant in the evolution of mankind; these, and these alone, can throw light on the rise and fall of nations, on racial progress and national degeneracy."[94]

Yet modern sentiments kept alive the weak and degenerate. Science, the discoverer of nature, would now replace nature's own workings, repair the damage that society had done by interfering with nature. "Race-culture," Pearson wrote, "will cope with the ills which arise when we suspend the full purifying force of natural selection."[95] As for the "lesser races," nothing at all could be done about them.

> How many centuries, how many thousands of years, have the Kaffir or the negro held large districts in Africa undisturbed by the white man? Yet their intertribal struggles have not yet produced a civilization in the least comparable with the Aryan. Educate and nurture them as you will, I do not believe that you will succeed in modifying the stock. History shows me one way, and one way only, in which a high state of civilization has been produced, namely the struggle of race with race, and the survival of the physically and mentally fitter race.[96]

And if one were to try to mix the races, the result would be utter disaster, the deterioration of the strong without the uplifting of the weak. Presciently and frightfully, Pearson maintained that "every remedy which tends to separate them [the "unfit"] from the community, every segregation which reduces their chances of parentage, is worthy of consideration."[97] He warned his countrymen that they were facing "race suicide" as they watched "the loss of our former racial stability and national stamina."[98] But if eugenics became the foundation of state policy and private behavior, then the future would be glorious indeed. A purified, powerful race would thrive and build an ever more prosperous, ever more creative, society. The Enlightenment belief in the perfectibility of humankind had a new foundation — in race science.

Pearson's German counterpart, Alfred Ploetz, was no less forthright in his calls for the placement of race at the center of national policy.[99] In the *Archiv für Rassen- und Gesellschafts-Biologie*, the journal that he founded in 1904, Ploetz argued that science had now proven the inextricable intertwining of body and spirit, physical and mental characteristics. "All spiritual and intellectual [*geistige*] developments are tightly bound up with our physical development." This was an "iron law" from which no human power can diverge.[100] These developments are themselves inseparable from "race," a grouping with similar life patterns, similar descent, and similar reproduction. A biological race is nothing less than the "maintenance of life in its entirety [*Erhaltungseinheit des Lebens*]" and the "development of life in its entirety [*Entwicklungseinheit des Lebens*]."[101] Morality, art, literature — these are the products of particular racial constitutions that are transmitted through the generations by heredity.

Ploetz, too, was keenly alive to the lurking dangers that threatened to dissipate the purity and quality of the inheritance matter that Aryans had passed on for generations. Race mixing, the protection of the feebleminded and the criminal, the limitation on family size practiced by the "better" elements — these were the dangers that Ploetz and his collaborators repeatedly identified in their research, writings, and lectures. Contributors to Ploetz's journal described a menagerie of well-endowed individuals, the finest elements of the race — lawyers, physicians, artists, scientists — who limited the number of their children or failed to reproduce altogether. Not rarely, they succumbed to a life of dissipation, their fine hereditary material destroyed by syphilis and gonorrhea.[102]

Like Pearson, many of the authors in the *Archiv für Rassen- und Gesellschafts-Biologie* advocated state policies to promote births among the better elements, to restrict births among those poorly endowed by inheritance. Should these measures not suffice, then more drastic ones, like compulsory sterilization of the unfit by castrations and ovariectomies, were required.[103] Progressive public health measures would round out the program. Underlying these state policies was a general science of racial biology. Ploetz proved positively inflationary in his advocacy of new, subsidiary disciplines. Along with "race biology," there would be race anatomy, race physiology, race pathology, race hygiene.[104] Race psychology and race sociology could not be far behind. Yet the presumed science of all this often degenerated into a collection of crass prejudices — the musical genius of Mozart and Beethoven rooted in their Aryan racial constitution, the formation of archery clubs as a means of reviving the vitality of the race.[105]

Ploetz also advocated an ethics of race that was derived from science.[106] The code mandated, especially for superior individuals, careful selection of one's partner and the couple's obligation to propagate. Racial ethics meant the promotion of state intervention in the very intimate realms of sexuality and reproduction to foster "*the widest possible dissemination of social virtues and the weeding out* [Ausjäte] *of persistent, debilitating characteristics* [dauernd Schwachen]."[107] Ominously, he wrote:

> The elimination of existing incurable diseases could occur only by extermination or expulsion [*Vernichtung oder Ausstoßung*]. . . . The deficient and defective individuals [*fehlerhaften und defekten Individuen*] that still emerge could only be removed by extermination or expulsion.[108]

Ploetz had imagined the fateful move: extermination of those with unwanted traits.[109]

NATION, STATE, AND EMPIRE

Far removed from the laboratories of London and Berlin and a few decades earlier, the prince-bishop Petar Petrović Njegoš of Montenegro had written *The Mountain Wreath* (1847). It is an epic poem that memorializes the Serbian defeat by the Ottomans at Kosovo Polje, the Field of Blackbirds, located in contemporary Kosovo. Njegoš tells the story of the epic hero Miloš Obilić, who supposedly slays the Turkish sultan Murat on the eve of battle in 1389. The poem also depicts the martyrdom of the Serbian prince Lazar, who refuses to betray his people and dies a hero's death in battle. Njegoš writes glowingly of the lands claimed by the Serbs, from the shores of the Adriatic to the mountains of Bosnia to the plains of Kosovo. The Serbs suffer terrible losses in battle, but they are the great defenders of the faith, those who fight the

. . . faithless Turk, with Koran!
Behind him hordes of that accursed breed,
That they might devastate the whole wide earth,
As locusts pestilent lay waste the fields! . . .
From out of Asia where they have their nest,
This Devil's brood doth gulp the nations up.[110]

Just a few years later, the Italian conspirator and publicist Giuseppe Mazzini wrote "Duties towards Your Country" (1854). It was a classic statement of liberalism that called on men to serve, first and foremost, the human family whose oneness derives from God. But God has also divided humanity into nations. Only the greed of governments and conquerors has prevented the realization of God's design — that each nation shall have its own state that extends to its natural geographic borders. When people act together, they will repair what kings and nobles have so unnaturally created. "Natural divisions, and the spontaneous innate tendencies of the peoples, will take the place of the arbitrary divisions sanctioned by evil governments. The map of Europe will be re-drawn. The countries of the Peoples, defined by the vote of free men, will arise upon the ruins of the countries of kings and privileged castes, and between these countries harmony and fraternity will exist."[111]

Njegoš and Mazzini represent the poles of nationalist thought in the nineteenth century, the one militant and exclusive, the other more humane and democratic. But both assumed it completely natural that a given state should be built upon an exclusive national group. Their sense of geography was necessarily expansionist, designed to include all Serbian or Italian speakers within the borders of the state. Njegoš provided a powerful story that bound — and continues to bind — the Serbian national idea to the Christian promise of redemption, but a redemption that can be achieved only through struggle and martyrdom against a foe that has been so vilified that he has lost any semblance of humanity. The epic poem also binds the national idea to a defined place, most immediately the battlefield of Kosovo Polje and, more generally, the Serb-settled lands around it. A medieval event related in written form in the mid–nineteenth century, *The Mountain Wreath* became virtually the official poem of Serbian nationalism in the nineteenth and twentieth centuries. Mazzini was a secular nationalist yet believed that a world composed of nation-states would fulfill the divine plan; he offered a political version of Newton's clockmaker universe. Mazzini also wrote glowingly of mountains and river valleys, linking the national idea to the warm emotions aroused by natural beauty and a sense of place. He made the nation-state the aim of democratic politics and the vehicle of eternal peace and fraternity among peoples. Yet he could never figure out how a state defined by a particular nationality could also encompass people of different linguistic and ethnic backgrounds. If Njegoš had no qualms whatsoever about eliminating foreigners from lands claimed for Serbia, Mazzini simply ignored the problem. Both articulations of the nation were, necessarily, exclusive, even if Mazzini's was far more humane and democratic.

From west to east in Europe, not only in Serbia and Italy, the idea of the nation took hold in the course of the nineteenth century. All across the continent, nationalist movements propagated the idea that a distinctive people (or nation) should have its own state. The advocates of the nation researched the historical origins of their people, wrote or discovered epic poems, developed dictionaries, and modernized languages. While they fostered the idea of the nation among many people, nation-states were made in the practical world of politics, and many different political ideologies intersected quite easily with nationalism. The coloration of the nation and nationalism was socialist, liberal, or conservative, depending on time and place. The nation found concrete manifestation in the establishment of an independent Greece in the 1820s; in the carving out, later in the century, of other autonomous states in the Balkans, like Bulgaria and Serbia, that were formerly under Ottoman control; and in the creation of Italy and Germany in the 1860s and 1870s. In opposition to Mazzini's profound faith in popular action, many of these states were founded by modernizing elites whose political and social views were profoundly conservative, or by some combination of popular participation and elite direction. Conservatives recognized the power that could come from a population mobilized on behalf of the nation, and feared the consequences if liberals or socialists succeeded in becoming the spokesmen for the national cause. By establishing nation-states, the elites would be able to create, so they hoped, their own nationals, people whose understanding of the nation ran in suitably conservative paths. The nation aroused hopes of liberty and fraternity, but the nation-state was also a disciplining force, one that made nationals in the schools, the army, and the early welfare state pioneered by Germany and Britain. While much of the continent remained dominated by empires, by the turn into the twentieth century the nation had become a critical locus of identity for a great many people. And in the blendings and confusions so typical of the national form, its members were some-times considered a political community, sometimes an ethnicity, and sometimes a race—or some combination of all three.

"I would conquer the stars if I could," said the British explorer and businessman, the imperialist par excellence, Cecil Rhodes.[112] He never quite realized his dream of a British Africa straight from the Cape to Egypt. Then again, the British Empire celebrated at Queen Victoria's Jubilee in 1897 was quite an accomplishment, the most vibrant expres-sion of the Western drive to dominate the globe. Very quickly, in the last two decades of the nineteenth century, Europeans and North Americans divided most of the vast, remaining areas that had lain beyond their formal control. As with the discovery and conquest of the Americas, the motives were varied, from sheer economic greed to lofty impulses to uplift and Christianize other peoples. Certainly, the flurry to establish direct, formal control—in a word, to establish colonies—reflected a new, higher level of capitalist development and greater economic and strategic competition among the great powers. Once Belgium had staked out a claim in the Congo, and England had declared its predomi-nant interests in Egypt, the "structural logic" of the Western state sys-tem came into play: every other major European state, and soon the United States as well, felt compelled to aggrandize its own territory with colonies abroad. Not accidentally, imperialism and eugenics blossomed together. Eugenics provided an explanation for the domination of the "lesser" races—they were "by nature" inferior, hence could only exist to serve the well-being of those better endowed. At the same time, impe-rialism provided the intellectual material for eugenicism, the race-infused travel accounts, ethnographies, naturalist investigations, and poetry that demonstrated both fascination with and disparagement of other cultures and peoples.

Imperialism was a large, complex development, and the various impe-rial powers pursued different strategies of domination. But for all of its "civilizing" mission, imperial domination was often carried out with unspeakable cruelties.[113] Like New World slaves, Africans especially bore the signs of race on their bodies. The Belgian depredations in the Congo constituted one of the worst cases and appalled many Europeans when the news traveled back home. In their headlong exploitation of the Congo's immense resources, the Belgians did not shy away from amputating limbs, flogging backs, executing villagers en masse, and set-ting homes ablaze, all in the attempt to maintain their domination. The death toll ran into the millions. The situation was little better elsewhere on the continent. The Germans savagely repressed rebellions in Southwest and East Africa, carrying out one of the first genocides of the twentieth century against the Herero. All of these forms of repression were public acts—domination required public humiliation as well as direct violence. British conquerors forced indigenous leaders to crawl before them on all fours as they sat regally above them. They executed elders in front of their children and barred the "colored" from the public spaces reserved for white Europeans and Americans.[114]

But for so many of its European practitioners, imperialism was also a sporting game. Winston Churchill reported from the Sudan in the 1890s for the *Morning Post*. He later described the Battle of Omdurman, at which the British routed the Sudanese, as "[one] of those spectacular conflicts whose vivid and majestic splendour has done so much to invest war with glamour." Britain's "little wars," the colonial conquests, were "only a sporting element in a splendid game"; those were "light-hearted days" and "everyone" (on the British side) who was about to participate in the battle "was in the highest spirits and the best of tempers."[115]

As Hannah Arendt understood, the actions of Europeans abroad could not be separated from politics at home. It is, then, in the context of Gobineau's claim that history is defined by race, of Darwinism and Social Darwinism, of imperialism and eugenics, that antisemitism, that particularly deadly form of race thinking, first emerged. The term itself was coined in 1879 by Wilhelm Marr, a German whose life amounted to a catalog of failures in journalism, business, politics, and marriage. Marr drew upon the philological studies of the preceding one hundred years that had first distinguished between Indo-European and Semitic languages. However tainted the source, it is useful to follow Marr's invention and distinguish between antisemitism, with its clear racialist meanings, and the centuries-long Judeophobia of Christian society. One can scour the literature and find traces of a racialist conception of Jews in medieval Europe. The Spanish Inquisition, in its hunt for *conversos*, certainly came to define Jews as a racial group, whose Jewishness was constituted "in the blood," not by a freely chosen lack of faith in Jesus. Bishops and priests used a language of vilification barely surpassed by the Nazis, and Jewish communities often endured the most brutal persecutions. Yet the overwhelming reality remains that the universalist teaching of the Church prevented a racialist understanding of Jews. Race thinking in general and antisemitism in particular became possible only with the advance of secular society and Enlightenment thought, which proclaimed the formal equality of men and enabled Jews to move out of the confined spaces of the ghetto.[116] Except in Iberia, the path of conversion always remained open to Jews. Few took the path until the Enlightenment and the French Revolution fostered Jewish emancipation and created the dilemma of assimilation.

Initially, in the late eighteenth and early nineteenth centuries, assimilation was a problem only for Jews—the agony of deciding whether to convert to Christianity to remove the stigma of Jewishness and to enhance one's possibilities in a more mobile, but still largely Judeophobic, society. The advance of race thinking over the course of the nineteenth century made assimilation a problem for the general society, because now race thinkers cast Jewishness "in the blood." Jews became a constant, pulsing threat to the purity of the racial group, the "hidden Jews" particularly dangerous because they steadily and secretively worked their degenerative impulses into the noble, upstanding, Aryan racial body.

The specific charges against Jews were hardly new. They drew upon long-standing Christian Judeophobic myths. Jew were accused of rituals in which they murdered Christian babies on Passover and used their blood in the making of matzos (the "blood libel"). The "wandering Jew," condemned to a rootless existence because he had helped in the crucifixion of Jesus, haunted the imagination of a world that placed great value on "rootedness"—literally, to the soil and property; metaphorically, to a fixed and secure place in a world in which so much was in flux. Jews were accused of an unrelenting drive toward economic domination, of concern merely with material matters, of sexual licentiousness, particularly with Aryan girls and women. The language was virulent, as bad as, or worse than, that used about African slaves. But the bodily metaphors used in medieval society about Jews became even more dangerous when articulated in conjunction with the germ theory of disease and eugenics. Now it was possible to imagine the "therapies" that could deal with the "diseased microbes" and the "parasites" that sucked the life out of the healthy host. As ever, these virulent epithets are far more revealing about the accusers than about the accused. They betray the most deep-seated psychological anxieties—about sex; bodily pollution, whether through blood or semen; gender, with Jews often depicted as weak and grotesque, at times in a feminine manner, the diametric opposite of the noble and virile romantic-racial hero. To extirpate the Jews, to remove or exterminate them, would purify the Aryan race and open up unlimited vistas of happiness. In the antisemitic vision, racial warfare against the Jews would resolve not only all political and social problems, but also—though this went unspoken—the most profound psychological and sexual anxieties.

Yet from the outset a curious contradiction marked antisemitic thought. How could anyone truly fear the decrepit, bent-over creature that was invariably depicted as the Jew? A lurking, if grotesque, admiration is evident in the writings of Gobineau, Chamberlain, and even Hitler, who saw in the decrepit Jew evidence that Jews had maintained their racial purity. The imagination of antisemites was boundless; the political will and techniques had to await the twentieth century.

CONCLUSION

Historians like to be attentive to the openness of the past. They strive to consider the variety of possibilities present at any given moment, the "paths not taken" as well as those that were traveled. But the categories of race and nation became such powerful currents of the modern world, principles so fundamental to the organization of state and society and to the self-conception of so many people, that it is almost impossible to imagine our contemporary world without them. So many diverse strands—political, social, intellectual—went into their making, and they came to fulfillment in the twentieth century with the extension of the nationalities principle around the globe and the organization of "overtly racist regimes" like those of the United States in the Jim Crow era, apartheid South Africa, and Nazi Germany.[117]

The New World discoveries, the utter strangeness of the Americas and the revelations of the immense diversity of the world's population, resulted in vastly altered ways of understanding difference and of exercising domination. New World plantation owners did not invent slavery, which had existed in biblical times and in virtually all societies. But the scale of New World slavery and its association with one, phenotypically distinct group, black Africans, meant that New World slavery became an institution of a radically different order. To explain their degradation of this land with slavery, a land first thought to be a Garden of Eden, the fertile, life-giving "nipple" of the earth, as Columbus called it, slaveholders and their apologists formulated an understanding of black skin as the mark of sin and submission, both seen as innate, inheritable characteristics.[118]

These views commingled with the great intellectual advances of the

Scientific Revolution and the Enlightenment of the seventeenth and eighteenth centuries, which forged new ways of categorizing human beings. A culmination of sorts came with the emergence of anthropology: the definition of humankind's place in nature was the very raison d'être of this new discipline. To understand man-in-nature required developing a paradigm of order out of the diversity of humankind, a diversity ever more evident and expansive as Europeans continued their explorations of the globe. Theorists in the eighteenth and nineteenth centuries made that order hierarchical on a racial scale marked by gradations of inferiority and superiority. Nationalism, also postulated upon difference — often of a "natural" kind based in language and an unchanging culture — lent added credence to anthropology.

In the course of the nineteenth century, national and racial thinkers further replaced the notion of community based on politics or religion with the idea of the unbreakable national or racial bonds among distinct peoples. Upon that basis physicians and scientists layered a new understanding of the human body and human evolution that seemed to confirm racial categorizations. Although Darwin's ideas were in eclipse among scientists by the turn into the twentieth century, his revolutionary theories had become immensely popular.[119] Race theorists argued by analogy, substituting races for species and turning all of human history into a struggle among races for the survival of the fittest. Through biology and medicine, race thinking infiltrated the professions and state bureaucracies. Race thinking rose from street politics and penny pamphlets to the highest echelons of society and was as much, perhaps even more, the province of the "better" classes as it was of the popular classes.[120] In the racial-scientific agglomeration postulated by race theorists, inheritance determined all the essential characteristics of human beings. And the quality of inheritance rested not only on individuals and families, but on the entire racial group to which they belonged.

Darwinism and then eugenics joined science and medicine to the Enlightenment sense of the perfectibility of humankind — even if Darwin himself posited only a nonteleological progression, not perfectibility.[121] From the mid–eighteenth century, the prescriptions for perfectibility were many and varied, ranging from the virtue of the French Revolution to Hegel's unfolding spirit to Marx's masses of proletarians mounting the barricades for socialism. Ploetz and Pearson gave a new dimension to such sentiments, one rooted in the popularization of Darwinism and medicine. As ever, the path to perfection was not easy; there were enemies along the way, and they had to be vanquished. To flee the contest was to flee from history-as-nature, and the consequences could only be, at best, a kind of purgatory, a long stagnation in the languid world of racial imperfection. Imperialism, overtly organized around the domination of non-European peoples, lent credence to the popularized views of Darwinism and eugenics. Race thinking, around 1870 a history, mythology, and anthropology of the human species, had become, by 1900, a science as well. More dangerously, science and medicine had begun to provide the ideas and techniques by which the population could be manipulated, purged of its ailing elements and refined to the lofty stage of pristine purity. Biology had developed techniques of immunization against harmful bacteria; it was now possible to imagine biological-political techniques for dealing with the harmful scourges of human society.

Certainly, not all adherents of the theory of natural selection were racists, and the pioneers of the bacteriological revolution were generally liberal minded. Thomas Huxley, so ardent a defender of Darwin's theory of evolution, was no less ardent an opponent of Social Darwinism. He argued vociferously for the autonomy of the ethical realm.[122] Franz Boas, for decades the dean of American anthropologists, challenged the notion of immutable racial traits, emphasizing, in opposition, the role of environment in the shaping of human cultures.

Nonetheless, by 1914 race thinking and nationalism had become predominant and pervasive in the West. At all levels of society, many people believed that racial characteristics were hierarchical, inheritable, and immutable, and that they entailed not only physical but moral and intellectual qualities as well. Many also took it for granted that at least among Europeans, nations should have their own states, and the regnant multinational empires — Ottoman, Habsburg, and Russian — were considered relics of the past that could not long last in the twentieth century.

The cataclysm of World War I only intensified the tendency to think in racial and national terms. The first total war in history required the full mobilization of all of society's resources, human and material, for the practice of violence. Total war required total victory; amid the massive death toll, a war of empires and nation-states became a war of nation as race versus the racial enemies. According to George L. Mosse, propaganda attacks on the enemy in previous wars had only exceptionally involved complete, all-encompassing condemnations of a people.[123] But total war meant also the total dehumanization of the enemy in official propaganda, which lent a fateful tenor of racialization and brutalization to the conflict.[124]

Moreover, the postwar settlements enshrined the nationalities principle in the political map of Europe. In the American view so forcefully
advocated by President Woodrow Wilson, only within a nation-state
could democracy flourish. The Great Powers, then, produced a settlement that affirmed the rights of some self-proclaimed nations to establish their own states. Despite the platitudes of protection in the treaties,
the very notion that states should be the exclusive representatives of
particular nationalities presented grave problems for specific populations throughout central and eastern Europe. It is perhaps no surprise,
then, that the situation of Jews deteriorated markedly all over the region—not just in Germany—in the 1920s and 1930s, because they
were the consummate outsiders wherever the nationalities principle was
affirmed.[125] Nor is it a surprise that the 1923 Treaty of Lausanne legiti-
mated both the forced removal of some 800,000 ethnic Turks from an
enlarged Greece and 1.2 million Greeks from their historic homelands
in Anatolia, and, in effect, the genocide of Armenians by abandoning
the Armenian state that had been recognized in the prior Treaty of
Sèvres.[126] In light of these developments, it might not have appeared so
strange to Soviet officials in the 1930s and 1940s that they should brutally remove from border areas entire populations whom they considered security threats, or to the Nazis that there was anything so amiss
about organizing massive migrations of ethnic Germans into the Reich
from all over central and eastern Europe as a corollary to the forced
expulsions of Jews.

World War I had other effects that were decisively related to the subsequent escalation of genocides in the twentieth century. The war established a new model of a powerful interventionist state that tried to manage everything in sight, because only the state had the capacity to
mobilize resources on the scale required by total war. Afterward, both
Soviets and Nazis would look back with admiration upon the powerful
World War I states, Imperial Germany in particular, which they then
sought to replicate.

World War I also created an aesthetics of violence that reverberated
through the postwar period.[127] The massive death toll of the war made
violence on such a large scale almost normal and, to some, a necessary,
even desirable way of shaping the future society and the character of the
new man and new woman who would inhabit it. For every Erich Maria
Remarque, the soldier-turned-pacifist author of *All Quiet on the Western Front*, for every Wilfrid Owen, the English poet who so powerfully
depicted the brutality of warfare and the tragic waste of death, there
were at least as many like Ernst Jünger and Gabriele D'Annunzio, the

men who in their postwar writings continually returned to the theme of heroic combat, ennobling death. In his books *In Stahlgewittern* (Storm of steel), *Das Wäldchen 125* (Copse 125), and many, many others, Jünger wrote glowingly of the machines of death, the tanks, cannons, guns, and railroads that he naturalizes and aestheticizes, imparting an almost erotic sensibility to the practice of killing.[128] Large segments of the Left, long considered antiwar in its predominant sentiments, came to idealize political violence as the path to the future. Even the political and social center, especially in Germany, but also elsewhere, become radicalized by the unprecedented scale of wartime killings and deprivations, a process that found expression in dreams of ever greater victory over a racialized enemy.

And out of the war came a series of revolutions, the most profound societal transformations that penetrate to the very core of individual and collective existence. The crises of World War I provided both Bolsheviks and Nazis with the opportunities to seize power. The Bolsheviks acceded to power in 1917, aided by the enormous popular discontent with the deprivations of war, which ultimately deprived the czarist system of all legitimacy. The Nazis came to power amid the immediate crisis of the Great Depression, but also because the Weimar Republic could never quite master the immense social, economic, and political issues that the war had left in its wake. Absent World War I, it is hard to imagine either movement's coming to power. From the legacy of World War I, both Soviet and Nazi leaders adopted a casual attitude toward human life, a willingness to countenance death on a massive scale; a model of a powerful, interventionist state; a commitment to political violence as the means of societal progress; and, each after its own fashion, the ideologies of race and nation.

two

Nation, Race, and State Socialism: The Soviet Union under Lenin and Stalin

Dossier number 24260 of the NKVD, the Soviet secret police, concerned one Vassili Klementovitch Sidorov. The police, writing in 1938 on a standardized form, listed the usual information: name, age, birthplace, education. Certain questions concerned Sidorov's political background—previous party affiliation (none), service in the czarist army (1915–16, infantryman), Red Army service (none), White Army service (none). His property holdings at the time of his arrest were detailed—all of a wooden house eight square meters, a partly covered courtyard thirty by twenty meters, a few animals—and were compared with his holdings in 1929 and 1917, presumably on the basis of Sidorov's own testimony. The form also called for information on nationality (Russian) and "social origins," to which Sidorov replied, "I consider myself the son of middle peasants."

In his interrogation, Sidorov was asked to give explanations concerning "your social origins, your social and patrimonial situation before and after 1917." He explained that his father had owned a small shop in Moscow and made do without employing hired labor. Ultimately, he could not maintain his business against the competition of larger merchants. The father returned to the countryside and worked two plots of land with the help of one person whom he employed for many years. After his father's death in 1925, Sidorov and his brother divided the land, and each worked his own plot.

Sidorov was accused of "evil intentions" toward Soviet power in general and the party in particular, and of systematically expounding "anti-Soviet propaganda." He denied any wrongdoing but was "exposed by several witnesses." This particular "troika," one of the infamous boards of party and state officials that decided the fate of millions of individuals, concluded its decision with reference to Sidorov's social background.[1] He was a former "merchant," who had engaged in counter-revolutionary propaganda, defeatist expressions, threats against communists, and criticism of the policy of the party and government. Sidorov was shot on 3 August 1938 and posthumously rehabilitated on 24 January 1989.[2]

Sidorov's case, one lone incident among millions of others, demonstrates the Soviets' compelling drive, obsession even, to categorize and classify the population. Unlike the Nazis, the Soviets were concerned with a variety of ways to identify people, not just by their race. They were certain, though, that individuals did not exist unto themselves, but only in relation to their class and national backgrounds and their political perspectives. The Soviets, seeking to construct a socialist society in immensely difficult conditions, sought to identify their friends and enemies. Certain favored categories, like the proletariat and clearly defined nationalities, would provide the institutions and the culture through which people would become good Soviet citizens with a developed socialist consciousness. Membership in other categories could land an individual in the camp of the enemies, which could make one subject to relentless pursuit by the state. Virtually none of the categories in which people were placed were "objective"; all were the result of ideological and political considerations, and the parsing of individuals into particular categories was often arbitrary. Sidorov's supposed grumblings about the Soviet system might have been the final cause of his execution, but there is no question that his family's social background—onetime merchant, owner of a few animals, hence a *kulak*, a "wealthy" peasant—made him immediately suspect in the eyes of the authorities. His Russian nationality seems neither to have helped nor to have hindered him. But at the very time he was under investigation, particular nationalities were coming under suspicion as "enemies" of the Soviet Union. In their entirety, they would soon be forcibly deported in conditions of great privation and brutality.

POWER AND UTOPIA

The Bolsheviks took power in 1917 with enormous confidence that they could implement their version of utopia. They had a capacious vision.[3] By clearing away the rubble of the past, they believed, they would open the path to the creation of the new society that would permit the ultimate efflorescence of the human spirit. In Marxian terms, the realm of necessity would finally be surmounted by the realm of freedom; material prosperity in conditions of social equality would finally lay to rest all the pathologies of class-riven societies and the nefarious traits of individual human beings. As socialism developed, rough speech patterns would disappear, women would become equal with men, and social relations all around would take on a pleasant, friendly air. Literature, art, music, and science would flourish.[4] Alcoholism and crime, even envy and arrogance, would disappear, along with the degrading servility portrayed by countless Russian novelists. Within the harmonious socialist society, all sorts of possibilities for human development would become the order of the day.

Communists were to be individuals involved in society, working to make it better, desiring that "all people should live well and be happy."[5] Private and social life would be merged together, and the most committed would derive joy from their involvement in the collective, the knowledge that they were helping to build the new society.[6] For some Bolsheviks, even sexuality would be subordinated to the demands of party work, because a "disorderly" sexual life prevented one from working well and effectively for the collective. Others, at least in the early years of the revolution, argued that socialism would finally set eros free. Sexual and marital relations would no longer be governed by material requirements and outmoded religious codes of behavior. Individuals would at last be able to find true satisfaction and love in their sexual lives.[7] Socialism would eliminate burdensome labor, especially by women in the household; they would be freed to participate in the building of the new society by the dissemination of communal, state-run laundry, feeding, and child-care facilities. Alexandra Kollontai, one of the few women in the top ranks of the party, expressed the heady, optimistic vision of the revolution's early years, a vision, depending on one's perspective, that now appears charmingly naive or chillingly totalitarian, when she proclaimed that "a comradely workers' state will overcome the family. Society is taking upon itself little by little all concerns which previously were parental."[8]

Utopia signified not only individual advancement and emancipation. The social dimensions of utopia were, for communists, always paramount. Socialism meant, first of all, that Russia would become a modern nation with all that level of attainment implied economically. The Soviet Union would develop and possess the most advanced technology, and the riches of society would have the widest possible distribution. The Soviet Union would become a fully urbanized society supported by an efficient, prosperous collectivized agriculture. The very move from country to city, from peasant to proletarian, constituted a critical element of the socialist utopia. Factories, massive in scale, would not be subject to the vagaries of an inequitable market but would work under a rational plan. They would reach unimagined levels of production. The "USSR on an automobile, and the *muzhik* [peasant] on a tractor"—so Stalin depicted the symbols of the new Russia, attainable, it was believed, within a generation.[9] Rationality was perhaps the key term, because it signified the application of science, supposedly, embodied in the economic plan, to development. As Stephen Kotkin writes, "Soviet industrialization could be 'utopian' . . . precisely because it was 'scientific.' "[10]

Especially under Stalin, the socialist utopia meant that Russia would at last and unquestionably secure its great power stature. Stalin was fond of invoking the countless foreign rulers of the past who had beaten and humiliated Russia—Mongol khans, Turkish beys, Swedish feudal lords, Polish and Lithuanian gentry, British and French capitalists, Japanese barons. "All beat her—for her backwardness: for military backwardness, for cultural backwardness, for political backwardness, for industrial backwardness, for agricultural backwardness. She was beaten because to do so was profitable and could be done with impunity."[11] Soviet power and socialist modernity would ensure that these defeats would not be repeated. Moreover, Russia would now serve as the model for socialists around the world. Great power stature would be achieved through support of communist movements as well as through the normal realms of foreign policy. Ultimately, the world would be joined in a free commonwealth of peaceful, egalitarian communist societies.

This utopia, in all its dimensions—individual, societal, state, international—required a race against time. Compared to the decades of industrialization in the West, the workers' state would create in a few years a powerful economy and state based on socialist principles. "We are fifty or a hundred years behind the advanced countries," Stalin stated in a speech to industrial managers. "We must make good this distance in ten years. Either we do it, or they crush us."[12] To catch up and pass the capitalist countries was only a matter of will. "We have all the 'objective' opportunities [for this pace of development]. The only thing lacking is the ability to make proper use of these opportunities. And that depends on us. *Only* on us!"[13] Workers inspired by the vision of socialism would bend time to their wills, just as the powerful blacksmith of so many Soviet posters bent the iron hot out of the forge. One propagandist wrote of the labor at the giant Magnitogorsk works, where dams had also to be constructed: "The Magnitogorsk dam was a school at which people began to respect Bolshevik miracles."[14] "Utopia has become a reality," exclaimed one Soviet newspaper, when the state abolished Sunday as a universal day of rest and introduced continuous production. Workers were supposed to work four days at a stretch, followed by one day off. "The continuous-production week has knocked time out of the calendar saddle. . . . [T]he country has entered a state of permanent waking."[15]

As these quotations from Stalin make clear, the optimism of the revolution did not die with Lenin and the New Economic Policy (NEP) of the 1920s, even if its advocates were chastened by the difficulties of actually implementing socialism. Instead, as Kotkin also argues, the Stalin "revolution from above" revived utopian desires that had waned in the NEP years, when many committed communists watched with grave mistrust the reemergence of a bourgeoisie and private peasant agriculture.[16] The Stalin revolution gave utopian strivings an even more solid grounding in production and state power, but also in the efforts to formulate a specifically socialist culture in daily life and in the arts. Magnitogorsk, the huge metallurgical complex built in an undeveloped area in the Urals, would produce both steel for economic development and a new socialist culture. Communal apartments with common eating and laundry facilities and public baths were supposed to forge the new collectivist consciousness. "Red corners" in apartments and housing barracks, socialist clubs organized among groups of workers, theater performances and film showings, celebrations of public holidays like May Day—all were to serve as educational and cultural centers that would train the peasant recruits to the industrial mammoth to be modern proletarians. They were to be skilled at work, committed to the cause, engaged in the trade union and party section: the very image of "What a Communist Ought to Be Like."[17] Even Stalin waxed melodic about a rural life set free by the flourishing fields and hefty cattle grown and raised on the collective farms, where meals would be taken communally and the burdens of household labor eased by public bakeries and central laundry facilities.[18] "Life has improved, comrades. Life has become joyous," he concluded.[19]

The realities of utopia-in-the-making fell far, far short. Life did not become "more joyous"; eros was not set free. There were few signs that drinking fell into abeyance, or that the use of the Russian language had become more elevated. The immense transformations of the 1930s—

forced collectivization of agriculture and the rapid acceleration of industrialization—caused unfathomable hardships. People could not find basic goods to purchase, and famine swept over the Ukraine, north Caucasus, and other regions. In places like Magnitogorsk the newly built apartment complexes were shabby, the most basic sewage and water services prone to disruption. The public baths were unsanitary, the apartment buildings crowded. Communal living seems to have inspired more an intense desire for privacy than a joyful collective life. Party cadres were impatient with the tendency of workers, both the newly recruited and the experienced, to spend their time drinking, playing cards, and laughing over raw humor instead of engaging in high-minded devotion to the cause. The dam built in "miracle" time at Magnitogorsk leaked and soon had to be replaced by a much bigger one.

Nonetheless, the vision of the socialist utopia could be quite inspiring.[20] From a vantage point that looks, first and foremost, at the collapse of the Soviet system in the last decade of the twentieth century, it is perhaps too easy to forget the great hopes that animated the involvement of so many people in the socialist project, and not just in the Soviet Union but also around the world. The utopian vision inspired thousands upon thousands of participants, who sought to build something new out of the morass of old Russia, dominated by aristocrats and capitalists and peopled by backward peasants. The notion that everyone, from party cadres to the masses, could undergo a profound inner transformation, could become a better human being, the "new Soviet man" or the "new Soviet woman," gave many people confidence in the future. The building of giant factories and canals, the conquering of nature, also meant that "man himself is being rebuilt."[21] Workers and peasants would "become Soviet" through the brick and steel of planned factories, the organized sowing of collective farms, a life lived in planned communal apartments and planned cities.[22] Those who joined the effort—produced beyond their norms, volunteered for extra shifts, or went to dig sites, railroad lays, or factory constructions on special assignments—received material privileges and honored status. They had their names inscribed in ledgers, their lives written up in the local newspapers, their clothes adorned with special medals. They rose in the social hierarchy, the Soviet system, especially under Stalin, a giant engine of social mobility.[23]

But were these utopian hopes related to the population purges that were also a central feature of Soviet life from the civil war that began in 1918 to the death of Stalin in 1953? In the case of Nazi Germany—and of the former Yugoslavia, as we shall also see later—the link between ideology and population removals was immediate and direct. The future society was always meant to be a society for one group alone, Aryans or Serbs, whose movement toward utopia depended upon the mass deportations and killings of "alien" national or racial groups. But the Soviets promised a bright future for all peoples; the utopian vision was inclusive, at least once class and political enemies had been removed from positions of power (not necessarily physically eliminated). Clearly, the enormous chasm between the promises of its rhetoric and ideology and the realities of political repression and population purges has been one of the key problems that has driven the ever intense political and historical debate about the Soviet Union. Some observers (and participants) have looked to the overwhelming weight of Russia's economic backwardness and Russia's authoritarian traditions to explain the shift from the halcyon hopes and promises of 1917 to the brutalities of forced collectivization, the Great Terror, and the ethnic and national purges. Others have argued that utopian convictions necessarily resulted in the mass deportations and killings of the Soviet period because to implement their ideology, the Soviets had to ride roughshod over human frailty and diversity of all kinds—political, social, religious, and ethnic. The utopian promise, in this view, was fatally flawed from the outset because it violated the realities of human nature and posited an impossible world of harmony and uniformity. The utopian endeavor could result only in its antithesis, continual repression and terror.[24]

Between these polarized positions some middle ground needs to be found. The Soviets could never simply implement their ideas; they operated on an immensely difficult historical terrain that necessitated constant political adjustments. The linear view that utopian ideology led directly to terror is far too simplistic; ideology was always mediated by the political and social situation in which the Soviet leaders found themselves. That situation was of course complex and constantly changing. It was composed of the weight of historical traditions, such as economic backwardness and political authoritarianism; the consequences, often unintended, of the Soviets' own policies; and the actions of hostile foreign powers. At the same time, a position that explains the worst aspects of Soviet history only by reference to the historical context in which the Soviet leaders operated misses the very dangerous potentials that the utopian vision contained despite all its alluring promises for the future.

The first problem with utopia lay in the reliance upon, indeed, the veneration of state power as the agent that would "build socialism." The emphasis on the state created a huge burden for communist systems in the twentieth century and is the root cause of their eventual demise. The second problem, perhaps more complicated, had to do with the vision of a society shorn of substantive difference (aside from gender distinctions), a society composed of a harmonious "family of nations," in the Stalinist phrase, that celebrated the fairly innocuous items of diversity—national cuisines, folk dances, epic poetry, and the like—but presumed that the forms of cultural expression would be subsumed within societies marked by the same essential structure. However distinctive the poetry of each nationality, the Soviet view expected that all of them would possess collectivized agriculture, planned economies, and communist party predominance. The first of these two problems necessitates some commentary here; the second will be addressed in the subsequent sections of this chapter.

The socialist utopia, it was clear, would not emerge by proclamation alone. Like all the cases discussed in this book, the Soviet Union was to have a strong unitary state that would secure party power, transform the social order, and reshape the population in an appropriate fashion. It was the state that would assume control of the economy to foster development in a rational, that is, planned, manner; this would enable the Soviet Union to surmount the anarchy of the capitalist mode of production and serve as a model for the rest of the world. The state would also promote the arts and bring "culture" to the farthest reaches of the Soviet Union. Schools, trade unions, and neighborhood organizations would all be subsumed under the state and would be the sites of training for the new Soviet man and woman. In its full-blown rendition, the Soviet view signified the virtual collapse of any distinction between state and society.

The implementation of these momentous transformations required not just policy pronouncements but the thundercrashes of state-directed violence, especially in view of the large and powerful hostile forces that the Soviets faced, both domestically and internationally. In an oft-quoted letter, Lenin already in October 1914 advocated the transformation of World War I into a civil war between the proletariat and the bourgeoisie, a point to which he returned repeatedly in the next few years.[25] Indeed, if there is any constancy in Lenin's politics, it lies in his conception of revolution as civil war, as a bloody, violent confrontation that required the most severe determination on the part of the Bolsheviks and their possession of the state to secure the victory of socialism.[26]

He proudly trumpeted these views in public, even boasted about them: "In answer to all reproaches and accusations of terror, dictatorship and civil war, we say: yes, we have openly proclaimed what no other government would ever proclaim: we are the first government in the world which openly speaks of civil war; yes, we started and continue to wage war against the exploiters."[27] Total war turned into total revolution could be carried out only by that construct advocated by Lenin, the dictatorship of the proletariat, "an unlimited state power based on force in the most literal sense of the word, and not on law."[28]

Within weeks of the seizure of power, the Bolsheviks introduced the category of "enemy of the people" and within a few months, on 20 December 1917, created the Extraordinary Commission to Combat Counterrevolution and Sabotage, or Cheka, the first in a long succession of internal security agencies imbued with nearly unlimited powers. Feliks Dzerzhinsky, the Cheka's first head, argued that the enemies of Soviet power had to be destroyed by systematic, state-directed violence. "We should send to this [domestic] front [of revolution] the most determined, hard, and solid comrades, without feelings of pity ready to sacrifice for the safety of the revolution. . . . We are at war, at the cruelest front. The enemy advances in disguise. This is a struggle to the death!"[29]

The level of violence only escalated as full-blown civil war erupted in the late spring of 1918. As Nicolas Werth argues, the extraordinary brutality on both sides of the civil war, Red and White, resulted from the convergence into one dramatic, cataclysmic upheaval of various forms of violence—urban workers' hard-bitten protests against the brutalities of capitalist exploitation; "traditional" cruelties of rural peasants against landlords and outsiders; the impact of World War I, which made modern, organized, massive violence an everyday, accepted part of life; and the Bolsheviks' own ideological commitment to violence as the necessary, indeed, heroic, means of societal transformation.[30] The Bolshevik leaders looked always to the most radical phase of the French Revolution, the period of the Committee of Public Safety and the Terror, as a model. Lenin's orders to party institutions evince a fearsome brutality, a cool indifference when it came to the shedding of blood, with order after order to shoot, take hostage, or deport any opponents of the revolution. "Find the hardest people," he said in one telegram, "act resolutely," "hang one hundred of the rich, bloodsucking *kulaks* (*and in a fashion that the people can see them*)."[31] Lev Trotsky displayed a cavalier willingness to shoot without question Red Army deserters or villagers who harbored White supporters or even proletarians, the class in whose name the Bolsheviks pursued revolution, if they challenged Bolshevik power. As he wrote: "Intimidation is a powerful [instrument] of policy. . . . War, like revolution, is founded upon intimidation. A victorious war . . . destroys only an insignificant part of the conquered army, intimidating the remainder and breaking their will. The revolution works in the same way: it kills individuals, and intimidates thousands."[32] And Lenin was not above deploying a dehumanizing, biological language, which we shall also see in the subsequent cases discussed in this book. The Russian land, he wrote, had to be purged "of all kinds of harmful insects."[33]

Stalin's assumption of the Bolshevik mantle signified an even greater readiness to use the weapon of state violence to consolidate party power, force-pace the transformation of Soviet society, and institute broad, violent population politics. Lenin and Trotsky had no hesitations about exercising violence, and they used military metaphors for every conceivable policy, but they at least imagined violence and militarization as part only of the initial phase of the revolution, and Lenin sought in his final months to convince the party to exercise some restraint.[34] Stalin had not even these compunctions. The "socialist offensive" that Stalin initiated in late 1928 implied the exercise of violence against all sorts of opponents, real and imagined. The massive, internal, state-directed transformations of forced collectivization of agriculture, rapid industrialization, and the Great Terror reinforced the proclivities toward the exercise of force that the Bolsheviks had already displayed in the civil war. At the same time, the polices of the socialist offensive created such havoc that the powers of the state grew ever greater. By its drive to transform society so rapidly and so fundamentally, the Soviet state created nearly permanent instability, which led Stalin and the other leaders to assume ever greater — and more arbitrary — powers in the effort to contain and manage society.[35]

Moreover, Stalin's own particular ideological contribution to Marxism-Leninism — the closer the final victory of socialism, Stalin proclaimed, the more desperate and dangerous the enemy becomes — provided almost unlimited license to the exercise of state violence.[36] Stalin's penchant for biological metaphors, greater than Lenin's, evokes some of the worst horrors of this century: *kulaks* were "bloodsuckers, spiders and vampires."[37] Cadres who did not take up the struggle against the opposition drive "the sores into the inside of the party organism, and the party falls ill."[38] Even worse: "Our party is a living organism. As in every organism a metabolism takes place: old, obsolete stuff falls off (applause); new, growing things flourish and develop (applause). Some leave the stage, at the top and at the lower levels. New forces grow up, at the top and at the lower levels, and carry forward the work."[39] If the "stuff" did not fall off quickly enough, then a state-directed population politics, replete with violence, would accelerate the process.

The Soviets understood their efforts in world-historical terms (as did the Nazis from a different ideological vantage point). They were fighting with the march of history and against the weight of a past marked by class struggles. The confidence of the Soviet leaders and the attraction of their efforts lay precisely in this sense of history writ large, of the epoch-making transformations that the Soviet Union had initiated. Like the socialist movements before World War I, they displayed the promise of the blissful utopian future in the metaphors of illumination, of sunlight, of sparkling seas of red banners.

But that bright and attractive vision, offered to all people regardless of ethnicity, nationality, or race, was stalked by the Soviets' veneration of the state, their open advocacy of violence and terror as the necessary means of creating the socialist future, and their vision of an essentially homogeneous society. While it is too simplistic to argue a straight line of continuity from the brutal political repression of the early years of the revolution to the still more systematic violence practiced under Stalin, it is also clear that the Bolsheviks' willing exercise of force created a set of dispositions that made possible the fearsome actions of the 1930s and beyond. The internal contradiction between utopian promise and systematic political violence runs through the history of the Soviet Union, and it helps explain how the regime that promoted ethnic and national cultures could also use all the powers of the state to suppress and deport in the worst conditions imaginable particular nationalities.

CATEGORIZING THE POPULATION

The Bolsheviks seized power in a huge, complex, and diverse empire. They could count on only a thin stratum of loyal supporters, mostly radicalized urban workers and a few peasant soldiers and sailors. Even this base of support was decimated by the ravages of the civil war and popular hostility toward many of the state-centered policies that the Bolsheviks enacted.[40] By 1921 and the waning of the post–World War I revolutionary wave in the rest of Europe, the Bolsheviks had become isolated internationally as well as domestically.

That sense of isolation and insecurity contributed mightily to the regime's constant drive to identify the friends and the enemies of the revolution, a tendency that would last through all of Soviet history and would reach its most virulent stages in the period between the very end of the 1920s and Stalin's death in 1953. But the Soviets were also intent on reforming men and women, making them into socialists Soviet-style. This was not a regime that could leave its population alone. The state had to be ever vigilant against presumed enemies, but it also had to work on those thought to be friends of the revolution, to instruct and refashion them into good Soviet citizens.[41]

The Soviet Union, in short, was both a repressive and a tutelary state. To enact its dual mission, it categorized all of its citizens along the lines of class, nationality, and politics. To use James Scott's terminology, the Soviets sought to make society "legible" so it could be administered.[42] This was no easy matter. To be sure, the proverbial steelworker was easily labeled a proletarian, a smallholder in the countryside a peasant, a person born of two Russian parents and living in Voronezh a Russian. But too many people straddled different categories, moved from one part of the Soviet Union to another, changed class positions, or married someone of a different nationality. The world was never as simple as Marxian categories presumed, especially in a country thrown into disarray by war and revolution and composed of hundreds, if not thousands, of ethnicities and nationalities. The Soviets created a veritable industry of categorization; in every program and in every decision, a profound tension existed between the assertion of the malleability of individuals, the belief that people could change and become good Soviet citizens no matter what their class or national identity, and the weight of inheritance, the understanding that a particular class or national background forever shaped an individual's and group's relationship to the Soviet project. Amid the most intense crises of the 1930s and 1940s, aspersions would be cast onto entire nationalities, and virtually every individual member of those nations would suffer the consequences.

The Bolsheviks, in Sheila Fitzpatrick's words, "reclassed" society. They established legally defined social groups that, in some ways, reprised the old Russian estate system.[43] Initially, proletarians and poorer peasants were the only members of society granted full citizenship rights, including the right to vote. Given the straitened conditions of the Soviet Union generally, they did not necessarily receive material benefits, nor did they possess democratic liberties in the Western sense. But they did acquire the status rewards bestowed upon them by the "workers' and peasants' state," and many of their number had opportunities for upward mobility within the system. Their ranks were expanded by party members, who automatically became proletarians-in-essence, even if their social origins lay in the intelligentsia or the nobility — a sign of the malleability of class categorizations, of the absence of any clearly "objective" definitions.

The peasants, meanwhile, were divided into poor (*beredniak*), middle (*seredniak*), and wealthy (*kulak*) strata. The regime touted the virtues of the poor peasants, but it was preoccupied by the *kulaks*, who, though few in number, fulfilled a critical economic position since they brought the largest proportion of grain to market. To the Soviets, *kulaks* were the nucleus of the antisocialist forces in the countryside, and society's economic dependence upon them was very troubling. But the real material differences among *beredniaks*, *seredniaks*, and *kulaks* were usually slight and unstable.[44] Often enough, *kulak* came to be a term of opprobrium bandied about in local feuds and political conflicts. Any sign of hostility, even of a lack of assent, to the regime's policies in the 1930s could land one in the category of *kulak*, with dire consequences. Such labeling had little or nothing to do with class as a "real," objective category.

The *kulaks* were among the *lishentsy*, those who in the 1920s and early 1930s were legally disenfranchised, subject to all sorts of discriminations in the public realm, and generally dishonored.[45] The *lishentsy* included, along with *kulaks*, czarist officers, priests, the petty traders and industrialists of the New Economic Policy, and the bourgeoisie and nobles of the old regime. In the early 1930s the ranks of the *lishentsy* grew ever larger, the sanctions against them even greater. *Lishentsy*, including former *kulaks*, now faced difficulties even finding work; many were fired, evicted from their homes, denied rations, or barred from education. Although the category of *lishentsy* was formally abolished with the proclamation of the 1936 constitution, many of them continued to face severe discrimination. Moreover, the state formulated a new classification in the 1930s, "social marginals," a highly fluid category that largely overlapped with *lishentsy* and demonstrated disturbing similarities with the "asocials" targeted by the Nazis.[46] Even earlier, in the 1920s and early 1930s, the Soviets had considered sending into exile "socially dangerous" and "undesirable elements," including the Roma and Sinti. In the mid-1930s these approaches assumed concrete form. Outward behavior — alcoholism, vagrancy, job shirking, individual self-assertion — was often taken as a sign of internal, almost biological deficiency that could be remedied only through exile or execution. Stalin himself signed a secret order in July 1937 condemning social marginals, and the directives issued by the NKVD chief, N. I. Yezhov, slated 70,000 of them for immediate execution and 186,500 for deportation.[47]

The categorization of the population by social class had immense consequences for individuals. Placement in the proletarian or poor peasant categories enhanced the possibilities that one could claim political influence, basic goods, and access to jobs and apartments, no small matters in a country still stricken by so much poverty. *Lishentsy* and social marginals faced enormous difficulties securing resources and opportunities and, in the worst cases, encountered deportation, imprisonment, and execution. Moreover, the classifications were recorded in an array of documents that constituted a virtual archive of the individual. Most infamously, the regime reinstituted internal passports for urban residents in 1932. The measure was designed to fortify internal security by enhancing the regime's control over the movement of the population. But the passports listed individuals' class and national identities. Moreover, every application for every position or benefit interrogated individuals about their class backgrounds. Every arrested individual, however specious the charges, faced a battery of questions about his or her social background. According to Aleksandr I. Solzhenitsyn, the Chekist M. I. Latsis wrote early in the revolution that the first questions to pose in an interrogation should concern the individual's origins, including his or her education and upbringing, a practice continued in succeeding years.[48] All these questions and documents made it clear that there were no "pure" individuals in the Soviet Union; an individual existed only as a member of a particular class.

But class was not the only criterion of categorization. The Bolsheviks assumed power in an empire with a dizzying array of nationalities and ethnicities. Just as classes had to be defined and filled with appropriate individuals, so nations, too, had to be defined and classified, and individuals assigned to their proper nationality. In the 1920s and 1930s, the Soviets set to work hordes of statisticians, ethnographers, linguists, and geographers and a variety of state and party agencies. Their task was to define, categorize, and count the population according to nationality, a process that was even more complex and difficult (and often arbitrary) than defining classes and their members. In conjunction with the censuses, the experts fiercely debated the appropriate criteria for nationality. Language, culture, geography, and biology all came into play.[49] The major guide to the deliberations was none other than Stalin, the key figure in the Bolsheviks' nationalities policy.

At Lenin's behest, Stalin had written *Marxism and the National Question*, published first in 1913.[50] As a good Marxist, Stalin argued that the nation is a form of political organization specific to the period of capitalism. Yet he also gave to the nation a certain stability over time. Writing in the catechismlike style he preferred, Stalin produced the ultimate, oft-cited definition: "A nation is a historically constituted, stable community of people, formed on the basis of a common language, territory, economic life, and psychological make-up manifested in a common culture."[51] "'National character,'" Stalin claimed, is not fixed for eternity. It is "modified by changes in the conditions of life; but since it exists at every given moment, it leaves its impress on the physiognomy of the nation."[52] With these statements, Stalin argued that the nation: (1) is a historical reality — it cannot simply be wished away; (2) evolves historically — its form is not constant over time; and (3) has a certain stability that is reproduced among its members through culture. Proletarian power, in Stalin's view, would contribute to the "blossoming" of national cultures. Once they were fully developed, then the preconditions would exist for their ultimate "fusion into a single, common, socialist (both in form and content) culture, with a single, common language, when the proletariat is victorious throughout the world and socialism becomes an everyday matter."[53] Yet even after the worldwide victory of the proletarian revolution, national differences "are bound to remain for a long time."[54] Since the order of the day was building "socialism in one country," the prospects of a unitary world culture and language were so abstract that they hardly needed serious consideration. Instead, the immediate task was developing cultures that were "national in form, socialist in content," as the slogan went. In other words, the nation would be a critical element in the fostering of Soviet citizens. Where nations had not yet emerged among the peoples of the Soviet Union, where tribes or ethnicities languished in backwardness, then the state would force-pace their development into modern nations, just as the state had to promote the development of the proletariat through forced industrialization.

Stalin's formulation and subsequent Soviet deliberations about the meaning of the nation and nationalities were firmly embedded in the general Western discourse on race and nation. The multinational and imperial character of both the czarist and Soviet systems made these deliberations even more complicated.[55] It should come as no surprise, then, that the same ambiguities and ambivalences that haunted this discourse — the tensions between relatively open and inclusive and harshly exclusive articulations of the nation, between belief in the malleability of humans and the firm conviction that certain recalcitrant types had to be purged from society, between social and biological categorizations of populations — were replicated in Russian and Soviet discussions as well, though with their own coloration, of course. Stalin, for example, offered no biological concept of nationhood. Yet as with the German theorists of the late eighteenth and early nineteenth centuries, Johann Gottfried von Herder and Johann Gottlieb Fichte, his defense of the reality of the nation and its rootedness in culture easily lent itself to the sense that the nation possessed certain timeless, essential qualities, and this entire perspective could slide easily into a racially based understanding of nationality.

PURGING THE POPULATION

Purges were a part of the Soviet project from the very beginning and were intimately connected with the veneration of the state and the categorization of the population into social classes and nationalities. Categorizations enabled the regime to identify those who were on its side, those who were potential supporters, and those whose possibilities for redemption were so slight that they had to be removed entirely. Purges had their roots in Lenin's conception of the party as a unified, disciplined organization that would serve as the vanguard of the proletariat and the "general staff" of the revolution. Even when the seizure of power was a distant dream and the Bolsheviks only a few thousand strong, Lenin was quick to expel this or that individual or faction from the party when, in his view, they threatened its disciplined bearing or disputed its strategic direction. Immediately after the revolution, the Bolsheviks began to exercise severe political repression, a trend that became still more pronounced in the course of the civil war. Lenin's and Trotsky's orders to hang those who took up arms against the young Bolshevik state and seize the families of counterrevolutionaries as hostages are only among the best-known of the repressive actions that the Bolsheviks initiated to save their regime from the hostile forces all around them. Even in the 1920s, the most liberal decade in Soviet history, the Soviet regime maintained its strict watch against political enemies real and imagined. Within the party the purge of factional opponents constituted a normal aspect of life. Under Stalin's rule, all these trends became still more extensive and severe.

But purges entailed much more than removing from power political opponents — again, real or imagined — and they extended well beyond the ranks of the party or active counterrevolutionaries. The purge was a complex, multidimensional phenomenon that in its most extensive reach encompassed entire social groups, like the peasantry and particular nationalities. It was an intrinsic part of the process of making Soviet citizens, of creating the new society by destroying the foundations of life that the regime deemed to be anti-Soviet, and by refashioning people into dedicated communists. Crises and instabilities of the 1930s and 1940s contributed to the virulence of the purges, but the Soviet leaders also drew upon and perfected practices and policies that had developed in the party and state from its earliest years.

Already in 1919 and 1920, in the midst of the civil war, the Bolshevik regime exercised massive violence against the Don and Kuban Cossacks as a group.[56] "Cossack" came to mean anti-Soviet, a synonym for "enemy" that carried an implicit racialization of a group defined not even by ethnicity but by its special service relationship to the czarist state. According to Peter Holquist, once the Cossacks rose in revolt, they came to be seen, at times, as a "biological . . . rather than juridical category."[57] To be sure, intensive arguments took place within the Bolshevik leadership, with some individuals condemning the slide into "zoological" terminology as un-Marxist. As Holquist also points out, the total biological categorization of the Cossacks lasted only a few months. Practical policy zigzagged between massive repression that included forced deportations and efforts to incorporate the Cossacks into the Soviet world. Nonetheless, the policy set at the center opened the way for all sorts of atrocities committed by local Red Army units, including arbitrary executions and the deportations of entire villages, many of whose residents were sent to the mines of the Donets Basin. Out of a population of 3 million, 300,000–500,000 were killed or deported in 1919 and 1920.[58] A barrier had been broken with the actions against the Cossacks, which demonstrated how easy it was to condemn a particular population group in its entirety and to presume that every single member of the group was a real or potential opponent, no matter what actions an individual had undertaken.

The victory in the civil war gave the regime a respite from the most overt and dangerous challenges to Bolshevik rule. Lenin's New Economic Policy, decreed in March 1921, allowed for the return of small-scale private commerce and production, which revived the economy that had been devastated by war, revolution, and civil war. Of course, the Soviet system was not a liberal democracy, and political opponents still suffered active repression. But the most severe political conflicts moved within the party, and there the tendency to demonize enemies and remove them completely from political influence only intensified. The factional conflicts of the 1920s were marked by militaristic language and by all-encompassing charges against opponents, which established dangerous precedents for the future. The situation was exacerbated by the absence of any clear checks on the exercise of party power except by the party itself, an institution over which Stalin wielded ever greater control.

For the Soviet leadership in the course of the 1920s, the truly great, massive obstruction on the road to the socialist future was the peasantry. Even those Soviet leaders who were advocates of the rural population, like Nikolai Bukharin, recognized that the peasantry had to be transformed. Given land by the revolution in 1917, the rural population, in Soviet eyes, represented a dangerous mix of private proprietorship capitalist-style with the dull drag of communal village control inherited from the czarist system.[59] Three or four times in the 1920s, the peasants, primarily *kulaks*, had withheld their grain from market in the hope of driving up prices, to the regime a dangerous assertion of economic and political power by a group it already suspected of disloyalty.

The problem, though, was not only the economics of peasant agriculture, which hindered the country's transformation to a fully industrial and prosperous society. The problem was also the peasants themselves, who still constituted the vast majority of the population. In the Soviet view, the individual peasants had to be radically transformed alongside the structure of agriculture. Their old practices and customs—Christianity; slow-witted, slothful work methods; attachment to nothing larger than the village—all the traits that the great Russian novelists of the nineteenth century had depicted with either admiration, irony, or loathing, all this the Soviets wanted to uproot. They wanted to make proletarians out of peasants—real proletarians who went to work in industry or proletarians on the land who worked in socialist collective farms. Set off on either road, they would at last develop socialist consciousness. At the end of 1929, Stalin argued that "the great importance of the collective farms lies precisely in that they represent the principal basis for the employment of machinery and tractors in agriculture, that they constitute the principal base for remolding the peasant, for changing his psychology in the spirit of proletarian Socialism."[60] Collectivization "turns [the peasant] towards the town," from which he derives productive assistance and, no less important, culture, socialist culture in particular.[61]

Under Stalin, then, the Soviet state launched a "veritable war" against the entire population of small peasant proprietors.[62] The official goal was the "liquidation of the *kulaks* as a class," according to Stalin's pronouncement of 27 December 1929, and the collectivization of peasant agriculture.[63] This was the most radical form of population politics yet practiced in the Soviet Union, one infused with the language and tactics of a military campaign. "[W]e must," Stalin wrote, "*break down* the resistance of [the *kulak*] class in open battle and *deprive* it of the productive sources of its existence and development."[64] To carry out this policy, the state mobilized committed communists, the Komsomol (Young Communists) in particular, and sent them out into the countryside to aid local party officials. But these dedicated activists hardly sufficed, and the state also dispatched Red Army units into action against the recalcitrant peasants, who sought desperately to maintain their individual holdings. Ultimately, the regime deported in horrendous circumstances more than 2 million peasants, accused of *kulak* status, from their villages to resettlement areas, while millions of others were herded into collective farms. As a consequence of their brutal and radical uprooting in the early 1930s, probably 6 million Soviet citizens died of famine, and perhaps 300,000 died in deportations.[65] Yet as we have already seen, *kulak* status was by no means self-evident, and the term proved enormously elastic. In many instances, mere opposition to collectivization landed one in the camp of *kulaks*. Local officials used the chaos of collectivization to settle old scores. People who did not fit easily into village life — supposedly promiscuous women, self-willed individuals, outsiders, many of them dubbed "social marginals" — often became engulfed in the whirlwinds of collectivization and terror in the countryside.[66]

The Soviet state halted mass peasant deportations by the mid-1930s. Many deported *kulaks* were allowed to return to their villages, and many of their children had their rights (to the extent that the term had meaning in the Soviet 1930s) restored. According to the regime, enemies now moved on the sly, infiltrating the very institutions of Soviet society and state, hence were more dangerous than ever. But as we shall see, the techniques of mass deportations that the state initiated in the campaigns against Cossacks and peasants—in particular, the combination of party and popular mobilizations and the use of heavily armed security forces—would be revived against other segments of the population, especially the suspect nationalities, and would be implemented in an even more complete and efficient manner.

Close on the heels of the forced deportation of peasants came the Great Terror of 1936–38, which marked the ultimate consolidation of Stalin's power. It also moved population politics to yet another, more radical level. Despite the assertion of some historians that the repression was "massive against all social categories," or that "practically the entire population was potential Purge fodder," more recent research indicates that certain population categories were far more likely than others to become victims.[67] People of bourgeois or aristocratic origins, once again; those living in the border regions, especially minority nationalities; the "unproductive," social marginals, and former *lishentsy*; those with foreign contacts, including such dangerous characters as stamp collectors and ham radio operators—these categories of people were particularly susceptible to the ravages of the Terror.[68] En masse the intelligentsia were not targets, but those who worked in particular sectors, like the economy, military, and foreign service, or party cadres in the bureaucracy, were especially endangered.[69] Old Bolsheviks, those who had joined the party before 1917, suffered when they occupied elite positions or had taken oppositional stances, but not if they were just regular party members.[70]

The techniques of population purges evident in the Great Terror demonstrated the regime's tendency to enact policy in terms of population categories of various sorts, including social class (*kulaks*, former aristocrats), nationality (Finns, Poles), and behavior (*lishentsy*, even though the 1936 constitution had officially abolished the classification, and asocials). Even more or less explicitly political opponents, those charged with being "Trotskyites" or "Zinovievites," were turned into a population category, because the regime portrayed their crimes as so vast, so sweeping, that they lay not just in specific anti-Soviet actions but in the very essence of the accused. An assessment of individual guilt or innocence was never the principle at work here. Sabotage, murder, betrayal, all the charges leveled against the Terror's victims, were seen as the manifestations of a more deep-seated orientation that coursed through the entire being of the accused. Hence the accused had to be removed from society by deportation, imprisonment, or execution. Anyone associated with them, families, colleagues, and friends, also became ensnared in the whirlwind of terror. It was as if the accused bore an infectious disease. In this fashion, the regime came very, very close to racializing even political opponents, to rooting particular behaviors and ways of thinking in a kind of permanent identity shared by all individual members of the group. The vicious rhetoric used in the purge trials demonstrates this ominous tendency. A. Ia. Vyshinsky, prosecutor at the Zinoviev-Kamenev trial, infamously shouted, "I demand that these dogs gone mad should be shot—every one of them!" The utter, complete condemnation of the accused, their placement in a category of "other," certainly less than human, is also evident in the animal metaphors used, the charge that "alien elements" were "dogs," "reptiles," or "predatory beasts," or even worse, "vermin" and "lice."[71] Those confined to camps were also talked about as if they represented a form of subhumanity. "What people?" a camp administrator said to an interlocutor. "These are enemies of the people." Or as another told a foreign prisoner, "We are not trying to bring down the mortality rate."[72]

The orders that unleashed the Terror went out from the very center of the Soviet system, that is, the Politburo and, even more restrictively, Stalin and a few trusted aides, a process we shall also see in the case of Cambodia. Stalin took immense interest in the proceedings and personally signed tens of thousands of warrants for mass executions, as did V. M. Molotov. But the Terror, like the civil war and forced collectivization, was a societal process, an intrinsic element of the "project state." Stalin and his close collaborators could not control every single event that occurred; indeed, their very orders presumed the participation of tens and hundreds of thousands of people in the acts of repression. Terror, like the other forms of population politics, had a dynamic that unfolded from actions "on the ground," in the villages, provinces, and cities of the Soviet Union, as well as from orders decreed at the center.[73] Through all sorts of activities, the population became involved in the workings of terror even if, in the depths of their being, many opposed it. Within the factories, workers often denounced managers and other supervisory personnel, which helped to make these people one of the primary categories of purge victims.[74] Indeed, a party "democratization" decree in 1937 openly encouraged denunciations. Some people denounced neighbors or coworkers as a means of settling old scores. Individuals took over the apartments and the positions of those executed or deported to the Gulag, and did not necessarily welcome the return of those who survived. At mass meetings in factories and offices, people were called upon to pass resolutions condemning others as Trotskyites or Zinovievites or many other terms of opprobrium. The proceedings of the infamous show trials at which political luminaries were badgered and humiliated by the prosecutor were widely reported in the Soviet press. In all the institutions of Soviet life, people were called upon to pass resolutions supporting the convictions of the accused. Through these many actions of daily life, the Terror became a societal phenomenon that incorporated large segments of the population, not only as victims, but also as perpetrators or as those simply complicit with the regime's actions. Whether undertaken willingly or out of fear, their activities helped sustain the system.

The impact of the Terror penetrated deep into Soviet society, even though the exact number of victims remains subject to dispute.[75] But for all its brutalities, the Terror lacked the total character of other twentieth-century population purges, including the Holocaust. A substantial movement to and from the Gulag existed. Many people were released after relatively short sentences, only to be replaced by others. The ideal, however perverted in action, that people could be "reformed" through labor and turned into good Soviet citizens, did not completely die. People could be "redeemed"; the purge was not final and total for all its victims, as was deportation to Auschwitz. But like forced collectivization and the deportation of purported *kulaks*, the Great Terror represented an enormous violation of basic democratic and human rights and a vast expansion in the powers of the state. It also imposed immense hardships on a very large segment of the Soviet citizenry. In this manner, the Terror established dangerous precedents for how supposedly suspect populations could and should be handled in moments of extreme instability.

THE ULTIMATE PURGE: THE NATION AS RACE

By the late 1930s, the Soviet Union was well on its way to becoming an urban, industrialized power. A certain "euphoria of victory" reigned among the Soviet leaders and committed communists, who were convinced that the socialist offensive had moved the entire system much closer to the final victory of communism.[76] The 1936 constitution, with its proclamation of the victory of socialism, articulated the heady sense of triumph over immense obstacles and optimism about the future.

At the same time, social instabilities and economic inefficiencies had reached towering levels. This was the "quicksand society," in the words of Moshe Lewin, a society of fantastic movement and mobility, from countryside to city and back again, from home to Gulag and back again, where nothing seemed quite secure and discontent was rife.[77] Food was still scarce, the harsh conditions of everyday life enervating. The immense instability was, of course, largely generated by the Soviet system itself—by the massive, forced transformations associated with collectivization and the five-year plans, by the continual removal of elites and even regular individuals by the Great Terror and more "normal" repression and purges. It is no surprise that the leadership had a palpable sense of insecurity, intensified no doubt by Stalin's personal psychology, which led to the ever more sweeping hunt for enemies and the ever more arbitrary exercise of power. The euphoria of victory and the dread fear of chaos and defeat ran hand in hand in the Soviet Union.

The Nazi assumption of power in 1933 served only to escalate the fears of the Soviet leaders. It was, after all, the German invasion in World War I that had led finally to the demise of the Romanov dynasty. The Nazis made absolutely clear their hostility to communism and to the Soviet Union. Incessantly, they linked communism and Jews as the ultimate enemy of the Aryan race. Germany's rearmament through the 1930s made its intentions crystal clear, and the invasion that finally came in June 1941 marked the most massive mounting of troops and armaments ever seen. The impact on the Soviet Union was immediate and devastating, and it aroused enormous fears of betrayal from within, especially from members of diaspora nationalities who, in some cases, had cross-border ties to the military enemies of the Soviet Union and had demonstrated particular hostility toward the "socialist offensive" of the 1930s. In this context of crisis and instability, the Soviets mounted yet another purge of the population designed both to move the country further down the path of socialist homogeneity and to create domestic security in the context of total war. But this purge was carried out through the lens of nationality. Before examining its unfolding, we need first to consider the evolution of Soviet nationalities policies.

The Soviet Union was formed as a federation of nationalities, and from 1923 to around 1937, the Soviets actively promoted nationalities, even where they had not previously existed. Soviet policy meant that "socialist content was only accessible to nationals in national form."[78] One

American historian has even termed the Soviet Union in this period "an affirmative action empire."[79] The hallmark of this approach was *korenizatsiia*, or indigenization, which promoted national languages and national elites. "Real Sovietization" of the nationalities, Stalin argued, is inconceivable without their "native schools, courts, administration and government bodies recruited principally from among the native people . . . acquainted with the life and language of the population." The Soviet system granted members of the nationalities preference for administrative positions; established quotas for them in higher education; and founded newspapers, theater companies, and publishing houses in the particular language. Soviets, the supposedly representative bodies that functioned as the basic political institutions of the state, were established for all the nationalities. The Soviets even promoted small-nation, indeed, small-tribe, nationalism within the republics.[80] Soviet scholars developed written languages for populations that numbered fewer than one thousand, and consolidated some groups and handed them one common language.[81] Through the use of native languages, the various peoples would also learn to "speak Bolshevik," in Steven Kotkin's phrase.[82] They would become the grateful recipients of the Soviet version of the "civilizing mission." For some of the more underdeveloped peoples of the Soviet Union, *korenizatsiia* even entailed receiving Komsomol activists, who were sent out to teach them to brush their teeth, bathe, and read.[83] For all groups, the trend signified a certain homogenization of life forms. All the national groups, it was presumed, would arrive at the same social structure and have the same reverence for the improvements the Soviet state had brought to them.

With the state itself promoting nationality as a category offering access to power and privilege, nationalist intellectuals and party leaders in many areas fought over the ranking between *narodnost'* (people) and *natsional'nost'* (nationality), the latter suggesting a higher stage of development.[84] On a more ominous level, policies of the republic governments and popular actions in Kazakhstan and Kirgizstan, for example, led to expropriations and expulsions of Russian colonists, a form of "popular ethnic cleansing."[85]

To mark the "triumph of socialism" that supposedly resulted from the policies of the 1930s, forced collectivization and crash industrialization, the regime proclaimed a new constitution in 1936. It marked a significant transformation in nationalities policy, just as it did in relation to the *lishentsy*.[86] With the new constitution, the regime claimed that the cause of socialism had triumphed in the Soviet Union. The nobility, then the bourgeoisie and the *kulaks*, had been vanquished. No internal *class* enemies existed any longer. Despite the triumphant tones of the constitution, the policies of the 1930s had resulted in enormous instabilities and discontents. Danger loomed across the borders from Nazi Germany. Stalin became increasingly paranoid the more powerful he became. The Soviet Union could not rest secure, and it found enemies among individual "saboteurs" and "wreckers" and among particular nations, some of whom would now be accused, collectively, of threatening the very existence of the Soviet Union. Ironically, the very importance granted to the nationalities principle through *korenizatsiia* now underpinned the attack on "suspect" nations. Over the course of the 1930s the objects of persecution shifted from class enemies to "enemies of the people," a concept that slid easily into "enemy nations." As Amir Weiner shows, by the mid-1930s Stalin was proclaiming that "the nationality question . . . harbored the clearest and most present danger to the moral-political unity of the people," which resulted in a significant shift in the category of enemies from class and political to ethnic and national groups.[87]

Beginning in the mid-1930s, then, the state limited the proliferation of nationalities without abandoning the nationalities principle. But it also asserted the cultural and political superiority of Russia.[88] The consolidation process deprived many diaspora nationalities of their institutions, such as their national soviets and publishing houses, theater groups, and so on, in their own languages. Cultural Russification, marked especially by the mandatory teaching of Russian, became the watchword. Stalin justified these policies by proclaiming that the former "feeling of mutual distrust [among the nationalities of the Soviet Union] has disappeared, a feeling of mutual friendship has developed, and thus real fraternal co-operation among the peoples has been established within the system of a single federated state."[89] "Friendship of the peoples" served as the new slogan, repeated through all the media and expressed at one rally after another. Stalin and many others invoked warm family metaphors to represent the unity, emotional and political, of the Soviet peoples under the aegis of their "genial leader." In countless programs and proclamations, the Soviet Union celebrated folkloric elements, previously condemned as the residues of backwardness, as the expressions of culture, "national in form, socialist in content." Folk dances and music, national dress, epic poetry — all the manifestations so beloved by nineteenth-century nationalists — were honored and celebrated in the Soviet twentieth century as the exotica of the Soviet family of nations. An essentializing rhetoric emerged in the mid-1930s, crass to the very core, that, for example, associated "sunny Georgia with its joyful art." The Russian people and culture were seen as manifestations of primordial being and the model for the other nationalities. The party's theoretical journal and school textbooks trumpeted the achievements of the Great Russian people and their history of heroic battles for independence and freedom against innumerable enemies.[90] In World War II, this kind of rhetoric only intensified as the Soviet state articulated the war as a racial battle between Slavs and Germans and explained the ultimate victory as a result of the inherent superiority of Russians and their Slavic brethren.[91] In conjunction with these views, traces of race entered into Soviet rhetoric, with at least one argument that "Germans were more Mongoloid than eastern Europeans, especially those from Hannover and Baden."[92] Like Herder, the German theorist of the eighteenth century, the major Soviet linguist, N. Ia. Marr, condemned the whole notion of race yet argued for the division of humankind into nations, with language and culture as the expression of the national essence.

Alongside the elevation of Russians into an essentialized, virtually racialized nation came the escalation of ethnic and national purges.[93] Already in the 1930s, security and domestic political concerns resulted in the forced removals eastward of *kulak* families from Belorussia, whose major form of identity was the fact that they were of Polish nationality.[94] The regime instituted similar measures a few years later against Germans and Poles in the Ukraine and Belorussians, Latvians, Poles, Estonians, and Finns from the Leningrad border region.[95] These groups were not deprived of their civil rights, nor were they labeled counterrevolutionary, only "unreliable." But the removal of entire national and ethnic categories was a clear sign of the stigma of collective guilt that the Soviets assigned to suspect populations and a fateful move on the way to the "racialization" of enemies. Amid the collectivization campaign, the regime deported Kuban Cossacks en masse, charging them not just with resistance to socialism but with Ukrainian nationalism. This event marked a critical transition from "class-based deportations, which predominated prior to 1933, to the ethnic deportations that predominated from 1933 to 1953," as the historian Terry Martin argues.[96]

These first ethnic deportations were directed against diaspora nationalities with ties across the Soviet borders to their fellow ethnic groups, and they were not total in nature.[97] They could be explained on the basis of security concerns, that is, on putatively political rather than racial grounds. But a major shift occurred with the forced removal of Koreans in 1937—in the midst of the Great Terror and when the prospects of war with Nazi Germany were becoming ever more likely. War with Imperial Japan was also a possibility, and clashes had already erupted along the Soviet border with Manchuria, which Japan had occupied since the early 1930s. The Soviet regime feared that Koreans would serve as Japanese spies, despite the fact that Japan had also conquered and colonized Korea. Now, in 1937, the Soviets for the first time conducted a population purge that involved an entire ethnically defined group. The Soviet regime sought out nearly every single Korean for removal.[98] Like other ethnic deportees of the decade, the Koreans were declared not an "enemy nation" nor "special settlers," the term applied to deported *kulaks*, but "administratively resettled." The regime provided them with compensation and their own collective farms and cultural institutions. The relocation seems to have been carried out relatively efficiently. But the Koreans endured inhumane conditions, including a month spent in barely heated freight cars. Then they were deposited into open areas in Uzbekistan, Turkmenistan, Kazakhstan, or Kirgizstan without any shelter or food. Many died from epidemics and hunger. In 1943, the government even demobilized 20,000 non-Russian soldiers from the army, including Koreans and Chechens, and shipped them to resettlement sites.[99] Deportations of a few remaining Koreans continued as late as 1946.[100]

In the Great Terror, about one-third of the total victims, 800,000 people, were arrested, deported, or executed on national grounds.[101] During the war years, the purges escalated still further as the Soviet Union reeled from the massive force of the German invasion, and the leadership feared betrayal from within. Germans, some of whose families had lived in Russia and the Ukraine since the eighteenth century, became immediately suspect, and the regime initiated their deportations in late summer 1941. Almost 82 percent of the Germans in the Soviet Union were removed, not just those in the Volga republic.[102] The initial decree issued by the Presidium of the Supreme Soviet accused the Volga Germans of harboring thousands of "saboteurs and spies . . . [the] enemies of the people and of Soviet power," which necessitated transferring "the entire German population" living in the region.[103] Other great waves of deportations unfolded in the southern regions from November 1943 to June 1944 and from July to December 1944, and involved Chechens, Ingush, Crimean Tatars, Karachai, Balkars, Kalmyks, and Meskhetians, all of whom were deported to Kazakhstan, Uzbekistan, or

Kirgizstan.[104] These measures affected about 900,000 individuals and were followed, from July to December 1944, by "cleansing" actions in the Crimea and Caucasus against "suspect" nationalities and "anti-Soviet elements," including Greeks, Bulgarians, and Armenians of the Crimea, and Turkish Meshkites, Kurds, and Khemchines of the Caucasus. As with the Koreans, soldiers of the affected nationalities were dismissed from the Red Army and sent to the resettlement areas; some 40,200 freight cars, presumably vital for military operations against the Germans, were diverted to the deportations from the North Caucasus and Crimea.[105] After the war, yet another round of purges affected populations in the western borderlands, especially in the reannexed Baltic republics. The Russian historian N. F. Bugai counts in total fifty-eight peoples (3 to 3.5 million individuals) deported on ethnic and national grounds, including 478,479 Chechens and Ingush and 1,084,828 Germans.[106] At the outset of the 1950s, more than 90 percent of those classified as "special deportees" were members of ethnically defined populations.[107]

The regime charged some of these people, like the Volga Germans, Crimean Tatars, Balkars, Kalmyks, and Chechens and Ingush, with direct collaboration with the German invaders. There were, indeed, instances of cooperation with the Germans, but no wholesale collaboration of entire nationalities. The regime's hostility toward many of these peoples was accentuated by their resistance to the policies of the socialist offensive, forced collectivization in particular, in the 1930s. A number of them, like the Kalmyks, were largely nomadic. Some groups, the Chechen and Ingush, for example, lived in fixed settlements but also herded flocks in the highlands. Their agriculture system combined individual and clan control of the land. These people's entire way of life ran against the collectivization drive and the effort to impose a uniform social structure upon all groups of the Soviet Union. Into the 1940s they had managed to hold on to some of their traditional patterns.[108] Other groups aroused the regime's suspicions because of their cross-border ties and other traditions that conflicted with the Soviet vision of socialism. The Greeks and Armenians seemed too Christian and too commercially minded, Jews the epitome of cosmopolitanism, and all three groups were presumed to be closely linked to their national or racial compatriots abroad. In the eyes of the regime, all of these groups threatened the great achievements of the 1930s. Their ways of life were outside the bounds of uniformity—collectivized agriculture, massive industrial enterprises—that constituted socialism Soviet-style. They threatened the "euphoria of victory" that the regime had trumpeted in association with the socialist offensive and the 1936 constitution, as did, even more directly, the invading German forces. Soviet confidence in the future coupled with the dread fear of defeat at the hands of enemies at home and abroad resulted in the radicalization of population politics and the turn against particular nationalities.

The manner of deportations bears all the characteristics of other ethnic cleansings in the twentieth century, including the Holocaust, just short of the actual and deliberate killings.[109] The operations were all highly organized, and Stalin was kept informed on an almost daily basis of their progress.[110] In fact, the ethnic and national deportations seem to have been carried out far more efficiently than the earlier ones against the peasants, indicating that the regime had learned from its prior efforts. They were also far more total in nature. As NKVD chief L. P. Beria expressed it in orders to local NKVD officials in the Caucasus in May 1944, they were to search out and deport members of the targeted nationalities, "not leaving out a single one."[111]

Typically, NKVD troops arrived in force in full display of the symbols of power at their disposal—uniformed and heavily armed troops, fast-driving cars and trucks, rapidly moving men. They sealed off a town or neighborhood, then went door-to-door telling people that they had forty-five minutes (sometimes less) to gather their belongings. Sometimes they simply grabbed people from fields and factories. The troops herded victims onto trucks and then into sealed freight cars, where they sometimes languished for a month before being deposited under open skies in their place of deportation. Following the population removals, place-names were changed, buildings destroyed, and cemeteries bulldozed in an effort to erase the visible signs of a once extant people and culture.[112] In many of the transports, children and the elderly composed around 50 percent of the deportees.[113] Evidence exists that the troops shot people too weak to move, and that guards threw out of trains the bodies of those who had died in the overcrowded boxcars.[114] Mortality levels as a result of the harsh conditions of resettlement and transfer, estimates at best, vary widely. On the basis of Soviet documents, Aleksandr Nekrich asserts that 17.7 percent of the Crimean Tatars deported to Uzbekistan died between 1944 and 1946.[115] According to Bugai, NKVD documents show that 23.7 percent of the Chechens, Ingush, Balkars, and Karachais died between 1944 and 1948.[116] By 1948, according to Nicolas Werth, the mortality rate of the 600,000 people deported from the Caucasus between 1943 and 1944 had reached 25 percent.[117]

At the end of the 1940s another decree declared that the peoples deported between 1941 and 1945 would retain that status "in perpetuity."[118] They would, in effect, carry racialized stigmas for generations. This applied to the 2,342,000 "special colonists" as of 1946, a figure that reached 2,753,000 in 1953, augmented especially by "*kulaks*" and "bandits" from the Baltic lands.[119] According to one report, Stalin regretted that it was "impracticable" to deport the entire Ukrainian population, as had been done with the Chechens and Kalmyks.[120] Yet as late as 1948 Turks, Armenians, and Greeks in the Black Sea region were deported.[121] And it is grimly appropriate that the very last Stalinist attack on an ethnic group, an attack imbued with racialist elements, was directed against Jews.[122] All the repressive measures and charges, symptomatic of the worst excesses of the Stalinist imagination, were, in all probability, the steps toward a revival of terror on a grand, societal scale, which would certainly have extended beyond Jews. But the charges of "cosmopolitanism," leveled throughout Stalin's last years, were also redolent of Nazi-style antisemitism. Moreover, in the weeks just before Stalin's death, reports circulated of a plan to deport eastward the entire Jewish population.[123] Fewer than ten years after the end of World War II, the scheme raised the specter of the worst actions of both the Nazi and Soviet regimes.

The Soviet state created nationalities by implementing a dual principle: the country was established as a federation of national territories and, beginning in the 1930s with the introduction of internal passports, every individual became the carrier of a prescribed nationality.[124] To be sure, a strong ethnic and national consciousness existed before 1917 among a number of groups, particularly in the European parts of the Russian Empire. But the entire thrust of Soviet policies was to affirm nationality as an organizing principle. In the Soviet view, progress toward socialism could come only in the national form — infused, as the saying went, with socialist content.

But the meanings the Soviets ascribed to nationality were highly ambivalent, even contradictory. The Soviet regime promoted nationalities, gave people freedom to choose their national identification, and, for the most part, supported a diversity of cultural and linguistic expression. Yet at the same time, in the period from 1937 to 1953, the Soviet state

also defined certain nations as suspect and dangerous, and those characteristics were seen to inhere in each and every member of the group.
Just as every individual had a certain, nearly irrevocable class background, so everyone possessed a national identity, one that had evolved
historically but also had a timeless, essential character. This position
blurred the boundaries between biological and cultural-based criteria
for categorizing the population. The entire ideological construction of
nationalities in the Soviet Union oscillated between an understanding of
nationhood as historically conditioned and subject to individual choice,
and of nationhood as a primordial, virtually racialized essence. Stalin in
1950 finally decided that nations were long-lasting, essential and permanent, a position far more categorical and one-sided than his original
formulations in 1913 in *Marxism and the National Question*.[125] His
1950 position affirmed the worst manifestations of Soviet policies that
had made every member of a national or ethnic group the bearer of the
characteristics ascribed to it by the state—heroic and virtuous in the
case of the Russians, suspect and dangerous in the case of Koreans,
Chechens, and others. Virtually all Poles or Germans or Koreans were
subject to the charge that they were at least security risks, if not outright enemies of the people. Yet at the same time, individual Jews could
occupy high positions in the Soviet state, and even a few members of
other suspect groups could escape the net of deportation.

The purge of nationalities took place under conditions of extreme
deprivation in a society already enduring the upheavals of forced collectivization and industrialization, and then, from 1941 to 1945, total war.
Total war in particular certainly lent a tenor of hysteria to Soviet policies, an intense fear of betrayal from the rear as a mighty army advanced against the Soviet Union. Rank brutality and incompetence,
well-known features of Russian bureaucracy attested to by almost every
nineteenth-century Russian novel, also contributed to the brutalities of
nationalities policy.

But these features—deep-seated insecurities in wartime, bureaucratic
incompetence—had such dire consequences because they were linked
also to the massive state project of building socialism, which encompassed the unending fear of enemies within and outside the Soviet borders and the enormous importance placed upon the nationalities principle. Policies of exclusion constituted a fundamental aspect of the
building of state socialism and a federated nationhood in the Soviet
Union. By the mid-1930s, virtually no one could escape categorization
by nationality, which offered some people access to resources and op-

portunities for advancement, while for others it meant classification as an enemy and forced deportation. A state that had already assumed such massive powers could carry out the policies of exclusion with impunity. The populations that became targeted as "enemy nations" were seen to lie outside the realm of reform. Their ways of life were too rural, too nomadic, too commercial, too individualistic, too religious, or some combination of the above, or they purportedly had cross-border ties to conationals, some of whom were at war with the Soviet Union. Ultimately, each and every member of the "enemy nation" populations was identified as a carrier of the same suspect traits that he or she transmitted, necessarily, to the next generation. Under Stalin, the Soviet regime condemned entire generations of particular nationalities, not on the basis of what they actually did (despite official propaganda that they had engaged in treason), but on the basis of who they were. That is a racial logic at work.

RITUALS OF POPULATION PURGES

In Vasily Grossman's novel *Forever Flowing*, the main character, Ivan Grigoryevich, returns to Soviet society of the 1950s after spending nineteen years in the Gulag. He feels out of place, alone and isolated amid the bustle of Moscow streets and the nicely appointed apartment of his scientist cousin. His very presence evokes unease—a lowered gaze, a nervous cough, a turn in the conversation. Ivan Grigoryevich is the spirit that haunts the conscience of those who managed to escape the various purges instigated by the Soviet system. All those actions that they had pushed to the dim corners of memory come flooding back in Ivan Grigoryevich's presence—the individuals they denounced to the authorities; the letters and petitions they signed, supporting the show trials of the 1930s and the purge of Jewish intellectuals in the 1940s; the friends, colleagues, and relations they shunned on the streets, or whose letters from the camps they left unanswered.

In Grossman's account, there are no innocents. The actions of the state have penetrated deeply into the sinews of society, implicating virtually everyone as either victim or perpetrator or, most often, both. While wandering around Leningrad, Ivan Grigoryevich comes upon the famous statue of Peter the Great. Never before has Peter appeared "so mighty as today. There was no power in the world so immense as that which he had gathered unto himself and expressed—the majestic power of the divine state. . . . It had come to reign . . . not only over an area which was vast in its physical, geographical expanses, but also over the innermost, deepest heart of each hypnotized human being who was willing to offer up to it as a gift, in sacrifice, his freedom, and even his very wish for freedom."[126] The state brings into its realm even those who live apparently normal lives. For Ivan Grigoryevich's cousin, Nikolai Andreyevich, the path to the very apex of the scientific community is finally opened by the removal of Jewish scientists. He relishes the recognition now bestowed upon him, soothes his conscience by finding bits of work for his former colleagues.

The human motivations, Grossman tells us, are many-layered. Some people seek career opportunities and recognition, like Nikolai Andreyevich. Others act out of fear of "starvation, torture, and Siberian hard labor," but also "of receiving red caviar in place of black caviar."[127] Sometimes the fear is very immediate, as with those who felt harassed and persecuted because of their social origins. They want nothing so much as to be accepted, like the character Grossman dubs "Judas 2," the son of a wealthy family that had supported the Whites in the civil war. "From his very childhood he had lived in terror. His mother had been frightened to the point of trembling before all authority. . . . Each day and each hour he and his kinfolk had been made to feel their class inferiority and their class depravity."[128] So he made a career of denouncing others.

So, too, did another type depicted by Grossman, the activist, the man from poor working-class and peasant backgrounds who joined the party in the Stalin years. He is told that the party needs his services, that progress is being derailed by those older members who are actually "enemies of the people." "He carried out his duty. He was not settling personal accounts. But he wrote denunciations out of a feeling of self-preservation as well. He was accumulating capital more valuable than gold and land—the trust of the Party."[129] Then there are those who are complicit merely for personal gain, who, in Grossman's words, reverse Kant's categorical imperative and see their fellow human beings only as means for their own advantage, while others relish the power they now possess. In the prisons and camps, the state gives them freedom to exercise whatever brutalities they wish, and their very being is nourished by the violence they dispense.

Literary accounts like Grossman's tell us what the historical scholarship has barely begun to investigate: the orders to repress the Cossacks, expropriate the peasants, purge party officials, and deport the

Chechens and Tatars came from the central state. But the execution of the orders involved the participation of hundreds of thousands, probably millions, of Soviet citizens. They denounced fellow citizens to the authorities and took the land, apartments, and positions of those expelled to the Gulag or to the "administrative" or "special" settlements in the east. As members of the security organs of the Soviet state, they herded, guarded, and killed the victims. However much the population's inner face was a mix of distance, hostility, opposition, and support, its outer face was one largely of compliance with the regime—exacted through fear and terror, or offered willingly in exchange for the regime's promises of progress and its cultivation of a sense of belonging and power. As Grossman's literary rendering of Soviet history makes clear, the line between the two—compliance attained by fear or won by acclamation—was anything but hard and firm. The "gray zone" that Primo Levi depicted for the world of the Nazi concentration and extermination camps was perhaps even greater—and grayer—in the case of the Soviet Union.[130]

. . . .

> They took you away at daybreak. Half waking, as though at a wake, I followed.
> In the dark chamber children were crying,
> In the image-case, candlelight guttered.
> At your lips, the chill of an ikon,
> A deathly sweat at your brow.
> I shall go creep to our wailing wall,
> Crawl to the Kremlin towers.[131]

Arrest is an "instantaneous, shattering thrust, expulsion, somersault from one state into another."[132] Most often it occurred in the middle of the night or as here, in Anna Akhmatova's *Requiem*, at daybreak. The officials sought deliberately to cause fear and disorientation, and the quotient rose dramatically when the victims were roused in the middle of the night, under the shroud of a darkness—the Soviet version of the Nazi reliance on "night and fog"—made even more fearful by dimly lit Soviet towns and villages. Had the officials come in the day, few neighbors would have been around to hear the Black Marias—the name given to the NKVD's automobiles—careening their way through the streets or the tramp of boots up the stairs. The officials loudly ring or knock, heralding the "insolent entrance of the unwiped jackboots of the unsleeping State Security operatives."[133] The officials search the apartment; one is flooded with a sense of utter helplessness as all of one's belongings come under police scrutiny. "Nothing is sacred" in the search, and the jackboots crush things, obliterating the objects of family life.[134] The accused is hurriedly taken away, given little or no time to pack any belongings.

No orders went out from Stalin's pen concerning the arrest procedures. He did not tell the NKVD agents to drive swiftly through the streets or to arrive ostentatiously with loud steps and powerful knocks. These were the inventions of nameless, countless police officials who sought to demonstrate unequivocally their own power. Every action they took displayed their domination over life, the abject helplessness of the accused. Over time, such procedures became standardized — ritualized — demonstrated to new agents their first time out on an arrest, written up in the myriad handbooks that came to guide a recruit's training.

Knowledge is also a tool of power, its absence a sign of utter powerlessness. Typically, prisoners were not informed of the charges against them. The interrogations often began, "Do you know why you're here?" Prisoners were moved around, completely unaware of the final destination. In Varlam Shalamov's story "The Lawyers' Plot," one of his harrowing *Kolyma Tales*, the narrator is moved blindly from one prison to another, one camp to another. Guards come and go; prison cell gates clang shut; the rasping of metal on metal indicates that they are about to be opened, sending him on another leg of a journey whose destination is unknown. Guards take him to the latrine, offer him a loaf of bread, order him into a truck, order him out, shuttle him in and out of offices, place him in an unheated stockade where all his toes become frostbitten. At every stop he has to respond to the same questions — name, crime, sentence, profession? He is too experienced to bother to ask where he is being taken, until other prisoners join him. "To be shot," they respond matter-of-factly to his query "Where are they taking us?" This story ends on a high note, of sorts. He and his fellow inmates are not shot. Their denouncer himself becomes caught in a web of accusations, and all those he had denounced are "freed," that is, just returned to their old camps. But the overwhelming sense of the story is of bleakness, the surrender to conditions over which one has no control, the anomie that arises when one has no knowledge of what lies ahead — indeed, loses even the desire to know since one is, in any case, utterly powerless to affect the conditions of life.[135]

In the cities, among the loved ones of inmates, the absence of knowledge has similarly enervating effects.

And if ever in this country they should want
to build me a monument

I consent to that honour,
    but only on condition that they

Erect it not on the sea-shore where I was born:
My last links there were broken long ago,

Nor by the stump in the Royal Gardens,
where an inconsolable young shade is seeking me,

But here, where I stood for three hundred hours
And where they never, never opened the doors for me.[136]

The women waited on line for hours, as did Akhmatova, day in and day
out, moved in packs from one prison to another, one office to another,
hoping for information about their loved ones, trying, often in vain, to
pass along packages of warm clothes and food. Rarely did they know
for certain the whereabouts of their sons, husbands, and fathers. The
only power that existed was of witness, the drive that led Akhmatova to
write *Requiem*, her searing poem of the Stalin years. Once they were
sentenced, the situation became even worse, since the inmates would be
removed to more distant, still unknown, places. The wives, mothers,
and daughters often lost jobs and apartments, had to scrounge for a
living, and faced arrest themselves.

Here, too, no one, at least initially, issued orders that knowledge was
to be withheld from the arrested and their families, that women were to
be kept waiting endlessly on endless lines. Police officials invented the
procedures. They relished their possession of knowledge, the power to
dispense it at will. And its possession was one key element in the formation of the secret police as an elite, the protectors of the revolution, a
sense that sometimes imbued the consciousness of even a lowly guard.
N. I. Yezhov, the head of the NKVD during the worst years of terror,
called for the creation of "chekists" as a "closely-welded, closed caste
which will unconditionally fulfill my orders and be faithful to me, just
as I am faithful to Comrade Stalin."[137] Yezhov himself did not last very
much longer, and many other, less powerful secret police officials would
be purged. But before their fall, they were rewarded with all the benefits

of a closed caste, including the best apartments, rations, and other items in the straitened Soviet 1930s.[138]

When the arrests were collective in nature, as was the case with the deportation of nationalities, the display of power and the circles of complicity became even greater. The residents of a particular area had no knowledge of the planned action. Aleksandr I. Solzhenitsyn describes the situation in one of the volumes of his acclaimed novel, *The Gulag Archipelago*:

> Armed divisions enter the doomed people's locality by night and occupy key positions. The criminal nation wakes up and sees every settlement ringed with machine guns and automatic rifles. . . .
>
> From the air or high up in the mountains it was probably a magnificent sight. The whole Crimean peninsula (newly liberated in April, 1944) echoed with the hum of engines and hundreds of motorized columns crawled snakelike, on and on along roads straight and crooked. The trees were just in full bloom. . . . The motorized columns did not go right up to the settlements, but stayed at the road junctions while detachments of special troops encircled villages. Their orders were to allow the inhabitants an hour and a half to get ready, but political officers cut this down, sometimes to as little as forty minutes, to get it over more quickly and be on time at the assembly point. . . . Hardened villages like Ozenbash, near Lake Biyuk, had to be burned to the ground. The motorized columns took the Tatars to the stations, and there they went on waiting in their trains for days on end, wailing, and singing mournful songs of farewell.[139]

After the long wait, the trains were finally set in motion.

> It was February 1944. The cattle wagons were filled beyond capacity, without light or water. We traveled for almost a month to an unknown destination. . . . Typhus broke out. There wasn't any kind of medicine. The war continued. . . . During the short stops at the remote, deserted stations, they would bury the dead in the snow that was black from all the engine soot. (If anyone ventured further than five meters, they were threatened with death on the spot.)[140]

These kinds of mass purge operations expressed the highly organized, militarized elements of the Soviet system. Lenin, as we have seen, was enthralled with the notion of revolution as civil war, and the military style became deeply embedded in the Soviet state as early as the real civil war from 1918 to 1920. Forced collectivization and industrialization and, ultimately, mobilization for total war against the Germans in the 1940s only elevated further the model of social development as a disciplined, tightly organized military campaign. It did not take much for this kind of logic to be applied to actions against the Tatars and other suspect nationalities. After the experience with forced removals of the Cossacks in the civil war and millions of peasants in the collectivization drive, officials had learned how to conduct these operations more efficiently. As Solzhenitsyn describes the situation, only a few high-level officers possessed knowledge of the operation, which enhanced the aura of power that surrounded them. The troops moved in rapidly and forcefully. Military discipline ensured that the NKVD troops and auxiliary personnel would carry out their tasks without opposition—they had either assimilated fully the discipline taught them in training, or they feared the consequences of violating martial law, or, most likely, some combination of the two. The Crimean Tatars, like Shalamov's narrator, were rendered completely powerless both by the phalanx of force arrayed against them and by the complete absence of knowledge concerning their destination and the nature of the "charges" against them.

The numbers involved in these actions were not small. For the operations against the Chechens and Ingush, N. F. Bugai, as mentioned above, notes that nineteen thousand NKVD troops were deployed, and that does not even include officials at various levels of the party and state bureaucracy; railroad engineers, stationmasters, and signalmen; and all sorts of bystanders. Aleksandr M. Nekrich notes that along with NKVD troops, the regime deployed regular army units, convoy guards, and border guards in the operations.[141]

Not only the dedicated or disciplined servants of the state—activists, security police, or army troops—were involved in implementing policy. Many peasants and workers became more actively complicit. They carted off the possessions of those who were deported—or at least what was left after the activists got to them—and, later in the 1930s, opposed the return of fellow villagers who had been dekulakized, who might claim some of their possessions or the support of the collective.[142] Red Army veterans and regular citizens, often Russians, moved into the houses and land that Chechens, Tatars, Germans, and others had occupied before their deportations. Many people took advantage of the opportunities for mobility—and higher pay, better housing, and other material advantages — offered in exchange for their becoming a collective farmer or party bureaucrat, a skilled worker with the Machine Tractor Stations, or a Stakhanovite, those who were decorated for far exceeding the output specified in the five-year plan.[143] Some took an active, public role in lauding the Soviet system, like the peasants and workers who participated in the Congress of Outstanding Kolkhozniks (collective farm workers) and Stakhanovites, or who allowed themselves to be interviewed for the endless newspaper articles and radio broadcasts about the building of socialism, the great accomplishments of the revolution, the "genial" leader of the Soviet Union and the world proletariat, Comrade Stalin. In the industrial sector, the Stakhanovites were the most famed of these, the individuals who performed nearly superhuman tasks on the job and contributed especially to the "construction of socialism." The utopia of socialism was evident in their grand efforts of will that surpassed all known limits of time and materiality.[144] Such efforts were also accompanied by the language of militarism, the "socialist offensive," "assaults" on the capacity of machinery, voluntaristic acts of will that decided the "battle."[145] At the local level, they gave the toasts at public functions, expressed gratitude for the awards they had been given. These "Potemkin villages," as Sheila Fitzpatrick has named them, presented an idyllic image of everyday life. No doubt such efforts bred great cynicism, but they were also an ideological mechanism that bound people to the regime, and many of them at least hoped that the real course of development would someday meet the idyllic image disseminated through the country.[146]

Denunciation was probably the most widespread form of complicity with the regime. Grossman provides a powerful depiction of it:

> At one end of the chain two people drank tea and talked across a table. Then afterward, in cozy lamplight, an intelligently phrased report was composed. Or perhaps it was merely a speech delivered by a Party activist at a collective farm assembly. And at the other end of the chain were crazed eyes; smashed kidneys; a skull pierced by a bullet; rotting, infected, gangrenous toes; and scurvy-racked corpses in log-cabin, dugout morgues. In the beginning was the word: truly, truly.[147]

Like the Third Reich's Gestapo, the Soviet secret police could hardly have functioned without the hundreds of thousands of people who accused their neighbors, colleagues, comrades, and relations of crimes against the Soviet state.[148] Denunciations were a traditional practice, a

means of appealing to the authorities in a society with few legal mechanisms for the resolution of conflicts or forms of public representation.
But like so much under the Soviet system, "traditions" of an authoritarian society became systematized and radicalized—to such a degree
that they took on an altogether new character. Building on past practices, the state devised denunciations as a set of rituals that mobilized
the population, willingly or not, to the Soviet cause. In turn, countless
citizens used denunciations to settle private scores, win favor with the
authorities, or promote the building of socialism—or all of these at
once. Soviet citizens wrote letters to the newspapers or to Stalin, con-
tacted the secret police and other state organs, and gave public speeches
or testimony. Some individuals denounced scores, even hundreds, of
others.[149] They denounced the factory director who failed to reach his
quota, the party boss who abused workers or drank too much, the
neighbor who had expressed reservations about Stalin, the engineer
who ridiculed communists, the *kulak* who hid his grain, or the son of a
merchant who now cheated the kolkhoz. As Grossman depicted it in the
passage above, denunciations occurred in private, but also in mass
meetings on the shop floor or in the meeting hall of the collective farm
or the local party organization. In the new cities of the 1930s like Magnitogorsk, barracks commandants and house managers provided information to the police—a more extensive and sinister version of the classic concierge who knows everything that goes on. Crowded, communal
living conditions made the task of surveillance that much easier, but the
willing "complicity of the residents" was even more important.[150]

Denunciation led to arrest, arrest to interrogation. The whole process
was designed to elicit a confession, the distorted reflection of denunciation. And interrogation meant, quite often, torture, especially during the
Great Terror. The gruesome brutality of it can barely be described, and
we shall see it manifested again under another communist system, that
of Cambodia. Like arrest, interrogation most often took place at night.
Prisoners on the way from their cells to the site of interrogation were
not allowed to look at anyone else, and vice versa. Guards made a
sound with their buckles or tongues to warn other prisoners of their
approach. Then came the interrogation, which first involved questions
about why they thought they had been arrested. A revolver lay on the
desk. In many cases, family members or colleagues would, at some
point, be brought before the accused, either already bearing the signs of
torture or threatened with its horrors. Everything about the procedure

emphasized the power of the interrogator and the utter helplessness of the accused, their inability even to protect their families.[151]

At least some of the guards and interrogators were convinced of the justness of their cause. Like Arthur Koestler's Gletkin in *Darkness at Noon*, they believed they were exercising revolutionary justice on the order of Robespierre and St. Just, and if the particular individual might not have been guilty, certainly enemies were abroad in the land and the larger cause demanded individual sacrifice.

The confessions extracted from some victims, especially Bolshevik leaders, served the clear political purpose of discrediting Stalin's opponents. But the practice extended far beyond a few Old Bolsheviks, and its meaning ran far deeper than factional conflicts within the party. The show trials of the 1930s were monumental public events, and they were replicated on lesser scales in communities, factories, and collective farms all over the country. Great and minor, show trials provided a politics of display and spectacle that involved virtually the entire country, and "assumed a carnivalesque function (the powerful become villains, the 'simple people' become the guarantors of justice). . . . These public trials serve [then] as . . . 'a formidable mechanism of social prophylaxis.' "[152]

The combination of tradition (carnivalesque) with the modern (the biologically tinged notion of "social prophylaxis") gave the trials their power and their hold on the popular imagination. And they had a theological element as well. It is perhaps easy to attribute the Soviet preoccupation with confession to Stalin's theological training, to a reinscription of Christian practice into modern communism. Those whose deeds and thoughts have been so depraved can return to the community only through abject repentance. Confession marked the ultimate rejoining of the community, and of course only the great power, priests or pope, party or leader, could bestow grace once again upon the flock. Yet confession was demanded even from those bound for execution, a kind of deathbed plea for the removal of sin. Confession marked the ultimate assertion of a homogeneous community differentiated, not even by life and death, but only by the power of he who bestowed or withheld grace.

And confession was not simply an individual act, signed after threats and torture while powerful interrogators looked on. At the infamous last show trial in 1938, Bukharin and his codefendants were accused of plotting the murders of Lenin, Sergei Kirov, and Maxim Gorky and his son, among others. They were further accused of "wrecking," which entailed, according to the prosecutor Vyshinsky, mixing glass and nails into butter. The language was designed to condemn the accused forever.

> The Trotskites and Bukharinites [are] a band of felonious criminals . . . who have sold themselves to enemy intelligence services, criminals whom even ordinary felons treat as the basest, the lowest, the most contemptible, the most depraved of the depraved.[153]

They formed "a foul-smelling heap of human garbage" that "must be shot like dirty dogs! Our people are demanding one thing: crush the accursed reptile!"[154]

The fantastic, otherworldly nature of the charges bore distinct similarities to the totalizing, all-encompassing "denunciations" of subordinate racial groups, because they were designed to castigate for eternity the victims and everyone even remotely associated with them. The circle of coconspirators radiated outward to family, even distant relations, and coworkers, and, in some instances, to entire political groups. Bukharin's wife, Anna Larina, spent months in prison in horrendous conditions, then eighteen years in labor camps and exile.[155] His first wife had a surgical brace taken from her, leaving her in continual pain. She was arrested and shot, and her brothers and other relatives languished in prison and labor camps or were shot. The families of other onetime Bolshevik leaders suffered similarly. A. I. Rykov's wife died in prison; their daughter was sentenced to eight years. M. P. Tomsky's two older sons were arrested and shot, his wife and younger son sentenced to prison.[156] Individual assessments of guilt these were not.

The Soviets had no extermination camps on the order of Auschwitz. Yet millions died in the waves of population purges, sometimes by direct killings, more often by neglect. The rigors of transport were killers, the bodies of the deceased unceremoniously discarded along the way. As one deportee to a Tatar settlement described the situation:

> We were forced to repair our own individual tents. We worked and we starved. Many were so weak from hunger that they could not stay on their feet. From our village they deported thirty families, and of these only five families, themselves stricken with losses, survived.
>
> My cousin . . . and her eight children were deported with us. . . .

[O]nly one daughter . . . survived, crippled by the horrors and hunger she had experienced.

Our men were at the front and there was no one who could bury the dead. Sometimes the bodies lay among us for several days. . . . [T]he owner of one house threw two little infant corpses out onto the street, on the edge of an irrigation canal.[157]

In the camps, prisoners might be summarily executed for violating the rules, or to serve as examples for other prisoners. During the Great Terror the camps had to fulfill execution quotas, leading to a wave of deliberate murders. If not done in by execution, prisoners were often felled by disease, tuberculosis, pneumonia, and scurvy especially rampant. In the Arctic camps like Kolyma, the extreme cold, down to minus seventy degrees Celsius at times; the nearly complete absence of sunlight in the winter, swamps and mosquitoes in the summer; and vast labor requirements to extract gold and lumber and to build railroads in the most inhospitable terrain made conditions particularly excruciating. The death rate from the gold field camps reached as high as 30 percent per year; few seem to have survived the labor in lumber camps for more than two years.[158] Construction work on the infamous Baltic–White Sea Canal was also a killer. By 1938, the death rate was running at about 20 percent a year; those who arrived in 1936 were almost all dead by 1940.[159]

In another of his stories, Shalamov describes the discovery of a mass grave as a bulldozer clears the way for the men to log a new area of the forest.

From a distance, from the other side of the creek, I had previously seen these moving objects that caught up against branches and stones; I had seen them through the few trees still left standing and I thought that they were logs that had not yet been hauled away. Now the mountain was laid bare, and its secret was revealed. The grave "opened," and the dead men slid down the stony slope. . . .

The bulldozer scraped up the frozen bodies, thousands of bodies of thousands of skeleton-like corpses. Nothing had decayed: the twisted fingers, the pus-filled toes which were reduced to mere stumps after frostbite, the dry skin scratched bloody and eyes burning with a hungry gleam. . . .

Grinka Lebedev, parricide, was a good tractor driver, and he controlled the well-oiled foreign tractor with ease. Grinka Lebedev carefully carried out his job, scooping the corpses toward the grave with the gleaming bulldozer knife shield, pushing them into the pit and returning to drag up more.[160]

Like the body of a Crimean Tatar thrown from a train taking its passenger-load to the place of exile, the bodies of the Kolyma laborers served as the mark, real and symbolic, of the worst aspects of the Soviet state's population politics. The corpses of the ensnared individuals — thrown, deposed, shoved, slashed — were denied the barest shred of respect. They were, indeed, like the logs Shalamov first took them to be. Violated in life, the bodies were degraded in death. And the degradation did not occur anonymously, but at the hands of a guard on a transport leading a population into exile or a fellow inmate who wielded the controls of a tractor.

CONCLUSION

The future envisaged by the Soviet Union was radically different from the Nazi utopia. The Soviet utopia was to be egalitarian and inclusive. Yet population purges were a central feature of Soviet life until the mid-1950s. These purges were entwined with the obsessive drive to categorize every member of the population, to determine their class, national, and political affiliations. On the basis of such extensive information, the regime hoped to determine its allies and its enemies among the population. It sought to use the information to form people into good Soviet citizens. But those whose attachments to older ways were considered too profound or whose association with conationals beyond the Soviet borders made them immediately suspect had to be removed from society by deportations and executions. The drive to reshape the behavior, the thought patterns, and the very composition of the population was an intrinsic aspect of Soviet socialist modernity, the effort to create "a quintessential enlightenment utopia" that would result in a "conflict-free, harmonious body."[161] This social engineering drive was not unique to the Soviet Union, but under Stalin it became particularly systematic and virulent, precisely because of the system's totalizing claims and the absence of the legal and cultural limits imposed upon the state in liberal regimes. For all the talk about the malleability of human beings, in the immediate present of the Stalin period, which placed such a premium upon uniformity and adherence to the socialist project, many of those considered outside the pale became enemies in toto. The Soviet version of the "civilizing mission," which had accorded the nation such a prominent role, meant, for some groups, forced deportations in conditions that led to extremely high mortality rates, because they were seen to stand in the way of "building socialism" or were suspected of collaboration with the enemy, Nazi Germany in particular.

A whole variety of experiences and activities—class background, political affiliation, "asocial" tendencies, sheer bad luck—could land people in the vortex of purge operations. But by the mid-1930s, national identity had become one of the key criteria by which the regime categorized and evaluated its population. Soviet nationalities policies were immensely complex, ambiguous, and even contradictory. The Soviet Union actively promoted the development of national institutions and national consciousness. "National in form, socialist in content" remained the guiding principle of its policies. The Soviets explicitly and loudly rejected the ideology of race. "Zoological" thinking, as it was sometimes termed in the Stalin period, was characteristic of the Nazi system in particular, degenerate bourgeois society in general, the Soviets claimed.

Yet traces of racial politics crept into the Soviet system even though one would hardly expect to find them here, in a polity that very explicitly rejected the entire ideological corpus and terminology of race. At the more open and tolerant end of the spectrum, the Soviets allowed people to choose their nationality upon reaching age sixteen. In its most exclusive and racialized articulation of the meaning of nationality, the regime came to define groups as the bearers of an inheritable, and sometimes immutable, essence that might not be marked by skin color or even biology but had a cultural form so deep-seated that it was transmitted—automatically, inevitably—through the generations. Hence the regime rounded up and deported virtually every member of targeted populations, stamping them with racial stigmas. In its oscillation between open and inclusive and harshly exclusive, racialized understandings, the Soviet experience demonstrated all too vividly the ambiguities inherent in the national form.

The Bolsheviks took power in an immense, varied, and poverty-stricken society, and one that was always under siege from a hostile, capitalist world. In the 1930s, that sense of endangerment took on a new reality with the emergence of a powerful and belligerent Nazi Germany. The situation in which the Bolsheviks took power and Stalin secured his dictatorship was not auspicious for the development of a harmonious, prosperous, and peaceful socialist society. When some population groups were perceived to be particularly recalcitrant, particularly resistant to the siren song of socialism, especially in the context of the huge social upheavals of the 1930s and the immense danger posed by the German invasion in the 1940s, the ideological belief in the malleability of human beings weakened and sometimes utterly collapsed. The fraught instability of these years only heightened the Soviet state's drive for political and social uniformity, which helps explain the increasingly radical application of population politics that resulted ultimately in a kind of racial typing of particular nationalities. While the preceding purges had been based on purported class and political identities, the national purges were both more systematic and more total, reflecting both the regime's perfection of purge techniques and the ideology of nation as race. Ultimately, there was no escaping the charge that one was at least a security risk, if not an outright enemy of the people, if one was Tatar or German, Korean or Chechen, or any of a host of other nationalities. The attacks on these people went far beyond mere security concerns, however real these were, especially in light of the cataclysmic scale of the German invasion. Security policies were enacted through a racial lens that captured in the range of vision every member of the targeted groups. No less than the internment of Japanese Americans by the United States in World War II, the ethnic and national purges in the Soviet Union demonstrated the workings of a racial logic.

Yet it needs to be said, once again, that race was by no means the only logic of the Stalinist system. As recent scholarship has emphasized, the Soviet regime also held out the possibility of redemption for those purged from society and from their historic sites of settlement, as evidenced by the movement in and out of the Gulag, by the possibilities for redemption offered by wartime service, by the oft-repeated claim that sons should not pay for the sins of their fathers and the release of children of *kulaks* from special settlements, and, following 1956, by the removal of disabilities from some (though not all) of the purged national groups.[162] Stalin and many other Soviet leaders were, of course, non-Russians. Even among those populations trapped in the racial logic, anomalies could appear—the Jew Lazar Kaganovich at the seat of power while the official discourse on Jews was saturated with racial antisemitism, a few Koreans who managed to escape the total deportation of the population. But even that most systematic of overtly racial regimes, the Third Reich, had some anomalies—German Jewish men who were spared deportations because they were married to German

Christian women; a Bosnian Muslim brigade in that most elite of Aryan formations, the Waffen SS.[163]

The Soviet utopia, like the Nazis' utopia, was a social project, very much a twentieth-century enterprise that, by its very nature, entailed popular participation. The Soviet regime, to be sure, exercised a war against society, as Nicolas Werth depicts the history of the Soviet Union.[164] Yet this war encompassed a very substantial segment of society as its perpetrators, the people who followed orders to repress the Cossacks, expropriate the peasants, purge party members, and deport the Chechens and Tatars. Though the orders came from the central state, their execution involved the participation of hundreds of thousands, probably millions, of Soviet citizens. At the very top of the Soviet hierarchy under Stalin, there remained few individuals whose revolutionary credentials went back to the pre–World War I period. Following the Great Terror with its radical purge of the party, it was mostly the interwar generation that occupied key positions both at the top and in the middle levels of the system. The midlevel functionaries had experienced enormous social mobility, and they came together in party institutes where they received their training and in the great campaigns of the 1930s, forced collectivization, rapid industrialization, and purges and terror. They were socialized into an ethos that memorialized the civil war as the great heroic engagement of communism, which necessitated tough masculine struggle and disciplined combat. If they read anything, it was Gladkov's *Cement* or Nikolai Ostrovsky's *How the Steel Was Tempered*, in which the heroes are, inevitably, Red Army veterans of the civil war. If they did not read, they would have seen the countless posters of heroic male combatants, sometimes with women at their side, though rarely were women depicted alone.[165] They imbibed an ethos of male camaraderie and masculine toughness — despite the official ideology of gender equality — that contributed to their willingness to exercise violence on a broad societal scale.

The partisans of the Soviet order were "new people," not the old elite and not, by and large, the experienced conspiratorial revolutionaries of Imperial Russia. They were bound together by their commitment to the Soviet cause (in its Stalinist guise) or simply by their desires to stay out of trouble and advance their careers. As members of the security organs of the Soviet state, they herded, guarded, and killed the victims. Along with everyday people, they denounced fellow citizens to the authorities and took the land, apartments, and positions of those expelled to the Gulag or to the administrative or special settlements in the east. From

the vantage point of common citizens, the act of denunciation or participation in the roundup of Koreans, Chechens, and Tatars might simply
have been a means of protecting one's own position or securing material
benefits by pillaging those less fortunate. From a larger perspective,
such actions performed multiple purposes: they served as the means of
implementing policies decreed at the center, whether the building of
canals or the removal of suspect nationalities; they bound the participants to the regime; and they marked the outer manifestation of transformed inner lives, the "making" of Soviet citizens. At the same time,
such actions made victims out of distinct population groups. In other
words, the process of mobilizing the population was a mutual one: victims and perpetrators were made together, and the same rituals that
bound one side to the regime made the others into the objects of population politics.[166]

But did the Soviets engage in genocide? If one does use, with all its
problems, the United Nations definition (as I suggested in the introduction), then one has to conclude that the Soviets engaged in some genocidal actions. The UN Convention, again, defines genocides as "acts
committed with the intent to destroy, in whole or in part, a national,
ethnical, racial, or religious group." The specific actions can range from
deliberate killings to causing "serious bodily or mental harm to members of the group" or "inflicting on the group conditions of life calculated to bring about its physical destruction in whole or in part."[167]
There can be little doubt, I think, that the Soviets imposed conditions of
life that they knew would result in severely high mortality rates of particular national groups, like the Chechens, Ingush, Tatars, and Koreans.
If they did not seek the actual physical annihilation of each and every
one of these people, they certainly presumed the death "in part" of
significant segments of the targeted populations. Moreover, while some
groups, like the Koreans, were granted national institutions in their new
settlements, others, notably Chechens and Ingush, were barred from
using their language in schools or from engaging in other public forms
of cultural expression.[168]

The Soviet Union under Stalin did not become a "genocidal regime,"
one in which the actual physical annihilation of defined population
groups moves to the very core of state policies, to such an extent that
the entire system revolves around human destruction. The absence of a
fully developed racial ideology, and the belief—though intermittently
applied—in the malleability of human beings, acted as a brake on the

Soviet regime's population politics, preventing the unfolding of a full-scale genocidal program along the lines of Nazi Germany. As a result, the state supplied purged groups with provisions, however minimal; granted some of them ethnic institutions in the places of deportation; and, after Stalin's death, could evolve into an authoritarian but not murderous regime, which even granted apologies and reinclusions to some of the groups purged in the 1930s and 1940s.[169]

At the same time, the purge practices of the Soviet Union under Stalin brought the system uncomfortably close to the Third Reich, though vital distinctions remained as well. The racial politics of the Stalin era were not predetermined and were never a fixed, continual characteristic of the Soviet system. But they were not an aberration or accident either. They sit firmly in the mainstream of modern history, marked by the easy slippage between open and harshly exclusive articulations of the nation, by the fateful ubiquity of racial politics, and by the Soviet Union's own commitment to creating a uniform society.

three

The Primacy of Race:
Nazi Germany

Johannes Paul Kremer received his doctorate in 1914 for a study on the tissue structure of insects, and his doctor of medicine degree in 1919. In 1927 he became head of the Anatomical Institute of the University of Münster; by 1936 he had become a senior lecturer as well. He joined the Nazi Party in 1932, the SS in 1934, rising to the rank of Oberst-sturmführer in the Reserve Waffen-SS. Throughout the Third Reich he maintained his university activities. During semester breaks he was dispatched on various assignments, often to SS hospitals to care for the wounded or ill men.

Kremer was an assiduous diarist. He kept detailed track of his own comings and goings, his assignments, his diet. On 29 August 1942, he notes in his diary, he received orders to proceed to "Auschwitz concentration camp, which reportedly is one doctor short due to illness." On 31 August, he records his first meal at the camp: pickled duck's liver, stuffed tomatoes, and tomato salad. Two days later, on 2 September 1942, he writes: "3:00 a.m. attended my first *Sonderaktion* [gassing of camp inmates]. Dante's Inferno seems to me almost a comedy compared to this. They don't call Auschwitz the extermination camp for nothing!" On 5 September he attended two more *Sonderaktionen*, which he finds dreadful. The following day, he notes in his diary, "excellent luncheon: tomato soup, half a chicken with potatoes and red cabbage (20 g fat), dessert, and wonderful vanilla ice cream." That same evening, he attended another *Sonderaktion*. On 9 September he received "excellent news" from his lawyer: "from the first of this month I am divorced from my wife. I can now see life in all its colours again. A black curtain has risen from my life! Was later present as the doctor at corporal punishment of eight prisoners and an execution with small-bore rifle." Next day: "In the morning attended a *Sonderaktion* (5th)."

The entries go on, the mundane seamlessly interspersed with the murderous. He orders clothes from Berlin, records the weather, bemoans an illness that lays him up for a few days. He fixes the wounds of an SS man hurt in a motorbike accident, praises the fine Bulgarian red wine and Croatian plum brandy available at a fellow officer's lodgings. At his sixth and seventh *Sonderaktionen*, he proudly notes that a guard snapped to attention before him. Immediately afterward he writes of a "real feast" in the officers' mess, with baked pike, "as much as you wanted," real coffee, excellent beer, and sandwiches. All told, he records attendance at fourteen *Sonderaktionen* during his two-and-a-half-month stay at Auschwitz. And he records several times that he "fixed fresh living material from human liver and spleen as well as pancreas." He is researching the effects of malnutrition on the human body. To get his specimens — he reveals later, after the war, not in his diary — he selected prisoners from the sick bay, who were then killed by injection, their organs removed immediately.[1]

The casual tone of Kremer's diary entries, the easy blend — after an initial unease — of mass killings and gastronomic delights, of family matters and murderous experiments, was all too typical of social life in Nazi Germany. Population purges of the most extreme kind had become routine, the order of the day. For men like Kremer, members of the professional classes who chose to make or continue their careers in Germany after 1933, the Third Reich offered unprecedented opportunities for state-supported research and career advancement. Professional prospects no doubt blunted the sense of moral outrage that one might expect from such men, physicians in particular. But the professions were also deeply implicated in the revolutionary characteristics of the Nazi regime: the movement of race thinking and racial policies, antisemitism in particular, to the very epicenter of state and society.

POWER AND UTOPIA

On 30 January 1933, President Paul von Hindenburg named Adolf Hitler chancellor of Germany. Every other government amenable to Germany's large, powerful, multifarious antidemocratic and anticommunist coalition had failed to master the economic collapse and political paralysis of the Weimar Republic's last years. Hitler, the head of a powerful movement, a man seemingly committed to order, had become acceptable. The transition of power occurred in a formally legal, constitutional manner. The government was composed of nine conservatives and only three Nazis. Many Germans were reassured.

Hitler's victory pronouncement was a model of restraint. As thousands of Storm Troopers marched through Berlin holding torches, Hitler decried the depressed and demoralized condition of the country and the power of communism that had sapped the moral order of Germany and Europe. He promised full employment, national unity, the safeguarding of eternal values, Germany's return to great-power status.[2] Hitler, at this moment, evinced none of the revolutionary grandstanding of the Bolsheviks, as when Lev Trotsky unlocked the Foreign Ministry's safe, published the secret treaties the czarist government had concluded, and declared the work of the ministry over. For the Bolsheviks, flush with the sense of victory on 7 November 1917, the proletarian revolution had made diplomacy superfluous.

Yet Joseph Goebbels, the chief of Nazi Party propaganda, soon to be minister of propaganda and popular enlightenment, recorded, on the same day as Hitler's restrained speech, an emotionally laden entry in his diary. "Germany stands before a historical transformation," he wrote. Observing the huge torchlight parade of Nazi supporters, he was exuberant. "An indescribable jubilation prevailed. . . . This is the uprising [*Aufbruch*] of the nation! Germany is awakened!"[3]

Goebbels was the more accurate reporter. Hitler, ever the consummate tactician, knew that his power base was still fragile. He sought to allay fears and keep the wavering middle and upper classes on his side. But underneath lay his rapture with power and his determination to reshape the world. No less than Lenin, Hitler had a clear ideological vision; he was never only concerned with power for its own sake, despite what many early observers thought.[4] If class was the central element in the Bolsheviks' worldview, race constituted the essence of Nazism, and Jews the premier racial enemy. The specific policies, even genocide, were not preordained; they would emerge in the context of political and social developments — including, critically, total war — in the 1930s and 1940s. But a society in some way purged and purified on the basis of race was the lodestar of Hitler's politics, and the state would be both sextant and sail, the instrument that would. chart and implement the course.[5]

In Hitler's own account, he became an antisemite in Vienna. In an infamous passage in *Mein Kampf*, he describes walking in Vienna and suddenly encountering a black-haired, caftan-wearing apparition.[6] First astonished, he claims, he then discovers that this nonhuman human being is a Jew. Hitler then comes to understand that everything he despises in Vienna — modern art, prostitution, the liberal press, social democracy — is controlled by the Jews. "Was there any form of filth or profligacy, particularly in cultural life, without at least one Jew involved in it?" he wrote in 1924.[7]

Biographers have cast doubt on Hitler's story of encountering a Chasidic Jew on the streets of Vienna. He may not have become a serious antisemite until Germany's defeat in World War I. Yet there is no doubt that Vienna was crucial to Hitler's formation, and that his experience there enabled him, after the fact, to embellish the story of his encounters with Jews. Pre–World War I Vienna had a substantial Jewish population and a cityscape strewn with antisemitic ideas and movements.[8] To Hitler writing retrospectively, "the giant city seemed the embodiment of racial desecration."[9] As his own life, filled at first with grand artistic ambitions, declined into the vortex of men's shelters and pittances earned from selling his trivial paintings on the streets, he picked up the antisemitic ideas so widely available in leaflets, rallies, and the press. As his most recent biographer, Ian Kershaw, suggests, antisemitism provided him with the means to vent his fury over the decline in his own personal fortunes, the grandiose plans that he had no possibilities of fulfilling, all because of "the Jew." But antisemitism as a fully worked-out worldview lay in the future. For Hitler, Germany's defeat in World War I was not just a political and military disappointment, but an unsurpassed personal disaster.[10] In the army he had found a place in the order of things — to fight for Germany in camaraderie with his fellow soldiers. Now this was taken from him. The movement he would build would, in some senses, serve as the stand-in for his army experiences. The National Socialist German Workers Party (NSDAP) had an ideological goal and a firm structure, at least at the top, which gave Hitler a renewed sense of purpose in life.

The main expression of his ideology came, of course, in *Mein Kampf*. It was written at a decisive moment, and not just because Hitler in 1924 languished in jail after his first, failed attempt to seize power. More significantly, *Mein Kampf* marked the synthesis of various strands of Hitler's beliefs, notably the equation of Jews and communism, the definition of the nation in racial terms, and the absolute centering of the race principle and antisemitism.

In *Mein Kampf*, Hitler made of Jews a race from which no individual member of the group could escape his or her benighted condition. Biological metaphors permeate the text, as they do the rhetoric of each of the cases discussed in this book. Jews were the maggots feeding on a rotting corpse, the parasites that had to be surgically removed, the sexual predators preying on German women, a spider that sucks people's blood, a plague worse than the Black Death, the sponger who spreads like a noxious bacillus and then kills his host.[11] In another nefarious, oft-quoted passage in *Mein Kampf*, Hitler wrote:

> With satanic joy in his face, the black-haired Jewish youth lurks in wait for the unsuspecting girl whom he defiles with his blood, thus stealing her from her people. With every means he tries to destroy the racial foundations of the people he has set out to subjugate. Just as he himself systematically ruins women and girls, he does not shrink back from pulling down the blood barriers for others, even on a large scale. It was and it is Jews who bring the Negroes into the Rhineland, always with the same secret thought and clear aim of ruining the hated white race by the necessarily resulting bastardization.[12]

Nazis high and low gave continual expression to this kind of biological and sexual imagery. At a medical lecture in 1936, one professor even depicted cancer cells as Jews, the X rays deployed against them as Nazi Storm Troopers.[13] Near the very end of the Third Reich, Hitler claimed that he had "lanced the Jewish abscess. . . . For this, the future will be eternally grateful to us."[14]

Hitler's vitriolic antisemitism was but one element, albeit the most virulent, in the larger complex of Nazi race thinking, which was itself little different from the wider currents of antisemitism and racism that had become prevalent in Europe prior to World War I. Like the class revolution of the Bolsheviks, the race revolution propagated by the Nazis offered a distinctive anthropology and history of humankind. In this view, human society was divided into a hierarchy of races. Each race bore particular characteristics that were transmitted, completely, ineluctably, from one generation to the next. The lofty accomplishments of human beings, from the architecture of the ancient Greeks to the classical music of nineteenth-century Germans, were the results not of isolated instances of individual creativity, but of a genius bred and sustained by the racial characteristics that lay "in the blood." The Nazis' terms of identification switched effortlessly from "German" to "Aryan," indicating their blending of the concepts of nation and race. That creative race was, of course, the Aryans. "All human culture, all the results of art, science, and technology . . . are almost exclusively the creative product of the Aryan. . . . He is the Prometheus of mankind from whose bright forehead the divine spark of genius has sprung at all times, forever kindling anew the fire of knowledge which illumined the night of silent mysteries and thus caused man to climb the path to mastery over the other beings of this earth."[15] Through a "unique pairing of the brutal fist and the intellectual genius," the Aryan "created the monuments of human culture."[16] Heinrich Himmler, the head of the SS, was even more blunt: "We are more valuable than the others, who are and always will be more numerous than we. We are more valuable because our blood makes us capable of inventing more than the others, of leading our people better than the others, because our blood enables us to be better soldiers, better statesmen, to reach a higher level of culture and a higher character. . . . We will maintain this quality so long as we keep our blood and our people healthy."[17]

Just as the traits of the great culture-creating race passed from one generation to the next, so the "culture-destroying" traits of the Jews coursed through their bodies and were passed on to every one of their descendants.[18] These nefarious groups, Jews in particular, did not exist in pristine isolation; they could not be blithely ignored. Instead, they actively threatened Aryan domination.

For the Nazis, race conflict was the driving motor of history. Hard, vigorous, masculine struggle against degenerate races, and against the degenerate members of their own group, marked the synthesis of race-based history and anthropology, a particularly radical, Nazi version of Social Darwinism. Each group, in this view, had an inherent drive to flourish, which necessitated expanded living space and continual conflict with other races. Out of the harshness of struggle, a still more vital and creative race would emerge. Since nature is "aristocratic" in essence, it favors the victory of the strong while it demands the "annihilation or unconditional surrender of the weaker."[19] Indeed, Judaism is nature-destroying, because its ideology, Marxism, "rejects the aristocratic principle of Nature and replaces the eternal privilege of power and strength by the mass of numbers and their dead weight. Thus it denies the value of personality in man, contests the significance of nationality and race, and thereby withdraws from humanity the premise of its existence and its culture."[20] History was fast approaching that cataclysmic moment of decision, a fateful clash worthy of Revelations.[21]

Never a consistent doctrine, race theory of this sort revealed traces of begrudging, perverse admiration of Jews, who had supposedly maintained their racial purity over the generations of the diaspora.[22] Yet at the same time, Jews, without a territory of their own, incapable of culture creation, lived as parasites off other races, surreptitiously inserting themselves into the land, state, and blood. Ultimately, Jews sought to denationalize other races, to reduce them to their own level, a task they accomplished by burrowing into the literal and metaphorical veins of the host population. The Jews' ambient character, everywhere and nowhere, made them especially dangerous.[23]

But the enemy was spatially located to the extent that the Soviet Union became, in effect, the Jewish empire. This was Hitler's other fateful invention, after the melding of nationalism and socialism — the identification of Judaism and Marxism, Jews and communists. As Hitler wrote in *Mein Kampf*, a victory of Bolshevism over Germany would not lead to a Versailles-like settlement, a political and economic oppression of Germany, "*but to a final annihilation, yes, the extermination* [Ausrottung] *of the German people.*"[24] The fight against Bolshevism "signifies an annihilation struggle."[25]

The fight against Jews was, then, an existential one in the most basic sense of the word, the conflict of two irreconcilable world forces, one culture-creating, the other life-destroying. While the Soviets envisaged a political struggle between two irreconcilable social systems, the Nazis clearly imagined a violent conflict between peoples. In one particularly chilling comment, Hitler said to Himmler in 1942: "[T]he discovery of the Jewish virus is one of the greatest revolutions that has taken place in the world. The battle in which we are engaged today is of the same sort as the battle waged, during the last century, by Pasteur and Koch. How many diseases have their origin in the Jewish virus! . . . We shall regain our health only by eliminating the Jew."[26]

But Nazi racial policies were never directed only against Jews, and the immense elasticity of race thinking is evident in an array of other comments and programs. The "defectives" within the ranks of the Aryan population had also to be purged. This included the mentally and physically handicapped, and also the broad, loose category of "asocials" — those who shunned work, alcoholics, vagrants, promiscuous women, jazz fans. Political opponents also could fall into this category, though less consistently. They did, nonetheless, have to be expunged from the population. In this way, the Nazis demonstrated the easy slippage between biological and cultural definitions of race. Outward behavior became the sign of internal, biological deficiencies, which mandated either forced reeducation in concentration camps — a kind of neo-Lamarckism premised on the belief that the environment could force changes in the bodily constitution—or worse, the forced prohibition on reproduction via compulsory sterilization. Such ideological positions were conveyed even in school textbooks, where a math assignment asked students to compute the cost of care and sustenance for a mentally ill or crippled person compared to the wages of workers and civil servants. Or the following: "The construction of a lunatic asylum costs 6 million RM. How many houses at 15,000 RM each could have been built for that amount?"[27]

To Hitler and the Nazis, race struggle was simply the manifestation of nature. And since that struggle was always a violent one, war, too, was the expression of nature, and politics merely the means of pursuing war. In this way, Hitler naturalized history by making its course an unmediated result of the laws of nature—of racial purity, racial conflict, and the struggle for existence. Nature, like races, was a fixed entity, a primeval, timeless determining force in human affairs.[28] If Aryans were not victorious, or if they failed to take up the struggle expected of them, Nature itself would be violated. Tragedy would loom large, the utter destruction of the species the likely outcome. Hitler seemed haunted by the possibility of a world depopulated of humans, a return to a past so distant that the world would be covered in ether, or would become a desert, a point he makes a number of times in *Mein Kampf*.[29] If not utter depopulation, then the next worst development would be the racial degeneration of a people via mixing: "[History] shows with terrifying clarity that in every mingling of the Aryan blood with that of lower peoples the result was the end of the cultured people. . . . To bring about such a development is, then, nothing else but to sin against the will of the eternal creator."[30]

But Hitler and the Nazis fully expected to emerge victorious. At the end of the struggle would come the glory days, years of unprecedented bliss and prosperity. Nazism had always a messianic character, no doubt part of its great appeal. The German people were not uniformly antisemitic, and physical annihilation was hardly a popular goal, or even a concept, prior to the outbreak of World War II. Rather, as Saul Friedländer has so cogently argued, Nazi antisemitism had a "redemptive" quality.[31] Only through the elimination of the Jews, whether by forced emigration or mass murder, would Germans reach the Elysian fields of the Thousand Year Reich. Unlike communism, which postulated an inclusive utopia—at least once the inequities of class privilege had been abolished—Nazism always envisaged a society of domination and subordination, with the inferior races providing much of the menial labor that would allow Aryans to pursue higher pleasures. The efflorescence of Aryans required the suppression of others. With final victory, Germany as a nation would be powerful, its rule uncontested, its domination feared. As a people, Germans would be productive and prosperous, the masters of nature through engineering and science, yet at the same time they would be able to revel in the retreat to a pristine natural order. Everyone would be joined together in a racially homogeneous grouping, all the members healthy, the elderly well cared for.[32]

This was the Nazi ideal of the *Volksgemeinschaft*, the organically unified, racially select, people's community.[33] While the substance of this ideal community was very different from the Soviets' imagined utopia, the rhapsodic language used to describe a harmonious society of new men and women was at times quite similar. The Nazi world purged of the racial others would have at its center "a new culture . . . rooted in the living nationality [*Volkstum*]."[34] Labor in the Third Reich would be defined by "the comradely experience of work and the equally comradely experience of leisure time [that] belong together; in them lies the idea of social life itself. . . . [A] new type of culture is in the process of being born."[35] It was to be one that joined rural and urban, manual and intellectual workers, all under the rubric of a purified national community. Membership in the national community would surmount all the differences of class and status and region.[36] There was, said Hitler in 1937, "a new feeling of life, a new joy in life" in the air; a "new human type" was emerging, men and women who would be "healthier and stronger."[37] Comprehensive public health measures, including dietary reforms like the promotion of whole-grain bread and greater consumption of fresh fruits and vegetables, were intended to increase productivity, in both production and reproduction. *Leistung* (performance or productivity) became a key word in the Nazi lexicon, spurring on numerous coinages like *Leistungsmedizin* and the related (and more ominous sounding) *Selektionsmedizin*, which would improve the work environment, weed out the weak, and match people's capabilities to labor tasks, all in the context of raising individual productivity.[38]

A product of World War I, the Nazi movement glorified male physical combat as the essence of revolution. The new man of this vision displayed martial as well as productive values: "[W]e like to see not the man who can hold his drink, but the young man who can stand all weathers, the hardened young man. Because what matters is not how many glasses of beer he can drink, but how many blows he can stand; not how many nights he can spend on the spree, but how many kilometres he can march."[39] Membership in the Nazi Party was open only to those men who were "swift as greyhounds, tough as leather, and hard as Krupp steel."[40]

For all its concentration on masculine glory, National Socialism was ever mindful of women. For them, the realm of combat was in the home and family, and any effort to overcome this division was yet another violation of the fixed order of nature. National Socialism therefore promoted marriages and honored motherhood. For the new Nazi man there was a new Nazi woman, who birthed and raised genetically correct children, maintained the household, and taught the family to honor Fatherland and Führer. The household presided over by the mother would be sustained by wholesome foods that would nourish productive and fertile Germans, food appropriate for a lean hardness geared to struggle and an appropriate roundedness suited for fecundity. Language in the home was to be purified, purged of its "non-German" elements and made clear and clean, while the rhetoric of racial struggle permeated daily life and the professions.[41]

The *Volksgemeinschaft* with its new men and women would not emerge easily: it had to be crafted through a determined politics of social and biological engineering. Amid the transcendent views about Nature, History, and Race, Hitler postulated politics "as the conduct and the course of the historical struggle of nations for life."[42] The state, of course, was the decisive instrument of politics.[43] Only through state action could the population be engineered to reach its lofty state of racial purity — by police and military struggles against the enemies, domestic and foreign, by social policies that promoted the well-being of the "Aryan" population.

This state had a number of particular characteristics. It was to be, first of all, a "total" state. Werner Best, deputy to Reinhard Heydrich, the second-in-command of the SS, held a doctorate in jurisprudence and was always quick to provide the intellectual rationale for the National Socialist state:

> National Socialism's political principle of totality corresponds to the ideological principle of the organically indivisible national community. It does not tolerate within its sphere the development of any political ideas at variance with the will of the majority. . . . The National Socialist Führer State has created for the first time in Germany a political police which we regard as modern . . . which carefully supervises the political health of the German body politic,

which is quick to recognize all symptoms of disease and germs of destruction . . . and to remove them by every suitable means.[44]

As Best indicates, the total state would be characterized by an all-powerful, efficient police, whose job would entail far more than maintaining law and order. The police had to actively forge the healthy social body by purging errant elements.

At the same time, the total state was to be led by one man, who embodied the "will" of the people. The *Führerprinzip* mandated the subservience of the state to the will of the Führer, who had divined the historical task and the racial essence of the German people.[45] This apparent reinvocation of premodern charismatic beliefs led many early observers to conclude that National Socialism was a throwback to the personalized rule, and the personalized brutality, of the medieval era or, even earlier, of tribal societies. Yet what the Nazis really accomplished was a modernist revamping of charismatic rule, since the state and society Hitler presided over also included a large, complex bureaucracy, a highly developed industrial economy, and a population mobilized for a variety of social projects, from highway construction to total war.[46]

Hitler's seemingly otherworldly capabilities found deep resonance among the population. At some point, as Ian Kershaw observes, Hitler probably became convinced of his own creation, certain of his own infallibility. Bound and determined to take the nation on the path he had divined, Hitler fused the personal and political in an uncanny, and also highly effective, fashion. For Hitler himself, there came to be no question that his person and the destiny of the nation were one. He "subordinate[d] history to autobiography," in the keen words of Sebastian Haffner.[47] And it is not too much to conclude, then, that so many of the major decisions undertaken during the Third Reich—to go to war, to systematize the extermination of the Jews—were taken in the context of Hitler's sense of his own superordinate powers and his fears of his own mortality. He was resolved to be present for the glorious accomplishments of foreign conquest and the final solution.

The total state led by the Führer was, however, never simply a dictatorship of one man. The new politics advocated by the Nazis, the vast project of social and biological engineering that they instigated, required popular participation. Goebbels, as minister for popular enlightenment and propaganda, made clear that the regime, the express "will" of the nation, also had to win to its side those elements of the national community that still resisted the siren song of National Socialism. They could not just be "terrorized" but had to be won over through hard work, including propaganda.[48] But dissent could not be tolerated. The claims of the Nazi movement and state upon the individual were total. The National Socialist Revolution, asserted Goebbels, "does not stop for [the realm] of private life."[49] These totalizing ambitions required not just obedience but also participation. The state had to "set the masses in motion," as Goebbels put it.[50] If Hitler did not deign to intervene directly in every policy matter, Hitler's followers believed that "working toward the Führer," pursuing his goals without his express orders, placed them in accord with the movement of history.[51]

Nazi views on the total state and popular mobilization concurred with strategic doctrine, Hitler's as well as the Wehrmacht's. In Nazi doctrine, war would allow the race to flourish; to pursue the war successfully, the race had to be purified. Since the coming conflict was never simply a campaign of territorial conquest but always a racial, ideological war, the links between domestic and foreign policy were particularly tight in Nazi Germany.[52]

Were the utopian goals of the Nazi leadership replicated in the population? At the very least, vast segments of the population viewed the movement "as a source of rejuvenation" and as a "great and radical surgery or cleansing," as Robert Proctor writes.[53] Germany would be purged of all its ills—foreigners, immorality, weakness, unproductive members, cancer, Jews, Bolsheviks. And this "cleansing" would open up vistas of happiness. The Nazis' promotion of vegetarianism and wholegrain bread, campaigns against alcohol and tobacco, support for research into occupationally induced diseases, promotion of screening tests and self-examinations for cancer, advocacy of saunas—these were not incidental to the regime, even when the exigencies of war made such efforts inconsistent. They were all part of the endeavor to purify the population, to create a "healthy" social body that was an intrinsic element of the happy, productive, and fertile society the Nazis aimed to create. Hence slogans like "Nutrition is not a private matter!" "You have a duty to be healthy!" and, most ominously, "Your body belongs to the Führer!" were as much a part of the Third Reich as "One people, one empire, one Führer!" or "Jews out!"[54] And the legion of ultimate or final solutions is a clue to the utopian aspirations of Germany under the Third Reich. The term's deadly implications were clearest in relation to Jews, of course. Yet there would also be "solutions" to the "women question," the cancer question, the smoking problem. If these were not immediately and once and for all "solved," they would soon face their "twilight," as in the *"Tabakdämmerung."*[55] Whole-grain bread was called the "final solution" (*Endlösung*) to the bread question. Even the great health scourge of the modern era, cancer, would be vanquished by the comprehensive programs of the Third Reich, just as alien racial elements would be purged from the social body by state action.

Hitler's racial ideology, with antisemitism at its core, was by no means unique. Everything he wrote or said could have been expressed, almost word for word, by antisemites all across Europe. The elements had all fallen into place before 1914. The real differences were political — specifically, that German race thinkers had taken power in a country with a highly sophisticated and capable bureaucracy, military, and economy, and they demonstrated a relentless ambition to implement their ideology. Their aims, while different in content, were as dramatic and totalizing as those of the Soviets, which places the Third Reich firmly in the camp of twentieth-century revolutionary states.

CATEGORIZING THE POPULATION

On 7 April 1933, the Third Reich issued the Law for the Restoration of the Professional Civil Service, the regime's first formal antisemitic act. Paragraph III.1. declared that "officials who are of non-Aryan descent are to be retired."[56]

But who was an Aryan, who a non-Aryan? After nearly 150 years of Jewish assimilation and intermarriage in Germany, how was a German Jew to be distinguished from a German Christian?

In 1938, a father wrote to Hitler, requesting that the Führer permit the legal murder of his severely handicapped child. The son, wrote the father, consumed resources yet would never be a productive member of society. He was a burden on the family and the state. Hitler instructed his physician, Karl Brandt, to examine the infant and consult with the physicians on the case in Leipzig, and to kill the child if their diagnosis concurred with the situation described by the father. Brandt traveled to Leipzig and authorized the killing. So began the formal process of "euthanasia," the murder of those deemed the carriers of genetically transmitted mental and physical handicaps.[57]

But how precisely were the handicapped to be defined, especially in a society populated by so many wounded World War I veterans? Who was handicapped by dint of genealogy?

To purify the society, to determine those elements to be purged, those to be honored, the Nazis obsessively categorized the population. The goal, it should be underscored, was the classification of the entire population, Aryan and non-Aryan, according to racial criteria. To accomplish this task, the Nazis did not engage in long intellectual disputations about the meaning of race and nation, as did the Soviets in the 1920s and 1930s. The Nazis assumed, simply and brutally, that they understood race, and it remained the underlying principle of virtually every social program, every political campaign in the Third Reich. But they did have to define the criteria that made one a Jew, Roma or Sinti, degenerate, or Aryan. In formulating and implementing their racial criteria and policies, the Nazis drew upon a very substantial scientific and pseudoscientific literature, and upon the work of learned professionals — doctors, jurists, anthropologists, historians, and many others — who promoted the concept of race. As the examples of Jews and the handicapped indicate, the Nazis quickly discovered that the biology of race could never be the sole criterion of identification. Biology and culture slid easily into one another as the Third Reich set out to define its enemies, demonstrating, once again, the highly malleable and mobile — and deadly — potentials of race thinking.

The Nazis assumed power in a society with a highly developed bureaucratic tradition. Many of the techniques for legal categorization of the population were not new. There already existed censuses, tax forms, birth and baptismal records, registries of the Roma and Sinti. These documents now could be mobilized for the work of purging the population. But the Nazis also established new registries and made use of new technologies, like tabulation machines that read punch cards. While categorization was fundamentally a legal, bureaucratic process, the Nazis also made widespread use of physical signs, most infamously with the revival of the yellow star as the marker for Jews. Soon such markers extended to other groups of the population. In the Third Reich, categorizations, legal and visual, marked the first steps on the path to annihilation.[58]

But first the Nazis had to define the criteria of membership in various races. A few days after the pronouncement of the Law for the Restoration of the Professional Civil Service, the state issued a supplemental decree that defined a non-Aryan as anyone with one non-Aryan grandparent. Two months later, those married to non-Aryans were also included among the officials to be purged from the civil service.[59]

The definitions became more precise with the infamous Nuremberg Laws, decreed initially (and supplemented many times) on 15 September 1935. Formally, the Law for the Protection of German Blood and German Honor banned marriages and any kind of sexual relations between Jews and Germans and prohibited Jews from employing female Germans under forty-five years of age. The Reich Citizenship Law, issued on the same day, defined a citizen as a subject of the Reich "who is of German or kindred blood and who, through his conduct, shows that he is both desirous and fit to serve the German people and Reich faithfully."[60] Here again the Nazis introduced both racial and cultural or behavioral criteria into the definition of citizenship. Jews were completely banned from the category of citizenship, but so were Germans who strayed from the proper National Socialist course.

Not even the Nazis sought here to define in detail the criteria of proper conduct. But they were quickly compelled to elaborate upon the citizenship law by defining who was a Jew. In a supplemental decree of 14 November 1935, the regime defined a "full Jew" as one descended from three "full-blooded" Jewish grandparents. Grandparents were considered full-blooded if they belonged to the religious Jewish community. But in addition, an individual descended from two full Jewish grandparents was a full Jew if he or she belonged to the Jewish religious community, was married to a Jew, or was the child of at least one Jewish parent. The decree also defined various categories of *Mischlinge* (people of "mixed race"), the most basic definition of which entailed descent from one or two "racially full" Jewish grandparents. *Mischlinge* were further subdivided into categories depending on whether they had one or two Jewish grandparents, though in reality all sorts of behavioral and cultural criteria came into play.[61]

Individual cases could become quite complicated. One man had two Jewish grandparents, one Aryan grandmother, and a half-Aryan grandfather, the latter having become Christian only late in life. The person in question was, technically, 62 percent Jewish. But was he a *Mischling* or a full Jew? The Reich Association of Non-Aryan Christians answered that the person was a Jew because one of the grandparents was a practicing Jew. If that grandparent had been Christian at birth, the grandson would be a *Mischling* of the First Degree.[62] Clearly, how one *acted* — practicing Jew or not — was, in some cases, as significant as who one was, at least in the Nazis' early discriminatory measures.

The definition of a Jew or any other "alien" was but the first step. The individuals who filled the category had to be found, and phenotypical markers — the "Jewish nose," the dazed look of the "feeble-minded" — were not always so clear. How did the Nazis actually find the people they sought to purge?

By and large, the task was rather easy. In the case of Jews, some were denounced by neighbors, a common enough practice in the Third Reich.[63] More typically, the Nazis simply made use of existing documentation, the most important being censuses, police registrations, and baptismal records. A vast number of party, SS, and regular governmental agencies compiled the information, and much of it came together in the 1939 census, in which workers used punch cards and tabulating machines to keep track of Jews in the population.[64] Private associations also aided the effort. The Evangelical Church in 1939 enforced the provisions of the civil service law by compiling a list, passed on to the government, of clergy and employees of Jewish background. Various genealogical associations were coordinated and their data passed on to the Reich Office of Statistics. Goebbels went on continual hunts for remaining Jewish influence in the arts. He had his subordinates compile list after list of artists and writers suspected of Jewish ancestry. Alfred Rosenberg, one of the other leading Nazi ideologues and Goebbels's competitor for control of German cultural life, did the same.[65] When the deportations of German Jews began in 1941, officials in Berlin issued orders decreeing the number of Jews to be deported from each locality. Gestapo officers in collaboration with the local police and other officials implemented the orders.[66] No doubt, the number specified to local officials was derived from the census and police registration data along with the earlier lists submitted by the Jewish community.

All of these efforts were not restricted to Jews. According to official interpretation, the Nuremberg Laws were to encompass "Gypsies, negroes, or their bastards," as well as Jews.[67] The identification of the Roma and Sinti was largely coordinated by Dr. Robert Ritter, a physician-anthropologist, who was appointed in 1936 to head the Racial-Hygienic and Heredity Research Center (RHA) in the Reich Health Office. Partly subsidized by the Criminal Police and the Reich Main Security Office of the SS, the RHA's task was to investigate and clarify basic "racial and criminal-biological issues" for an intended law on the Roma and Sinti.[68] Ritter built a veritable empire of racial research on them and the asocials, with at least seven major sites. He played a key role in forging, by the late 1930s, a "scientific-police complex," a tightly wound nexus of cooperation between highly trained academics and the SS, that investigated, formulated, and implemented racial policy toward the Roma and Sinti.[69] By 1941, the RHA had information on twenty thousand individuals, who were carefully divided into full-race Gypsies, *Mischlinge*, and non-Gypsies. The final determination as to whether one was Gypsy, *Mischling*, or a person who "behaved like a Gypsy by moving around" was made by the Reich Criminal Police Office on the basis of affidavits compiled by the RHA.[70]

Ritter maintained that Gypsies had indeed been Aryans but in their migrations north and west had interbred with lesser races. This "asocial and useless" population, the source of criminal and degenerate behavior, should be gathered in large camps where the individuals would be put to work and prevented from procreating. "Only then will the future generations of the German people be truly freed from this burden."[71] "Pure" Gypsies — estimated at only 10 percent of the thirty thousand living in Germany — would be allowed to follow their practices under controlled conditions. Himmler supported Ritter, but other Nazis thought that the entire Roma and Sinti population, pure and mixed, had to be purged completely. Ominously, Reich Health Officer Leonardo Conti stated that "an ultimate solution to the Gypsy problem can occur only by making Gypsies and Gypsy *Mischlinge* incapable of reproducing."[72]

Similar thinking went into the identification and registration of those thought to be the bearers of congenital mental and physical handicaps. Within six months of assuming power, the Nazis issued a law that mandated the sterilization of those deemed to be suffering hereditary illnesses, including "congenital feeblemindedness," "hereditary blindness," "manic depression," "schizophrenia," "serious physical deformities," and chronic alcoholism. A 1935 amendment authorized compulsory abortions for women placed in these categories who had somehow managed to escape sterilization. These radical interventions in the bodies of hundreds of thousands of Germans, a substantial majority of whom were women, were to be carried out without the approval of families, let alone the individuals involved. The law specified that if needed, "the use of force is permissible."[73] These measures set the precedent for the still more radical program of euthanasia, initiated in 1939. An array of state agencies and professionals charged with health and well-being — doctors, nurses, midwives, and social workers — provided the pages of documentation that flowed into the Ministry of Interior's Health Office in Berlin and to the more secretive "T4" agency (so named because of its address in Berlin, Tiergartenstraße 4) that directed the euthanasia program. Physicians staffed the review panels that determined the fate of handicapped individuals — whether or not they would be forcibly sterilized and, later in the decade, killed.[74]

The elasticity of racial categorizations, the easy slippage between biology and behavior, the conviction that outward antisocial behavior was a sign of a degenerate inner constitution, is even more evident in the treatment of "asocials." The Third Reich never passed a comprehensive law regarding asocials. Instead, a variety of arbitrary police measures, draft laws, and haphazard definitions characterized policies toward them.[75] Nazi officials typically listed an array of behaviors that were "hereditarily determined and therefore [display] an irremediable attitude."[76] These included alcoholism, work avoidance, vagrancy, prostitution, promiscuity, criminality, and homosexuality. Even more fluidly, the display of various "attitudes," not just actions, could mark one as an asocial. Himmler offered one such list, which included indifference toward the war; preference for English ideals, speech, behavior, and clothing; and attraction to jazz, "hot" music, and swing dancing.[77]

As all these examples make clear, the Nazi regime relied on the cooperation of a wide array of individuals and institutions, public and private, to compile racial registries. Clearly, even the Nazis could not adhere exclusively to a biological definition of race, which indicates just how specious are the term and the category. An Aryan who married a non-Aryan was not alien by birth or bloodline. But by dint of behavior—relations with a Jew or another member of an inferior race—one became a non-Aryan. Behavior was a broad, general category that could become subject to all sorts of arbitrary determinations and could determine whether one received the full protection of the Reich or incurred discrimination as an "alien" element.

PURGING THE POPULATION

"All evening there was only one subject of conversation, the frightful one. We make jokes and laugh and are basically all in despair."[78] So wrote Victor Klemperer, a Jew married to a Christian German, who chronicled a world closing in around him, removing from him, step-by-step, his liberties and his livelihood. He was a professor of French and despaired over his vanishing prospects of publication, the possibilities of dismissal from his position, and the foreclosure of his ability to procure a mortgage for the country house his wife wanted so desperately to build. These were rooted in the normal worries of a professional but now wildly exacerbated by the discriminatory measures implemented by the Third Reich, which made race the key criterion that governed access to positions and resources. In class he worried over every sentence he uttered, fearful that one of the students would denounce him to the Gestapo. Already in 1933, he was deprived of the right to sit on student examination boards. In January 1934 he received the official notification: "The Ministry has decided to cancel your appointment to the Examination Board . . . with immediate effect."[79] Some months later, he entered the lecture hall on the first day of class and found it totally empty, not one student present. "A crushing experience," he wrote.[80]

Klemperer managed to hold on to his post until April 1935, when he received a curt, formal notice of dismissal. Although he was able to procure a loan through acquaintances, so the house could be built, his economic standing plummeted. No longer able to afford new clothes, he worried over every frayed collar, every stain. His movements became more and more circumscribed. By the late 1930s, Klemperer feared even going to the marketplace, wondering whether he would be beaten or suddenly picked up and transported to a concentration camp.

Right alongside the bureaucratic and legislative categorization of people, the Nazis instituted an array of policies and procedures that demarcated Jews, Roma and Sinti, the handicapped, and asocials from the rest of the population. Like Victor Klemperer, these groups found their movements limited, their access to resources and opportunities, even to the bare necessities of life, severely restricted. Visual markers facilitated the segregation of Jews. Decrees issued by the Ministry of Interior in 1938 first required Jews to turn in their passports and to carry identification documents that specified the bearer as a Jew. Those without easily recognizable Jewish names were given the added appellations of Israel or Sarah.[81] Then the regime ordered physical markers: the wearing of a yellow Star of David with "Jude" inscribed in the middle. Nazi officials had first ordered Polish Jews to wear the badge, a measure that they extended to German Jews in September 1941. Victor Klemperer described the humiliation:

> I ask myself today . . . what was the worst day in those twelve years of hell? . . . 19 September 1941. From then on one had to wear the Jewish Star, the hexagonal Star of David made of yellow coloured cloth, which today still signifies plague and quarantine, and which in the Middle Ages was the identifying colour for Jews, the colour of envy and of bile in the blood; the yellow cloth with the boldly-printed letters in black: "Jew", the word bounded by the lines of the two intersecting triangles, the word formed from thick capital letters, which in their isolation, and in the broad exaggeration of the horizontal, pretended to be Hebrew characters.[82]

Like Klemperer, other Jews in letters and memoirs recorded the excruciating realities of exclusion as they were removed from every realm of public life and were subjected to all sorts of violent acts.[83] As early as March 1933, the Jewish residents of Gladenbach, a small town in Hesse, found their homes invaded and ransacked by Nazis. In public a few days later, a Jewish man was beaten, another forced to renounce his alleged defamations of Hitler. Violence of this sort surfaced randomly. Again in 1935, Jewish homes in Gladenbach were ransacked, Jewish men beaten on the streets. Some were thrown into jail. Everywhere in Germany Jews stopped going out, fearful that they would be accosted on a streetcar or thrown out of a theater. One young Jew could no longer go to her favorite café since the owners no longer wished to serve Jews, while the cinema put up a sign, "Jews not wanted here."[84] In school, Jewish children found themselves shunted to corners, barred from field trips, and forced to hear endless descriptions of the Jewish menace. Former friends avoided them. And perhaps most excruciating of all, families broke up, as parents sent children abroad for safety. "Children turned into letters," as the expression went.[85] Families that managed to emigrate were spared the worst, but they left, in most instances, impoverished. The Gestapo in Berlin had an emigration bureau. When Jews entered, "[they were] still . . . the owner[s] of an apartment, perhaps a business, a bank account and some savings. [When they left, they had been] reduced to . . . stateless beggars."[86] Amid the slew of decrees that followed Kristallnacht in 1938 — the Nazis' organized destruction of synagogues and Jewish businesses — the regime deprived Jews of driver's licenses; forbade them to enter theaters, concert halls, or exhibitions; and banned them from the dining and sleeping cars on trains.[87] They were barred from virtually all employment and business activity and found their remaining assets seized or blocked by the state.

For Roma and Sinti, the full force of the population purge came later but no less virulently. Wanda Michaelis was Sinti, and the reality of Nazi purges came in 1940 or 1941 when her father was told by the police that as a "non-Aryan," he could no longer work in the postal service.[88] One week later, the authorities took him away. He was released after an Aryan family vouched for him. But a few weeks later, the police came again and ordered the entire family to pack their belongings. Along with other Sinti and Roma, the Michaelis family was interned in a camp in Frankfurt, which had been established by the local authorities in 1937 — no orders from Berlin were required. Initially, the police rounded up Roma and Sinti who lived in wagons, but then they moved those who lived in houses and apartments out of their homes and into the camp. Many more families were now crowded into wagons, some of which had to be rented or purchased by the city. Surrounded by barbed wire, it became a macabre parody of a Gypsy encampment. Michaelis and the other internees could leave only for work or school. They could shop for food and other necessities only one hour a day. As at a regular concentration camp, the inmates had to stand for roll call twice a day. Survivors recalled especially long roll calls in the rain and snow. Those who did not give the Hitler salute in proper fashion were forced to run backward until they collapsed. Forced labor at nearby factories and in the camp exerted a frightful toll on bodies already worn down from inadequate nourishment and overcrowding. The camp guard, known for his brutality even before the Nazi period, "struck the children with his whip at every trivial incident." For the slightest infractions the guard threatened Roma and Sinti with far worse — that they would be turned over to the SS and sent to a concentration camp, which happened in numerous instances. "You're going to the camp and you're never coming back," the guard told one young man, who returned one hour late from school. He was deported to Sachsenhausen.[89] In other cases, officials threatened Roma and Sinti with sterilization or the concentration camp; often, they got both.[90] In the autumn of 1941, Roma and Sinti were banned from the Wehrmacht. An unknown number of Roma and Sinti had been sterilized in the early 1930s, a procedure that became even more widespread in the late 1930s and early 1940s, especially as more and more of them were deported to concentration and extermination camps.[91]

The racial purge did not stop with Jews and Roma and Sinti. In the late 1930s and in the war years, many "asocials" were shipped to labor camps, supposedly for reeducation. But certain of them, considered unreformable, were to be "annihilated through labor," as Himmler told Reich Justice Minister Thierack, who evidently had no objections.[92] Many others were sterilized, and some women had their babies forcibly aborted.

These extreme efforts to prevent reproduction are also evident in the formal euthanasia program that began in 1939, with the killing of children first, then adults.[93] The endeavors led to the creation of a new kind of institution, the killing center for the handicapped, which would lead directly to the establishment of the extermination camps for Jews.[94] The euthanasia program remained lodged in the Führer's chancellery, though its implementation depended on the close cooperation of the Ministry of Interior, especially its Health Office, and police and Gestapo units. A very high proportion of the program's directors were physicians, and, as with compulsory sterilization, boards composed of physicians made the determination to kill. As mentioned, the vast majority of health-care personnel at hospitals and long-term care institutions, including physicians, nurses, social workers, and public health officers, cooperated with the program, first by filling out the forms, then by transferring the children and adults to the killing centers. Typically as well, a number of the leading physicians also held officer rank in the SS. Almost all of the physicians invited agreed to participate in the adult euthanasia program.[95] Eventually T4 operated six killing centers that "processed" about eighty thousand patients over the next year and a half. Despite much self-serving testimony after the war by the physicians and bureaucrats involved, the killing process was by no means "clean" and "painless." At the Hardamar killing center, the handicapped were killed by gas. As one employee later reported:

> I . . . looked through the peephole in the side wall. Through it I saw 40–45 men who were pressed together in the next room and were now slowly dying. Some lay on the ground, others had slumped down, many had their mouths open as if they could not get any more air. The form of death was so painful that one cannot talk of a humane killing, especially since many of the dead men may have had moments of clarity. I watched the process for about 2–3 minutes and then left because I could no longer bear to look and felt sick.[96]

Only after the killings had occurred were the families informed, and always with a faked cause of death.

As would be the case with Jews and Roma and Sinti, the bodies of euthanasia victims were used for research purposes. Among others, the Kaiser Wilhelm Institute (KWI) for Brain Research received brains from euthanasia victims for research. Typically, interlocking directorates existed: two of the physician board members of the KWI were also members of T4. The KWI had a branch for dissections, which received more than six hundred brains. Julius Hallerworden, the senior physician responsible for the collections, testified in July 1945:

> I had come to know that they were planning the euthanasia project. That's why I went there in order to offer my assistance with the following words: Look guys, if you're going to kill these people, then you should at least take out their brains so that this material

can still be used. I was then asked how many of them I should examine. And I answered: As many as you have, the more the better. . . . Among these brains there were wonderful ones, terrific cerebral mutations, deformities, diseases of early childhood. Of course, I accepted these brains with pleasure. Where they came from and how, that was really none of my business. The whole thing was really great.[97]

The brains of thirty-three children killed in one action were all sent to the KWI, and the specimens were still being used decades later.[98] Living patients endured numerous experiments prior to their killing. In some instances, SS physicians removed their organs and brains for further research, much of it of a highly dubious kind.[99]

In implementing its purge policies, the Nazi regime moved somewhat carefully so as not to alienate the broad middle of the German population. The rowdy, public disruptions of some of the first antisemitic actions in 1933 displeased many Germans, and euthanasia in particular violated Christian norms concerning the sanctity of life. But it is hard to resist the interpretation of an inexorable logic to Nazi policies, which became increasingly radical over the course of the 1930s as Hitler felt his power more and more secure, even unassailable. The population purge combined legislated discrimination, confinement in concentration camps, public humiliations, forced sterilizations, and legally sanctioned murders, and, for the racially elect, access to resources and public recognition. Only the combination of race thinking, the utter conviction that the racially degenerate represented a *Lebensballast*, a burden on the population at large, coupled with a bureaucratic mentality, made possible such rapid implementation of racial policies. And the most radical of the prewar measures, euthanasia, served as the model for an even grander effort to purify the population by mass killings.

THE ULTIMATE PURGE:
FROM DISCRIMINATION TO GENOCIDE

By the winter of 1940/41, the second winter of World War II, Jewish life in Germany had been reduced to a confined, impoverished, frightened existence. As the Nazis began the invasion of the Soviet Union in June 1941, even these radical population policies would be surmounted by the move toward killings on a massive scale. In the confused, chaotic, and stimulating context of total war, Nazis at both the middle and top ranks seized the initiative and launched the systematic killing of Jews. Some acted out of enthusiasm, others out of frustration; some thought they were engaged in a grand historical venture, while others merely followed orders. Together, they created the Holocaust.

In October 1939, right after the victory over Poland, Hitler appointed Heinrich Himmler Reich commissar for the strengthening of German nationhood (*Reichskommissar für die Festigung des Deutschen Volkstums*), a post he held in addition to his role as Reichsführer of the SS and chief of the German police. Hitler charged him with the task of ensuring "the final return into the Reich of ethnic and racial Germans [*Reichs- und Volksdeutschen*] abroad," including the creation of settlement areas for them. His mandate was also to ensure "the elimination of the harmful influences of racially alien population groups, who constitute a danger for the Reich and for the German racial community [*Volksgemeinschaft*]."[100] Always direct in his lectures to fellow Nazis, Himmler made it clear that National Socialist occupation policy was designed carefully to distinguish the different peoples of eastern Europe — and to eliminate the inferior ones, physically or culturally or both.[101]

Other key institutions and individuals shared Himmler's perspective. In an order of October 1941, the command of the Sixth Army in the Soviet Union told its troops that the ultimate goal of the campaign against the "Jewish-Bolshevik system" was "to free the German people *for once and for all from the Asiatic-Jewish danger*."[102] A host of civilian officials elaborated upon the vision of a clear-cut, racially ordered imperium. They developed and began to implement plans for population removals and in-migrations of ethnic Germans in conjunction with the economic exploitation and development of central and eastern Europe. These officials were highly educated; they composed an intelligentsia of lawyers, economists, geographers, historians, and many others. They staffed such respectable-sounding institutions as the Reich Council for Productivity (*Reichskuratorium für Wirtschaftlichkeit*), the Institute for German Labor in the East (*Institut für Deutsche Ostarbeit*), and many others.[103]

In short, all levels of the Nazi hierarchy, from the very top leadership to midlevel functionaries, from the army to the planning intelligentsia, envisaged a vast reordering of the population of central and eastern Europe, ethnic cleansings and in-migrations on an immense, hitherto unimagined scale. Like the Soviets, the Nazis had no compunction about moving around entire populations. Both systems viewed social engineering in this very basic sense — determining who should be included in society, who had to be excluded through deportations — as a necessary element of the drive to create utopia. But Nazi plans were even grander, the outcomes more deadly, than Soviet population politics.

The Nazi process began with the outbreak of World War II. The invasion of the Soviet Union offered still greater and more exciting opportunities for this kind of engineered population politics. The "Generalplan Ost," widely discussed in the Nazi hierarchy, made more systematic and radical ideas that had circulated within the regime for years. The plan, formally drafted in July 1941, envisaged drastic depopulation of the lower races through birth control, sterilization, abortions, deportations, deliberate neglect, and murders, and the active repopulation of the area with German elements.[104] Whole areas — Byelorussia, the Ukraine — would be emptied of a good portion of their existing populations and would be repopulated by German colonists. This is a critical point: forced emigration of Jews and the in-migration of ethnic Germans — around 500,000 — were linked processes, and both were based on a racialized conception of society and history.[105] Ultimately, ethnic Germans would be moved from South Tyrol, Bukovina, Bessarabia, Lithuania, Byelorussia, the Baltic lands, even from outside Athens, where there lived the descendants of Bavarians who had gone with King Otto to a newly independent Greece in the 1820s.

These population transfers had begun in the early years of the war. By the winter of 1940/41 about 250,000 ethnic Germans sat in around 1,500 "resettlement camps" (*Umsiedlerlager*), and the Germans had signed an agreement with the Italians for the resettlement of an additional 200,000 ethnic Germans from South Tyrol.[106] Hundreds of thousands of Jews were languishing, and dying, in the crowded and deprived conditions of the ghettos into which they had been forced in the area the Nazis termed the "General Government," the large occupation zone in central Poland. Local Nazi officials had already begun to establish ghettos in late 1939, right after the defeat of Poland.[107] Some Jews had been moved out of the Warthegau, the western part of Poland, now directly annexed into the Reich; some 70,000 Jews, Roma and Sinti, asocials, criminals, mentally handicapped, and nationalists from Alsace-Lorraine, and a few thousand Jews from western Germany, the Saar and Baden, had been deported to Vichy France.[108] The case of Lodz is typical: 160,000 Jews were confined to the ghetto; 30,000 Poles, slated for deportation, were confined to a camp; and around 30,000 ethnic Germans occupied another camp, waiting for their final destination.[109] Reflecting the chaos of these operations, even the Nazi officials did not know the final destination point for the various people under their authority.

These forced population movements, especially in the General Government, created severe logistical and financial problems for the SS. In many cases, individual commanders took matters into their own hands. While still somewhat hesitant and incomplete, the rush of extreme, deadly actions against civilians in all realms of German control in central and eastern Europe set the precedent for more systematic actions.[110] The invasion of the Soviet Union only intensified the sense of chaos as ever more Jews and ethnic Germans came under Nazi control, and as the exigencies of warfare placed new demands on the resources of Nazi Germany. Amid this growing sense of chaos and of strained resources, but also of elation at the opportunities created by German domination, officials at all levels of the Nazi hierarchy began to radicalize their measures against the Jews under their control.

In June 1941, right after the invasion and close on the heels of the Wehrmacht, SS Einsatzgruppen began to implement the infamous Commissar Order, which mandated the killing of Soviet officials and "Jews in the service of the Party or State."[111] Many of the SS officers understood the original order as a license to kill almost any Jewish man, and by mid-August, Jewish women and children as well— "useless eaters," in the words of countless Nazi documents.[112]

From mid-July and August, Himmler also dramatically added to SS manpower in the East, including security and reserve police battalions and police units of Ukrainians, Lithuanians, and others, all of whom operated in conjunction with the Einsatzgruppen.[113] By September 1941, ghettos in Lithuania were being emptied of their Jews, who were taken out and shot.[114] By mid-October, Einsatzgruppe A officers stated that "the cleansing operations" undertaken by the security police, "in accordance with basic instructions, have as their objective the total elimination of the Jews."[115]

In Serbia, the process of mass murder was underway by the autumn of 1941, and directly involved the Wehrmacht as well as the SS, both of which were involved in mass shootings of Jews and others. In spring 1942, the Nazis began to use mobile gas vans to kill Jews interned in concentration camps. SS-Gruppenführer Harald Turner, the military administrative chief of Serbia, reported in August 1942 to the Wehrmacht commander that "Serbia is the only country in which the Jewish question and the Gypsy question have been solved." He was not quite correct: after Estonia, Serbia was the second country under Nazi rule to be made "Judenfrei."[116]

In eastern Galicia, which came under German control in the summer of 1941 and was then attached to the General Government by order of Hitler on 16 July 1941, pogroms and mass murders began immediately. In the first half of July, 10,000 Jews had fallen victim to Einsatzgruppe C.[117] In September 1941, the police initiated more systematic killings of Jews and Soviet prisoners of war in this area. In Lemberg (Lvov) and numerous smaller towns, the SS, with the help of Ukrainian units, began to ghettoize and then kill Jewish populations as early as October 1941, under the curious gaze of regular soldiers, railroad workers, police, and residents, some of whom sometimes lent a hand. On one "bloody Sunday," some 10,000 Jews in the town of Stanislau were killed by security and reserve police.[118] In November 1941, the authorities leveled a "shoot order" against all Jews living outside the cities. By the end of 1941, 60,000 Jews, including women and children, had been killed just in eastern Galicia.

And in the autumn and winter of 1941, the Nazis built in Chelmno (also in the General Government) the first extermination camp. Officials who had directed the euthanasia program led the effort. The first mobile gas van was tested on Russian prisoners of war in Sachsenhausen in the autumn of 1941, and more were then deployed by the Einsatzgruppen in the Soviet Union from December 1941 onward. They also were deployed at Chelmno, where the first Jews to be exterminated by gas were killed in early December 1941. These killings occurred not on orders from Berlin but on the initiative of Artur Greiser, Gauleiter of the Warthegau, who wanted to clear his area of Jews, especially in Lodz, the deportation terminus for 20,000 German Jews and 5,000 Roma and Sinti. All told, over 150,000 people were gassed at Chelmno, the vast majority Jews, and also Roma and Sinti, Poles, and Russians.[119]

By the autumn of 1941, three to four months into the Soviet invasion, two processes, usually considered separately, had come together — first, what Christopher Browning has very aptly termed the "euphoria of victory," and, second, the dismal recognition of defeat once the Nazi invasion had slowed down by the late summer, and then, by mid-October, had became halted outside Moscow.[120] *Both* processes together created the Holocaust.[121] Among the Einsatzgruppen and other SS units, and probably for Himmler himself, the initial, dizzying successes in the Soviet Union offered them the opportunity, at long last, to implement on a grand scale their vision of a racial utopia. This was the "euphoria of victory," and it is evident in Himmler's assignment of additional SS police forces in the occupation areas and in indications that he gave some units, in midsummer 1941, orders now to kill Jewish women and children as well as the men. Still, at this point, the "final solution" probably signified transport behind the Urals combined with high death rates that resulted from mass shootings and the rigors of deportation.[122] The more Jews killed by the Einsatzgruppen and other SS detachments, the fewer who would have to be deported. And it was commonly understood that a high percentage of the Jewish population would die in the population transfers — "natural decimation through resettlement," in the words of one document.[123]

But the intent to move vast numbers of Jews to the east very quickly evaporated as the rush toward victory in the Soviet Union slowed down by the late summer. Within a period of eighteen months, the Nazi leadership had sequentially considered Lublin in the eastern part of the General Government, Madagascar, and the general "East," somewhere in Siberia, as places for Jewish resettlement. None of these plans had proven feasible, while the forced migration into the occupation zones of ethnic Germans had further complicated matters. Eichmann had gone from counting 5.8 million Jews (in late autumn 1940) who had to be removed (*ausgesiedelt*) from the "living space of the German people" to counting 11 million in the summer of 1941 — that is, following the invasion of the Soviet Union — whom he now targeted for the "Endlösung."[124]

With resettlement options closed off, executions seemed the only way to deal with the "Jewish problem." A mutually reinforcing radicalization process came into play at both the middle and the top levels of the hierarchy.[125] The initiatives for mass killings had already been taken by planners and SS officials all over central and eastern Europe. Alongside those infused with the "euphoria of victory," others struggled with the chaos and confusion in the occupation zones and initiated the killings out of a sense of frustration and of strained material resources. No doubt, they all thought that they were doing Hitler's bidding, or at least they felt they had license to do whatever they wanted with their Jewish populations.[126] Indeed, Berlin ratified their actions when Hitler, presumably informed of the killings in Galicia, in Byelorussia, in Serbia, and elsewhere, took no counteraction. Given the way the Nazi system functioned, with Hitler only rarely intervening with a direct order, such silence could only be understood as approval.

At the same time, the changing course of the war provided added impetus for Hitler to systematize the killings.[127] The Blitzkrieg against the Soviet Union had initially been intended to last no longer than four months. In July, a number of generals thought the war would last only another two weeks. Hitler on 14 July 1941 spoke of another six weeks' duration to the war. In his original plans, the Jewish matter would be settled after the defeat of the Soviet Union.[128] But with the Blitzkrieg over, Germany now faced a long land war in Eurasia, and the intent to deport Jews east of the Urals could not be realized.

In Hitler's view, his "prophecy" of 1939, repeated many times afterward, had come to pass. The Jews had unleashed another world war, and Hitler's intense fears of the destruction of the Aryan race—of a depopulated world "moving through the ether," as he expressed it so often in *Mein Kampf*—took hold. The other part of the prophecy had to be fulfilled: the outcome of a world war, Hitler had warned, would be not the defeat of Germany but the annihilation of the Jews. In the compelling interpretation presented by the historian Tobias Jersak, Hitler, in the wake of Pearl Harbor, took the wild leap into the future utopia of German world domination and racial purity: he declared war on the United States, ordered the extermination of the Jews, and took over supreme command of the Wehrmacht.[129]

In this context, Reinhard Heydrich, the SS second-in-command, convened the Wannsee Conference in late January 1942.[130] The meeting had been planned originally for 9 December 1941, but the Japanese attack on Pearl Harbor and Hitler's subsequent decisions forced a delay. In the interim, the agenda for Wannsee expanded far beyond the original task of deciding the ultimate fate of German Jews. By late January, the task at Wannsee was to make more systematic and comprehensive the mass killings of Jews that had already begun "on the ground" all over central and eastern Europe. For Heydrich, and presumably Hitler and Himmler, all these partial but bloody executions provided the basis for implementing the full-fledged, utopian goals of National Socialism.

The move, then, to killings in gas chambers began in the late winter of 1941/42 and the spring of 1942.[131] Following the Wannsee Conference, the formidable resources of state and society were mobilized for the systematic annihilation of Jews. The SS expanded killings by gas, begun against Jews at Chelmno in December 1941, as the most efficient method to carry out this immense project of human annihilation. Scores of T4 personnel, experienced in the use of gas for mass killings, moved eastward and deployed their expertise in the extermination camps. In the General Government, Jews deemed incapable of work were the first selected for extermination. In mid-March 1942, the ghettos of Lublin and Lvov were cleared out (though not completely) and the Jews sent to Belzec. The action in Lublin under Odilo Globocnik was particularly brutal. Similar events then occurred in the smaller towns and cities of the area. In May–June 1942, the next phase began, the full clearing of the ghettos — though selections were still made partly on the basis of work capabilities — and the shipment of Jews to Treblinka, now a bigger extermination camp than Sobibor or Belzec, and ultimately, of course, to Auschwitz.[132] With Wannsee, then, the entire apparatus of the state became mobilized behind deliberate annihilation, and the Nazis began the more systematic applications of killing by gas and built the first extermination camps. Still, all along the way, mass shootings were also applied against Jews.[133]

As the campaign against Jews radicalized, so did the measures directed at the Roma and Sinti.[134] With the onset of the war, they became more subject to deportation and to the rigors of concentration camp existence. Some Nazi officials in the General Government, like Hans Frank, refused to accept additional Roma and Sinti because of the already strained and chaotic situation in their areas of control. A number of intended deportations were delayed because priority was given to the deportation of Jews. As mentioned, a group of 5,000 Roma and Sinti, deported from western Germany to Lodz, were gassed at Chelmno in January 1942. Even earlier, the Einsatzgruppen had taken it upon themselves to shoot en masse the Sinti and Roma in the Soviet Union, possibly as many as 250,000. Himmler wanted to keep some "pure" Gypsies alive, as much for curiosity as anything else, a move opposed by Martin Bormann at the Führer's Chancellery. On 16 December 1942 Himmler signed an order that authorized the transport of the Sinti and Roma to Auschwitz. Following the guidelines promoted by Ritter and his staff at the RHA, Himmler exempted "pure race" Roma and Sinti as well as "good *Mischlinge*" married to Germans and a few other groups. Yet in the chaos of deportations, local officials often ignored the exemption categories and deported populations en masse. Of the 23,000 Roma and Sinti interned at the special "Gypsy camp" at Auschwitz, 20,078 were killed. Wanda Michaelis, whose testimony was cited earlier, was among those deported with her family from Frankfurt to Auschwitz. Of twenty-nine family members, only four survived. The rest were killed at Auschwitz or other camps.[135] Many Roma and Sinti worked as slave laborers, and still others were subject to gruesome medical experiments at Dachau and elsewhere. The Dachau hypothermia experiments alone resulted in the deaths of eighty to ninety inmates. In Ravensbrück and other camps hundreds, perhaps thousands, of Sinti and Roma suffered compulsory sterilization, some with the promise of freedom, which was never actually granted. Not rarely, complications led to the death of the individuals, especially women who had been injected with radioactive material.[136]

As Dieter Pohl writes, the move to the Holocaust has to be explained as a "mutual communication process between center and periphery . . . in which both sides forced the radicalization process, and intermittently stopped it."[137] Ideology — race thinking in general, racialized antisemitism in particular — played a central role in this escalation into "the unthinkable."[138] But the context of total war was also critical. The violence of war removed whatever barriers might have existed to mass killings of civilians. The war was a coveted opportunity for some of the Nazi leaders; for others, the chaos, confusion, and fear of defeat led them to lash out at their perceived enemies. The primacy of race thinking joined the various levels of the Nazi regime in distinct but common moves toward intentional annihilation of European Jews and a significant segment of Roma and Sinti, once deportation had been closed off and the fortunes of war had shifted. Many groups suffered enormously from Nazi racial politics, but only in relation to Jews, the objects of "redemptive antisemitism," and Roma and Sinti did these policies escalate into genocide.[139]

More than any other regime discussed in this book, Nazi Germany formed a "racialized social system," a polity and society consciously shot through and through with race.[140] The primacy of race — as an ideology, as a set of social practices, as state policies — helps explain the origins of the genocide and how it could continue even when it was, in strict terms, irrational in relation to military strategy and economic planning. The genocide was, however, fully "rational" from the vantage point of a racialized social system, as certainly was the Third Reich.

RITUALS OF POPULATION PURGES

The genocide of the Jews was a state-directed process that involved Nazi officials "on the ground" and then the central leadership in Berlin, which made the process more systematic and efficient. But the implementation of the policies involved thousands upon thousands of people, probably even more extensively than in the Soviet Union, where the ethnic and national purges were more organized and always centrally directed. By their involvement in the genocide, large segments of the population in the Third Reich became tied to the regime. Sometimes they followed orders and sometimes they developed their own procedures; once routinized, the procedures of killing became rituals that bound perpetrators together through the violence they inflicted on their victims. The seam of corruption ran deep, implicating substantial segments of the population in the racial practices of the regime that created unbridgeable chasms between the superior Aryan population and the racial outcasts below them. The social death and physical annihilation of Jews and others became a mass project.

A physician who selected prisoners at various concentration camps for euthanasia wrote from Ravensbrück on 19 November 1941:

My dearest Mummy,
   It is 17:45. I have finished my day's work and am once more sitting in my hotel. The result of my day's work is 95 forms completed. . . . The work speeds along thanks to the fact that the headings have already been typed and I only have to write in the diagnosis. . . .
   Everything is going perfectly. I am having my meals in the camp: for lunch in the mess there was lentil soup with bacon and omelette for pudding. I finished at 17:00 and had my supper in the mess: 3 sorts of sausage, butter, bread, beer. I sleep marvelously in my bed.[141]

For physicians allied with the Nazi regime, the selection of prisoners, Jews and the handicapped, for execution was simply one task among many in a day punctuated by a sumptuously laid table, a stirring concert, and a refreshing hunt. Mass murder had become routine, a part of everyday life, an act of professional responsibility and of loyalty to nation, race, and Führer. Other Germans, less educated perhaps than physicians or lawyers, made mass murder ordinary by manning the trains, serving in the army, denouncing neighbors, and guarding camps. Before discrimination had turned to genocide, the averted glance, the jeer at a Jew on the street, the happy acquisition of an apartment or a couch once owned by a Jew marked the populace's complicity in the practices that sustained the Nazi regime.

These daily discriminatory practices began as soon as the Nazis took power and continued throughout the Third Reich. In March 1933, less than two months into the regime, the *Vossische Zeitung* reported that in a town in Silesia, "a large number of young men entered the court building and molested several Jewish lawyers. The seventy-year-old legal counselor Kochmann was hit in the face and other lawyers punched all over."[142] In another instance, a Czech Jew and Holocaust survivor remembered, many years later, that the Germans had seized her family's home, forcing them to crowd into the back rooms. One day a Gestapo officer came in back and asked what smelled so good. The mother was cooking potato soup and asked the officer if he would like some. She ladled out a plate and handed it to him. He dropped it straight on the floor. The soup splashed his pants. The officer told the woman to clean him up. She got a towel and, on her knees, began to clean off his pants, when he kicked her in the face—all in the full view of her children.[143]

Violence was an intrinsic, ever-present element in the process of exclusion.[144] The exertion of violence causes, most obviously, deep physical pain. But its effects are far more lasting. Acts of violence were a kind of "propaganda of the deed" that turned the victims into pariahs, isolating Jews, Roma and Sinti, and others from their fellow Germans. Collective violence—whether by groups of Storm Troopers; crowds that suddenly gelled, stimulated by official actions like Kristallnacht; or units of uniformed security forces like the Gestapo, SS, or Wehrmacht—bound perpetrators together. While a few individuals occasionally shrank from the exercise of violence, and some later claimed guilty consciences, many perpetrators, it seems, either simply followed orders or found intoxicating their complete power over the victims, their unlimited ability to violate the integrity of another's body. The beating of Jewish lawyers or a Jewish housewife was a random act but could occur with legitimacy only because of the larger frame of state violence.

By the later 1930s, the regimen of violence in the concentration camps had sunk to new depths. The specific acts were not decreed in Berlin. Camp guards and commanders proved enormously inventive in the physical pains they inflicted. In Buchenwald, Sinti and Roma, alongside the usual beatings, had to remain standing in the cold, sometimes with heads held in the snow for minutes, because their beds were not properly made. In the heat they were forced to wear coats; in the cold, they had to stand naked. Overworked and exhausted, many who made the march back from quarry or road to the camp hospital through the aid of friends were then killed the next morning by injections. In Ravensbrück, Roma women and children sat for two days and a night in the open, where the SS guards, men and women, "jeered, spit, beat, and trampled" them. Probably half of the Burgenland (Austrian) Roma interned at Buchenwald in 1939–40 died there. Of 250 Roma and Sinti sent to work in the infamous Mauthausen quarries in August 1938, 140 had died by the beginning of October 1941, the victims of violence and deliberate neglect.[145]

Despite still prevalent views that the Holocaust was a "secret" process unknown to most Germans or other Europeans, the violence associated with it was often quite public in nature:

> While I was traveling through [Kovno] I went past a petrol station that was surrounded by a dense crowd of people. There was a large number of women in the crowd and they had lifted up their children or stood them on chairs or boxes so they could see better. . . . [W]hen I inquired what was happening I was told that the "Death-dealer of Kovno" was at work. . . .
>
> On the concrete forecourt of the petrol station a blond man of medium height, aged about twenty-five, stood leaning on a club, resting. The club was as thick as his arm and came up to his chest. At his feet lay about fifteen to twenty dead or dying people. Water flowed continuously from a hose washing blood away into the drainage gully. Just a few steps behind this man some twenty men, guarded by armed civilians, stood waiting for their cruel execution in silent submission. In response to a cursory wave the next man stepped forward silently and was then beaten to death with the wooden club in the most bestial manner, each blow accompanied by enthusiastic shouts from the audience.[146]

The most powerful form of violence is, of course, murder. The killing of Jews was never a clean, "sanitized" act, not even in the extermination camps. "Industrial killing" signifies that Jews were murdered on a massive scale through organized, repetitive procedures, but these actions were not devoid of personalized brutality or of public spectacle. In the case just quoted, the executioner and the crowds were Lithuanian; they claimed to be avenging their own horrendous treatment at the hands of Jewish communists. But the conditions that made possible the executions were the result of German policies that had deliberately destroyed the "thin crust" of civilization and encouraged the sadistic inclinations of particular individuals to flourish.[147] Whatever the motivations of the individuals, their violent tendencies were given free rein by a system with a utopian drive. The spectacle nature of the event provided the crowd with voyeuristic pleasures of sadism, the ugly side of human passions. The word used by an onlooker to describe the executioner appears in countless other documents: he was "at work," shaping and completing a task like any other, though this was a work of destruction inflicted upon human bodies, not a work of construction carried out on inanimate materials.

In Kovno, not only Lithuanians watched—so did regular Wehrmacht soldiers and officers, along with the SS, which had overall control of the town. Many other Lithuanians aside from the club and crowbar wielders participated directly in the killings. Within the ring of the SS a smaller circle made up of Lithuanian auxiliaries surrounded the area and guarded the space of Jewish execution. The small territory was theirs, a plot of land over which they exercised absolute control, but always within the structures, spatial and ideological, of the Germans. With one or two blows to the back of the head, the crowbar wielder murdered forty-five to fifty people within three-quarters of an hour.

Then came the finale. One of the executioners got hold of an accordion, climbed on top of a "mountain" of corpses, and played the Lithuanian national anthem. The crowd joined in the singing and applauded. The exclusive character of racialized nationalism perfectly expressed: one nation's triumph celebrated, literally, upon the corpses of another.[148]

In Kovno and elsewhere, collective killings and social pressure bound the perpetrators together. Otto Ohlendorf, commander of one of the four SS Einsatzgruppen that entered the Soviet Union right behind the Wehrmacht, stated specifically that he gave orders to his men to shoot simultaneously, "in order to avoid any individual having to take direct, personal responsibility."[149] Other volunteers sometimes joined in the shootings, as one SS officer testified after the war: "On some occasions members of the Wehrmacht took the carbines out of our hands and took our place in the firing-squad."[150] Male bantering amid the shootings provided another element in the bonding of the perpetrators and simultaneously constructed the chasm between killers and the killed. One army officer, witnessing a mass execution in the Ukraine, asked an executioner to finish off an old man still alive in the pit. The killer responded "in a jocular fashion, 'I've already shot him seven times in the belly, don't worry, he'll snuff it soon enough.'"[151]

In Nazi ideology and propaganda, the killers were heroes, men who surmounted the great stress of unrelieved bloodshed for the grand historical task, or simply to follow orders as good soldiers or party members or SS men. Such actions required "nerves of steel," "specially selected men" who "grasped [the] aims completely," men who carried out "their personal sense of duty . . . to overcome this pestilence [Jews] in the shortest space of time."[152] Some killers kept score sheets of the number of their victims, while the commanders of Sobibor, tallying their numbers, regretted that their 350,000 victims trailed behind the totals of Belzec and Treblinka.[153]

The treatment of bodies defined the ultimate pariah status of the victims.

> The moment one Jew had been killed, the marksman would walk across the bodies of the executed Jews to the next Jew, who had meanwhile lain down, and shoot him. It went on this way uninterruptedly, with no distinction being made between men, women, and children. The children were kept with their mothers and shot with them. . . .
>
> In addition to the two marksmen there was a "packer" at either entrance to the ravine . . . whose job it was to lay the victim on top of the other corpses so that all the marksman had to do as he passed was fire a shot.[154]

In the early killing operations, Jews were led out to the killing site on foot or loaded into trucks. Then they had to strip completely, placing each kind of clothing in a different pile. In many instances, Jews were made to stand or kneel over a ditch they had just dug. The force of the bullets sent their bodies into the ditch. At Babi Yar, the site from which the description above derives, the victims were led into a ravine, where they were forced to lie down on top of the bodies of Jews already killed. Then a police marksman came along and shot each one in the neck. In other instances, Jews were forced to undress and walk on a plank that straddled the mass grave. A bullet then sent the bodies plummeting.[155]

At the extermination camps also, the victims were first made to undress, then had their hair shorn. Certainly, an economic explanation is much too simple and mundane to explain this assault on the body. Shorn hair was processed into rugs and insulation material; clothes were recycled to slave laborers or even back to the Reich. But the forced undressing of the victims and the shaved heads marked the penultimate — just short of murder — demonstration of power, a symbolic rape of the victims in which nakedness became completely and absolutely nonerotic, only an uncovering that vividly displayed the victim's total lack of power. For the men observing the events, the thrill of such power freely dispensed could be intoxicating, as when Mengele and his aides casually inspected five hundred naked women, ordering them to turn around so they could have a total view of the bodies at their disposal.[156] Then he decided which were to be consigned to labor, which to immediate extermination. For women prior to gassing, their genital areas were shaved as well, as if a final assault on their sexuality just prior to their murder was also necessary — on women as reproducers, symbolically to ensure that no other Jewish children would emerge from their bodies, on women as sexual beings, to ensure that they could no longer entice German men from the path of Aryan rectitude to the sin of *Rassenschande* (racial defilement).

The corpses were then handled as material, the waste products of an industrial process. As we have already seen, at the shooting sites bodies were trampled upon by killers, new victims made to lie down on top of the still-warm victims who had immediately preceded them. The bodies of Jews who died en route to Auschwitz were simply thrown from the train cars.[157] At the first extermination camps, like Belzec, special Jewish detachments pulled the dead out of the gas chambers with long hooks, which they pushed into the victims' mouths. Then they examined the bodies for valuables; gold teeth were ripped out. Finally, they dragged the bodies to mass graves, poured gasoline over them, and set the entire heap ablaze.[158] At Auschwitz, when the crematoria were full, bodies were stacked on pyres. The fat from the burning bodies was collected in a trough, then poured back over to accelerate the burning process. Rudolf Höss, the commandant, testified: "After the trenches had been cleared the charred remains were crushed. This was done on a cement slab with wooden pounders. These remains were then taken to a remote part of the Vistula by lorry and poured into the river."[159] At Auschwitz a more automated process was also developed that directly linked the gas chambers with the crematoria via a conveyor. Here the bodies had only to be loaded onto the conveyor, not dragged to a ditch or pyre. In this way, Auschwitz did, indeed, signify the rationalization of murder, since automated conveyance was one of the major ways business applied mechanical motion to the industrial process, leading to great savings and the more efficient use of labor power. But still more primitive methods continued to be used. In 1942 Himmler ordered that all mass graves were to be dug up and the bodies burned. Temporary ovens or simple pyres were built, the ashes then ground to dust in a mill and scattered over the land.[160]

To purge the population meant not only to annihilate Jewish bodies but also to purge memory, to destroy the artifacts, the objectified traces, of Jewish life. The forms of attempted memory-destruction were many and varied. The infamous book burnings on 10 May 1933 provide one example, a true Savanarola-like scene straight out of the anti-Renaissance with its auto-da-fé of humanistic learning and pleasure. The Nazis destroyed books written by Jewish authors; moreover, given the identification of Judaism and Marxism, anything of a faintly socialist or pacifist tone could be classified as possessed by the "Jewish spirit," including books by Helen Keller, Jack London, and Thomas Mann. The burning of synagogues on Kristallnacht in 1938 and the deliberate desecration of Jewish holy objects — publicly burning or trampling on the Torah, for example — were also rituals of revenge, whose ultimate goal, if successful, would be to purge memory. The plan to establish a museum of Jewish life in Prague was only slightly different — a tour through the remnants of a destroyed civilization that would affirm the victory of the conquerors. This would be the ultimate "othering," the intentional destruction of a living civilization and its rendering into a museum exhibit, the artifacts of the dead.

Memory is not free-floating; it is tied to distinct places and objects. The plunder of their wealth sent Jews spiraling into poverty; it also deprived them of the deepest associations with home, family, and the rituals of religion. Plunder was a collective enterprise, a key element in the populace's collaboration with the exclusionary policies of the regime. Gestapo agents and civil servants took bribes to provide emigration papers, and agents rummaged through households, taking furniture, pictures, radios, and whatever else they desired. Sometimes Jews sold their precious belongings for a tiny percentage of their value because they were desperate for cash or because the buyers knew they were emigrating and could be cajoled or terrorized into the sale.[161] On a broader scale, "Aryanization" of Jewish businesses deprived Jews of their assets and enriched numerous German companies; it also destroyed the traces of an active and vibrant Jewish commercial life in central and eastern Europe. During the war, plunder kept German soldiers' families back home set in fine circumstances. SS Obersturmführer Karl Kretschmer, another member of the Einsatzgruppen, complained that he was unable to obtain a Persian rug for his wife — they were in high demand, and all of the Jewish dealers were dead. But he sent home from Russia butter, sardines, tins of meat, packages of sweets for the children, salami, French chocolate, flour, soap, and, around Christmastime, one or two geese.[162]

Violence and plunder were not the only means of exercising power. Knowledge is also power, and its possession bound perpetrators together. Conversely, the absence of knowledge bound victims together in a ring of fear and desperation. Survivors recalled that they had heard rumors and had vague knowledge that people were being transported somewhere, but they never quite knew the destination, nor its nature. As one woman noted: "We knew the name of Theresienstadt and later on Bergen-Belsen, but knew nothing about them. Later on we began to hear of camps in Poland, but always that they were work camps."[163] She had fled to Holland and was interned after the German occupation. "In Holland you didn't know exactly where you were sent. There were so many places which I found out later. . . . We didn't know anything about Treblinka, Majdanek, Stutthof. . . . This you found out later, after the war."[164] At Westerborg, the main camp for refugee Jews in Holland, the inmates one day saw the Germans at work. "They build train tracks into the camp. And we didn't know why they were building train tracks into the camp." The Nazis told them: "Juden, ihr kehrt zurück ins Reich." "Jews, you're returning to the Reich." Fear of the unknown gripped many of them, who expected the relatively decent conditions at Westerborg to deteriorate now that they were back under German control. They did not know where the transports were going, did not know about Auschwitz. They just knew that wherever they were being sent, "it wasn't going to be a good place."[165]

CONCLUSION

Germany under the Nazis was a "nation obsessed with tracking, diagnosing, registering, grading, and selecting."[166] The bureaucratic-scientific process of categorization rested on the principle of race and marked the first step in the policies of exclusion that entailed discrimination, internment, sterilization, deportation, and, ultimately, killing. While the Soviets classified people along a variety of axes, including ethnicity, nationality, race, and class, the Nazis were radical simplifiers—race alone was the important category.

Of all the cases discussed in this book, the Nazi regime demonstrated the clearest intent to destroy physically a defined population group in its totality. It is the case for which the term "genocide" fits most completely. But the move from discrimination to genocide still requires explanation. The discriminatory racial practices of the 1930s were "absolute prerequisites for the 'Final Solution,'" as Marion Kaplan writes.[167] Yet in and of themselves, those practices did not constitute genocide. For all of the brutalities of the Nazi system, the genocide was not the result simply of commands from the top. If there was any inevitability to the unfolding of the Holocaust, it was because war was inevitable. The Nazis were not just Versailles revisionists; they sought to overturn the entire Versailles system, indeed, the entire principle of state sovereignty in order to establish a racial imperium in Europe. In this sense also, the Nazis were radical simplifiers, who sought to overturn a continent of many sovereignties for total domination. Here, too, the contrast with the Soviet Union is strong, for despite communist rhetoric, the Stalinist system desperately feared war with Germany. Under Stalin, the logic of socialism in one country ran in precisely the opposite direction from foreign conquest — a hunkering down, a walling off of the socialist society so it could develop in an autarchic manner. But the Nazi revolution did mean war because of the fundamental, underlying belief in the sanctity of the race and the essence of history as a cataclysmic struggle between the races. The principle of race, tied to revolution, made genocide a highly probable option; it became reality in the situational context of total war, when both the chaos and the euphoria induced by Nazi aggression led individual SS and Wehrmacht commanders to take matters down a more radical course, and when the geopolitics of war foreclosed other options like the deportation of Jews.

The Nazi system revolved around the participation of the population, "a peculiarly perverted system of participation," as Michael Geyer stresses, one based on domination of others rather than democratic self-governance.[168] Robert Gellately notes that the Nazis "did not need to use widespread terror against the [German] population."[169] Ultimately, war became the substitute for democratic participation.[170] The regime encouraged the racially elect to pillage and purge, which made people complicit with the regime's policies. The Soviet system also thrived on popular involvement but, in the end, was much more centrally directed than the Third Reich. Middle- and lower-level officials in the Soviet Union could never have initiated deportations and mass killings, as did their counterparts in Nazi Germany. In that sense, population purges in the Soviet Union were more controlled. Perhaps that is one reason why they were also more limited in the Soviet Union: an order from Stalin or the Presidium of the Supreme Soviet could initiate forced collectivization or ethnic and national deportations, and orders from the same sources could put a halt to such operations. Moreover, as argued in the previous chapter, the Soviets were never driven by an explicit racial ideology even though their policies at times took on a racial character. In contrast to the Soviet Union's more controlled form of governance and its official egalitarian ideology, Nazi Germany's chaotic system of rule encouraged the mutual radicalization process of both the midlevel functionaries and the top leadership. This peculiar form of governance along with its racial ideology resulted in a system in which the physical annihilation of defined population groups moved to the very core of state policies. The Soviet system never quite developed the self-reinforcing dynamic of destruction that came to characterize the Third Reich in wartime and made it a "genocidal regime."

The people who directed the Nazi system, both the top and the middle ranks, were by no means street toughs. Among the few hundred men in the leadership corps of the Security Police and the Security Service, the key SS agency responsible for the mass killings and then the implementation of the full program of genocide, three-quarters were born between 1903 and 1915, and of these, four-fifths held an *Abitur*, the Gymnasium school-leaving certificate that one still needs in Germany for entrance into a university; two-thirds held a *Diplom*, essentially a B.A., from an institution of higher education, either a polytechnic or a university; and nearly one-third had a Ph.D.[171] Among the planners, the proportion with such high levels of education was even greater. They were men like Eugen Fischer, who had had an illustrious career as a physician and ethnographer even before World War I.[172] In 1927 he assumed the directorship of the Kaiser Wilhelm Institute for Anthropology, Heredity, and Eugenics and the chair of anthropology at the University of Berlin. Fischer's institute trained medical students, public health officials, and SS physicians, and he and his colleagues acted as consultants on racial policy to the Ministry of Interior and various SS agencies.[173] Otmar von Verschuer, who was mentor to the notorious Auschwitz physician Josef Mengele, succeeded Fischer as director of the Kaiser Wilhelm Institute.[174]

These people were not on the margins of German society; they were members of that group so esteemed in German culture and society, the *Bildungsbürgertum*, the educated middle class. They helped create the Holocaust and gave it that strange combination of personalized brutality and anonymous, bureaucratic process that accounts for its thorough and efficient character. Hannah Arendt has forever shaped our picture of the typical SS man through her portrait of Adolf Eichmann, a rather dull-witted, lumbering bureaucrat, who could not even get his antisemitism straight.[175] But it is a grave mistake to generalize, as Arendt did, from Eichmann to the entire machinery of annihilation. The Eichmanns were one type, but there were others, like Fischer, more intellectual, often from "better" social backgrounds, and they were probably more significant in the killing mechanism of the Third Reich. Most were a bit younger than Fischer and the top Nazis like Hitler and Hermann Goering. They constituted the Weimar more than the front generation. World War I was for them the great missed opportunity, which they spent their lives striving to recapture in their own ways. The imagining of the war produced among them an affinity for a tough, masculine, militant ethos, for a militarized conception of politics that infused the radical Right and the radical Left of the interwar years. They were reading Ernst Jünger, Ernst von Salomon, and others — the novelists and memoir writers who idealized male camaraderie, the violence of warfare, and the degradation of women, sometimes in quite beautiful prose.

As noted in the previous chapter, by the late 1930s, the officials in the middle ranks of the Soviet system were also members of the generation of the 1920s. With a few exceptions, the older, prewar Bolshevik generation had been purged. Soviet officials had undergone a very different kind of socialization process, but like their German counterparts, they had invested their hopes and their careers in the regime, and many had been rewarded with substantial social mobility. As the people at the center of the Soviet system, they had learned to adapt to and, in many instances, implement the repressive and violent practices of Soviet communism. While the Soviets, unlike the Nazis, expressed an ideology of gender equality, they also promoted tough masculine values as the expression of revolutionary virtue and fostered male camaraderie in the party and its security services. Women participated in population purges as spectators, denouncers, plunderers, and, occasionally, as camp guards, but the exercise of violence in both systems was overwhelmingly the work of men in their prime adult years. Many of the Nazi officials who directed the Holocaust adopted a rather cool, intellectualized attitude toward violence, as did Jünger in his novels and other writings. For them, race simply constituted the way of the world; the efflorescence of Germans required the removal of others, and a revolutionary right-wing state would be the agency to accomplish this task — by whatever means proved most efficient.

four

Racial Communism: Cambodia under the Khmer Rouge

Someth May was a young Cambodian living with his family in Phnom Penh. His father was a physician. Like all the other residents of the city, the family was forcibly deported to the countryside when Cambodian communists, the Khmer Rouge, seized power in April 1975. He recalls one incident when a party cadre addressed a crowd in the throes of the uncertainties and miseries of deportation:

"Friends and comrades, it gives me pleasure to introduce myself as the leader of this region. Welcome. As you all know, during the Lon Nol regime the Chinese were parasites on our nation. They cheated the government. They made money out of Cambodian farmers. . . . Because the politicians could never resist money, corruption spread through every ministry. Now the High Revolutionary Committee wants to separate Chinese infiltrators from Cambodians, to watch the kind of tricks they get up to. The population of each village will be divided into a Chinese, a Vietnamese and a Cambodian section. So, if you are not Cambodian, stand up and leave the group. Remember that Chinese and Vietnamese look completely different from Cambodians."

About ten people stood up and walked to the place reserved for them.

"Are there any more?". . . No one stood up. . . . Then the four guards were told to go through the crowd. Anyone whose face looked foreign was dragged out.[1]

The extent of mass killings in Cambodia under the Khmer Rouge was enormous, almost unfathomable. Estimates vary widely, but most likely around 1.5 out of 8 million people died in the short, brutal reign of the

Khmer Rouge from 1975 to 1979. They died from hunger, disease, and the rigors of mass deportations, the ravages of a forced, peculiar development policy that emptied the cities of people, closed off the country from Western medical supplies and knowledge, and imagined the tripling of rice production by mere acts of will. They died in executions because of their association with the ancien régime, with the Vietnamese communists, or with one or another party functionary who had fallen into disfavor. And they died, one way or another, because they were not Khmer, like the Chinese and Vietnamese in May's narrative. In this extraordinary killing operation, the Khmer Rouge managed to combine all the worst aspects of the twentieth century into one overarching system of compulsion and terror. The purifying ethos of revolution, the drive to create a homogeneous, perfect society, made the Khmer Rouge apply their proclivities with a frightening literalness.

The Khmer Rouge based their ideology and policies on standard communist politics, most notably that of China, itself modeled, to a significant extent, on the Soviet Union under Stalin. But the Chinese and Soviet models were also important to the Khmer Rouge because of their insufficiencies. According to the Khmer Rouge, in both socialist countries the correct policies had not been applied with sufficient rigor and determination. The Khmer Rouge would improve upon the Chinese and Soviet models and establish a truly egalitarian, communist society.[2] That approach they combined with an extreme nationalism that had deep roots in Khmer culture, but that also developed in the context of French colonial control and the decades-long struggle of Cambodians, including the Khmer Rouge, against French and American influence and intervention. In their drive to refashion radically Cambodian society, the Khmer Rouge created their own synthesis of communism and racialized nationalism.

POWER AND UTOPIA

World War II opened up new possibilities for Cambodia, as it did for so many places in the colonial world. Western colonial domination had been undermined by the burdensome costs of the war, by the West's own proclamations in favor of national independence and democracy, and, in Asia, by Japanese invasions. When the Japanese rapidly deposed French rule in Cambodia in March 1945, they did more than replace one colonial power with another — they destroyed the semblance of an ordered and stable world and evoked the possibilities of change. The French returned after the Japanese defeat, but to a world of burgeoning nationalist movements in Indochina, some of them, as in Vietnam, already marked by a strong communist dimension. Less developed politically than its neighbor Vietnam, Cambodian politics were more slow going, but on the move nonetheless. In the late 1940s, many future leaders of Democratic Kampuchea (DK)—the formal name of Cambodia under communist rule from 1975 to 1979—witnessed or participated in the first political demonstrations in Cambodian history. Young Cambodians took to the streets and the ballot box to demand the end of French control and the establishment of an independent Cambodia. They won their demands in the early 1950s, though the traditional authorities of palace and court retained their dominant roles. Under the mercurial Prince Norodom Sihanouk, Cambodia pursued an independent foreign policy, to the intense ire of the United States, which by the end of the decade had replaced Britain and France as the dominant Western power in Southeast Asia.[3]

Though France had been deposed as a colonial power, French cultural influence remained strong in Cambodia. Some of the men who would become leaders of the communist movement in Cambodia were among the first Khmers to receive a Western education. Pol Pot, Khieu Samphan, Ieng Sary, and many others attended a French-run collège and then a lycée or technical school in Cambodia, and then went to France in the late 1940s and 1950s for more advanced education and training.[4] They encountered through their education the specifically French version of nationalism and democracy founded on revolution. They learned about the French Revolution as a world historical event, the first defeat of a corrupt old regime and the model for other nations around the globe.[5] The future leaders of Cambodia also encountered the French fascination with the glories of the medieval Khmer kingdom. For the French, the Khmers were a distinctive and superior race among the peoples of Southeast Asia, a view absorbed by Cambodian leaders of all political persuasions, from royalists to communists.[6]

Almost one-quarter of the one hundred or so Cambodians sent to study in France in the late 1940s and 1950s, including Pol Pot, Ieng Sary, and Khieu Samphan, joined the French Communist Party, through which they again encountered French revolutionary republicanism but also, of course, Marxism-Leninism.[7] In a study group, they read Marx, Lenin, Stalin, no doubt the classic and popular works like Lenin's *Imperialism* and Stalin's *Foundations of Leninism*, as well as *Capital*.[8]

Ieng Sary studied Stalin's *Marxism and the National Question*.[9] Pol Pot's first published article, in 1952, "Monarchy or Democracy?" tellingly cited the examples of the French, Russian, and Chinese revolutions, which had overthrown corrupt monarchies and replaced them with democratic regimes.[10] Ieng Sary's deputy, Suong Sikoeun, later remarked that "the French Revolution influenced me very strongly, above all Robespierre. . . . Robespierre is my hero. Robespierre and Pol Pot: Both men have the same quality of decisiveness and integrity."[11] To mark his abiding affection for the French Revolution, Pol Pot chose for his wedding date Bastille Day 1956.[12] But a more important influence was the French Communist Party, which in the 1950s was marked by unswerving support for the Soviet Union and a highly undemocratic internal structure.

When these men (and a few women) returned to Cambodia in the 1950s, many of them served as teachers at the elite collèges and lycées. This group includes Pol Pot, Ieng Sary, Son Sen, Khieu Ponnary (Pol Pot's wife), Khieu Thirith (the wife of Ieng Sary and sister of Khieu Ponnary), and Yun Yat, the wife of Son Sen. The four men had studied together in Paris; they would become the leaders of the Khmer Rouge in power. They would also be joined by some men like Nuon Chea and Ta Mok who had never left Cambodia or Southeast Asia and had had a traditional Buddhist rather than a French education.[13] In the 1950s, most of them were formally members of the Indochinese Communist Party (and sometimes of the French Communist Party as well), and they seem to have resented Vietnamese domination of the party. When Prince Sihanouk in the late 1950s instituted a policy of repression against Cambodian communists, some of them fled to the forests, as did Pol Pot and Ieng Sary in 1963. Some of their students followed them, reproducing the very important teacher-student bond in Khmer Buddhist culture.[14] From the forests they launched a guerrilla war to create a communist Cambodia. By this point, they had separated from the Indochinese Communist Party and had formed their own Cambodian Communist Party (CPK).

Sihanouk's domineering ways and repressive policies created some new recruits for the guerrilla campaign, but overall, the CPK's successes were minimal until the Vietnam War spilled over into Cambodia. The United States launched waves of air strikes beginning in the late 1960s in an effort to disrupt North Vietnamese supply routes into the South that traversed Cambodian territory. The U.S. campaign failed in its stated goals. Instead, it wreaked havoc on Cambodian village life, killing and uprooting hundreds of thousands of people. Many of the survivors of the bombing raids fled to Phnom Penh, where they strained the meager resources of the city. Others fled to the jungle, a younger group of recruits to the Khmer Rouge guerrilla army.[15] In large part as a result of nearly indiscriminate American bombing in the eastern part of the country and then ground invasion in 1973, the Khmer Rouge became a formidable threat to the Cambodian government of General Lon Nol, who had replaced Sihanouk in a military coup in 1970.

On 17 April 1975, the Khmer Rouge marched into Phnom Penh, two weeks before the Vietnamese communists drove out the Americans and seized Saigon. The communist victory in Cambodia was, in many ways, a historical accident — but the same can be said of the Bolshevik triumph in October 1917 and the Nazi seizure of power in January 1933.[16] Each of these revolutionary events resulted from a combination of historical circumstances and political will; none was in any way inevitable. In both the Russian and Cambodian cases, the countries had been devastated by war, leaving large segments of the population hungry and uprooted and in mourning for the dead among them. War had dramatically revealed the ineptitude and corruption of the existing systems. Neither Czar Nicholas II in Russia nor Prince Norodom Sihanouk and his successor, General Lon Nol, could successfully conduct war, whether against foreign or internal enemies, let alone alleviate the enormous difficulties at home. The raging discontents of the population enabled the communists to mobilize a small but significant number of supporters, in the factories and naval installations of Petrograd, in the Cambodian countryside devastated by American bombing raids. Larger segments of the population, rural and urban, disoriented, discontented, disdainful of their own governments, were willing to tolerate a communist victory and hope for the best. Critically, at the moment the communists reached for power, other states were unable or unwilling to intervene directly in the events. In 1917, the European countries were still enmeshed in World War I. In the case of Southeast Asia, the U.S. Congress had forbidden further interventions in Cambodia, while the North Vietnamese were preoccupied with the final offensive against the U.S.-backed South Vietnamese forces. In spring 1975, Saigon was a much bigger prize than Phnom Penh.

Elated at their victory, the Khmer Rouge moved quickly to transform radically Cambodian society. In power they always claimed that they were creating something completely new and utterly Khmer. As Ieng Sary, the deputy prime minister for foreign affairs, stated in 1977, "the Khmer revolution has no precedent. What we are trying to do has never been done before in history."[17] Or as Pol Pot—"Brother Number One," as he was called, the leader of the party and state—put the matter in 1978, Democratic Kampuchea was "building socialism without a model."[18] Yet the idea of a fully autonomous Khmer revolution was sheer propaganda. For all the particularities of Democratic Kampuchea and the Khmer Rouge, its leaders were, first and foremost, twentieth-century communists.[19]

"In many places, water is flowing freely, and with water, the scenery is fresh, the plants are fresh, life is fresh and people are smiling," proclaimed Khieu Samphan, the president of Democratic Kampuchea, on the second anniversary of the communist victory.[20] The revolution, the Khmer Rouge believed, would create a prosperous, egalitarian society. Collective existence on every conceivable level would destroy the nefarious characteristics of the old society, like avarice and exploitation. Cambodians would live together as a virtual family whose collective labor would build the new society without any foreign aid or involvement. As Radio Phnom Penh reported, "our brothers and sisters of all categories, including workers, peasants, soldiers, and revolutionary cadres have worked around the clock with soaring enthusiasm, paying no attention to the time or to their fatigue; they have worked in a cheerful atmosphere of revolutionary optimism."[21] The self-sufficient society that they were creating would provide enough rice that no one would go hungry; indeed, Cambodians would be able to enjoy sweets whenever they liked.

The Khmer Rouge, then, focused on development for the future, not a mythical agrarian past. Often mistaken as a form of agrarian primitivism, these actions were really efforts to leap over bourgeois society into the communist future, "a forced march toward . . . communist modernity," as one scholar has described their policies.[22] Cambodian communists were, in essence, producing their own variant of a developmental dictatorship, complete with the standard communist practice of a Four-Year Plan, though their regime was too short-lived actually to implement it.[23] Upon the basis of a prosperous, collectivized agriculture, brimming with exports, Democratic Kampuchea would finance industrial development and the mechanization of agriculture.[24] Peasants were promised that the whole country would be electrified, and that draft cattle would soon be replaced by tractors.[25] "In the agricultural field," pronounced the leadership, "we are sure that we can achieve new progress by leaps and bounds. . . . [W]e should quickly change our beloved motherland from an underdeveloped agricultural country into a modern one and from a modern agricultural country into an industrial country."[26] And a modern country would be one that would be able to maintain its independence against adversaries of all kinds. Echoing one of Stalin's famous speeches in which he lamented Russia's backwardness and defeat at the hands of a succession of enemies, from Tatars in the thirteenth century to Germans in the twentieth (quoted in chapter 2), Pol Pot argued: "If we are not strong and do not leap forward quickly, outside enemies are just waiting to crush us. Enemies of all kinds want to have small countries as their servants. So, in order to prevent them from crushing us, we have to be strong. For that reason we must strive to move fast."[27]

Upon seizing power, the Khmer Rouge moved immediately to accomplish this "leap forward" — and the terminological similarity to the Chinese "Great Leap Forward" of the 1950s is not at all accidental.[28] The rapid and successful creation of this new, egalitarian, prosperous, and self-sufficient Khmer society depended upon four intertwined developments: the destruction of the preexisting class-riven society; the collectivization of all aspects of life; immense acts of will, especially in relation to labor; and the refashioning of individuals and ethnic and religious minorities into communist Khmers.

The first act in the drive to the future was the forced evacuation of Phnom Penh, the Khmer Rouge's best-known move, partly because foreign journalists were still present. The motives for the evacuation were unclear at the time, both to the deportees and to the observers. Cambodians were told that the Americans were about to bomb the city, and that they were being moved for their own protection. They would be allowed to return in just a few days. In reality, the evacuation was the first major step in the compulsory creation of an egalitarian society via a forced social leveling process. By ripping more prosperous Cambodians from their immediate surroundings, confiscating and ransacking their homes, the Khmer Rouge were destroying the foundations — and the trappings, like well-crafted furniture and more elegant clothing — of the wealthier groups of Cambodian society. The abolition of money was no return to primitivism but an attack on the middle and upper classes and a headlong rush into the socialist future.

Just as the Khmer Rouge attacked the foundations of class society by the forced deportation of the urban population, so they sought to undermine the traditional peasant organization of the countryside by the communalization of the land. Like the Soviets and Chinese but even more radically, Cambodian communists sought the abolition of private peasant agriculture as the means of fostering higher economic productivity (so they thought) and of making good communists out of individualistic peasants. The Khmer Rouge organized cooperatives in the countryside, at first of ten to fifteen families, then on a much greater scale, often involving several hundred people. Still larger "high-level cooperatives," seen as the acme of development, were accompanied by communal eating arrangements and a system of forced labor on large-scale projects.[29] The hostility toward any sign of individual property extended so far that even household items like pots, pans, and axes were made common property. Indeed, communal eating was lauded as one of the major accomplishments of Democratic Kampuchea, a great stride toward the elimination of all aspects of private, individualized life that, left intact, would inevitably form a beachhead for the return of capitalism.[30]

The elimination of existing classes was just the first step toward the building of the new society. Utopia, in the Khmer Rouge view, would entail the direct, unmediated relationship between "Angkar" — the Organization, as the party styled itself — and the population. Any institutions that fostered other loyalties the CPK sought to suppress. As a result, the Khmer Rouge closed monasteries and churches, even schools. But most significantly, they attacked the family — something even the Soviets shied away from — and, in so doing, struck at the heart of traditional Khmer society. As memoirs attest, teenagers and even young children were removed from their families and placed in labor brigades. In one group of forty-six Cambodians, interviewed in 1998, fully 80 percent said that they had been forced to live apart from their families.[31] The regime told Khmers to give up all their possessions and to surmount emotional feelings for spouses and children. The collectivist ethos espoused by the Khmer Rouge was so strong that any sign of overt affection, any effort to sustain family ties, made one immediately suspect.[32] "Mothers must not get too entangled with their children," warned one CPK document. "There should be time [for the mothers] to go and work."[33] In some cases, the Khmer Rouge arranged forced marriages for party cadres, and even weddings were collective events, presided over by party officials who lined up men and women facing one another and dispensed altogether with the traditional Buddhist celebrations.[34] After marriage, couples were often separated and worked in separate brigades. Even party cadres faced criticism for displaying too much "family-ism, sibling-ism, relation-ism," which "flouted the Party's criteria."[35] In perhaps the ultimate attack on the solidarity of the family, the CPK pronounced: "Children, you are the children of Angkar. Children, you should report to him all the activities of your parents!"[36]

Once the old society and its traditional loyalties had been destroyed, the path was open for immense acts of will that would literally transform the landscape of Cambodia. Heroic, collective human efforts would, in record time, clear forests, build irrigation systems, and vastly increase the rice crop yield. Collective organization and labor inspired by the vision of a new society would produce three tons of rice per hectare where, formerly, the average yield had been one ton per hectare. On some occasions there was even talk of raising the harvest to eight or ten tons per hectare.[37] The entire population would be mobilized to create the new society, with tens and hundreds of thousands of people moved around the country on gigantic labor projects. "When a people is awakened by political consciousness, it can do anything," claimed one party spokesman.[38] Cambodians were to become "masters of the earth and of water," "masters of the rice fields and plains, of the forests and of all vegetation," "masters of the yearly floods."[39] With the correct political line, Democratic Kampuchea would create a modern agriculture in five years.[40] "There are no longer diplomas; there are only diplomas of practice," ran another CPK slogan.[41] Revolutionary will and revolutionary politics were even more important than technical expertise. "Practice . . . teaches us technology. . . . By cultivating good political consciousness, we can all learn swiftly. . . . Formerly to be a pilot required a high school education — twelve to fourteen years. Nowadays, it's clear that political consciousness is the decisive factor. . . . As for radar, we can learn how to handle it after studying for a couple of months."[42]

These immense acts of will coupled with the immediate and dramatic transformations of Khmer society enabled Democratic Kampuchea to leap past even other communist states; it was thirty years *ahead* of China, Korea, and Vietnam, the Khmer Rouge claimed.[43]

> We have leaped over the neo-colonial, semi-feudalist society of the American imperialists, the feudalists and capitalists of every nation, and have achieved a socialist society straight away. The situation is completely different from other countries. . . . [In China] a long period of time was required. . . . [North Korea] needed fourteen years to make the transition. North Vietnam did the same.

As for us, we have a different character from them. We are faster than they are.[44]

Returning exiles heard the slogan "The Organization excels Lenin and is outstripping Mao" and the claim that Chinese experts in Cambodia had come "to study the Khmer Rouge system because it was superior to their own." The Chinese had made one Cultural Revolution, "but we are making a Cultural Revolution every day."[45]

Like the other parties and movements discussed in this book, the Khmer Rouge venerated the state as the agent that would create the future society. It was the state that depopulated the cities and collectivized the countryside, creating the conditions for communism. The state would also protect the revolution from the enemies who constantly threatened it. Like the Soviet state, the DK state would be a dictatorship of the proletariat, dispensing revolutionary justice to enemies and reeducating those who could still be saved.[46] The state's reach would be total. As one party document proclaimed: "Statepower in cooperatives; statepower in factories; and statepower throughout the whole country."[47] There would be no checks on this state power, no tripartite division of the branches of government, no effective parliament. The checks would come internally, by purges.

Violence was an intrinsic element of the Khmer Rouge view of the state. They had come to power through violence and would continue to exercise violence, real and metaphorical. They spoke of "smashing" and "destroying" "imperialism and its lackeys," and, again like the other parties and movements discussed in this book, made constant reference to struggles, battles, assaults — "to assault" the Four-Year Plan to bring it to completion, "to strongly assault" the requirements of the Plan for 1977, "to strike" at various "fronts."[48] The Northwest was to be the "number one battlefield" for economic growth; "we will . . . imme-diately launch the offensive in raising the level of dam water in order to double or even triple the harvest"; "our revolutionary army is launching a construction offensive."[49] The Khmer Rouge labeled the base group of ten families a platoon, the thousand-family grouping a regiment, larger collectives divisions.[50] Purges were called sweeps, and they required mo-bilization, as when the party recommended "constantly nursing the seething hatred and blood rancor against national and class enemies."[51]

Even more so than in other communist systems, the party, state, and army were almost indistinguishable from one another in Democratic Kampuchea. Pointedly, party leaders occupied the key positions not just in the state but in the army as well. Pol Pot, for example, was prime minister, secretary of the Standing Committee of the CPK Central Committee, and chairman of the General Staff of the Revolutionary Armed Forces of Kampuchea; Son Sen was deputy prime minister for national defense, a candidate member of the Standing Committee, and chief of the General Staff.[52] Because of this merger of institutions and personnel, slogans that honored the party — "Nothing is more precious and honorable than to belong within the party's ranks, and nothing is better than to be a communist," or "Long live the brilliant Cambodian Communist Party! Long live Marxist-Leninist doctrine, the strongest force!"[53] — rebounded onto the state as well. Even more fantastically, the Khmer Rouge claimed, "Angkar is ruler of the water, ruler of the land."[54]

The state was also the agency that would reshape individuals, developing their class consciousness and making them into Khmer communists. The destruction of private property was understood as the first step in this process, because however small the plot of land might be, possession of private property inevitably results in individualist, capitalist ways of thinking, while collective property ineluctably leads to socialist consciousness. However, even the Khmer Rouge recognized that this process would not occur immediately. "The feudalists and capitalist classes are, in fact, overthrown, but their specific traits of contradiction . . . still exist. They still exist in policy, in consciousness, in standpoint, and class rage."[55] The task of the CPK, then, was to "rid in each party member, each cadre, everything that is of the oppressor class, of private property, of stance, view, sentiment, custom, literature, art . . . which exists in ourselves, no matter how much or how little." In turn, "we must build a proletarian class world view, proletarian class life; build a proletarian class stand regarding thinking, in living habits, in morality, in sentiment etc." Because capitalist traits were often hidden, they were particularly dangerous.[56]

By eliminating the habits and consciousness of the old society, the Khmer Rouge were creating "purity" and "cleanliness," key concepts of the revolution. Pol Pot often spoke of the "*clean*" victory of the Khmer Rouge, which he contrasted with the degenerate habits of life under the old regime:

> Upon entering Phnom Penh and other cities, the brother and sister
> combatants of the revolutionary army . . . sons and daughters of

our workers and peasants . . . were taken aback by the overwhelming unspeakable sight of long-haired men and youngsters wearing bizarre clothes making themselves indistinguishable from the fair sex. . . . Our traditional mentality, mores, traditions, literature, and arts and culture and tradition were totally destroyed by U.S. imperialism and its stooges. . . . Our people's traditionally clean, sound characteristics and essence were completely absent and abandoned, replaced by imperialistic, pornographic, shameless, perverted, and fanatic traits.[57]

Radio Phnom Penh reported that "a clean social system is flourishing throughout new Cambodia." Villagers, it claimed, "have rid the areas of all vestiges of the old regime, cleaning up the village, wiping out old habits, and taking up the new revolutionary morals."[58]

To create "clean" and "pure" people required continual education. To transform people into solid party cadres, ran one document, "we must educate people over and over and yet again," which entailed "meetings, listening to radio broadcasts, studying short documents, by word of mouth itself, by documents from Regions or the sectors." People were expected to write their autobiographies, which were to be carefully scrutinized by party leaders. Those who demonstrated hostility to the revolution were "savage" and incapable of reeducation, hence had to be separated out. The party would continually "purify our state-power so that it is clean, tough and strong," and would "purify out the enemy among the people, to be clean, to be good, to be rough, to be strong."[59]

The enemies were at home and abroad, and the constant drive to search them out gave a special dynamism to the Khmer Rouge revolution, as it did to the Soviet, Nazi, and even Yugoslav revolutions. Responding to his own rhetorical question "Why must we move so swiftly?" Pol Pot pointed to the enemies abroad: "Because enemies attack and torment us. From the east and west they persist in pounding and worrying us. . . . If . . . we are strong and courageous . . . the contemptible people to the east and the contemptible people to the west will be unable to do anything to us."[60] The language of the Khmer Rouge bore all the biological symbolism of other systems of mass terror and population purges. They labeled their enemies "microbes" who caused an illness in the party. They are "buried"; they bore within and have to be ferreted out.[61] "If we wait any longer, the microbes . . . will rot us from within. . . . The old ones who remain in place give birth to new ones, one or two at a time, and so it goes on. . . . This is a life and death contradiction which must be firmly grasped."[62] Other typical DK slogans included these: "What is infected must be cut out"; "What is rotten must be removed"; "What is too long must be shortened and made the right length"; "It isn't enough to cut down a bad plant, it must be uprooted."[63] And in particularly chilling fashion, Pol Pot remarked in December 1976, "[S]ometimes there is no active opposition; there is only silence."[64] He meant that the party had constantly to seek out its opponents, even when only silence reigned. It meant, too, that the prosecution of actions did not suffice. The party had also to investigate the thoughts of people to see what the silence signified, a kind of theological investigation of consciousness.

For all that the Khmer Rouge adopted and radicalized standard aspects of twentieth-century communist politics, they also drew upon indigenous Cambodian beliefs and practices. Indeed, a good part of their popularity with some segments of the population, especially in the early months and in the years preceding the seizure of power, resulted from their mimicking of Khmer Buddhist cultural patterns. As one authority, François Ponchaud, writes: "Though the Democratic Kampuchean revolution appears to be the most radical revolution of the twentieth century, the behavior of the revolutionaries is not totally alien to Khmer culture."[65] The model of revolutionary self-denial, discipline, and internal transformation was also typical of Theravada Buddhism. The years the Khmer Rouge spent in the forests in the 1960s seemed to exemplify Buddhist lore, in which heroes wander in the forests, accumulating knowledge and skills that will serve them well on the eventual road to righteous power.[66] At least initially, the "exemplary behavior" of CPK cadres "fitted more closely with Buddhist ideals of propriety and social justice than anything emanating from Phnom Penh."[67] Khmer culture, Ponchaud also points out, was largely oral, rather than literate, and those who spoke well, "smooth talkers," were highly venerated.[68] Pol Pot inspired many of his followers, even amid the terrors inflicted by the Khmer Rouge, by his ability to speak in this traditional idiom, to convey his ideas "smoothly" and calmly. Even the communication of Khmer Rouge orders followed a largely oral pattern with relatively little in the way of formal government bureaucracy and written decrees and laws. Moreover, the Khmer Rouge leaders were faceless and nameless — a pattern of secrecy cultivated by the party, but one that recalls also the rituals of kingship and charismatic leadership in certain societies in which common people fear to look at the ruler or are prohibited from doing so.

The Khmer Rouge idealized the peasant world even as they radically transformed it, another point of contact with Khmer traditions that garnered them significant support. The hostility to urban residents, seen as the site of foreign influence and corruption, had affinities with the closed peasant world. The CPK idealized "natural" peasant knowledge. "The rice field is the university . . . the hoe is the pen," ran one slogan.[69] The forced relocation of urban residents and other presumed opponents of the regime into the countryside and a life of peasant labor would be the source of their regeneration, purging them of their corrupt past, teaching them the superiority of peasant ways — or, better stated, of peasant ways as understood by the Khmer Rouge. The common dress of loose-fitting black pants and shirts, short hair, and moral rigor imposed on the entire population all reflected a similar idealization of the peasantry and the insistence on a lack of social differentiation in the Cambodian countryside. As one person interviewed by the historian Ben Kiernan stated, "the real poor people liked the Khmer Rouge. . . . They liked the system and really hated the Phnom Penh people, because we had not struggled for the revolution and equality alongside the Khmer Rouge."[70]

For all their rootedness in traditional Cambodian society, the most striking feature of the Khmer Rouge was their attachment to communism. The utopian vision they espoused, with its promise of future prosperity and happiness for all in an egalitarian society, linked Cambodian communism back to the socialist ideology developed in nineteenth-century Europe. Yet the Khmer Rouge version had particular, fantastical elements to it. The notions that with the proper social conditions, correct political line, and immense acts of will, Khmers could quickly expand the rice yield, completely surmounting any real, objective limits of resources, human or natural, or that Democratic Kampuchea had in a matter of months surpassed all its communist predecessors — such notions display breathtaking bravado and absurd aversions to concrete reality, which led to the most tragic consequences.

But did it all have to be so deadly? Was there an immediate connection between the utopian strivings of the Khmer Rouge and the massive death toll of around 20 percent of the Cambodian population, including a number of genocides that were carried out against national minorities?

Ideology alone is never a sufficient explanation for such massive developments as genocide. Ideological inclinations intersect, roughly and unevenly, with politics, both at the center of power and "on the ground," and with international developments. As we shall see, by late 1976, the disastrous conditions at home—largely self-generated, to be sure—coupled with border conflicts, then full-scale war with Vietnam, created a crisis atmosphere at the very top of the CPK. The leadership responded with a vast expansion of purge operations. Democratic Kampuchea had its own version of the "euphoria of victory" coupled with the dread fear of defeat, that combination of reactions that moved the Nazi system from discrimination to genocide. Moreover, as the very last communist party to seize power in the twentieth century, the Khmer Rouge reflected in their practices their particular (and often peculiar) interpretation of the lessons, positive and negative, offered by their predecessors. The veneration of the state as the agent that would build socialism and of political violence as the favored technique to transform society flowed directly from the Soviet and Chinese models, sometimes mediated by the experience of CPK leaders in the French and Indochinese communist parties of the 1950s. Yet the lightning-like implementation of their ideology and the total, systematic character of their policies reflected their belief that even the Chinese had not moved quickly enough and had allowed capitalist forms to reassert themselves.

Still, it is hard to escape the conclusion that the specifically Khmer Rouge version of a communist utopia constitutes an enormous proportion of the explanation for the descent into mass killings and genocide, probably more so than was the case in the Soviet Union. After the Bolshevik victory, one can track disputes within the party for a good fifteen years, and the hiatus of the New Economic Policy in the 1920s is evidence for the possibility of an alternative, more peaceful and humane path of development than that followed by Stalin. While dissenting circles existed within the CPK, the rapidity and totality of Khmer Rouge actions suggests that there was little if any hope for a Khmer communism "with a human face" (to take the term of the Czech communist reformers in 1968), and that their specific version of communist ideology immediately endangered from the outset very substantial segments of the Cambodian population. As was the case in the Soviet Union, certain ethnic and national groups would come to be associated with hostility to the socialist cause, and every one of their members, no matter what he or she had done, came to be seen as an enemy who had to be purged.[71] Despite the claims that they were creating a completely egalitarian society, the Khmer Rouge were in fact establishing new lines of division and reasserting some older ones. In the process, large segments of the Cambodian population would lose their lives, and certain religious and national minorities would become the victims of genocide.

CATEGORIZING THE POPULATION

Immediately upon seizing power, the Khmer Rouge ordered the destruction of all identity papers.[72] In Phnom Penh, people threw their documents into fires strewn along the chaos-filled streets. It was an audacious act that reflected the Khmer Rouge's elation at victory and determination to build an egalitarian society. Inadvertently, the abolition of identity papers allowed many members of the old regime, especially low- and midlevel officials and soldiers of the Lon Nol government, to melt into the population at large.

Yet at the very same moment, the Khmer Rouge set off on a "a classification and elimination madness," as the French historian Jean-Louis Margolin describes their actions.[73] Like the Soviet Union and the Third Reich, a regime determined to refashion the thinking and behavior of the populace and to shape the very composition of society had to be able to identify its friends and enemies. It had to determine those upon whom it could rely, those whom it considered "educable," and those who had to be eliminated altogether. Also as in the Soviet Union and the Third Reich, the categories of identity developed by the Khmer Rouge were highly elastic and never self-evident and objective. They blended political, social, and ethnic criteria, and parsed individuals into particular slots often in a highly arbitrary manner.

The first and most fundamental delineation the Khmer Rouge adopted was that between "old" (also called "base") and "new" people. "Base people" were those who had been partisans of the Khmer Rouge or had lived in areas under their control before the seizure of power. Sometimes, though, poor peasants, no matter where they had lived, were considered base people. "New people" were city dwellers or those who had lived in areas under the control of the Lon Nol regime. Anyone who had served the old system, in however lowly a position, was also categorized as belonging to the new people.

The Khmer Rouge considered base people their loyal supporters. They were afforded vital privileges. They were not, by and large, moved en masse out of their villages and were able to retain their homes and even individual plots of land. They received more generous rations, and as conditions drastically deteriorated, even slightly more food could mean the difference between life and death. Many were recruited into the regime as soldiers. New people, who were thought to constitute about 30 percent of the population, had to be reeducated, primarily through labor and participation in mass meetings at which they listened to lectures and recounted their autobiographies for criticism. Between the two groups the regime erected a system of virtual apartheid. The two groups lived in separate places, ate in segregated eating halls, and labored in separate work gangs. New and base people were not allowed to marry or even to speak to one another.[74]

The division between new and base was only the starting point. In the Kong Pisei district in the Southwest, four thousand base people confronted three thousand new people, deportees from Phnom Penh. Typically, strict residential segregation prevailed. But within a few months the local cadres began further to divide the population. They categorized some as "full rights people," that is, base people with "good politics," those who displayed a willingness to work hard and had no relatives among new people or among those who had been executed by the regime. Base people with "bad biographies," those who failed to work diligently or had displayed some antagonism toward the new system, found themselves demoted to "depositee" and were forced to join the new people. Finally, the CPK cadres in the district established an intermediate group of "candidates"(or "probationary people"), new people who showed the promise of reeducation or fallen base people who strove to regain their former status.

The evaluation of an individual's labor served as the critical criterion that moved people up or down the hierarchy. If people worked hard and without complaint, they demonstrated their loyalty to the new system and might then become more privileged members of society.[75] Other districts had even more convoluted systems with up to nine categories that were based upon the cadres' evaluations of individuals' consciousness and labor. The lowest of the low were "bandits," those who had attempted to flee Democratic Kampuchea.[76] In other places, the cadres divided the population into work categories, "full strength" or "weak strength," which they then subdivided further. Some of the full strength people, generally those who were young and single, were organized into mobile labor brigades. The category of weak strength people comprised married men and women, young children, and the elderly. They were allowed to work near the village in work gangs generally divided by sex. All the groups were organized along military lines into platoons, companies, battalions, and regiments.[77] To make matters even more complicated, Pol Pot attempted to carry out a class analysis of DK society derived from Maoist China that involved classifying the peasants as lower, lower-middle, middle, or upper, and others as workers or "feudal people."[78]

Like the other cases described in this book, Democratic Kampuchea had an unrelenting drive to place every individual in a clearly defined category. In James Scott's words, the regime sought to make society "legible" so that it could be administered.[79] And as in all the other cases, the categories used to classify the population, to make it "legible," reflected an often arbitrary mix of social, national, and political criteria. Although social class was supposed to be the essential criterion of classification, in reality a wide variety of backgrounds, behaviors, and events—some totally beyond any individual's control—could land one in the honored or dishonored category. A poor peasant was an honored base person, a rice merchant immediately a dishonored new person. But almost irrespective of class, geographic variables—such as whether one had lived in the countryside or the city, in Khmer Rouge or Lon Nol regions—could be critical. A poor peasant with relatives who had served in Lon Nol's army became a new person. A peasant who failed to work hard—as defined by party cadres—or grumbled about the new system or even, in an act of humanity, aided deportees by giving them some extra food, if found out, would immediately be demoted into the new people category. Most of the CPK leaders were of bourgeois or wealthy peasant background, and some of them, as mentioned, had been educated in French-founded schools in the 1940s and 1950s, and in France itself in the 1950s. Yet they were categorized as "workers" simply by virtue of their party membership, and the same was true of people who served in the Khmer Rouge army.

Far from any kind of objective analysis of society, categorization was an ideological and political process by which the regime identified its supporters and enemies, real or imagined. Family and occupational background, political stance, labor output, and daily behavior all came into play in a confused jumble. One CPK document defined class as a "level of people with distinctive political tendencies," a curious confusion of social and political criteria.[80] As was the case with the Nazi category of "asocials" and the Soviet "*lishentsy*" (disenfranchised), the Khmer Rouge demonstrated the extreme elasticity of categorizations, which opened the way to an increasingly broad application of population purges. In the Khmer Rouge worldview, politics could determine being, just as being could determine politics.

Nationality was another critical element of categorization for the Khmer Rouge, and another one about which enormous confusion reigned. The CPK claimed that minorities constituted only 1 percent of the population, an effort to erase difference by fiat. In reality, the figure was closer to 20 percent.[81] The largest enclaves of non-Khmers were Chinese, Vietnamese, Chams (Muslims), Thais, and Laotians, along with some twenty others, many of them small distinct tribal groups. Under the new regime, the Khmer Rouge declared, "there are to be no Chams or Chinese or Vietnamese. Everybody is to join the same, single, Khmer nationality. . . . [There is] only one religion—Khmer religion."[82] Similarly, a survivor recalls a cadre saying: "Now we are making revolution. Everyone becomes a Khmer."[83] Chams were told that they had "to mix flesh and blood with the Khmer."[84] Khmers who had married Vietnamese or the children of Khmer-Vietnamese liaisons were often labeled "Vietnamese in Khmer bodies," and the implication was clearly that their "true essence" as non-Khmers had to be unmasked.

Without the developed documentation with which the Nazis and Soviets worked, the Khmer Rouge had to find other means of identifying non-Khmers. Often this was possible on the basis of physical traits, but the regime also tracked residential patterns, occupations, religion, and customs. Some of these characteristics were intermingled, making it even easier for the regime to find the people whom they considered suspect. Vietnamese and Chinese, for example, composed a large part of the urban population, and many of them pursued commercial and professional activities. On all three counts the regime considered them intrinsically hostile to the new society—as non-Khmers, urban residents, and members of the bourgeoisie.[85] The Chams not only were Muslim but tended to live in their own villages, and many of them labored individually as fishermen or farmers. They wore distinctive clothing and long hair. In all these cases, class came to be identified in national and then racial terms: virtually every Vietnamese, Chinese (at least those Chinese who had been living in Cambodia), and Cham was categorized as "bourgeois."[86]

In Khmer culture, family was the key institution that "underpinned the whole social structure" of the village. The inhabitants worshiped common ancestors, who protected the village and ensured it rainfall and an abundant crop. Ties of identity brought together family and village; "at a more general level, one could consider the Khmer people as comprising a vast single family," one built up from family to village to nation.[87] Cambodians traditionally addressed one another by relational ties, such as brother, mother, or nephew. These "names" clearly reflected the social hierarchy, demonstrating the ties that bound people to one another and the various levels of authority, with elders granted the greatest respect.[88] The Khmer Rouge drew upon these traditions and attempted to substitute Angkar, the Organization, for the family. Pol Pot's appellation of "Brother Number One" reflected both an outward modesty expected of people in Khmer culture — he was brother, not father or grandfather — and the authority vested in him as "Number One." Angkar, though, was referred to as the "dad-mom" of the people, military leaders as "grandfather."[89] "Angkar is the father and mother of little boys and little girls, and also of boy and girl adolescents," trumpeted one party slogan.[90] While the CPK went a long way toward destroying traditional family ties, it sought to replace them with the pseudofamily of the party organization, with its leading brothers, thereby making all Khmers, if not quite a family, at least a race bound by blood lineage. If race is a form of identity based on supposed biological ties among a group of people, then the CPK view of the Khmer people as one extended family constituted a form of racialization. As one party slogan expressed the matter: "Do you love your social class? Do you love your race? Do you love Angkar?"[91]

Indeed, Angkar assumed the power to determine who was legitimately a member of the family (or race) and who was not, who was honored by inclusion, who had to be purged. Because the honored group was bound by blood ties, so the characteristics of the dishonored were also seen to lie "in the blood," not just in the actions of particular individuals. "Counterrevolutionary elements which betray and try to sabotage the revolution," Pol Pot said, "are not to be regarded as being our people." Not only were they opponents of the revolution, a specific political event, but, he said, they were enemies of the Cambodian people.[92] Hence their wives and children also became enemies, as had been the case in the Soviet Great Terror. Photographs of Tuol Sleng prisoners, always harrowing, are especially poignant when they depict the young children — some looking no older than three or four — and wives of purged party members, soon to be executed.[93]

In racializing nationality, the Khmer Rouge drew not only on metaphors of the familial bonds among all Khmers. As mentioned, they also drew upon French colonial ideas.[94] French officials stereotyped Cambodians as lazy and passive, so they imported Vietnamese as officials and skilled laborers. But the French also posited the Khmers as a gentle, morally superior people, a sort of Aryan race among Asians, while the Vietnamese were believed to be mendacious and the Chinese untrustworthy. As the scholar Penny Edwards describes their views: "[French] scholar-officials fetishized those parts of Cambodia they found attractive—Angkor Wat [the medieval palace rediscovered by French archaeologists in the nineteenth century], fine arts, the royal dance—and roundly dismissed the rest. The present was thus dismissed as worthless entropy, the distant past reified as a golden era of high civilization, gleanings of which still shone on in a romanticized 'Khmer soul.'"[95] "Cambodia," then, was a French creation, and all of its modern, post-colonial leaders—Sihanouk, Lon Nol, Pol Pot—would invoke its past glory as a reason to resurrect a powerful, independent nation.[96] But this image of the past came bundled with intense hostility toward the Chinese and Vietnamese, a sense of utter difference between Khmers and their neighbors that was evident in the great achievements of the Khmer past—but also in the body, in the completely distinct lineages that supposedly constituted the three groups.[97]

PURGING THE POPULATION

In 1977 Pol Pot laid out, in starkly clear fashion, the population politics of Democratic Kampuchea.

> We must deal with [counterrevolutionary elements] the same way we would with any enemy, that is, by separating, educating, and coopting elements that can be won over . . . , neutralizing any reluctant elements . . ., and isolating and eradicating only the smallest number . . . who determinedly oppose the revolution . . . and collaborate with the foreign enemies to oppose their own nation.[98]

By identifying the Khmer people with the Khmer Rouge revolution, Pol Pot made any political opposition an act of betrayal against the Cambodian nation. Morever, in his view the political homogeneity that was an expected outcome of the revolution also implied national homogeneity. In Democratic Kampuchea, there could be no place for people of different ethnicities and nationalities, especially if they held on to their traditional beliefs and ways of life.

But what did "neutralizing" and "isolating and eradicating" actually mean? The Khmer Rouge did not, at first, organize a systematic campaign of genocide. Instead, they initiated a rapid, immense campaign of political, social, and economic transformation that led to the deaths of hundreds of thousands of Cambodians because of the program's sheer enormity, its total disregard for individual liberties, and its reliance on "will" and rejection of any rational assessment of resources. The CPK also carried out deliberate and extensive executions of perceived political opponents, especially the officials and soldiers of the old regime. But not all purported enemies of Democratic Kampuchea were killed. As Pol Pot's comment indicates, DK, like other communist systems before it, posited the possibility of reeducation. The act of labor carried out in conjunction with base people, the revolution's loyal supporters, would, presumably, purge false thoughts and capitalist sentiments from the minds and bodies of tainted individuals, remaking them into Khmer communists.

Yet by autumn 1976, a year and a half into the regime's existence, its policies had resulted in widespread starvation and a threatening war with Vietnam. Dissent had emerged even within the party. In this crisis context, when Pol Pot and his closest collaborators seem to have feared for their very existence, they escalated the level of violence, launching a preemptive strike at perceived opponents both within the party and in society at large. The last eighteen months of Democratic Kampuchea were marked by a cataclysm of deliberate killings and death from the privations of deportation, malnutrition, and harsh labor conditions. Within the overall campaign of political violence, the regime carried out genocides against distinct nationalities — Chinese, Vietnamese, Chams — that, to the Khmer Rouge, were by definition hostile to the effort to establish an egalitarian, homogeneous Khmer society.

The initial, infamous purge action instituted by the Khmer Rouge upon their assumption of power was the forced evacuation of virtually the entire population from Phnom Penh and other cities to the country-side.[99] Urban residents, including the elderly and sick, were set off on a journey, mostly on foot, to what destination they did not know. Perhaps as many as half of the entire population experienced the forced trek.[100] The number of deaths from this extraordinary operation seems not to have been very high — though no statistics are available — and there are some reports that Khmer Rouge soldiers acted politely and helpfully.[101] But other reports depict rank and arbitrary brutality. Certainly many ill and elderly individuals were felled by the privations of the evacuation.

This was not a onetime affair. The memoirs of Loung Ung, Someth May, and many others depict three or four or even additional forced relocations.[102] New and "unclean" base people from the southwestern region endured three deportations between 1975 and 1977. The third movement was accompanied by a political purge that removed the regional leadership in the Northwest, at least some of whom had protested the deportations. In 1975 alone, the northwest region absorbed 800,000 deportees.[103] With each deportation, the conditions worsened. Long Van, an airplane mechanic, was deported from Phnom Penh with an extended family of seventeen to his native village in the Southwest. The village could not support all of the additional people, and elderly individuals began to die of malnutrition and disease. Some of the deportees were accused of not working well. Even though Van's parents were base people, he and the rest of his extended family and other new people from Phnom Penh were deported again, this time to the Northwest. Van and his family walked for a day to a railroad station where, with many others, they waited for eleven days. They slept out in open fields, often battered by rain. A number of people died of pneumonia before they could even board the train and proceed to yet another site.[104]

Those who suffered from the forced deportations were by no means only long-term urban dwellers or officials of the old regime. Many villagers had fled to Phnom Penh to escape the multisided ground war that involved various armies, including those of the Lon Nol government, the Khmer Rouge, the United States, and Vietnam, and American bombing raids. When they returned to their home villages after the Khmer Rouge victory, they were castigated as "new people," or "Lon Nol people," or "the enemy," because they had fled the war rather than join the Khmer Rouge.[105] Educated Khmers, especially those who returned from abroad, were either sent for reeducation, which entailed hard manual labor, if they were sympathetic to the Khmer Rouge, or arrested, tortured, and killed.[106] Commenting on some of the returnees, Ben Kiernan writes, "[F]our hundred of Cambodia's most highly educated professionals and intellectuals were now growing vegetables in forest clearings, with three hundred more in work camps in Phnom Penh. Their foreign connections had ended their careers."[107]

The forced deportations were intended to level the population, homogenizing it by forcing former city dwellers into rural pursuits. The deportations also served as a means of political control. One cadre, interviewed later, said, "[T]he main thing was that we could not be assured who the people in Phnom Penh were."[108] The forced march from the capital city would break the remaining powers of the urban population — their economic bases, their social and familial networks, their lingering ties to the urban institutions of palace, bureaucracy, and army. The removal of the urban population would "wipe the slate clean" and permit agrarian and industrial development to proceed along communist lines. Moreover, the deportees would provide labor for the massive development projects that the Khmer Rouge launched, such as the felling of forests, the construction of dams, and the colonization of new agricultural areas. Sent to the countryside, organized into large collectives, even the deportees would learn to work efficiently, the CPK believed. They would contribute to the production of the large rice crop that would feed the population and provide the exports whose earnings would finance industrialization. This was state-directed development with a vengeance, an intensification of the Soviet and Chinese models.[109] Collectivization was so thorough that, by the estimate of Finnish experts, 95–97 percent of the population of Democratic Kampuchea lived on collective farms.[110]

In the context of forced deportation and resettlement, the Khmer Rouge carried out deliberate killings. Along the evacuation routes, they pulled out those whom they had identified as soldiers and bureaucrats of the old regime, who were then summarily executed. By some estimates, the number of deaths was about ten thousand out of two to three million inhabitants of the city and a few hundred thousand evacuees from smaller cities. Later, in the resettlement villages and camps, numerous individuals were "taken away" and never heard from again, as oral testimonies and published memoirs attest.[111] In some cases, individuals who had managed to survive for months, hiding their past of service to the Lon Nol regime and moving on countless times when they feared discovery, were finally identified and "taken away."[112] People who spoke out, failed to work hard, stole food, or became ill were also eliminated. At least one order explicitly advised cadres to "kill urban evacuees indiscriminately."[113]

The failure of the central leadership to halt such killings or to reprimand the killers no doubt encouraged cadres to act in as arbitrary and brutal a manner as they wished. Like the Nazi officials who believed they were "working toward the Führer" when they initiated the Holocaust, so CPK cadres believed they were fulfilling the leadership's goals when they acted on the fearsome, oft-repeated slogans, "If you die, it is no loss. If you remain alive, it is no matter."[114] Or "For the country that we are building, we need one million revolutionaries. We have no need of the rest. Better to kill ten friends than to leave one enemy alive."[115] Such attitudes also amounted to a form of selective euthanasia in which the cadres did nothing to prevent the death of the ill and elderly. In some instances, the handicapped and mentally ill were accused of willful acts of sabotage, or of being as "useless" as the new people.[116] These attitudes and policies recall Nazi Germany, with its emphasis on productivity and the deliberate policy of eliminating the handicapped, who were seen as "useless eaters," a costly burden on society at large.

Even in the first days of the regime, some CPK leaders opposed the forced evacuation of the cities and the abolition of money. Conditions in the eastern part of the country were notably better, the cadres more tolerant than in the Southwest, the core area of Pol Pot supporters. As conditions deteriorated drastically all over the country in 1976 and 1977, and as some officials, it seems, began to call more fervently for a change of course, the Pol Pot group launched a vicious purge that would cost the easterners not only their political power but their lives as well. Ultimately, the southwesterners would construct their domination over the entire country and would extend the purge from the party to society at large.[117]

The main agent of the purges was the Santebel, or the Special Branch, the CPK's security service. Presided over by Kaing Khek Iev, better known by his pseudonym, Duch, the Santebel was a stronghold of the Pol Pot group.[118] In May 1976 Duch moved his headquarters, the so-called S-21, to Phnom Penh and established the infamous prison at Tuol Sleng, the site of a former high school. By the last quarter of the year, Tuol Sleng was receiving scores of former party officials, many of whom would endure weeks and months of torture. In late December 1976, Pol Pot proclaimed that there was "a sickness inside the party," and despite strenuous efforts, "microbes" were still at large, lying buried within it. "If we wait any longer, the microbes can do real damage. . . . They will rot society, rot the Party, and rot the army." This was the clarion call for the escalation of political violence. "Don't be afraid to lose one or two people of bad background," Pol Pot advised. "Driving out the treacherous forces will be a great victory."[119]

In 1978, southwestern Khmer Rouge troops invaded the eastern zone. They carried out extensive massacres, deported thousands of people, and launched attacks across the border against Vietnam.[120] At the same time, the flow of inmates to Tuol Sleng escalated, and even top-ranked party officials endured internment, torture, and execution at the hands of Duch's agents. Ultimately, at least 14,000 people passed through Tuol Sleng, and only a handful survived. The purge took the lives of close to one-third of the original cabinet members of Democratic Kampuchea.[121] On a societal scale, the killings became increasingly indiscriminate, with base as well as new people counted among the victims. Minor complaints or work shirking could lead to executions. In one village, the CPK killed over 200 Phnom Penh people and about half the base people.[122] Ultimately, some 100,000 people may have been killed in this purge operation alone. However, death from privation remained the greatest killer. One physician who survived depicted conditions in the Northwest:

> Ninety percent of the women did not undergo menstruation. . . . The causes of this nearly general irregularity were evident: nutritional deficiency, forced labor, psychic traumas, etc. But to enumerate them in this way would mean to criticize the infallibility of the Angkar, a crime punishable by the death penalty. . . . In the "new villages," the mortality rate then reached more than 50 percent, and the survivors did not fare any better. Production, the main worry of the Angkar, went down to zero. [In the maternity hospital] most of the newly born died by accident from puerperal fever.[123]

Alongside all the violence and death, the regime kept up its belief in reeducation. The CPK expected the forests and rice paddies to transform Khmers with tainted pasts. The Khmer Rouge began to accumulate an enormous archive of life histories. Many of these were conveyed orally at mass meetings or to hostile officials. Those forcibly removed from Phnom Penh, for example, were often stopped along the road and asked about their backgrounds. In villages and factories, people sat through hours of meetings presided over by party officials at which individuals recounted their tainted past or faced accusations of undermining the revolution by poor work habits or excessive family sentiments. Sometimes, the meetings were a prelude to the execution of an individual who had stolen food from the fields or had engaged in sex. On other occasions, party cadres offered new people the opportunity to return to their home villages or to work in a cooperative with supposedly better conditions. But the point was only to get those who had not yet been reeducated to reveal themselves. Because of their "individualist inclinations," they were then sent off to villages with even worse conditions. "When we voluntarily registered ourselves," recalled one survivor, "we denounced ourselves."[124] The party members arrested and sent to Tuol Sleng wrote confession after confession, each time embellishing the traitorous deeds of their life histories as they suffered gruesome tortures.[125]

The population purges of Democratic Kampuchea were multifaceted. They entailed deliberate executions of political opponents, real and imagined, and the forced transformation of the life conditions of the Cambodian population, literally purging from existence entire social categories like urban residents. Life histories also constituted a key element of the world of DK population politics, for they signified the purging of an individual's bad traits by confession. Presumably, the mental act of thinking through one's life, presenting it as oral or written testimony under the watchful gaze of Angkar's cadres, would enable the individual to see the light and change his or her inner being. Communist systems, with their rhetoric of inclusion, of creating a better society for everyone, had to hold out the promise of transformed lives, of making good Khmers out of the detritus of the old society. Yet at the very same time, Democratic Kampuchea identified certain nationalities as intrinsically hostile to the revolution, its members, finally, incapable of reeducation. The only recourse, then, was to remove them entirely.

THE ULTIMATE PURGE:
THE FATE OF ETHNIC MINORITIES

The Khmer Rouge proclaimed that "there is in Kampuchea one single nation and one single language, the Khmer language. . . . The various nationalities no longer exist."[126] Yet it was not enough simply to declare the fact of national homogeneity. The Khmer Rouge repressed the languages and cultures of the varied ethnicities and nationalities that had lived in Cambodia in many cases for hundreds of years. They also launched a virulent propaganda campaign against the minorities and killed many thousands of them. They sought to destroy "ethnic, national, racial, or religious groups . . . in whole" and succeeded both "in whole and in part," to borrow the language of the United Nations Genocide Convention.

Twenty ethnic minorities composed 15 to 20 percent of the Cambodian population in 1970.[127] Chams, Vietnamese, and Chinese constituted the largest groups. The Vietnamese and Chinese, as mentioned, supported themselves predominantly by commercial and professional pursuits, while Chams tended to be small-scale hunters, fishermen, and traders, though some were farmers and others labored on rubber plantations. Some Chinese and Vietnamese and, more rarely, Chams, had intermarried with Khmers, and even in the top echelons of the Khmer

Rouge there were individuals of partly Chinese or Vietnamese background. Hundreds of Cambodian communists had gone to Vietnam in the 1950s and 1960s. Many returned to Cambodia in 1970 and 1971 to work more actively with the Khmer Rouge. They would soon find themselves purged, while Khmer Rouge of Chinese or Vietnamese ancestry, much like Soviet leaders of non-Russian background, willingly participated in the drive against particular national groups.

Prior to the seizure of power, the Khmer Rouge proclaimed their support for Cambodia's varied ethnic groups. At least some Chams who lived in areas under communist control in the early 1970s recalled that era fondly. Toward the numerous small, mountain tribal groups, the Khmer Rouge adopted no uniform policy, and some of the tribes were accorded significant privileges. Mountain tribesmen served as bodyguards for CPK officials, who might have favored tribespeople precisely because they seemed uncorrupted by material possessions and urban civilization. They existed in a world of primitive communism, which enabled them, Pol Pot and others might have thought, to be drawn directly into the world of advanced communism without the mediating, corrupting stage of bourgeois capitalism.[128]

But other events during the civil war in the early 1970s cast ominous shadows on the fate of Cambodia's minorities. Long-standing hostility toward the Vietnamese was becoming more pronounced as the Vietnam War spread over the border and North Vietnam sought to expand its influence in Cambodia. Even before the Khmer Rouge came to power, General Lon Nol, who in 1970 had established a military dictatorship, launched a pogrom in and around Phnom Penh in which thousands of Vietnamese were massacred, often with a high level of brutality. According to the historian David Chandler, the pogrom was a "racially based religious war against unarmed civilians whose families had lived in Cambodia for generations."[129] The regime then killed thousands more Vietnamese who lived in the border region, and expelled 500,000 of them to South Vietnam. On the other side, the Khmer Rouge in spring 1974 eliminated cadres of Thai ethnicity in the western regions. In some cases entire families were wiped out, hundreds in all.[130] In the Northeast, an ethnically diverse area and the region to which Pol Pot returned in 1966 from China and Vietnam, the Khmer Rouge forced semi-nomadic tribal peoples into collective farms and labor brigades. When faced with resistance, the Khmer Rouge initiated large-scale killings, especially of members of ethnic minorities who had had training in Hanoi.[131] Like the Soviets before them, the Khmer Rouge were certain that nomadic customs and religious beliefs represented backward ways of existence that had to be forcibly eliminated as part of progress toward the communist future. They blended together ethnic, social, and political criteria — the tribal people were suspect because of the ways of life associated with their particular ethnicity, and became even more dangerous when they proved hostile to the allure of the communist future.

These repressive measures escalated once the Khmer Rouge seized power. The forced evacuation of the cities was, to a significant extent, also an act of ethnic removal because of the large urban concentrations of Vietnamese and Chinese. The 1962 census, for example, revealed that 18 percent of Phnom Penh's residents were Chinese, 14 percent Vietnamese, and the figures probably increased over the succeeding years.[132] Survivors report that forced labor in the fields was particularly difficult for the deported Chinese because they were largely unused to agricultural work. In the villages and labor camps Chinese and Vietnamese were segregated from Khmers and were forbidden to speak their language.

The Chams, Muslim Khmers, endured a particularly tragic fate.[133] In 1975 the regime ordered them to change their names to conform to Khmer styles and sounds, and then purged all officials of Cham background. One CPK decree simply stated: "The Cham mentality [Cham nationality, the Cham language, Cham costume, Cham habits, Cham religion] are abolished. Those who do not abide by this order will reap all consequences."[134] In the northwestern region, those found speaking Cham were sometimes executed. The Khmer Rouge forbade Cham women to wear the traditional sarong or long hair. Cadres destroyed mosques and burned copies of the Koran. In spectacles of public humiliation and violence, the Khmer Rouge ordered Chams to eat pork or gave them the choice between eating pork and being killed. Numerous executions took place in full view of other villagers. In the last year of Democratic Kampuchea and in association with the general escalation of political violence, Khmer Rouge soldiers wiped out entire Cham villages. Estimates of the number of Chams in Cambodia before 1975 vary widely, but it seems likely that somewhere between 40 and 60 percent of the population did not survive the nearly four years of Democratic Kampuchea.[135]

The Vietnamese, though, were the prime national enemy for the Khmer Rouge. The more than one thousand Khmer communists who had been trained in Hanoi, many of them resident in North Vietnam since the mid-1950s, constituted the first target. As the Cambodian civil war escalated through the 1960s, many of the communist exiles left Vietnam and joined the Khmer Rouge guerrilla forces in their forest encampments. Almost immediately the cadres from Vietnam suffered a purge that would leave none of them in positions of authority; many would subsequently be killed.[136] Then right after the Khmer Rouge victory, the Vietnamese sent back to Cambodia not just party people but refugees of Chinese and Khmer descent. The Khmer Rouge massacred some of these people right away. The CPK even killed Khmers who had given shelter to Vietnamese communist forces. One month into the regime, Nuon Chea, the deputy secretary of the CPK and number two man in the hierarchy, and Pol Pot announced at a meeting plans to remove the entire Vietnamese population of Cambodia.[137] By late September, over 150,000 ethnic Vietnamese were rounded up and deported to Vietnam. The regime forced couples in mixed Vietnamese-Khmer marriages to separate or made the Khmer men follow their Vietnamese wives into exile.[138]

All of these measures reflected a combination of factors — resentment, dating from the early 1950s, of Vietnamese domination of the Indochinese Communist Party; political fears that Cambodian communists who returned from Vietnam would serve as agents for Hanoi; and general Khmer hostility toward the more populous and powerful country to the east. The situation would only worsen for the Vietnamese. By the end of 1976, almost two years into the regime, domestic conditions had deteriorated notably and dissension had flared up within the party. War with Vietnam loomed on the horizon, in part stimulated by Vietnamese military provocations along the border. In this context of dread fears coupled with wildly utopian hopes, the regime began to view elimination of the Vietnamese as a central element in the creation of the future society. The racial attitudes of the Khmer Rouge became so extreme that they took on a redemptive character — only through the elimination of the Vietnamese would Khmers be able to reach utopia. Vietnam was the "hereditary enemy," and only when "the Vietnamese are all gone" would Khmers be assured of survival and prosperity.[139] "Hit the Vietnamese, hit them until you break their backs!" ran one party slogan.[140] Pol Pot's fearsome rhetoric called on Khmer forces to wage guerrilla warfare deep inside Vietnam, and to "tie up the enemy by the throat, shoulders and ribs on both sides, his waist, his thighs, his knees, his calves, his ankles, in order to prevent his head turning anywhere and to increase the possibility of our large or medium-sized forces smashing and breaking his head."[141] DK forces would "kill the enemy at will, and the contemptible Vietnamese . . . will surely shriek like monkeys screeching all over the forest."[142] Phnom Penh radio called on Khmers to "fan the flames of national anger, class hatred and blood debts against the . . . expansionists and annexationists" and for "national and class indignation and blood rancour."[143] Maintaining in 1976 that the "national struggle is the same as the class struggle," a CPK journal placed Vietnam firmly in the counterrevolutionary camp.[144] Pol Pot's comment, "Vietnam is a black dragon that spits its poison," typified the CPK's approach not just to the state of Vietnam but to all Vietnamese people.[145] Even more ominous was the charge leveled against Khmers who were of mixed background or who had Vietnamese spouses, or even those who were accused of political sympathies toward Vietnam, that they were "Vietnamese in Khmer bodies." Such comments indicated racial thinking typical of other genocidal regimes, in which divergent ways of being were seen to be rooted in the body and carried through the generations. If the trait "Vietnamese" had infiltrated into Khmer bodies, then the only conceivable policy was to eliminate the tainted bodies, either by forced expulsion or by mass execution.[146]

On 1 April 1977, the regime ordered the arrest of all Vietnamese, who were to be turned over to central security officials. This included Khmers married to Vietnamese, even Khmers who spoke Vietnamese. As war with Vietnam escalated over the course of 1978, the actions against Vietnamese became even more systematic, resulting in extensive massacres all along the border regions where large numbers of Vietnamese lived. The extreme, racialized depictions of the Vietnamese in Khmer Rouge propaganda removed any barriers to the exercise of brutalities on the part of the troops.[147] As with other genocides, the sheer magnitude of killing resulted from the combination of directions from the center and the mobilization of popular support.

Ultimately, the Khmer Rouge, like the Soviets and Nazis and, as we shall see, Serb nationalists, came to define politics by being. Born a Chinese or Cham or, especially, Vietnamese, one was by definition at least suspect, and, by 1978, most definitely a traitor to the cause of the Khmer revolution. The Khmer Rouge racialized nationality by making every single member of the group the bearer of the same dangerous characteristics. To be sure, the promise of redemption was held out for some people, but at the cost of their completely abandoning their language, customs, and religion, their very membership in a defined community, and undergoing a process of reeducation in labor camps and mass meetings. By 1978, even the prospects of forced assimilation had been closed to Vietnamese, who were now pursued with a special virulence. Just as the Soviets thought that the entire way of life of the Chechens and Tatars ran counter to communist goals, particularly in the era of forced collectivization and rapid industrialization, so the Khmer Rouge instinctively distrusted the Cham, Chinese, and Vietnamese, whose culture was too urban, too commercial, too individualistic, or too religious, or some combination of all of these characteristics. The Khmer Rouge racialized class and nationality, making all members of the three groups bearers of identical characteristics, no matter what they had done.[148] And if they did resist, as did some Chams to CPK demands that women cut their hair, or if they had ties to conationals across the borders, as was the case with the Vietnamese and Chinese, they only confirmed the communists' deep-seated mistrust.

Clearly, difference, even on the level of the Soviet "family of nations," could not be allowed in Democratic Kampuchea.[149] By the time troops from Vietnam invaded Democratic Kampuchea and destroyed the regime, the only Vietnamese in Cambodia were those who had managed to hide their background. A once thriving community had been either killed or driven into exile over the border into Vietnam, and a similar fate had been suffered by the Chinese and Chams. Estimates vary, but of the pre-1975 population in Cambodia, somewhere between 50 and 62 percent of Chinese died, along with 62 percent of Vietnamese and between 50 and 60 percent of Chams.[150] Some were killed by deliberate execution, others by the privations of deportation, malnutrition, and forced labor. Whatever the method, the deaths were all part of a genocide designed to eliminate any cultural or physical presence of the targeted groups. The destruction of these communities constituted the regime's "macabre attempts at creation," as Penny Edwards writes. Out of the "ashes of 'otherness' a purely Khmer nation would arise."[151] For the CPK, the forced creation of a uniform Khmer society meant the revival of Cambodia's past glory, now in modern, communist guise.

RITUALS OF POPULATION PURGES

The vast extent of the population purges in Democratic Kampuchea was possible only because of the incorporation of tens of thousands of people into the regime. Like the other cases discussed in this book,

Democratic Kampuchea was a twentieth-century dictatorship, one that mobilized substantial segments of the population. The perpetrators carried out orders and also invented rituals that bound together the partisans of the regime and, at the same time, completely dehumanized the victims.[152]

Seng Horl was a teacher who was forced out of Phnom Penh. He returned to his native village in the Southwest, one of the key areas where DK policies were applied most radically. "My mother watched us arrive from a distance. . . . Mother did not dare come and ask me anything." The village chief confiscated his books, in Khmer and French, and his diploma, calling them imperialist objects. "My mother had never seen my children, but she did not dare approach us until the village chief and militia had left. She said to survive, you had to do three things: . . . know nothing, hear nothing, see nothing."[153] In the large commune Horl found teachers in one group, factory workers and doctors in another, ex-soldiers in still another. All of them were kept distinct from the base people. This kind of strict segregation was a means of recategorizing society after the initial flush of egalitarian enthusiasm, a way of identifying the people in need of reeducation or those who had to be eliminated altogether. All the people from Phnom Penh were called, simply, "enemies."[154]

The class resentments that Seng Horl described had provided the Khmer Rouge with much of their initial popular support and continued to feed the revolution after the conquest of power. The Khmer Rouge politicized the dislike and sometimes hatred of the peasantry for their social betters and provided an outlet for such sentiments in population purges. Seth Pich Chnay, an art student, was sent to a village of two hundred people that had become the site of residence for another five hundred deportees. The peasants had supported the Khmer Rouge and disliked the city dwellers as "oppressors." "You used to be happy and prosperous. Now it's our turn," they said. In a symbolic destruction of the upper classes, villagers cut in two a Mercedes 220 that had arrived with the urban residents, the metal used to fashion plows, the wheels put on an oxcart, and the engine adapted as a makeshift water pump.[155]

Yet at the same time, numerous survivors report good relations between new and base people, especially in the early months and years. There are accounts of local people being "hospitable" or "nice to us," and even sharing food with the new people. In the more moderate eastern zone, the Khmer Rouge commanders were also relatively tolerant, even helpful, and survivors reported no killings or excessively harsh conditions in the first two years of the revolution. Even people arrested were released after relatively brief internments.[156]

But others reported more gruesome experiences. One survivor named Lan, who spoke later with the historian Ben Kiernan, noted that she had first been deported in 1975. In 1978, thousands more arrived in her new village. Some were peasants; some were from Phnom Penh. All were "enemies," the earlier residents were told. Then the executions of the new arrivals started.

> At first they would just take away the husbands "to go and help start another cooperative." But the husbands never came back and after two or three months more the Khmer Rouge would come for the man's family as well, and take them away. People were told to get their things ready to go and rejoin their husbands and father. Fifty to one hundred people would set out at night . . . accompanied by four or five militia and two or three oxcarts. They put everything in the oxcarts.
>
> But the oxcart didn't follow the people. They went to the storehouse of the district officer. The people were all bashed to death. . . .
>
> The Khmer Rouge also asked some of us 1975 evacuees to kill Svay Rieng people [the newer arrivals]. They were unwilling young people . . . [who were] threatened with death if they didn't comply. . . . When these people came back they told me what had happened. Ten 1975 evacuees would be given axes and told to kill one hundred Svay Rieng people, who had been told to undress. They were meant to strike them on the back of the neck. They didn't want to kill them but they had no choice. They even killed young children with a single blow of an ax.[157]

Why, after deportations, after innumerable reeducation sessions, the descent into a spiral of such massive killings? Did the regime really fear political opposition? Surely the population, three years into Democratic Kampuchea, was too weakened by malnutrition and disease to constitute any serious threat of resistance. Part of the explanation has to lie in the extensive powers accorded CPK cadres in the villages and labor camps they controlled. They could act out their brutalities with no fears of legal or any other kind of sanction, since there were no limits upon party power. Like the Nazi camp guards who ran over the bodies of Roma and Sinti children or the Lithuanian auxiliaries who clubbed Jews to death in the market square, some Cambodian men became enthralled with the total power they exercised, the ability to grant or take life at will. Perhaps they also really thought that by physically eliminating the class or national enemy, they were building the better society of the future. And perhaps also, by late 1978, they feared that they too might be purged, and thought that brutal, radical actions could forestall that fate. At the same time, they deliberately incorporated other victims into the killing process, spreading the guilt so that no one could claim innocence.

In another instance, the Khmer Rouge chief of a village told his underlings, "Take him to the forest of the West," when they had caught a young man digging up a few cassava roots. Three executioners took him there.

> I stealthily followed them from a distance out of curiosity. Coming near the place, I hid in a thicket from which I could safely watch the "ceremony," but was so frightened by what I saw that I nearly fainted. The condemned lad was attached, nude from the waist up, to a tree, his eyes bandaged. Using a long knife, Ta Sok, the executioner, made a long incision in the abdomen of the miserable victim, who screamed with pain like a wild beast. (I can still hear the cries today.) Blood gushed out from all sides and from his intestines also while Ta Sok groped for his liver which he cut out, sliced into pieces, and started to cook in a frying pan already heated by Ta Chea. . . . They shared the cooked liver with a hearty appetite. After having buried the body they left with a satisfied air. I didn't dare leave my hiding place until they were far away, because if they happened to know that I had witnessed their criminal acts [that would have been it for me. That] evening, I could not sleep a wink [and] was haunted all night by the horrors [that I had seen].[158]

How can one possibly understand this instance of unspeakable cruelty, the violation of a taboo that exists in the vast majority of human societies? Human liver eating was certainly not typical, but it was not unknown in Cambodian and other Asian cultures.[159] In traditional Khmer culture, liver eating was understood to give the consumer great powers and courage. In the recent past, stories had circulated of Lon Nol soldiers eating the livers of Khmer Rouge soldiers they had captured, and vice versa, and at least a few communists kept up the practice once they were in power. The victim was reduced to animal-like status, his body the source of sustenance for his captors, his grievous howl as he was slaughtered like that of any butchered animal. As was the case with "simple" executions, cadres could cannibalize their victims because the regime had established policies that gave them absolutely free rein to perpetrate the worst excesses against their supposed enemies. The point seems banal, hardly worth writing, and one could say that cannibalism is no worse than torture or systematic execution by gas in the way it violates the most basic integrity of the human body. Perhaps therein lies the answer. Like rape, like torture, cannibalism symbolizes the utter, complete degradation of the individual, the utter domination of another through the decimation and consumption of the body. As an act of total power, nothing could be more complete than this.

The act, of course, inspired fear among other potential victims. Denise Affonço, the observer quoted above, trembled all through the night after watching the scene. Other survivors recall hearing cadres discuss their liver-eating episodes and debating the comparative merits of fat and thin people's livers. The cadres knew they could be heard; they luxuriated in their transgressions, and in the fear they inspired. They seemed, truly, all-powerful.[160]

Cannibalism might have been rare, but beatings were not. The family of Loung Ung, another survivor, was deported from Phnom Penh. In one of their places of resettlement, her brother worked as a servant for the CPK cadre who ran the village. His favored position brought the family the extra food that enabled them to survive for a time, but only at the cost of the beatings her brother endured nearly every day as the plaything of the cadre and his family.[161] Invested with so much power, Khmer Rouge soldiers and cadres sometimes beat harder still when the victim protested or cried out. They carried out mock executions to frighten people, thereby indulging their own pleasures. As yet a further violation of the body, the majority of executions came not from the "clean" and "efficient" bullet, but from beatings and worse. People suffered beatings and executions, mock and real, because they stole vegetables, roots, or crabs from fields; hoarded rice; visited family members; or had sex outside of marriage.[162] And sometimes, there was no explanation. "The Khmer Rouge kill, but never explain," ran one line among Cambodians living in Democratic Kampuchea.[163]

Only rarely did the Khmer Rouge carry out killings in public. Usually they took their victims away quietly, often at night. The next day they would not be there. Yet people certainly knew about the disappearances, just as Germans knew about euthanasia and the Holocaust, and Soviet citizens knew about the deportations, internments, and killings of all sorts of regime victims. "The soldiers came to take my grandfather.

They grabbed him and tied his hands behind his back. 'We know you were in the military,' they said to him. Grandfather did not struggle. But as he left, he turned to my grandmother and said, 'Would you take care of my family?' The soldiers slapped him in the face and marched him out. Many minutes went by. We heard a shot deep in the jungle. We knew grandfather was dead."[164] The semisecrecy of the process only added to the fear the populace experienced, as did its arbitrary character. Do what one could to stay alive, luck was the ultimate determinant. On some occasions, in fits of desperation, individuals performed traditional music or dance despite the fact that these forms of cultural expression had been outlawed. Sometimes, their performances swayed the cadres, who kept them alive and gave them extra rations. The individuals were surprised at their own lucky fates.[165] Yet this was part of the workings of terror and violence, namely, its arbitrary character, which only intensified the fear experienced by the populace. Secrecy, carefully cultivated by the CPK, gave an eerie, otherworldly quality to Angkar, the Organization, an aura of life-defying powers—and, of course, powerlessness to those living under its rule.

In every case discussed in this book, the desecration of the body was a fundamental feature of genocide. Even in death the body was violated, deprived of ritual burning or burial. It was not enough to kill; the dead body had also to be desacralized. Jewish bodies were burned; Gulag victims' bodies were thrown around by an earth mover like stacks of logs. As in many cultures, the manner of burial was highly ritualized in Cambodia and was a key element in the fulfillment of children's obligations to respect and honor their parents. The cremation of the body and burial of the bones provided the opportunity for family members to mourn the loss of a revered member. By prohibiting the practice, the Khmer Rouge sought in yet another way to destroy the bonds of family, the better to ensure the success of the collective and the all-powerful Organization. As another survivor reported: "After four months my father became sick and died. When he died, I did not even know where they took him. They just bundled him up in a mat and took him away. I was very hurt. I did not have a chance to bury him properly. My mother also died because of serious diarrhea. I was not able to bury her properly either. My husband had to take her away." The survivor continually regretted that she had not had "the opportunity to bury her parents properly."[166]

There were other ways of desecrating the body, notably through torture. Hu Nim was one of those interned at the infamous prison, Tuol

Sleng. He was a revolutionary of long standing. In the 1950s, he had been part of the anticolonial student movement and then went to France to study. He returned to Cambodia and served in the National Assembly and in government posts in the late 1950s and early 1960s, when many Cambodian leftists considered Prince Sihanouk an ally. As Sihanouk's regime turned on the Left in the 1960s, Hu Nim fled to the forests, where it was believed he had died. He surfaced after the Khmer Rouge victory in April 1975 and became minister of information.[167]

On 10 April 1977, Hu Nim was arrested. He was executed three months later. During his confinement, he was repeatedly tortured. In between, he wrote and rewrote his confession, seven times in all. Ultimately, the confession amounted to two hundred handwritten pages, each page signed and thumbprinted. In his confession, Hu Nim detailed his early years: a father who died when he was only six, a poor peasant mother, with whom he moved around selling their joint labor power, a sibling who died young. With patronage, he was able to obtain an education at the famed Lycée Sisowath, the training ground for the post-1945 Khmer political elite, communist, liberal, and royalist. He successfully completed the *baccalauréat*, the exams that, in the French system, enabled him to pursue higher education. And then he wrote, "I would like to tell the party with respect about my treacherous deeds." He chose the "wrong road" at the age of twenty-two, siding with the American imperialists and their Cambodian lackeys against the people of Kampuchea. For many pages, Hu Nim then detailed his "traitorous" behavior. "My political activities were to gather forces into the People's Movement in order to oppose the people's revolution and oppose communism." Wherever he was—studying in France, working in Phnom Penh, fomenting resistance in the forests, heading a ministry of the revolutionary government—he organized conspiracies, recruited other people hostile to communism, and maintained contacts abroad. He names scores, perhaps hundreds, of others involved in similar treasonous actions. One of his achievements was the organization of the "Marxist-Leninist CIA party." Interspersed in the narrative of treason are comments on his personal life—marriage, further education in France, aboveground politics, teaching, an extramarital affair. "I am a counterfeit revolutionary," he wrote; "in fact I am an agent of the enemy, the enemy of the people, and the nation of Kampuchea, and the Communist Party of Kampuchea. I am the cheapest reactionary intellectual disguised as a revolutionary." Through his legal and political activities, he says, he sought to hide his "reactionary, traitorous, corrupt elements representing the feudalist, capitalist, imperialist status quo and the CIA." At the end of the confession, he agrees that he has "served very cheaply the activities of the CIA and the American imperialists . . . and I have received my present fate. . . . Over the past month and a half I have received a lot of education from the party. I have nothing to depend upon, only the Communist Party of Kampuchea. My life is completely dependent on the party."[168]

Hu Nim's "confession" was extracted under brutal torture. He very likely had some differences with the Pol Pot group in the leadership of the Communist Party of Kampuchea, but a life of treason can be dismissed out of hand.

But why, then, was such gruesome torture inflicted and such abject confession required of a long-serving revolutionary? Why was Hu Nim forced into such total humiliation, into expressions of gratitude for the "education" he had received in captivity? Why the details about his marriage and education? Why the absurd stories about a "Marxist-Leninist CIA party"? The parallels with the Soviet show trials and the Chinese Cultural Revolution are obvious. On the surface, all these procedures can be understood as methods for eliminating completely any opposition, real or potential. The victims themselves would be destroyed, and their persons so humiliated, their legacies so tarnished, that even in death they would not be able to serve as the rallying points for opposition to the existing regime.

Yet somehow, this explanation seems insufficient. The autobiography, as mentioned earlier, was a fixed feature of life in Democratic Kampuchea. Even in the first days of the evacuation from the cities, cadres stopped refugees at crossroads and had them prepare autobiographies. Then the cadres sorted out the population, by class origins and by their ties to rural areas.[169] Survivors recall innumerable mass meetings at which individuals publicly reviewed their lives. "Everything was interpreted [at these meetings]: words, gestures, attitudes," recalled Ong Thong Hoeung, one of the radical intellectuals who returned from France to serve the revolution. "Sadness was a sign of spiritual confusion, joy a sign of individualism, [while] an indecisive point of view indicated a petty bourgeois intellectualism."[170] To destroy their individualism, people were told to "concentrate their memory" on their prior behavior and their class backgrounds. Hoeung was reminded of Buddhist meditation techniques.[171] At one mass meeting presided over by no less a personage than Ieng Sary, Pol Pot's longtime comrade and the deputy prime minister for foreign affairs, individuals were selected and ordered to speak their minds. Those who refused this "true application of democracy" were immediately expelled.[172]

The autobiography, recounted aloud in mass meetings, written down in confessions, was a central technique for categorizing the population. But confessions were also a means for reeducation and seem to have been particularly pronounced under communist regimes. "Exercise self-criticism, and criticize one another," ran one CPK slogan, and another admonished people, "If you commit a mistake, you should criticize yourself and punish yourself."[173] The Khmer word *kosang* means "to build," but the Khmer Rouge used it in relation to people, children especially but also adults. It conveyed "remolding," to shape people into proper revolutionary thinking and acting.[174] "Angkar wants you to come to a study session so you can remold yourself," ran yet another CPK slogan.[175] The fervent hostility such demands aroused in Cambodians comes through with crystalline clarity in virtually all the memoirs that have been published since the demise of the Khmer Rouge.

To extract confessions—forced autobiographies—the Khmer Rouge used torture systematically and extensively, more so than even in Stalin's Soviet Union. The major victims, like Hu Nim, were party cadres, the vast majority of them interned, tortured, and executed at the infamous Tuol Sleng prison. The wave of party purges intensified toward the end of 1976 and continued to the very end of the regime. Among the 1,622 prisoners who entered Tuol Sleng in 1976, 150 were themselves members of S-21, the security apparatus that ran the prison.[176] The prisoners were bound with iron chains on the feet, as though on a slave ship, elbows often tied behind the back, and lacked all sanitary facilities. In these conditions, it is not surprising that the captives lasted on average three months, and only a few survived. Children were not chained but received no care. In at least one instance, they were made the literal playthings of the guards, swung, beaten, and kicked around like soccer balls.[177]

Tuol Sleng was a prison, torture chamber, execution hall, and archive. Its store of written confessions—of which Hu Nim's is one example—provides chilling evidence for the realities of life in Democratic Kampuchea. The archive probably tells us more about the personnel who ran Tuol Sleng and their superiors, who included the very top leaders of the CPK—notably Pol Pot, Nuon Chea, and Son Sen—than it does about the victims. The guards tortured because they were ordered to do so, often with Duch's clear direction, sometimes scribbled in the margins of early drafts of the confessions. Like other Khmer Rouge cadres who took people away for execution, the guards also tortured because they thought such actions were expected of them, feared the consequences if they were not hard enough, and sometimes enjoyed and sometimes simply became immune to the horrors they were perpetrating. They might also have believed that they were, indeed, helping to create the new society. They are reminiscent of the "ordinary men," the reserve police officers in the Holocaust, studied by Christopher Browning.[178] The confessions they extracted served to humiliate completely the victims, rendering their entire lives worthless, so they could never function as rallying points for opposition to the center. Infused as they were with paranoid fantasies, the confessions, most important, provided justification for the brutalities approved by the CPK leaders and inflicted by mid- and low-level officials. The reasoning was circular but nonetheless compelling: if indeed so many and such dangerous traitors had infiltrated the ranks of the CPK, then extreme measures of compulsion were needed to ferret them out. In this way, the confession proved crucial to the ever escalating dynamic of political terror. Every confession not only constituted a document of forced self-humiliation but also named other people, sometimes scores of them, whom the security forces then had to locate and haul in to Tuol Sleng, keeping the entire process in motion.[179]

But as this chapter has demonstrated, party cadres were by no means the only victims of the CPK. As in the Soviet Union under Stalin and Nazi Germany, political terror was accompanied by genocidal actions against ethnic and national minorities: "[Ma] was born in China and moved to Cambodia as a little girl. . . . Ma . . . has to be extra careful because she speaks Khmer with a Chinese accent. . . . Ma is proud of her heritage but she has to hide it before it proves dangerous to us all. . . . The Angkar hates anyone who is not true Khmer. . . . To protect myself, I often have to rub dirt and charcoal on my skin to look as dark as the base people."[180] Loung Ung's family was endangered in many ways. They were Phnom Penh residents, and her father had been a police official in the Lon Nol government. Her mother, as this passage makes clear, was Chinese. They endured the usual sufferings — deportation out of Phnom Penh; relocation a number of other times, partly to try to hide her father's past record; separation of the family; death from malnutrition and disease. After a few successful deceptions, her father's past was discovered. Khmer Rouge soldiers took him away and killed him. Months later, they came for her mother as well. One family among many victims, their fate exemplifies the blending of identities practiced by the Khmer Rouge. They died because of their class and occupational backgrounds and the mother's ethnicity, all of which the Khmer Rouge racialized by extending the enemy category to all members of the family, no matter what any of them had done.

Blood serves as a powerful metaphor of race in so many situations, and it was a metaphor that permeated Democratic Kampuchea. The national anthem ran:

> Ruby blood that sprinkles the towns and plains
> Of Kampuchea, our homeland,
> Splendid blood of workers and peasants,
> Splendid blood of revolutionary men and women soldiers. . . .
>
> Live, live, new Kampuchea,
> Democratic and prosperous.
> We resolutely lift high
> The red flag of the revolution.
> We build our homeland,
> We cause her to progress in great leaps
> In order to render her more glorious and more marvelous than ever.[181]

Pol Pot provided a gloss on the anthem: "[O]ur national anthem was not composed by a poet. Its essence is the blood of our entire people, of those who fell for centuries past. This blood call has been incorporated into our national anthem. Each sentence, each word shows the nature of our people's struggle. This blood has been turned into class and national indignation."[182] Many survivors recalled the song "The Red Flag," in which blood flows out of the body and into the red flag, merging the struggle of revolution with the people's sacrifice.[183] Blood connected present-day Khmers to the achievements and struggles of the past; blood was the evidence, the very means through which Khmers forged the nation and achieved victory. Blood bound together class, nation, and people into a Khmer race.

CONCLUSION

The Pol Pot period, in the recollection of one survivor, "was beyond suffering."[184] The huge number of deaths, continual hunger, exhaustion from backbreaking labor—this is what most Cambodians remember of

Democratic Kampuchea. But more than anything else, the forced breakup of the family caused — and, for survivors, continues to cause — despair. As the anthropologist May Ebihara reports, "the separation of parents and children caused anguish, as did seeing family members die in terrible circumstances without being able to save them or even openly grieve their deaths."[185]

In the end, no exact reckoning of the death toll is possible. David Chandler, the American expert, offered in 1999 a conservative estimate of 800,000 to 1 million; the demographer Marek Sliwinski, the more commonly accepted figure of 1.5 million; and the Australian expert, Ben Kiernan, 1.7 million.[186] Another demographer, Patrick Heuveline, uses sophisticated statistical methods to derive the lower and upper possibilities of the "excess deaths" in Cambodia from 1970 to 1979. He arrives at the extraordinary range of 1.17 to 3.42 million deaths. Moreover, he concludes that fully one-third to over two-thirds of these deaths were the result of direct violence rather than malnutrition and disease, a much higher estimate than anyone had previously ventured.[187]

If one accepts Sliwinski's midrange figure, Cambodia lost 19 percent of its pre-DK population of 7.9 million, an astonishing proportion. If one uses Heuveline's median number, then the figure climbs to an almost unbelievable 32 percent. Strikingly, the death rate was highest among adults in the prime years of life — according to Sliwinski, 34 percent of the 20–30 cohort, 40 percent of the 30–40 cohort — and the elderly. Both men and women were killed, of course, but the population imbalance after 1978, 1.3 women for every one man, signifies a higher rate of loss among the male population. Kiernan concludes that the overall death toll includes 50 percent of the Chinese, 36 percent of the Cham, and 100 percent of the Vietnamese populations.[188] Not one Cambodian family emerged unscathed by the loss of members, whether from execution, disease, or starvation, or some combination of all of these factors.[189] No other country since 1945 has sustained such an enormous decline of its population.[190]

Cambodia also suffered great losses of its cultural heritage. Thousands of Khmer manuscripts were destroyed or deteriorated for lack of care. The CPK tore down Buddhist temples all over the country, and the few Catholic churches as well, notably the cathedral in Phnom Penh. Local knowledge died along with so many people — knowledge of long-standing agricultural practices, and also of Cambodia's traditional art forms, especially in dance and music.[191]

Under the Khmer Rouge, "politics became the continuation of warfare by other means," in the words of David Chandler.[192] The violence was so extensive, the loss of life so great, both because it was decreed from the center of power *and* because the regime had given completely free rein to cadres on the ground, many of them no older than teenagers, who decided on their own who could live and who should die. It was this combined dynamic, policies decreed by the leadership and the arbitrary exercise of power by lower-level officials, that helped make the four years of Democratic Kampuchea so deadly.[193] Interestingly, this particular dynamic bears comparison with the experience of Nazi Germany, even though the chronology was different, rather than with the Soviet Union, where the central government more tightly controlled the activities of its security forces. In Nazi Germany, midlevel officials on the ground initiated the Holocaust, which the center later systematized. In Democratic Kampuchea, both layers of the regime instituted the killings simultaneously. In both situations, top officials never ordered a halt to the killings, leaving lower-ranking officials with the clear sense that there were no limits to the brutalities they could exercise. CPK cadres understood themselves as "working toward Angkar" in the same way that Nazi officials were "working toward the Führer," which contributed to the unfolding of a dynamic of terror without any checks whatsoever. In a curious way, the relatively undeveloped state structure of Democratic Kampuchea facilitated this dynamic. While the population categories adopted by the Nazis and Soviets were highly elastic, those regimes by and large followed the lists they compiled. Without lists, Cambodians were subject to an even greater extent to the arbitrary determinations of individual cadres in the villages and labor camps in which they lived, who determined whether an individual labored well or believed fervently enough. Bureaucracies can be deadly instruments, but they also define the limitations of purges and exterminations, the people who are to be protected from the depredations of the regime. Cambodians en masse had no such protection.

It was finally only the army of Vietnam that could put a halt to it all. But even at the very end, in 1997, when Pol Pot was living in encampments on the Thai-Cambodian border, protected by various foreign powers and surviving on memories of the past and vain hopes for the future, he was capable of instigating one last paroxysm of violence, a bloody purge against other Khmer Rouge leaders and their families, some of whom he had known since the early 1950s.[194]

If any singular idea captures the essence of the Khmer Rouge revolution, it was homogeneity—the effort to create a population purged of difference, whether of class, education, political affiliation, ethnicity, or race. Accomplishing this goal required a monumental, state-directed effort of reshaping the population, and a state that was powerful and completely unchallenged. The CPK leadership took to the effort with enthusiasm and supreme confidence. As Chandler also writes: "[T]he fact that such a rapid and complete transformation of a society had never taken place anywhere else was viewed as an exhilarating challenge rather than as a warning of what lay in store for the country in 1977 and 1978. In a sense, therefore, some kind of 'culture,' a purely *Cambodian* ingredient never defined, was thought to be crucial to the success of the revolution."[195] In essence, the Khmer Rouge layered a racial concept of being Khmer—forged, as we have seen, partly out of indigenous Khmer ideas, partly out of the influence of French colonialism—upon the models of twentieth-century communist revolutions. The invocation of the glorious Khmer past and the still more glorious Khmer future that would emerge from the revolution entailed, in turn, the racialization of others, notably Chinese, Vietnamese, and Chams, as the unrelenting enemies who had to be eliminated altogether, either by forced assimilation, forced deportations, or mass killings, or some combination of all of these methods. The Khmer Rouge carried out a genocide of these groups; they intended to destroy "in whole or in part" population groups defined by ethnicity, nationality, religion, or race.[196] These specifically genocidal actions occurred in conjunction with mass political killings and mass deaths due to absurd development policies, all designed to create a leveled, homogeneous society. This pattern, too, is in keeping with the other cases discussed in this book: rarely, if ever, do regimes commit genocides outside of a more general political context of repression and violence. The most extreme form of population politics generally occurs alongside other types of highly repressive policies, including internments and executions of moderate members of the dominant group who may oppose regime policies.[197] As all the cases in this book demonstrate, the lines between race-based and political and social forms of population purges are fluid indeed.

The men who directed these policies constituted a closely linked group marked by a specific generational experience. They were born in the 1920s and early 1930s; some of them encountered French education and French communism. All of them were drawn into the Indochinese anticolonial struggles of the 1940s and 1950s. Many of them moved down similar educational, career, and political paths, and the bonds among them were strengthened by marriage and by the difficult years in the guerrilla movement and civil war.[198]

In spite of all their bravado about creating something completely new and utterly Khmer, the Khmer Rouge leaders actually drew upon a diverse set of lineages, including indigenous Khmer ideas about purity coupled with resentment against the seemingly more prosperous, sophisticated, and powerful Vietnamese; French republican ideas abut the nation and revolution that both the colonial authorities and the French Communist Party promoted; and twentieth-century communist models of revolutionary practice that moved through French, Soviet, Vietnamese, and Chinese examples. The Khmer Rouge were no more "true reactionaries" than the Nazis, despite the fact that both idealized, at least rhetorically, the countryside and the peasantry and a glorious past, for the Cambodians the period of Angkor Wat, for the Germans the Holy Roman Empire of the medieval era.[199] Everything about Democratic Kampuchea—the organization of the party-state, collectivization, purges, the racialization of nationalities—followed in the tracks of communist practices. The radical and virulent application of these policies in Cambodia resulted from two factors: the racial conception of Khmerness, and the CPK's analysis that preceding revolutions, notably in the Soviet Union and China, had not succeeded. Hence DK had to move with still greater speed and ruthlessness. Latecomers often have certain advantages, but in this case, the lessons learned from preceding models bore an enormous cost.

five

■ ■ ■ ■

National Communism:
Serbia and the Bosnian War

Dusko Tadić was born in 1955 in the Bosnian town of Kozarac. His
family was of Serbian background and well-respected around town. His
father was a decorated war hero from World War II. Tadić had opened
a café in Kozarac that both Muslims and Serbs frequented. The town
was heavily Muslim, and Tadić claimed that most of his friends were
Muslim.

But in 1990 he joined the Bosnian Serb nationalist party, and, increasingly, Serb nationalists gathered at his café. They dressed in Serb nationalist coats, sang Četnik songs, and gave the three-finger Serbian salute.
They were well armed and were heard to say things like "We are going
to kill all of the *balijas*," a derogatory term for Muslims. As the situation in Bosnia deteriorated, Tadić joined the Bosnian Serb Army and in
1992 served in the Prijedor region and at the Omarska and other concentration camps. There he delivered the most severe beatings to Muslim prisoners, often with an almost indescribable brutality. For these
actions, Tadić was indicted by the International Criminal Tribunal for
the Former Yugoslavia, established by the United Nations Security Council
in May 1993. His was the first trial held, and in 1997 he was found
guilty of crimes against humanity, war crimes, and other charges.[1]

Like so many other Serb nationalists, Tadić had lived an apparently
normal life. But when Yugoslavia began to disintegrate, he sided with
the Serbian cause. Whatever violent tendencies he might have had were
now given free rein—and political direction. The Serb regime in Belgrade and in Bosnian Serb territory actively encouraged the exercise of
utter brutality against Muslims and Croats. In the drive to establish a
completely homogeneous and "pure" Serbian state and society, nationalists adopted the most violent methods designed to make a multinational society unthinkable and, finally, unbearable.[2]

POWER AND UTOPIA

At first glance, Serbia evinces little of the revolutionary élan that characterized the Russian Revolution, the Nazi seizure of power, and the Khmer Rouge victory. There seem to have been no revolutionary heroics, nothing like the storming of the Winter Palace; the torchlight parade of thousands upon thousands of proud, disciplined Storm Troopers the day after Hitler was named chancellor; or the enthusiastic shooting in the air by troops who, after years of hard struggle in civil war, had finally taken Phnom Penh. The confidence that gripped the followers of the revolution in each of these cases, the sense that they were marching with History and were on the cusp of creating the new society, marked by unbounded prosperity and happiness — all that seems noticeably absent in Serbia, which appears, instead, to have undertaken in the late 1980s and 1990s a bumbling, cynical, and desultory march into war, ethnic cleansing, and genocide. Indeed, as Carla del Ponte, the chief prosecutor of the International Criminal Tribunal, stated as she launched the case against Slobodan Milošević for war crimes, crimes against humanity, and genocide: "One must not seek ideals underlying the acts of the accused. Beyond the nationalist pretext and the horror of ethnic cleansing, beyond the grandiloquent rhetoric and the search for hackneyed phrases he used, the search for power is what motivated Slobodan Milošević."[3]

Yet Del Ponte was not quite correct. Milošević, the head of Yugoslavia-become-Serbia, was certainly a supremely opportunistic politician. Nonetheless, he and his followers did articulate an ideology, actually, two ideologies. As the Yugoslav federal state system dissolved and communism collapsed all around Europe in the late 1980s, Milošević positioned Serbia as the last defender of the communist ideal, the worthy successor to the post–World War II Yugoslavia founded by Josip Broz Tito. He melded this claim with another ideology, one that might have lacked philosophical depth on the order of Marxism-Leninism but was, nonetheless, deeply rooted in modern European history and in the specific historical experience of Serbs. It was, of course, an ideology of nationalism. Other ethnic groups in Yugoslavia had their own nationalisms, notably Croats and Slovenes and, only much later, Muslims. The competing nationalisms among all these groups resulted in the dissolution of Yugoslavia. But it was Serbian nationalism that served as the pacesetter of events and as the ideology that, ultimately, underpinned the most extreme forms of population politics. By the mid-1990s, the original ideological synthesis of communism and nationalism seems to have faded and was replaced by a Serbian nationalism couched in such extreme terms that it barred the participation of other peoples in the exclusive Serbian state that Milošević and his supporters attempted to construct. Genocide was most likely not Milošević's original intent, certainly not in 1987 when he began to make his bid for power. As in the other cases discussed in this book, the genocide, in this instance of Bosnian and Kosovar Muslims, emerged at moments of extreme crisis, which were largely self-generated by the Milošević forces and their counterparts in Slovenia and Croatia. But the genocide also developed because of a set of deeper historical factors, notably, the potency of the ideology of nationalism, the continued commitment to communism on the part of important segments of the Serbian elite, and the typical — certainly by the 1990s — communist reliance on a powerful state to engineer the transformation of society.

On 24 April 1987, Slobodan Milošević was sent by his mentor, the Serbian president Ivan Stambolić, to Kosovo for talks with local party leaders. All through the 1980s tensions had grown between the largely ethnic Albanian population and the Serbian minority. The large demonstration that greeted Milošević was met by a strong police force. Rocks began to fly; the police responded with their clubs. As people were chanting and screaming, Milošević stepped out of the meeting room and yelled to the people gathered below, "No one should dare to beat you." His words had an electrifying impact on the crowd, Serbs who were trying to press their case that they were living under constant harassment from the Kosovars among them. In turn, the crowd's response had an electrifying impact on Milošević, who grasped immediately the power of nationalism. He went on:

> You should stay here. This is your land. These are your houses. Your meadows and gardens. Your memories. You shouldn't abandon your land just because it's difficult to live, because you are pressured by injustice and degradation. It was never part of the Serbian and Montenegrin character to give up in the face of obstacles, to demobilize when it's time to fight. . . . You should stay here for the sake of your ancestors and descendants. Otherwise your ancestors would be defiled and descendants disappointed. But I don't suggest that you stay, endure, and tolerate a situation you're not satisfied with.[4]

With these few words, Milošević captured all the essential themes of nationalism—the supposed timelessness of Serbian national identity, from past to present to future; the call upon heroic ancestors and the demands upon their descendants to fulfill their duty to the nation by defending their right to live in their historic homeland; the sense of aggrievement, that the nation is being oppressed by others; and the call to violent action to redress the wrongs with the promise of a better future.

The setting of this dramatic confrontation was highly significant. Milošević spoke near the battle site of Kosovo Polje (the Field of Blackbirds), where the Ottoman Turks had defeated Serbia in 1389. Kosovo had been the historic homeland of Serbs and the medieval Serbian kingdom. Only in the seventeenth and eighteenth centuries, under renewed pressure from the Ottomans, did Serbs move north in a great migration, shifting the focal point to the areas around Belgrade. But Serbian mythology always invoked Kosovo as the heartland of Serbia and the battle there against the Turks as the great national tragedy.[5]

Milošević did not, of course, invent Serbian nationalism, any more than Hitler invented race thinking and antisemitism. Serbs could claim something of a national tradition going back to the medieval Serbian kingdom. When that was destroyed by the Ottomans and by internal conflict, the autonomous Serbian Orthodox Church became the institution that carried Serbian national identity, intermixing religion and nationhood. Like other nationalisms, the Serb variant had its enemy, in this case, the Ottoman Turks; its legend, the battle of Kosovo Polje; and, by the mid–nineteenth century, its own epic poem, the prince-bishop Petar Petrović-Njegoš's *The Mountain Wreath*, which glorified the eternal struggle and ultimate redemption of the Serb people. Proverbially learned by every Serb schoolchild from the mid–nineteenth century onward, *The Mountain Wreath* relates the story of the hero Miloš Obilić, who fights alongside the Serbian prince Lazar and kills the Turkish sultan. Lazar, faced with the choice between losing his life and betraying his people, chooses death at the hands of the Turks. But Lazar was himself betrayed by the evil Vuk Branković. The epic unfolds in a Christian idiom as Lazar rises to heaven and Branković is revealed as a latter-day Judas. It is a powerful story, one that binds the Serbian national idea to the Christian promise of redemption, but a redemption that can arrive only through struggle and martyrdom. The story also binds the national idea to a defined place, most immediately, the battlefield of Kosovo Polje and, more generally, the Serb-settled lands around it.

Njegoš's epic was no simple brief for the national cause. It also celebrated what has come to be called ethnic cleansing, the forced removal (though not necessarily the killing) of a defined population group, and violent vengeance against Muslims.

> We put them all unto the sword,
> All those who would not be baptiz'd;
> But who paid homage to the Holy Child
> Were all baptiz'd with the sign of Christian Cross,
> And as brother each was hail'd and greeted.
> We put to fire the Turkish houses,
> That there might be nor stick nor trace
> Of these true servants of the Devil!
> From Cetinje to Tcheklitche we hied,
> There in full flight the Turks espied;
> A certain number were by us mow'd down,
> And all their houses we did set ablaze;
> Of all their mosques both great and small
> We left but one accursed heap,
> For passing folk to cast their glance of scorn.[6]

It would be much too simpleminded to draw a straight line from Njegoš's adoration of mosque burnings and the murder of Turks to the destruction of the wondrous Ferhadija mosque in Banja Luka in 1993 and the execution of over seven thousand Muslims by Serb nationalists in Srebenica in 1995. But *The Mountain Wreath* is a rather different foundational myth from the American Declaration of Independence or the French Declaration of the Rights of Man and Citizen or even, for that matter, the program of national self-determination enunciated by Lenin in the first few days of the Bolshevik Revolution.

The Mountain Wreath was but one sign of the emergence of modern nationalism in the South Slav lands in the nineteenth century. Serb nationalists could lay claim to the long tradition of Serbian self-consciousness wound up with religion and language and articulated especially through hostility toward Ottoman domination. But as with every other nineteenth-century nationalism, these traditional elements were recast by a new elite, one, in the Serbian case, often educated abroad in Vienna or Paris. The members served the state (rather than the church) in its expanding bureaucracy, and they sought to develop and modernize their lands. They promoted national independence, economic development, and compulsory education. Often — but not always — they invoked the language of democracy as well. Given the extreme hetero-geneity of the population in the South Slav lands, nationalist programs ran the gamut from harshly exclusive ones, which envisaged the terri-torial aggrandizement of Serbia or Croatia and its domination over other groups, to liberal romantic visions that imagined the harmony and equality of the various ethnic and national groups within a com-mon state, an incipient *jugoslovjenstvo* (Yugoslavism).[7] Under the state established by Tito at the end of World War II, national sentiments were to be represented within each republic but would also be entwined with communist ideology and a commitment to the larger entity of Yugo-slavia.

For all the varied strands of nationalist thought in the South Slav lands, it was clearly the most extreme, most exclusive, virtually racialized version that Milošević adopted and to which so many Serbs responded with enthusiasm. It was a nationalism imbued with a sense of aggrievement, of resentment over all the injustices supposedly perpe-trated against Serbs by a variety of forces — Croats, Slovenes, and Mus-lims within the Yugoslav federation, along with various Western powers, especially Italy, Austria, Germany, and the United States, that sup-posedly had designs on Yugoslav territory and sought to destroy its form of communism. Even before Milošević's 1987 appearance in Ko-sovo, this kind of nationalist thought had been gaining ground in elite circles. In 1986, someone leaked a memorandum drafted by the Serbian Academy of Sciences, a statement generally taken as the first public as-sertion of a new Serbian national program. The publication caused a public uproar and a great deal of condemnation, but the memorandum set the terms of discussion for the next months and years and was even-tually supported by Milošević. It offered one long lament about all the injustices done to Serbs, especially in postwar Yugoslavia. According to the memorandum, Yugoslavia under Tito had deliberately underde-veloped Serbia economically and had denied Serbs their own language and other forms of cultural expression, even denied them knowledge of their own history. The statement by the Serbian Academy referred con-tinually to the genocide of Serbs, in the past by Croatian fascists, the Ustaše, during World War II, in the present by Albanians in Kosovo.[8] In this fashioning of public discourse, Serb nationalists rekindled the worst fears of the Serb populace. The authors of the memorandum claimed for Serbia the status of the most oppressed nation within the Yugoslav federation; in some places, their statement seemed to claim for Serbia the status of supreme victim in all of history. "No other Yugoslav nation has been so rudely denied its cultural and spiritual integrity as the Serbian people. No literary and artistic heritage has been so routed, pillaged and plundered as the Serbian one."[9] Well before the outbreak of hostilities in 1990, the memorandum's authors claimed that "except for the period of the existence of the NDH [Independent State of Croatia, the Ustaše state established by the Nazis], Serbs were never so endangered as they are today."[10]

In the late 1980s, as we shall see in more detail below, the Yugoslav economic crisis deepened, the political system seemed gripped by paralysis, and Croats and Slovenes threatened to secede from the federation. In turn, Serbian nationalist rhetoric escalated. The self-pitying lament typical of the memorandum characterized virtually all statements issued by Serb nationalists. Serbs have never been a conquering people, while others have sought continually to oppress and subordinate Serbs, ran the typical line. In Kosovo — where Serbs dominated state institutions and repressed the Albanian Muslims, while nationalist Albanians exerted pressure and violence against Serb civilians — nationalists on both sides sought to inflame an already difficult situation. Raising fears that the Serb population was being overrun, one leading intellectual charged that Albanians "have developed an unprecedented campaign in support of the fecundity of their poor and miserable women . . . [and] have multiplied their number by 50, in only 40 years." "Bestial" Albanian terrorists break into Serbian homes and terrorize the rare people who resist. In Kosovo, "the terror of armed terrorists reigns."[11]

Milošević also kept up the nationalist rhetoric, becoming ever more dramatic and threatening. On 28 June 1989, Serbs commemorated the six hundredth anniversary of the defeat at Kosovo Polje. In the preceding weeks, Prince Lazar's bones were carried to various monasteries around Serbia, a medieval pilgrimage recast in modern terms.[12] The processions that accompanied the relics became a rallying point for Serbian nationalism, a ritual through which people summoned the distant past into the living present and projected into the future a new heroic age, the flowering of the Serb nation. On the Field of Blackbirds, hundreds of thousands of Serbs, perhaps over a million, gathered. *Politika*, the Belgrade daily, devoted its entire issue to the Kosovo myth. "The Serbian people," ran one headline, "has glorified and still glorifies its heroes and recognizes its traitors." The newspaper proclaimed that Serbs were "again living in the times of Kosovo, as it is in Kosovo and around Kosovo that the destiny of Yugoslavia and the destiny of socialism are being determined."[13] Many of the participants had come from abroad to be joined with their brethren in this national rite. The double-headed white eagle, the symbol of the Serbian royal family, which the Četniks, the Serbian nationalist forces in World War II, had adopted, blanketed the rally, as did the cross and other symbols of the Serbian Orthodox Church. Kosovo's Albanians stayed indoors, fearful of a pogrom. Summoning the ghost of Prince Lazar, Milošević proclaimed:

> Serbs in their history have never conquered or exploited others. Through two world wars, they liberated themselves and, when they could, they also helped others to liberate themselves.
>
> The Kosovo heroism does not allow us to forget that at one time we were brave and dignified and one of the few who went into battle undefeated.
>
> Six centuries later, again we are in battles and quarrels: They are not armed battles, though such things should not be excluded yet.[14]

The threat of violence was obvious. In Milošević's hands, Serbian nationalism was redemptive—it would bring together the far-flung Serb population and would restore the nation to its rightful, powerful place in the world. Through the national form Serbs would once again be safe and prosperous. If need be, the redemption of the nation would come through political violence. By assuming Lazar's as well as Tito's mantle, Milošević found himself riding a wave of popular enthusiasm. Laura Silber and Allan Little, two especially perceptive reporters, write: "Milošević attained almost divine status among the Serbs. . . . Suddenly he was everywhere. His photograph or portrait, often both, hung in every store window, in trucks, offices, and government buildings. . . . It was impossible to walk through the heart of Belgrade . . . without meeting Milošević's confident gaze. Tito's image began to disappear. Carrying his photo, at the scores of rallies . . . people would chant that Milošević had replaced Tito. Serbs loved Milošević for his pledge to protect them."[15]

A key element in this revived national discourse was the effort to make multinational communities "unimaginable," in the words of the anthropologist Robert M. Hayden. The rhetoric about the Jasenovac concentration camp is particularly significant in this regard. During World War II, the Independent State of Croatia carried out genocides against Serbs, Jews, and Roma and Sinti at its concentration and extermination camps, Jasenovac the most notorious among them. The numbers of victims are debatable, as they often are in these circumstances; the reality of the events is not. But for Serb nationalists, Jasenovac provided a case within the living memory of many people, who could recall the atrocities Croatian fascists, with some Muslim allies, had perpetrated against Serbs. Serb nationalists could arouse the most deeply felt fears of the Serb population. Yet Jasenovac was also a "positive" model for the Serbs, one that allowed them to make yet another claim for the establishment of an exclusively Serbian state. Genocide was supposedly the destiny of Serbs in any multinational state — a charge very provocatively raised by Milošević and his various allies, who bemoaned the fate of Serbs in present-day Kosovo and in the past in Croatia. Franjo Tudjman, elected the new leader of Croatia in 1990, publicly lauded the NDH and revived many of its symbols, actions that only accentuated Serbian fears.

Milošević and other Serb nationalists elevated Jasenovac into an exclusively Serbian symbol, second only to Kosovo Polje, despite the fact that Jews and Roma and Sinti had also been killed at the concentration camp.[16] In his Easter 1991 message, the patriarch of the Serbian Orthodox church compared the killing of Serbs at Jasenovac to the "genocide [presumably by Latin Christians] at the end of the Middle Ages. . . . in which in the course of eighteen years, 114,000 innocent men and women were burned at the stake." Jasenovac, where Serbs were tortured and annihilated, "was the new crucifixion of Christ." Moreover, the perpetrators of these crimes had never repented or atoned in any way. Instead, there are signs of "new, incurable intoxications, which lead to new crimes, to a new Deicide alongside the fratricide." Sounding the rallying cry, the patriarch called on the Serb people to "combat all that has been done to extinguish the memory and to underestimate the number of our victims, to erase our cemeteries, the places of execution and suffering, to destroy the documents that attest to the great suffering, which is without precedent in the history of the human species."[17]

But did Serbian nationalism mean anything more than a constant sense of aggrievement, of an unending stream of injustices perpetrated against Serbs? Did it possess a utopian element in the same fashion as did, say, Nazi racial rhetoric? Milošević and others were more prone to write and speak about the bedraggled state of present-day Serbia and to summon the heroes of the past. But every so often, images of a bright, glowing future appeared in the rhetoric of Serb nationalists. For centuries the Serbian Orthodox Church had viewed itself as the bearer of the national ideal, and it gave an intransigent and particularly mystical tenor to expressions of Serbian nationalism.[18] If Serbs lived in an oppressive present, a bright future awaited them in the afterlife. As Bishop

Jovan expressed the matter in the early 1980s, God looked down so gracefully upon Serbs and so many Serbs had been martyred through the ages that Heavenly Serbia "had become the largest state in heaven."[19] The novelist Dobrica Ćosić, one of the first Serb intellectuals to travel the road from communist—and high-ranking one at that—to extreme nationalist, spoke of the Serbian "calvary, humiliation, exodus," words that conjured up biblical stories but also the promise of ultimate redemption following the great sacrifices.[20] The Serbian symbol itself blended national and religious themes, four Cyrillic S's standing for "Only unity saves the Serbs" in the four corners of a cross.[21]

On a more earthly level, nationalists claimed that Serbs could flourish only by living together in their own state.[22] Many of its advocates also claimed that the heroic and emancipatory tradition of Serbian nationalism had to be retrieved from the past and reformulated for the present and future. The memorandum explicitly associated the Serbian national tradition with the liberal, progressive bourgeoisie of the nineteenth century. Ćosić, contending that Serbs had struck blows for freedom in two world wars and by their break with the Soviet Union after World War II, noted in 1991 that Serbs "by their great deeds in support of liberty, national and human dignity; by their great number of victims [have demonstrated] the greatest human courage for human value, have placed themselves at the summit of the European and world ladder."[23]

Milošević's nationalism found a broad range of support also because he promised to fight against corruption and inefficiency, presented himself as a strong leader, and, at least in the early years, appeared to be defending the unity of the country and its communist system. Indeed, for Milošević and other longtime party members in the League of Communists of Yugoslavia (LCY) and in the officer corps of the Yugoslav People's Army (JNA), the defense of "liberty" meant, precisely, defending Yugoslav communism.[24] Even as the federal system disintegrated around them, they remained firmly committed to the idea that the economy and society had to be based upon socialist property and Yugoslavia's own system of self-management. As the Yugoslav defense secretary General Veljko Kadijević stated in 1990: "The socialist idea cannot be rejected because of the crude failures of the real socialist model . . . [T]he idea of socialism . . . belongs to the future."[25] For JNA officers, already predominantly Serb by background, and for substantial segments of the LCY, democratic reform threatened both the return of capitalism and the end of their privileged positions in state and society. Career concerns were bundled together with the ideological commitments of an officer corps and party elite that had been schooled in Marxism-Leninism, along with the heroic deeds of partisan resistance in World War II, and remained deeply suspicious of the West.[26] Some fifty years after the Nazi invasion and occupation of Yugoslavia, they believed that Germany still coveted South Slav territory. Like Germany, Italy and Austria sought to make inroads against communism through Slovenia and Croatia, populated largely by fellow Catholics. And the United States signified capitalism writ large, an eternal enemy of the socialist project.

In the early 1990s, when their endeavor to maintain the integrity of Yugoslavia had failed, JNA officers and LCY leaders began to look to Serbia and Serbian nationalism as the means of sustaining communism. Many of them joined the successor party to the LCY, organized in Belgrade on 17 July 1990, which was named, significantly, the Socialist Party of Serbia (SPS). Most of the reformed communist parties in Eastern Europe after 1989 adapted to democratic practices; in Serbia, the SPS maintained the ideology, organizational structures, and political techniques typical of communist parties since the 1950s, including reverence for a strong state and opposition to an independent civil society. Milošević claimed at its founding congress that "the left wing's time is before us," and by that he certainly did not mean a future of democratic socialism.[27] As late as 1992, the SPS equated the cause of socialism and Serbian national interests. It claimed to be following a "national path" to socialism against an American- and German-led new world order and fought "against the unrestricted domination of capital over people."[28]

Other Serb nationalists, not necessarily committed to socialism, had their own suspicions of the West, sometimes rooted in Orthodoxy or in nineteenth-century-style Slavic romanticism. Much of their rhetoric had a profoundly antiurban tenor to it. The countryside was true Serbia; the city was Muslim or a depraved site of ethnic mixing. Some of the more extreme exponents of the Serbian cause described Sarajevo, Vukovar, Dubrovnik, and even Belgrade as places of pestilence and prostitution.[29] Their demands were remarkably simple: a Greater Serbia populated exclusively by Serbs.[30] The exact borders of this state varied depending on the speaker, but by almost all accounts it included at least the greater part of Bosnia, eastern Croatia (Krajina and Slavonia), Macedonia, and Montenegro, and extended north into the Vojvodina and perhaps parts of present-day Hungary. In more extreme versions, even Zadar and Trieste, both on the Adriatic, both at one time as much Italian as Croat, were considered part of Serbia.[31]

The implication of all this was that in their own state, possessed of security, freed from the exactions—economic, cultural, and spiritual—of the federal union, and protected from the depredations of capitalist countries, Serbs would finally flourish. Only an exclusive nation-state, it was claimed, would allow the potential of the people to burst forth in torrents of creativity and development. This was an old song, nineteenth-century nationalism played for late-twentieth-century audiences. But it formed the basis upon which communists, liberals, conservatives, and fascists joined together. In a country of immense ethnic diversity, where anyone could be a minority depending on background and location, the results of this kind of nationalist project quickly became dangerous. Slovenes, Croats, and, belatedly, Muslims also developed national programs. Each could claim, like Serbs, that it had been treated unfairly in the federation—even more, that its very survival as a people was at stake, threatened by this or that nationality.[32] Yet in this mix, it was Serbian nationalism that was most explosive—because of the number of Serbs, the size and power of Serbia, the extent of Serbian claims, and the virulence with which nationalists articulated their views.

But in a country of such diversity, where religious conversions had been a pronounced feature of the historical experience, and where, more recently, intermarriages had become common at least in urban areas, just how, exactly, was one to determine who was a Serb, and who was a Croat or Muslim?

CATEGORIZING THE POPULATION

As with the other cases discussed in this book, Serb nationalists, and their counterparts among Croats, Slovenes, and, finally, Muslims, sought to "fix" identities, to establish clearly and cleanly who was a member of what group. Only when that knowledge was firmly established could the state then determine those who deserved the rights and privileges conferred by membership in the nation, and those who had to be driven out and killed. In many instances, it proved quite easy to distinguish, for example, Muslims from Serbs in villages in northern Bosnia or Croats from Serbs in Krajina and Slavonia. But every act of identification entailed a particular scripting of history, an effort to obscure the complexities of a past and a present that were characterized by major population movements, fluid lines of division among groups, and long periods of tolerance and cooperation as well as conflict.

The major South Slav groups share a common ancestry. Serbs, Croats, Slovenes, and Bosnian Muslims all descend from Slavic tribes that migrated into the area of the former Yugoslavia in the late Roman period.[33] In the medieval and early modern periods, they became differentiated by religion, dialect, and customs as a result of the states that arose in the South Slav lands and the empires that ultimately destroyed or subordinated them. By the sixteenth century, the establishment of Ottoman Turkish and Habsburg Austrian domination over the area had made the region a borderland three times over: between Latin and Orthodox Christianity, between Latin Christianity and Islam, and between the Ottoman and Habsburg Empires. Under the empires, identities were more religious than national in character. The Ottomans explicitly organized their realm along religious lines, so that each religious community had a form of autonomy. Adherents of Serbian Orthodox Christianity predominated in the Ottoman realm. Among them, the intertwining of religion and nation had existed as far back as the medieval period, though a fully developed nationalism had to await the nineteenth century.[34] The link was not so strong in Croatia, where Roman Catholics predominated, because of the supranational character of the Roman Catholic Church, and because Croats had a form of representation through their political institutions that existed within the Hungarian kingdom from the medieval into the modern period. In Bosnia, many Slavs converted to Islam under Ottoman domination, making the population of the region even more complex. In Bosnia also the supranational character of Islam made it nearly impossible for a Muslim national identity to form prior to the modern period.

While Bosnia was the most diverse, all three major areas, Serbia, Croatia, and Bosnia, had substantially mixed populations and varied settlement patterns. Moreover, the settlement patterns were anything but static; they varied dramatically over the centuries, with formerly Serb areas becoming Muslim and vice versa, Catholics and Orthodox migrating with the shifting borders of empires. Populations adapted to new rulers or the scourge of war and repression sometimes by flight, sometimes by religious conversion. Migrations continued in the modern period: Muslims, for example, migrated in waves to Turkey after the Austro-Hungarian occupation of Bosnia in 1878, the establishment of Yugoslavia in 1918, and the communist victory in 1945.[35] Serbs migrated from Kosovo in large numbers in the latter part of the twentieth century as the Muslim population grew.

Only in the course of the nineteenth century, with the emergence of political struggles against Habsburg and Ottoman domination and of nationalisms throughout Europe, did religious identities become fully intermingled with national ones, so that by definition, a Catholic was also a Croat; an Orthodox, a Serb.[36] In Bosnia the situation remained far more complex, and no one could really articulate a Bosnian nationalism, given its great population mix and the absence, except for a very brief period, of a historical tradition of statehood.[37] Instead, nationalists from the nineteenth century onward asserted that Bosnian Muslims were simply wayward Serbs or Croats, the descendants of those who had wrongly adopted Islam and who now needed to be brought back into the fold. Even in the late 1980s, an anthropologist conducting fieldwork among Bosnian Muslim villagers was told by colleagues in, respectively, Belgrade and Zagreb, that her informants were "really" Serb or "really" Croat. In their view, Muslim identity was not "natural" since it was not based on lineage, as was supposedly the case for Serbs and Croats.[38] Bosnian Muslims did tend to base their self-conception on their religion and a set of related customs and, in contrast to Croats and Serbs, rarely thought of "blood" descent as the determining factor.[39] But that did not make any of these identities more or less natural; they all were the result of historical factors and ideological constructions.

For official purposes in Yugoslavia, individuals were free to choose their own ethnic and national identity. The 1961 census permitted for the first time the self-identification of "Muslim," but as an ethnic, not national, category, because "nationality" would then qualify Muslims for their own republic. However, in 1971, so that a somewhat equal balance among the various groups in the federation might be maintained, "Muslim" did become an officially recognized nationality. At around the same time, some Yugoslavs were abandoning their particular identities. In the 1981 census, 20–25 percent of the population in Bosnia's five largest cities identified themselves as "Yugoslav" instead of providing an ethnic or national identity. They constituted 7.9 percent of the overall population in 1981, 5.5 percent in 1991, and were overwhelmingly urban-based. Mixed marriages made up 15.3 percent of the total in Bosnia, but the great majority of these were between Serbs and Croats. Over 90 percent of Muslim marriages were endogamous.[40]

All the complexities of ethnic and national identities in the past and the present — shifting borders, population movements, religious conversions, mixed marriages — were, to nationalists, obstacles that had to be removed or ignored. As the Yugoslav crisis deepened in the late 1980s and early 1990s, and increasingly loud calls were voiced for separate, nationally defined states, Serb and Croat nationalists sought to erase ambiguities. Their goal was to define, once and for all, who was Croat, Serb, or Muslim, and thereby to determine people's fates. As nationalists moved into control both of the central states and of localities in Bosnia (as we shall see below), they went around affixing permanent, indelible categories upon individuals and families. Despite all the talk of Bosnian Muslims as "really" Serbs or Croats, any belief in the malleability of identities vanished in the firestorms of forced deportations and mass killings. If there were any cases of Muslims' being offered the possibility of conversion as a way of saving their lives and property, they were minuscule in number. In the course of the war, Croatia would make a political and military deal with the Muslim-led government of Bosnia against Serbia. But for Serb nationalists, Muslims, by their very being, were seen as constituting a threat to the Serbian future, and it required the full power of the state and its security forces to remove them.

Like the Soviets in the late 1930s and 1940s and the Nazis and Khmer Rouge throughout their reigns, Serb nationalists used whatever forms of knowledge were available to slot people into distinct categories. In the highly mixed regions of Slavonia and Krajina in Croatia and in Bosnia generally, particular villages or neighborhoods were simply known as Muslim, others as Serb or Croat. Very often, people's names identified them as members of one or another group.[41] All sorts of state records identified people by their nationality, from individual identity cards to job applications, and the documents were often scoured by nationalists when they entered a locality. People in mixed marriages came under immense pressure; spousal violence intensified as men blamed their wives of a different nationality for destroying their prospects for the future.[42] Individuals could sometimes be distinguished by their dress or by their homes. Standing in the hills over Banja Luka in more peaceful days, a friend was able to point out Muslim houses because their roofs were four-sided.[43] In the midst of the conflict, Serb nationalists in Prijedor (in Bosnia) ordered Muslims to mark their homes with white sheets and then to wear white armbands, an identifying badge no less nefarious than the yellow star Jews had been forced to wear in Nazi Germany.[44]

The knowledge available from official documents and informal, local sources enabled Serb (and Croat) nationalists to place people in fixed categories. Like the Nazis, Serb nationalists were radical simplifiers, who ignored, disdained, and, finally, obliterated other forms of identity, like class or locality, and the complications that arose from mixed marriages and conversions. Ultimately, they reduced all Muslims, like Jews in the Third Reich, to a biological category from which there was no escape. Muslims had to be either driven out or killed. But to reach the point where that kind of radical transformation of society was possible, Yugoslavia had first to descend into a crisis for which nationalists claimed to have the solution.

PREPARING FOR POPULATION PURGES: THE YUGOSLAV CRISIS

The cases of genocide discussed in previous chapters developed at moments of severe crisis, both domestically and internationally. Wars in particular created grave insecurities but also provided revolutionary elites with grand opportunities for asserting their powers and reshaping their populations. At the same time, the moments at which the situations "tipped" over into genocides had deeper roots in the ideologies and institutions of the various regimes.

The specific nature of the Yugoslav crisis was somewhat different. Yugoslavia was not at war, and the system was not in the throes of vast social and institutional transformations on a par with those engineered by the Soviet Union and Nazi Germany in the 1930s or by the Khmer Rouge in their first months of power. But Yugoslavia did face its own combined domestic and international crisis that rapidly undermined the premises of the existing system. The collapse of communism and the increasing power of globalized capitalism destroyed the Cold War umbrella that had given Yugoslavia its protected and privileged place in the international order. Its economy stagnated and lacked the flexibility to function effectively in the more competitive global markets of the late twentieth century. As the communist system's ability to provide for its people deteriorated, and the political order became mired in internal conflicts and incompetence, people turned to extreme nationalism for solutions. But the dissolution of Yugoslavia and the transition to violent population politics were not the result of age-old ethnic hatreds, as the popular media and government circles in the West often proclaimed. At a moment of crisis, in large part self-generated, nationalist leaders opted to destroy the system. To accomplish their aims, they mobilized long-standing national sentiments but also drew upon the very character of Yugoslavia as a federation of nationally based republics and as a communist society.

In comparison with other Eastern European countries, Yugoslavia in the 1960s and 1970s seemed like a model of prosperity. A visitor in the 1970s and very early 1980s could see well-stocked shops and markets and many houses in varying states of construction, the labor provided by the owners themselves on weekends and vacations, the money accumulated from the marks they had earned as workers in Germany. But the oil shocks of the 1970s led to severe inflation. Indebtedness spiraled upward, greatly burdening the economy, while unemployment rose into the double digits. In some areas, like Kosovo, close to one-quarter of the workforce was unemployed by the early 1980s, also because West Germany, long an outlet for surplus Yugoslav labor, began to limit and even repatriate foreign workers. The Yugoslav system of combined central planning and self-management at the enterprise level had worked well enough in the early stages of economic development in the 1950s and 1960s, but not in the more intensely competitive international situation of the 1980s. As in the other European socialist states, real living standards began to stagnate and then decline. According to some calculations, real personal income declined by one-quarter over the period from 1979 to 1985, by one-third in the decade from 1979 to 1988.[45] To the extent that the Yugoslav regime had staked its legitimacy on providing ever higher standards of living for the population, stagnation and decline had nearly immediate political consequences.

Yugoslavia's immersion in the international economic order only intensified its problems.[46] Since the break with the Soviet Union in 1948, Yugoslavia had been able to raise funds in Western capital markets and had been granted favorable trading relations by the European Community (EC) and the United States. In the 1980s, the International Monetary Fund (IMF) and the World Bank imposed austerity measures— their standard formula—on Yugoslavia and demanded political and economic reforms in return for the restructuring of Yugoslavia's extremely high indebtedness. The results were mass unemployment, hyperinflation, and steep slashes in social welfare programs, as well as substantial cuts in the long-sacred defense budget. New IMF conditions in the late 1980s sought to enhance the powers of the central state, yet in the general context of dissolution, such moves only provoked outrage from the constituent republics. Meanwhile, the end of the Cold War deprived Yugoslavia of its room for maneuver between the two blocs. Indeed, the collapse of European communism and of the Cold War meant that from an international standpoint, Yugoslavia had as little reason to exist as did East Germany.

The nature of the Yugoslav political order elevated the problems to crisis level, because no individual or institution proved able to manage the situation and institute a viable program of reform. In its structure, Yugoslavia, like the Soviet Union, affirmed the saliency of ethnic and national identities. Both systems implemented a dual principle of nationality: the countries were created as federations of national territories, and every individual was the carrier of a prescribed nationality.[47] Like the USSR, Yugoslavia was organized as a federal system of nationally defined republics, six in all. And like the Russian Socialist Republic within the USSR, the Serb Republic contained within it two ethnically defined provinces, Vojvodina and Kosovo.[48] The initial constitutions defined the republics as the political expressions of sovereign nations, to which the ethnic groups outside the republics were also linked. Serbs in Bosnia, for example, were considered part of the Serbian nation represented by the Serb Republic. Within each republic, political positions were distributed according to national criteria.[49]

The League of Communists of Yugoslavia and the Yugoslav People's Army were the two very powerful institutions that maintained the cohesion of the system.[50] Yet even before Tito's death, the federal structure had enabled the particular republics to exercise greater authority at the expense of the LCY and JNA. In the words of the historian John Lampe, the "mind-boggling complexity" of the political system made any resolution of economic or political problems exceedingly difficult, if not quite impossible.[51] The constitution of 1974 and various amendments worsened matters by giving the six republics and two autonomous provinces firm legal status as the constituent elements of Yugoslavia. As one Serb legal expert remarks, "the principal message [of the 1974 constitution] was that, in spite of class oratory, the federal state was based on national arrangements."[52] After 1980, the complex and highly inefficient political system Tito had insisted upon as his legacy — designed to provide checks on the accumulation of too much power by any one republic or any one faction — only accentuated political paralysis and fragmentation. A dizzying array of institutions, including all sorts of cross-republic committees, proved increasingly ineffective in managing the ever more severe economic and political problems of the

1980s, which resulted in a precipitous decline in public confidence.[53] Even within the LCY the individual republican and provincial parties became more important than the federal one in the course of the 1980s.

In short, the institutional structure of communist Yugoslavia sustained and developed particular national identifications.[54] In the Soviet Union, as we have seen, the recognition of nationalities as the constituent elements of the union led to a policy that both fostered national development and treated some groups as enemy nations that had to be removed in toto. In Yugoslavia, a similar system led to an even more radical outcome. As one scholar writes, the federal structure based on national republics had the result that "every question was by necessity 'nationalized.'"[55] For some years Yugoslavia was able to muddle along. But by the late 1980s, economic decline, political paralysis, and a rapidly shifting international situation had brought the domestic situation to a crisis level. As the central government proved increasingly unable to fulfill its role as guarantor of the living standards and protector of the population, the system devolved to its constituent elements—the six republics and two autonomous regions, with the JNA sometimes referred to as the "ninth federal unit"—each of which raised its own demands. The dissolution became so dangerous in Yugoslavia because there, unlike the other communist societies in Eastern Europe, no viable, democratically minded civil society had emerged that stretched across the entire country, not just among a particular nationality. Only in Bosnia did the Muslim leadership, along with a few Croat and Serb allies, try desperately to maintain the republic's multinational character, its stature as the "true" Yugoslavia.

In contrast to Poland, Czechoslovakia, and East Germany, where a broad-based, grassroots reform movement came to the fore (if only temporarily), in Yugoslavia political leaders in each of the republics, Bosnia excepted, began to formulate particular national programs as the solution to the crisis. Nationalist leaders—one still a communist (Milošević in Serbia), one a communist on the road to becoming a liberal (Milan Kućan in Slovenia), and one an ex-communist (Tudjman in Croatia)— successfully galvanized their own populations with nationalist sentiments. Groups with long-standing grievances could easily be mobilized—Croats and Slovenes for being "taxed" to support the less developed parts of the country, Serbs for their supposed suppression by the numerically dominant Albanians in Kosovo, Albanians because of their exclusion from power in an area in which they were, by far, the largest population group. Grander historical claims were also revived.

Serbs, as we have seen, called for continued struggle against Muslim influence and for a Greater Serbia; Croats demanded a Greater Croatia as a bastion of "Western civilization." Tudjman, for example, commented, in typically grandiose fashion, that "Croats are part of Western Europe, part of the Mediterranean tradition. Long before Shakespeare and Molière, our writers were translated into European languages. The Serbs belong to the East . . . like the Turks and Albanians. They belong to the Byzantine culture."[56] Only Slovenes, residing in a nearly homogeneous republic, demanded just secession, not an expanded territory.

Serb, Croat, and Slovene politicians were able to mobilize highly diverse elements of their societies around the national cause. As mentioned, LCY bureaucrats and JNA officers conceived of Serbia as the last defender of communism in Yugoslavia and even in Europe. All three national leaderships also welcomed the cooperation of other extreme nationalists, including right-wing émigré Serbs and Croats in Australia, North America, and Europe and criminal elements, like the infamous Arkan, who would lead one of the major paramilitary units of the Serbian campaign. Alongside the regular armies and bureaucracies of the states, criminals and some émigrés would provide men, money, and munitions for the national program of ethnic cleansings and genocides.

THE ULTIMATE PURGE: DISSOLUTION, WAR, AND GENOCIDE IN BOSNIA

Slovenia and Croatia took the lead in demanding independence, even though some Albanian radicals, as early as 1981, had raised a similar demand. But the Serbs were the driving force behind the dissolution of Yugoslavia. As Silber and Little write, it was Milošević who, failing in his attempt to preserve the integrity of the state, "chose an alternate project, the creation of a new enlarged Serbian state, encompassing as much territory of Yugoslavia as possible."[57] From 1987 onward, Milošević, acting like any communist leader, used the instruments of party and state to extend his own power and promote the nationalist cause. First he deposed his mentor, Serbian president Stambolić, and then moved his own supporters into positions deep within the bureaucracy.[58] The Serb leadership inflamed nationalist sentiments by staging pro-Serbian rallies, depicting in the party-controlled media the dangers faced by Serbs outside of Serbia, and threatening military intervention if Serbian demands for greater authority within the federation were not met. Milošević also carried out a very significant rapprochement with the Serbian Orthodox Church, to the extent of permitting Orthodoxy to be recognized as "the spiritual basis" for the national identity of Serbs.[59] In March 1989, Milošević promulgated a new Serbian constitution that gave Serbia direct control over Vojvodina and Kosovo, which enabled Serbia also to dominate federal institutions, including the eight-member presidency. The assertion of Serbian power signified to Croats and Slovenes that they would never be able to pursue their republics' interests within the federation. As a result, they moved ever closer to outright secession.

Elections in 1990 in each of the republics brought smashing victories to newly formed nationalist parties in Croatia and Slovenia. A shifting set of tacit alliances — Slovenia and Croatia, Croatia and Serbia, Slovenia and Serbia — led, step-by-step, to the deliberate destruction of Yugoslavia, abetted by confused signals emanating from the United States and outright support emanating from Germany and other EC countries.[60] As a result, Bosnia was left in an exposed and tenuous position. In this most ethnically mixed republic, no single group could claim domination. Within the major cities, Sarajevo especially, a culture of tolerance and diversity had long existed. Members of the different communities lived side by side in Sarajevo, and intermarriage rates were on the rise. In the countryside, villages tended to be predominantly Serb or Muslim or Croat, but few villages were populated exclusively by one ethnic group. Bosnia-Herzegovina could exist, even thrive, in Yugoslavia. Outside the federation, its chances were slim. Both Serbia and Croatia coveted its territory and sought to bring their respective conationals into a single state. Indeed, at a secret meeting, Tudjman and Milošević had clearly formulated plans for the division of Bosnia.[61]

But war erupted first in Croatia, in Krajina, the old frontier region between the Habsburg and Ottoman Empires that was heavily populated by Serbs. In the face of Tudjman's ever more radical Croatian nationalist policies, and ever more fervent summoning of the symbols of the Ustaše, Serbs in the region had begun to organize, politically and militarily. Support for the Croatian Serbs poured in from Belgrade. The local Krajina leaders were feted by Milošević and others. Individuals in the JNA and Interior Ministry freely dispensed arms to them, with tacit approval from on high.[62] The Krajina Serbs had announced a referendum on autonomy, which amounted to virtual secession from Croatia. Tudjman demanded that the vote not take place, and, in response, the first fighting of the Yugoslav wars broke out in August 1990. Local

Serbs, with the support of Belgrade, were able to establish effective control in Krajina.[63]

In this period, 1990–91, the JNA was still committed to the integrity of Yugoslavia. Milošević kept up the pretense of defending Yugoslavia. But all the while, he was destroying federal institutions from within, trying to get them to follow Serbia's bidding and, when they did not, ignoring them. In reality, by 1990 he had already given up on the idea of Yugoslavia for a Greater Serbia. He was willing to let Slovenia become independent and Croatia as well, so long as it was a truncated Croatia, and the Serb-populated areas like Krajina were separated off and joined to Serbia. When the Federal Presidency refused to countenance a state of emergency so Milošević could use the army against student demonstrations, he declared on 15 March 1991 that "Yugoslavia is finished" and Serbia was no longer bound by federal decisions.[64] The same day, Krajina Serbs declared independence from Croatia. A few days later, raising the stakes yet again, Milošević said: "If we have to, we'll fight. I hope they won't be so crazy as to fight against us. Because if we don't know how to work and do business, at least we know how to fight."[65]

In the following months of spring 1991, the situation deteriorated further, especially in Krajina. The Serbian secret police were actively organizing Serb communities in Croatia and Bosnia, and Serb paramilitaries seized control of police stations.[66] As tensions and fears escalated, the most extreme elements of both communities gained the upper hand. Moderates were forced out and sometimes executed. The JNA lent continued support to the activist Serbs. The media in Zagreb and Belgrade screamed atrocities and published lurid stories — exaggerated, at least at this point — of tortures and mass executions. Amid all this, on 19 May 1991, a Croatian referendum in favor of secession from Yugoslavia won 90 percent of the votes. One month later, on 25 June 1991, Slovenia, assured of German support, declared its independence by a nearly unanimous vote of its parliament, and Croatia soon followed with a similar declaration.[67] The JNA invaded Slovenia, but this was a sham war that lasted only ten days: "a Serbian-Slovene pact," according to Silber and Little, "to facilitate the secession of Slovenia, humiliate the JNA, and destroy what was left of . . . [the] Federal Government. It had succeeded in all three respects."[68] Croatia and, especially, Bosnia would pay the bill.

While the war in Slovenia was limited, fighting now spread rapidly into Croatia. Serbia's intent to expand its borders and bring all Serbs into one state escalated the character of the conflict into a war over populations as well as territory, a war that became inextricably entwined with forced deportations and genocide. Through the summer and fall of 1991, an undeclared war raged in Krajina and Slavonia. The battles took on a standard format. The JNA, with no Yugoslavia left to defend, its officers desperately searching for a way to maintain their prestige, resources, and careers, was transforming itself into the army of Greater Serbia.[69] JNA troops took up positions around a town and launched artillery barrages. Serb paramilitaries and local Serbs, sometimes with JNA infantry support, entered the town, scoured through it, looting and burning Croatian property and driving Croats into exile. On many occasions, the violence took a more brutal turn, as paramilitaries killed people outright. The goal was obvious: to clear a historically mixed territory of Croats and others, and to make the population homogeneously Serb. At Vukovar, a lovely, historic city virtually leveled by Serb artillery barrages, the JNA commander, General Zivota Panić, integrated the paramilitaries directly into the JNA command structure. In a pattern that would become all too familiar, Serb forces, once they had finally taken Vukovar, separated the men from the women and children. The women and children were asked whether they wanted to be evacuated to Serbia or Croatia. Those who chose Serbia were allowed to leave; those who chose Croatia were turned over to Croatian authorities. Some of those under Serbian control were taken to a detention center where they were stripped and beaten.[70] Meanwhile, Croats retaliated against Serbian ethnic cleansing by driving out and, in some instances, massacring Serbs in towns in Croatian-held territory. By the end of November 1991, some 500,000 Croats and 230,000 Serbs had been displaced from their homes, some having fled in fear of what was to come, others directly forced out by the deliberate violence of nationalist forces.[71]

In essence, a mutual radicalization process developed, not unlike the one that resulted in the Holocaust. Serb activists "on the ground" in Croatia as well as the military and political leadership in Belgrade were both pushing the situation forward, supporting one another ideologically and materially. With no one applying the brakes or searching for a moderate solution, violent methods of dealing with Croats and Muslims became the favored policy. The mutual process then moved, almost inevitably, to Bosnia and became still more radical. Serb nationalists could not be content with the territory they had seized from Croatia; they also wanted a significant portion of Bosnia.

In the late spring and summer of 1990, in the immediate aftermath of elections in the other republics, political leaders of the three major communities in Bosnia had organized separate, nationally defined parties. Elections were held in November 1990, and the vast majority of the electorate voted along national lines, which led to a deeply divided parliament with a slim Muslim plurality.[72] For over a year, from December 1990 until March 1992, an uneasy truce reigned as the war continued in Croatia, and Serb and Croat nationalist leaders within Bosnia continually escalated the crisis. Serb nationalists deliberately sought to make Bosnia ungovernable, as the Nazis had done to the Weimar Republic. Serb deputies boycotted sessions of Parliament and challenged the legitimacy of Aliza Izetbegović, the leader of the Muslim party and now president of Bosnia. Serb paramilitaries seized control of villages and towns and declared them Serbian autonomous regions, virtually seceding from Sarajevo, much as the Croatian Serbs had done in Krajina. Serb forces conducted pogromlike raids of Muslim villages. Through all available media, Serb nationalists spread the word that the very existence of Serbs was in danger in Bosnia, especially if it were to become an independent state. They demanded the right to join their Serb brethren in a common state. The JNA had large troop concentrations and supply depots in Bosnia. Under orders from Belgrade, non-Serb officers were transferred out and replaced by Bosnian Serbs. By the end of December 1991 JNA forces in Bosnia were 85–90 percent Bosnian Serbs. The JNA was transferring military supplies to the Bosnian Serbs, and they and the Croatian paramilitaries were arming their supporters all over Bosnia. Long dominated by Serbs but committed to Yugoslavia, the JNA had incontestably become the Serbian national army.[73]

In autumn 1991, Bosnian Serbs convened their own parliament and held their own plebiscite, which demanded union with Serbia proper.[74] On 15 December 1991, the Bosnian Serb Assembly promulgated the Serb Republic of Bosnia and Herzegovina, which it declared independent on 9 January 1992. Its territorial claims were extensive, even beyond those Serbian autonomous regions that the paramilitaries had established over the previous months. In January 1992, the European Community countries recognized Slovenia and Croatia. The two events — the declaration of a Bosnian Serb Republic and EC recognition of Croatia and Slovenia — presented Bosnia with a stark choice. If it remained within rump Yugoslavia, it would no doubt be reduced to a Serbian-dominated dependency, much like Kosovo. A declaration of independence would bring down upon it the wrath of Bosnian Serbs and their allies in Serbia and Montenegro. The Bosnian Serb leader, Radovan Karadžić, had already threatened that if Bosnia were recognized as an independent state, it would not survive one day and would "lead the Muslim people into annihilation."[75] But independence was the only path left to Izetbegović. Bosnia became an independent state in early April 1992, and it, too, on 6 April 1992, was duly recognized by the EC countries.

Serb nationalists made good on their threats. First they initiated discriminatory measures that echoed the policies of Nazi Germany in the 1930s. Non-Serbs found their movements restricted, and they were bound by curfews. Local governments under Serbian control dismissed Croats and Muslims from their jobs and prohibited them from opening businesses and their children from attending schools. Many were deprived of their social and health insurance, the benefits — soon nonexistent anyway — made available only to loyal Serbs. The Serb authorities banned Muslims and Croats from swimming and fishing in the local rivers, and from gathering in groups of more than three. Muslim religious and cultural institutions were destroyed. Constant police harassment only added to the sense of terror. Muslims and Croats in Banja Luka were picked up arbitrarily and taken to a special building for beatings. In northern Bosnia, areas of major Croat and Muslim populations, Serb nationalists also developed a bureaucratic form of ethnic cleansing that again is reminiscent of Nazi efforts in the 1930s. In Prijedor and other towns, Croats and Muslims were allowed to leave Serb-controlled areas only after they had turned over any assets they held and had signed documents surrendering in perpetuity their rights to their property. In some places, people were packed into sealed trains, another specter of the Holocaust and of the deportation of "enemy nations" in the Soviet Union.[76]

But that was not all. In April 1992, Arkan's Tigers and other feared Serb paramilitaries moved into Bosnia from Krajina and continued the tactics they had perfected there. All over northern and eastern Bosnia, Serb paramilitaries, the JNA, and Ministry of Interior forces, acting in conjunction, laid siege to towns and villages, driving out Muslims in a firestorm of brutality. On 20 May 1992, General Ratko Mladić, since indicted as a war criminal by the Hague Tribunal, was named commander of the Republika Srpska (that is, the Bosnian Serb Republic) Army. He brought a high level of professional expertise and ruthlessness to the Serb nationalist forces.

Everywhere the pattern was the same — artillery barrages that laid waste to people and buildings; sieges that went on sometimes for months, even years, reducing the populations to a starved, diseased, and fearful existence. When Serb nationalist troops entered a town, the suffering became even worse. The fate of Bosanski Novi, a town in northern Bosnia, was typical. Serb paramilitaries and police herded the Muslim residents of eleven villages into this one village. For over two weeks they were kept in houses, as many as thirty to one house. After more than two weeks, the people were packed into freight train cars, the men separated from the women and children. Serb forces fired wildly, leaving thirty or forty dead, according to one witness. Up to three hundred people were forced into each wagon without food or water for days. Some young women were taken away and not seen again and were presumably raped. After five days' traveling, the Serb nationalists sent the men back and interned them at a sports stadium, while they expelled the women and children to Croatia. Serb forces blew up mosques and Muslim-owned shops and sprayed houses with bullets. They rounded up the remaining Muslim men and took them to the stadium. There the men were forced to kneel with their hands behind their backs and were beaten. Members of the local Muslim elite were interned in a hotel where they, too, were beaten. After five days Serbs released many of them — the experience of terror was enough to drive the victims out of the area. They sold off their remaining property at expropriation prices to get exit permits. And they had to pay for their bus fare, just as the Nazis had made Jewish communities collectively pay for their transport to the death camps.[77]

In Bijeljina, one of the first towns taken by Arkan's Tigers, and in other localities, paramilitaries murdered Muslims outright.[78] As in the other cases discussed in this book, political murders took place alongside the genocidal actions. In Bijeljina a number of local Serbs tried to halt the massacre of Muslims and were themselves killed by Arkan's Tigers.[79] In some communities — Tuzla, Vareš, the Bihać region, Fojnica — local residents of different nationalities continued to work together and tried desperately to stave off the violence.[80] Ultimately, they fell victim to the stronger forces around them and became engulfed by the tidal wave of ethnic cleansing and genocide.

Serb paramilitaries, again with clear support from the JNA, also laid siege to Sarajevo, one of the events that remains a poignant and tragic symbol of the war. The Bosnian Serb leader Radovan Karadžić — like General Mladić, since indicted as a war criminal — announced a plan to partition the city into three sectors, Serb, Croat, and Muslim. The Serb segment was to be the largest and most prosperous; Muslims were to be crowded into what was, for all intents and purposes, a ghetto. "They like to live on top of one another," was the justification issued by one of Karadžić's advisers.[81] A de facto partition emerged, defined by a line Serb forces had managed to reach while a Serb army held the commanding heights above the city. They would never be able to seize the city in total. But they were able to cause immense destruction. As Silber and Little remark, "Serb and JNA forces had proved themselves almost incapable of capturing urban territory without first reducing it to rubble."[82] The siege of Sarajevo was carried live on television and splashed across the front pages of newspapers around the world. As the scholars Steven L. Burg and Paul S. Shoup write, "the callousness of the Serb shelling and sniping from the surrounding hills provided a dramatic contrast to the courage of the Sarajevans under siege. It turned world public opinion decisively and permanently against the Serbs."[83]

The U.S. government and others had intelligence reports on the atrocities being committed but tried to keep the information under wraps, fearful of being drawn into the conflict. Instead, it was reporters who broke the news of the appalling conditions in Serb-dominated areas.[84] Roy Gutman of *Newsday*, in a set of searing dispatches, described the scenes he first encountered at the Serb concentration camp Manjača. Karadžić, in London for more negotiations, was enraged by the reports. Enveloped by his own hubris, he had the temerity (and stupidity) to invite journalists to come to Bosnia to see that there were no concentration camps. They came and found out that there were. Some two weeks after his first report was published, *Newsday*'s headline ran, "The Death Camps of Bosnia." Gutman, along with the British television news station ITN and the *Guardian*, also broke the news of the horrific conditions at the Omarska concentration camp, where Muslims were constantly beaten and tortured, and executions were a regular occurrence. The prisoners often had only scraps to eat, and sanitary facilities were nonexistent. Soon it became clear that there were at least three other concentration camps where Muslims languished in similar conditions, along with countless smaller, sometimes temporary, ones.[85]

Even these atrocities did not encompass the full range of Serb nationalist actions. At Srebenica in July 1995, the Bosnian Serb Army under the direct command of General Mladić massacred over seven thousand Bosnian Muslim men, the worst such event in Europe since World War II and now recognized as a genocide by the International Criminal Tribunal for the Former Yugoslavia (ICTY, also known as the Hague Tribunal). According to the ICTY, the Bosnian Serb leader Karadžić had already given orders on 8 March 1995 that the Drina Corps of the Bosnian Serb Army should, "by well thought out combat operations, create an unbearable situation of total insecurity with no hope of further survival or life for the inhabitants of Srebenica and Žepa," two of three Muslim enclaves in northern Bosnia that the UN had proclaimed "safe areas" (along with Sarajevo).[86] Within four days of the attack, on 12 July, the Bosnian Serb Army, aided by JNA and Ministry of Interior troops, military police forces, and paramilitaries, had captured the city in toto. Once again, Muslim men were separated from women and children, who were herded onto buses and trucks and transported out of the area. The remnants of the Bosnian (Muslim) Army tried to break through Serbian lines, and some of the troops were successful. Large numbers of other soldiers, however, were ensnared by the Serbs. The vast majority of Muslims were civilians, but the Serb forces made no distinctions. They rounded up Muslims in the town and hunted them down in the woods; they then deliberately killed the men and buried them in mass graves.[87]

The massacre at Srebenica was a tragedy for Muslims. It was also a political disaster for the West and the UN, which, however reluctantly, had become drawn into the Yugoslav conflict. Dutch troops operating as UN peacekeepers were present at Srebenica, and they endured the worst catastrophe in the history of UN peacekeeping operations. The Dutch forces were understaffed, underarmed, and undersupplied. They were fired upon by the Bosnian Serb Army, and on more than one occasion, General Mladić had them held as hostages, even chaining them around Serbian positions to prevent NATO air attacks. In the end, the Dutch troops simply watched the Serb forces deport and kill the Muslims of Srebenica.

But Srebenica also marked the point at which the West finally intervened more forcefully in the Yugoslav conflict. At different junctures in the war, the UN, NATO, the EC, and, finally, the United States, had taken initiatives to mediate the conflict. The efforts had often been half-hearted, haphazard, or ill-conceived. Even the best-intentioned mediations were stymied by the complexity of the situation, the intransigence of the three major parties — Serbs, Croats, and Muslims — and the internal divisions within each camp, and the disagreements and conflicts among the Western nations. None of the major powers wanted to lose troops or reputations in the Balkans. Each sought to pursue an "even-handed" approach that, in essence, signified support for the strongest of the parties, Serbia for the first years of the conflict. The arms embargo imposed by the UN Security Council on 25 September 1991 was easily evaded by Croatia, and Serbia had the very substantial resources of the JNA, but the embargo fatally hampered Muslims and the Bosnian Republic under Izetbegović. When the Security Council in 1992 finally established a peacekeeping force (UNPROFOR, the United Nations Protection Force), its commanders clung tightly to the Security Council strictures for the operation, which was defined as "peacekeeping" and not "peace enforcement." Yet force was needed just for the delivery of the humanitarian aid that was the express purpose of the mission. As a result, their own troops and other UN personnel were placed in highly precarious and dangerous situations. Cease-fires brokered by a variety of mediators never held but made UN forces in effect the legitimators of territorial changes accomplished by force. In the seesaw operations typical of the war, Serb forces would launch offensives and seize more territory, then agree to a cease-fire monitored by UN troops, which the Serbs would break sooner or later. It was a calculated and cynical policy used by Milošević and the more radical Bosnian Serbs.[88] By providing safe routes and camps for refugees—intermittently, never adequately, never on a scale that could really protect the endangered, largely Muslim, populations—the UN and then NATO also became party to ethnic cleansing. It was a devil's deal that brought agony to UN officials on the ground. "We're becoming collaborators," one UN official said. "It's blackmail. The choice we face is either to become agents of ethnic cleansing, or to leave tens of thousands of people to continue living their nightmare."[89]

But the agony was not always shared by government leaders in Europe and North America, who had long ago determined that Yugoslavia could not survive, and believed that the only way to end the conflict was to accept the creation of more homogeneous entities.[90] While Western leaders condemned the atrocities at Srebenica, they had also determined that the town would have to go to the Serbs; sotto voce they expressed the view that the peace process could now move forward, that drawing the maps would be easier.[91] By this point, Milošević had decided that his Bosnian Serb allies were more trouble than they were worth. They had rejected one peace plan after another, and their continual flouting of the international community—tying and chaining up UN troops, deliberately antagonizing Western diplomats—had created severe problems for rump Yugoslavia. Not least important, UN-imposed sanctions, passed on 30 May 1992, had sent the Serbian economy reel-ing, and Milošević needed some relief from their effects if he were to retain his popularity.

In August 1995, yet another Serb mortar attack on Sarajevo finally led to major air strikes against Serbian positions by mostly U.S. planes operating under NATO command as a UN-designated force. The threat of a still wider war with NATO intervention did not bode well, not for Serbia and not for Milošević, who decided to break with the Bosnian and Krajinan Serbs. By so doing, Milošević became the man with whom Western leaders could negotiate, the man, they believed, who would help bring peace to the region. Yet only the shifting balance of power had forced Milošević into this position. In late July 1995, Croatian forces, with tacit (and perhaps more active) American support, swept into Krajina and Slavonia.[92] The Serb disaster was total. The Serb Re-public of Krajina fell; its leaders fled, trying to save their own skins. Knin, the town where the Yugoslav wars had begun, fell to Croat forces on 4 August 1995. Serbs now became subject to the ethnic cleansing that Croats and Muslims had experienced through four years of war. Close to 500,000 Serbs fled and were forcibly deported from Krajina and Slavonia, one of the largest ethnic cleansings since World War II.

Now the scene shifted to U.S.-led negotiations. As the war dragged on, the costs to the United States had escalated significantly. President Bill Clinton and his advisers worried about the political damage he might have to weather in the 1996 presidential elections. Most impor-tant, the standing of NATO, the linchpin of American strategy since 1949, was endangered by its inability to create a settlement in the Balkans, its internal divisions over proper strategy, and its humiliation at the hands of the Bosnian Serbs. Moreover, the United States's NATO allies were threatening to withdraw their troops from UNPROFOR. U.S. ground troops would inevitably be drawn into the conflict, since the United States would have to help guarantee the safe withdrawal of UN forces. American policymakers preferred to set the terms of Ameri-can involvement rather than get drawn in by events and parties over which they had no control. American intervention, diplomatic and mili-tary, had become a necessity.[93]

In early October 1995, combined European and American pressure finally resulted in a cease-fire, and on 1 November 1995, the leading figures—Tudjman, Milošević, and Izetbegović—met at Wright-Patter-son Air Force Base in Dayton, Ohio, under the forceful negotiating of Assistant U.S. Secretary of State Richard Holbrooke and U.S. Secretary of State Warren Christopher. After more than two weeks, the parties finally came to a settlement. As a result of the Dayton Agreement, Bosnia remained in existence, its borders intact, its formal name now the Republic of Bosnia and Herzegovina. But internally, it comprised two separate entities, a Serb one, the Republika Srpska, and a Muslim-Croat one, the Federation of Bosnia-Herzegovina. According to the constitution determined at Dayton, each entity is granted the right to establish "special parallel relationships" with neighboring states, and each was also a signatory to major aspects of the agreement. The central state is very weak, with major powers left to localities and to the Federation and the Republika Srpska. These were all major concession to Serbs, granting them in fact some of the powers, if not all the territory, for which Serb nationalists had fought. In the words of the political scientists Burg and Shoup, "the constitution institutionalizes the ethnic division of the state."[94]

In the Yugoslav wars, all sides committed atrocities, including Muslims. But Serb nationalists were the pacesetters, and Serbia, the largest and most populous of the republics of the former Yugoslavia, had the greatest power at its disposal. The goals of Serbian actions were clear: to expand Serbian territory; to create an ethnically homogeneous country through mass murder and forced deportations; to terrorize Croat and especially Muslim populations in neighboring towns and villages so that they would depart even before Serb troops arrived; to make the very idea of Yugoslavia unthinkable, indeed, unbearable, because of the memory of the losses and brutalities that the survivors would always carry with them—the murder, often in front of their eyes, of loved ones and compatriots; the rapes of family members; the "little Četniks," the fetuses Muslim victims of rape carried to term or had aborted, either destiny a revisiting of the traumas they had endured.[95] Serbian policy was also designed to render the past unimaginable or unrecognizable. Serb forces destroyed mosques and libraries indiscriminately and changed town names and street names, much as the Soviets had done to the homelands of Chechens and Tatars. The mosque in Banja Luka, one of the treasures of Ottoman architecture, was reduced to rubble, as were scores of others throughout Bosnia. By the end of 1992, the combined impact of these policies had made two million Bosnians, almost half the population, homeless.[96] For many Muslims (like other Yugoslavs), it had taken years of their own labor and careful savings to build their homes. Many of them had gone to work in Germany and Austria for just that purpose. The destruction of so many homes by Serb nationalists had a devastating impact on survivors that extended far beyond the sheer lack of shelter.[97]

As in the other cases discussed in this book, forced deportations and genocide were social projects that involved the participation of many thousands of people. First there were the armed men, the JNA, Serbian Ministry of Interior troops, the Bosnian Serb Army, and various paramilitaries like Arkan's Tigers. In general, but not always, ethnic cleansing was engineered from the outside by armed units, not by local residents. But local populations quickly became complicit in the actions. In Krajina, local Serbs took over the property of Croats who were forced out; when the Serbs suffered a similar fate in 1995, Croats returned and did the same to Serbs. In towns throughout Bosnia, local Serbs joined in the looting and confiscation of Muslim property, as well as in more brutal actions against people. As towns and villages changed hands or were relegated to one group or another on the basis of negotiations, the locals tried to prevent the return of those previously forced out. They feared the loss of the property they had stolen and more violent retaliation. Ethnic cleansing created a new reality on the ground, caused immense personal tragedies for those driven out or who watched their loved ones brutalized and killed, and had a deeply corrupting impact on those who remained.

The Dayton Agreement brought peace to Bosnia, but an uneasy one. It affirmed national identity as the basis of political organization, thereby granting the nationalists the essence of their programs, if not in fully flowered form. And it could not, of course, undo the tens, perhaps hundreds, of thousands of deaths and the forced displacement of upward of two million people. It could not banish the memories of mass killings and rapes, the traumas that will stay with the many survivors throughout their lives.

And Dayton could not stop Serbia from launching one last campaign of ethnic cleansing, again with the most dire consequences, this time for Muslims in Kosovo.[98] For at least a decade, Kosovars had endured the most severe repression by Yugoslavia and Serbia, although some Serbs also had suffered violence at the hands of nationalists in Kosovo. Kosovars were driven out of positions in the university, state, and economy. The population as a whole found itself removed from the state-sponsored social security and health insurance systems. Security forces conducted arbitrary arrests. The plight of Kosovo received no mention at Dayton, to the dismay of Kosovo Albanian activists. Partly as a result, Kosovar radicals organized the Kosovo Liberation Army in the early 1990s. It carried out some terrorist attacks on Serbs, which successfully provoked Serbia into a massive response. As in the Croatian and Bosnian wars, the Serb attack utilized regular army, Interior Ministry, and paramilitary forces. The intent was, again, to cleanse an area by force, and to visit such terror upon the inhabitants that others would flee in advance. The result was a forced deportation of hundreds of thousands of people, along with many murders and rapes. What Milošević had not counted on was seventy-eight days of NATO air strikes that killed around twenty-six hundred Serbs, more civilians than soldiers, and destroyed a good part of Serbia's infrastructure.

RITUALS OF POPULATION PURGES

The genocide of Bosnian Muslims, like that of Chechens and Tatars in the Soviet Union, Jews in Nazi Germany, and Chams and Vietnamese in Cambodia, was a state-directed operation. It was not an eruption of age-old hatreds, a kind of natural disaster that every so often swirls up from the landscape, but a policy conducted by political and military elites. But as in these other cases, the successful implementation of genocide in Bosnia required the cooperation and even the initiative of people at many levels of Serbian society. They beat and raped, took the property of those forced out of their homes, and pointed out Muslim homes to troops who entered a town or village. These particular acts of violence and complicity were not always the result of orders from Belgrade or even Pale, the headquarters of the Bosnian Serb government. Participants invented their own forms of action, but these were always social acts conducted in the presence of other perpetrators and bystanders and often in full view of other victims. In this way, the perpetrators deliberately spread fear among the victims and made genocide a social project.

To carry out extreme violence on such a widespread scale, Serb nationalists had first to dehumanize their victims, to make them completely "other." They used all sorts of derogatory terms for Bosnian Muslims, like *balijas* and "dogs." At General Radislav Krstić's trial before the ICTY, Presiding Judge Almiro Rodrigues noted at his conviction that one of his subordinates had "asked for your help in dealing with '3,500 packages.' You knew exactly what was meant by 'packages,' General Krstic—Bosnian Muslims who were to be executed."[99]

With this kind of language, Muslims had become not even animals but inanimate objects.

The procedures of roundups and separations of men from women and children also reflected a total dehumanizing process. Serb nationalists herded, shoved, and beat people as if they were cattle. A witness at the Krstić trial described his experience:

> I got off the bus . . . with my child in my arms. My wife had her backpack on her back, and she was supporting my mother because she was old and very frail. My child was five years old. After we had got off the bus and had made just a few steps . . . one of those Serb soldiers pulled me by the shoulder and said, "Give the child to your wife and you come with us." I had to do that. So I gave the child to my wife. I tried to turn once again, because I knew that was the last time I would see my child. As a matter of fact, I was about to say something. I wanted to say anything, but then I couldn't. At that moment, the Serb soldier pushed me with his rifle and said, "Move on."[100]

Like other people forcibly deported at different times and in different places, the Muslims who were rounded up were utterly powerless before the armed might of the guards and troops around them. Their families were sundered, a deliberate tactic designed to heighten fear and, at the same time, weaken the ability to resist, since the victims could no longer rely on even the most basic resources of the family.

The extreme violence that Serb nationalists enacted upon Muslims was also a means of dehumanizing the victims and, of course, of spreading fear. One witness at the Hague Tribunal described his experience at the Omarska concentration camp:

> Senad Muslimovic . . . had already been much beaten . . . [when] he was called out of his room in the hangar, beaten as he went down the stairs to the hangar floor and met by a group who beat him severely, tied him to a large tyre bigger than himself and there beat and kicked him into unconsciousness. When he regained consciousness he was on his knees and a man was holding a knife to his throat and threatening to cut it but was told to "leave him for the end." That man then made to cut off his ear but instead stabbed him twice in his shoulder. He was then beaten again into unconsciousness and when he came to found himself hanging upside down suspended from the hangar roof, in which position he

was again beaten and kicked until he fainted. When he came to again he was lying on the floor, was beaten again, fainted yet again, came to once more and this time found himself lying in an inspection pit let into the hangar floor. He was taken out of the pit and allowed to return to his room in the hangar. He had suffered knife wounds to his right shoulder, knife cuts along his arms and feet, bruising, head pains and a broken jaw.[101]

How can one possibly explain the utter and complete brutality of Muslimović's beating at the hands of Serb nationalists? Yet it was not even the worst event to occur in Omarska.

Witness H was threatened with a knife that both his eyes would be cut out if he did not hold Fikret Harambasic's mouth closed to prevent him from screaming; G was then made to lie between the naked Fikret Harambasic's legs and, while the latter struggled, hit and bite his genitals. G then bit off one of Fikret Harambasic's testicles and spat it out and was told he was free to leave. Witness H was ordered to drag Fikret Harambasic to a nearby table, where he then stood beside him and was then ordered to return to his room, which he did. Fikret Harambasic has not been seen or heard of since.[102]

Women were also beaten:

A woman from . . . north-west Bosnia who had been kept in a primary school and had been exchanged for a Serbian army officer trembled as she described how she had been hit in the face by guards and how they had stamped on her feet: "My husband was next to me, he shook like a reed as they did this to me. We thought they would execute us. You cannot imagine the fear. He was a teacher and many of the guards had been his pupils. Some of them got very bad marks so they made him wear a woman's wig. They beat him every day.[103]

As with the other cases discussed in this book, the dominant regime established conditions that gave individuals free rein to enact their sadistic tendencies. Their violent actions, though, had political meaning. They were designed to terrorize the Muslim population, so that if not killed outright, they would flee in terror from the areas Serbs claimed as their own. Moreover, the utter humiliation and degradation experienced by Muslims, who not only endured the violence of Serbs but were forced to inflict acts of violence upon one another, could only destroy any sense of community among them. The destruction was total — of bodies, of conscience, of the sense of sociability that makes human life possible.

Serb nationalists also separated men and women because they treated them differently. In the wartime deportations in the Soviet Union, it seems that mostly women, children, and the elderly were rounded up, because many of the men were soldiers in the Red Army who only later were sent to the places of deportation. At Auschwitz, pregnant women or those with young children were slated for immediate execution. In Bosnia, it was men who were designated for execution. The ICTY's judgment in the Krstić trial described the process at Srebenica:

> Most of the mass executions followed a well-established pattern. The men were first taken to empty schools or warehouses. After being detained there for some hours, they were loaded onto buses or trucks and taken to another site for execution. Usually, the execution fields were in isolated locations. The prisoners were unarmed and, in many cases, steps had been taken to minimise resistance, such as blindfolding them, binding their wrists behind their backs with ligatures or removing their shoes. Once at the killing fields, the men were taken off the trucks in small groups, lined up and shot. Those who survived the initial round of gunfire were individually shot with an extra round, though sometimes only after they had been left to suffer for a time. Immediately afterwards, and sometimes even during the executions, earth moving equipment arrived and the bodies were buried, either in the spot where they were killed or in another nearby location.[104]

This action was, most obviously, a deliberate act of mass killing that had no military significance. In fact, as noted by Richard Butler, a U.S. intelligence officer and the prosecution's military expert, the Bosnian Serbs had a prime opportunity to use the Muslim men as a "bargaining chip" with the Bosnian government and the international community.[105] But that was not their intent. The point was to annihilate physically a significant proportion of a community.

Fear was an essential part of the killing process. At Srebenica, witnesses to the Hague Tribunal reported that some of the soldiers were dressed totally in black and walked around with dogs. Witnesses labeled some of the soldiers "Rambo types" who plundered houses, then burned them as well as crops in the fields, and dragged people off for beatings and killings. The so-called Drina Wolves wore an insignia depicting a wolf's head. Other paramilitaries covered their faces with scarves or stockings, or wore knit ski masks, adding a fearsome, anonymous aura to their presence.[106]

Even when they intended to kill their victims, Serb nationalists systematically humiliated them. The Hague Tribunal relayed the story of one witness who along with a few others had managed to survive a killing operation.

> Witness J somehow escaped injury and spent the night inside the warehouse hiding under a dead body. The next morning, the soldiers called out to see if any of the wounded men were still alive. Upon identifying some wounded prisoners, the guards made some of them sing Serb songs and then they killed them. After the last one had been killed, an excavator began taking the bodies out of the warehouse. A water tank was used to wash the blood off the asphalt.[107]

The perpetrators reveled in the power they exerted over the victims, which perhaps enabled them to justify to themselves their own wild transgressions of the normal rules of human interaction. And they forced even moderate Serbs to take part in executions. At Srebenica, General Mladić's men commandeered buses in Srebenica to deport women and children. The Serbian bus drivers, who were noncombatants, were "terrified," according to an eyewitness. They were each ordered to kill at least one Muslim. That way the soldiers would be sure that they would not testify against them. It also made the killings a communal event that bound all Serbs together.[108]

Guards and troops also dragged out the process of killing to humiliate the victims. As the judgment in the Krstić trial related:

> Another large group of about 1,500–2000 prisoners from Bratunac was driven north to the Petkovci School on the afternoon of 14 July 1995. As at the other detention sites, the conditions at Petkovci School were deplorable. It was extremely hot and crowded, the men had no food or water and some prisoners became so thirsty they resorted to drinking their own urine. Periodically, soldiers came in and beat the prisoners or called them out to be killed. . . . Eventually . . . the men were called out in small groups. They were told to strip to the waist, take off their shoes and their hands were tied behind their backs. Sometime during the night of 14 July 1995, the men were taken in trucks to a stony area near the

Petkovci Dam. As soon as they saw their destination the prisoners recognized their fate. Witness P recalls seeing a large "field" already filled with dead men lying face down with their hands tied behind them. Groups of five or ten prisoners were taken off the trucks. They were then lined up and shot. Some begged for water before being killed, but none was provided. Witness O recalled . . . "I was really sorry that I would die thirsty. . . . And then I thought that I would die very fast, that I would not suffer. And I just thought that my mother would never know where I had ended up." . . . In fact Witness O was only wounded and lay still expecting another round of gunfire to end his life. When the soldiers were finished with a round of killing, they laughed and made jokes: "Look at this guy, he looks like a cabbage."[109]

The victims were "packages" or "cabbages," anything but humans. The final act of humiliation and dehumanization came in the treatment of dead bodies. After managing to survive the killing operation, the witness quoted above crawled across a field that contained, he estimated, fifteen hundred to two thousand dead bodies. Hiding in the forests, he watched the next morning as earth-moving equipment scooped up the bodies to deposit them in mass graves.[110]

Execution was not the only fate of Muslims. The transcripts from the Hague trials describe in excruciating detail the rapes that many Muslim women suffered for days, weeks, and months on end. Sexual violence certainly occurred in the other cases discussed in this book, but Serb nationalists made it a systematic component of their genocidal practices. In convicting three Serbs for war crimes and crimes against humanity, the judges declared:

What the evidence shows, is that the rapes were used by members of the Bosnian Serb armed forces as an instrument of terror. . . . Serb forces . . . set up and maintain[ed] a detention centre for scores of Muslim women . . . from which women and young girls were taken away on a regular basis to other locations to be raped. . . . The authorities who were meant to protect the victims, such as the local police which had been taken over by the Serbs, turned a blind eye to their suffering. Instead, they helped guard the women, and even joined in their maltreatment when approached by them for help against their oppressors. . . . Muslim women and girls, mothers and daughters together, [were] robbed of the last vestiges of human dignity . . . treated like chattels, pieces of property at the arbitrary disposal of the Serb occupation forces, and more specifically, at the beck and call of the three accused.[111]

Like plunder, like executions, rape was a social act that involved large numbers of men. "Of the women and girls so detained," the judgment goes on, "one was a child of only 12 years at the time. She has not been heard of since she was sold by one of the accused. The women and girls were either lent or 'rented out' to other soldiers for the sole purpose of being ravaged and abused. Some of the women and girls were kept in servitude for months on end."[112] The rapists seem never to have been disciplined by higher Serbian authorities, which the men could only have understood as approval of their actions. At the same time the tribunal specifically stated that the men were not following orders to rape and doubted that such orders existed. "The evidence shows free will on their part."[113]

As if the physical violations were not enough, the women were continually taunted—that their bodies would be mutilated, that they would be killed, that the rapists had killed their brothers or uncles.[114] The Hague Tribunal could barely contain its rage at the accused. As Presiding Judge Florence Mumba declared in the decision against Radomir Kovač:

Particularly appalling and deplorable is your treatment of 12-year-old A.B., a helpless little child for whom you showed absolutely no compassion whatsoever, but whom you abused sexually in the same way as the other girls. You finally sold her like an object, in the knowledge that this would almost certainly mean further sexual assaults by other men.

You knew that any chance of her being re-united with her mother, whose immense grief the Trial Chamber had to countenance in the hearing, would thus become even more remote than it already was. At the time of trial, some 8 years later, the child had never been seen or heard of again. . . .

But what you did to the other girls is no less severe. You kept them as your and Jagos Kostic's slaves. . . . When they had served their purpose, you sold them, too.[115]

Judge Mumba accused Kovač of a "morally depraved and corrupt character." But it was, of course, the state-directed policies of war, forced deportations, and genocide that enabled people like Kovač to enact such brutalities against Muslim women. Serb nationalists eliminated physically Muslim men and raped Muslim women to prevent any semblance of a normal family and community life. Vive Žene is an independent social welfare agency in Bosnia that has dealt with the survivors of the Bosnian war. Its director testified at the Hague Tribunal that many child survivors show "low levels of concentration, nightmares and flashbacks." Health and social workers describe a "Srebenica Syndrome":

> The fate of the survivor's loved ones is not officially known: the majority of men of Srebenica are still listed as missing. For Bosnian Muslim women it is essential to have a clear marital status, whether widowed, divorced or married: a woman whose husband is missing does not fit within any of these categories. Moreover, on a psychological level, these women are unable to move forward with the process of recovery without the closure that comes from knowing with certainty what has happened to their family members and properly grieving for them. The Trial Chamber also heard of the collective guilt experienced by women because they survived the events in Potocari and their husbands, brothers and fathers did not. . . . This heartbreak and anguish is no better reflected than in the words of Witness DD whose young son was torn away from her in Potocari: "I keep dreaming about him. I dream of him bringing flowers and saying, 'Mother, I've come.' I hug him and say, 'Where have you been, my son?' and he says, 'I've been in Vlasenica all this time.' "[116]

To a certain extent, Serb nationalists were successful. They destroyed Muslim lives — including those of the survivors, haunted by the traumas of the past — and demolished multinational Yugoslavia, making its reconstruction impossible.

CONCLUSION

The number of dead and wounded from the Yugoslav wars remains disputed, as is generally the case with events of such magnitude. In November 1995 the CIA estimated 156,600 civilian deaths in Bosnia, which did not even include the more than 7,000 men still missing from Srebenica and Žepa, and 81,500 combatant deaths (45,000 Bosnian government, 6,500 Bosnian Croat, and 30,000 Bosnian Serb).[117] Others contend that these numbers are much too high, but a figure of around

200,000 deaths, around 50 percent Muslim, 30–35 percent Serb, 15–20 percent Croat, is probably correct.[118] The number of rapes is even harder to determine. The UN Human Rights Commission found evidence of approximately 12,000 rapes, the majority committed by Serbs. The political scientists Burg and Shoup consider this figure a "conservative estimate."[119] The CIA estimated that 900,000 to 1.2 million refugees had fled Bosnia for other countries, and an additional 1.3 to 1.5 million within the country, almost half of whom were Muslim, had also been forced out of their homes. Nearly 500,000 Serbs and 150,000 Croats had also been made refugees.[120]

These are staggering figures. More than one-half of the total prewar population of Bosnia had been displaced. The economic disaster was no less staggering: the World Bank estimated that war damage in Bosnia amounted to $50 billion and includes half the capital stock. To this one has to add losses of $20 billion in the Croatian war and $30 billion in Serbia and Kosovo in 1999.[121] Serbia, meanwhile, experienced a hyperinflation that was one of the worst ever recorded. From October 1993 to January 1994 the inflation rate reached 500 trillion percent; on 12 January 1994 it ran at 338 percent per hour.[122]

How can these events be understood? In contrast to the three other cases discussed in this book, the forced deportations and genocides conducted by the Serbian state seem to have revolved less around a heady, revolutionary ideology directed toward the creation of a utopian society populated by the new man and woman, more around the desperate efforts of an old elite to hold on to power as the ground shifted from under them. The potency of the national idea provided them with a formidable means of popular mobilization, through which they hoped to maintain and expand their authority.

Yet Milošević, his allies, and his adversaries carried out in the former Yugoslavia such a fundamental transformation of state and society, one that reached down so deeply into every aspect of people's lives, that their efforts bear the appellation of "revolution."[123] At the federal level, they conducted a political revolution that dismantled the existing state structure and placed, in its stead, particular national states. In Serbia they sought first to sustain communism via Serbian nationalism, then essentially abandoned communism, as the legitimating ideology, for an extreme nationalism that led easily into ethnic cleansing and genocide.

Within the republics, the particular leaders also carried out revolutions, but ones that did not always entail a frontal assault on existing institutions. Milošević's Serbia is, again, the best example. As was the case with the Third Reich, the state, army, and party were all recast from within, and parallel institutions like paramilitary units were established alongside existing agencies. In all the republics, and especially Serbia, the leaders purged the state administration and army of political opponents and people of a different nationality. Significantly, the newly elected Serbian legislature of the early 1990s was older, more politically experienced, and far more masculine than its predecessor, indicating Milošević's political base among old-line communists who were opposed to the reform efforts sweeping through the Soviet bloc.[124]

At the same time, "new men" came to the fore, notably Franjo Tudjman and Alija Izetbegović, nationally minded politicians who had served prison terms under the old regime. Many Serb nationalist leaders in Bosnia and Croatia were professionals and midlevel functionaries. Like the Bosnian Serb leader and psychiatrist Radovan Karadžić, they were people who occupied positions of standing but were far from the very top in the former Yugoslavia. Others, like the infamous Arkan, were criminals who found war profiteering a lucrative activity that they conducted alongside ethnic cleansing.[125] The revolutionary transformation of state and society in the context of war offered all these people a great opportunity to assume leadership roles and to revel in the prominence, power, and wealth that they achieved. It also gave their followers a newfound sense of purpose: Arkan's Tigers absorbed gangs of soccer hooligans, who were transformed into disciplined soldiers for the Serbian cause. Their inclination for violence moved from brawls at soccer stadiums to the more systematic, lethal campaign of genocide directed against Muslims.[126]

Most significantly, Milošević and Tudjman and their respective allies pursued the revolutionary transformation of society. Whatever their motivations, be it desire for power or ideological commitment, they sought to create ethnically homogeneous societies, a Serbia only for Serbs and a Croatia only for Croats. They sought to remake radically patterns of mixed settlement that had existed for centuries, and to reverse more recent innovations like mixed marriages. Especially in Bosnia, communities existed side by side with varying levels of tension, but also cooperation, even to the extent that Muslims and Catholics in one village supported one another's construction of mosques and churches.[127] In the sharpest contrast, Serb nationalists refashioned a significant segment of the Serbian population into the willing agents and bystanders of radical population politics, ultimately succeeding in breaking the bonds of tolerance and even cooperation that had existed in some towns and villages. Milošević and Tudjman both launched massive projects of demographic engineering, and it is hard to imagine anything more revolutionary — and more dismaying — than the state-sanctioned massacres at Srebenica, the forced removal of hundreds of thousands of Kosovars, or the seesaw pattern of ethnic cleansings in Krajina, where first Croats and then Serbs were forced out of areas they had populated for generations. By making multinationality unthinkable and unbearable, Serb and Croat nationalists sought to create radically new societies in the South Slav lands. They promised their respective followers that in a nationally pure state, their own people would flourish as never before. Freed from mundane exactions — monetary transfers to the less wealthy Yugoslav states, for example — as well as the supposed oppression of a federal state supposedly dominated by the other nationality, Serbs or Croats would become prosperous, and their cultures would flower. Territorial aggrandizement formed a key element of these national dreams. Expansion, ethnic cleansing, and genocide went hand in hand — just as it did for the Nazis, though, admittedly, the Nazis claimed as their own and expected to conquer a far larger territory.

The national ideology was couched in such extreme terms that it can properly be called a racialized nationalism. Unlike, for example, the perpetrators of the Armenian genocide, some of whose potential victims could escape death by adopting Islam, Serb nationalists offered Muslims no way out. To be sure, some ideologues asserted that Bosnian Muslims were "really" Serbs who had adopted the wrong religion. Theoretically, they could abandon Islam and revert to being the Serbs that they supposedly were in essence. But on the ground, there seem to have been no such cases in which Muslims were offered the choice of conversion. For all intents and purposes, they were categorized as a race with all the stigmas associated with racial typing. In toto Muslims were charged with being corrupt and mendacious; with the desire to swamp Western, Christian civilization through their high birthrate; with harboring designs upon Christian women; and with all sorts of horrendous acts against Serbs.

Enveloped in the world of extreme nationalism, Serb nationalists practiced in reverse the very acts of which they accused Bosnian Muslims. It was Serbs who carried out mass rapes, making sexual violence an intrinsic part of genocide. Rape had been the fate of numerous Armenian women. The Nazis had been preoccupied with Jewish sexuality, and despite the *Rassenschande* (race defilement) laws, sexual violence against Jewish women (and boys) certainly occurred and constituted a fixed feature of the occupation practices in general in eastern Europe. But in no other case discussed in this book was rape practiced so systematically as in Bosnia by Serb nationalists. The "little Četniks" they gloated about producing were never, ever intended to become members of a future Serb society.[128] Rather, rape served as the ultimate act of humiliation, an act that inscribed Serb nationalism in masculine terms, and that made multinationality completely unthinkable, because the survivors would always carry the trauma with them.

Modern Serbian and Croatian nationalism emerged in the nineteenth century, though both groups could claim a much longer history. But it was also the communist system itself that promoted nationalism despite Tito's repression of its overt expressions. The Yugoslav system had institutionalized national identities as the basis of politics and the key criterion for the distribution of resources. The goal was to maintain a carefully calibrated balance among the groups, but the result was to support the saliency of national identities and to create competitions based upon nationality. When shorn of the communist emphasis on solidarity, nationalism manifested its worst excesses.

Moreover, the new leaders could not easily shed the trappings of communist power. Tudjman paraded around like a parrot-Tito, resplendent in a military uniform bedecked with medals. Milošević and the JNA officers had a commitment to communism based both on ideology and on the privileges they had been afforded by the Yugoslav system. Almost alone among communist party leaders in the wake of the revolutions of 1989–91, they were able to retain their hold on power, first by melding communism and Serbian nationalism and then by relying solely on nationalism. They demonstrated one very deadly way of managing the transition from communism.[129]

But did Serbian actions constitute genocide? There can be no question that the actions of the Serbian state and its allies entailed ethnic cleansing, but did they warrant the more serious historical and legal charge of genocide? The Hague Tribunal has answered in the affirmative by delivering a genocide verdict in one case and by indicting Milošević on an array of charges, including genocide. The tribunal delivered its verdict against Radislav Krstić, successively the deputy commander and then commander of the Drina Corps of the Bosnian Serb Army, specifically for the mass killings in Srebenica. In so doing, it held to the UN Convention's standard that killing a defined community "in part" falls under the definition of genocide. The Hague Tribunal maintained that the prosecutor did not have to demonstrate an intent to kill every last Muslim in Bosnia. A concerted effort to kill a portion of the community satisfied the legal definition. In describing the tribunal's reasoning, Presiding Judge Almiro Rodrigues noted that the Trial Chamber was not asserting that a prior plan of genocide existed. Nor did the fact that some Bosnian men survive mitigate the severity of the crime. Only the Serbian forces' military inability to pursue every single individual accounts for the fact that some Muslims survived. Rodrigues also noted that women, children, and the elderly were separated from adult men and were deported from Srebenica rather than killed. But the deliberate killing of around eight thousand Bosnian men constituted genocide because its results could only be the physical destruction of the community. As Rodrigues stated in the tribunal's summary judgment, "by deciding to kill all the men of Srebenica of fighting age, a decision was taken to make it impossible for the Bosnian Muslim people of Srebenica to survive."[130]

In the former Yugoslavia, the policies of discrimination and genocide virtually ran together. Unlike in Nazi Germany, where the genocide of Jews began eight years after increasingly severe discrimination, Serb nationalists banned Muslims from positions and public facilities at about the same time they initiated systematic deportations, killings, and rapes. But as in Nazi Germany, a mutual radicalization process was at work. Midlevel and rank-and-file nationalists in the JNA and the paramilitaries engaged in extreme violence; to the extent that their actions were not countermanded by higher officials—and they never were until late summer 1995 when Milošević finally felt compelled to break with the Croatian and Bosnian Serbs—they must have felt fully justified and supported. They probably thought that they were "working toward Belgrade" or "working toward Pale" (Bosnian Serb headquarters), just as Nazi officials thought they were "working toward the Führer." At some moments, express orders for extreme violence were given by the Bosnian Serb authorities, while Milošević generally supported the actions on the ground through his constant rhetoric about the Serb nation and, more efficaciously, with the supplies and free rein he gave to the JNA and paramilitaries in Croatia and Bosnia. It seems clear that the intent of the Yugoslav government and its allies was to create an ethnically homogeneous state through the most violent means possible, including forced deportations; massacres of the Muslim elite and, in some instances like Srebenica, the entire male population; and the exercise of terror against those who remained, including the systematic practice of sexual violence against women. Certainly, there were oppositional elements in Serbia and high levels of desertion from the JNA during the war. Yet as an eminently twentieth-century dictatorship, Serbia made ethnic cleansing and genocide a cause not only of the state but of the population as well.

Violent conflict in the Balkans, in the 1990s and in earlier periods, the historian Mark Mazower writes, "was not . . . the spontaneous eruption of primeval hatreds but the deliberate use of organized violence against civilians by paramilitary squads and army units; it represented the extreme force required by nationalists to break apart a society that was otherwise capable of ignoring the mundane fractures of class and ethnicity."[131] Serb nationalists not only destroyed people and communities. At Omarska, Srebenica, and all the other sites of systematic terror, they destroyed the very idea of a multinational Yugoslavia. It is difficult to imagine that idea's returning anytime in the foreseeable future.

Conclusion

The movements and regimes discussed in this book all articulated powerful visions of the future. Each of them promised to create utopia in the here and now. There were, of course, profound differences in the contours of the future societies they intended to create. The Thousand Year Reich was to be an explicitly racial order presided over by Aryans. More focused on race than on economics, the Nazis maintained key elements of the existing economic and state structures, though transforming them from within, and the traditional elites became, by and large, deeply complicit in the practices of the Third Reich. The Soviets, in contrast, claimed to be creating an egalitarian future for all peoples. To do so required that the state wrest the factories and estates from the hands of capitalists and aristocrats. Unlike the Nazis, the Soviets destroyed the power of the old elites and instituted a far more thorough transformation of the social structure. In the drive to create their own egalitarian order, the Khmer Rouge reproduced and radicalized Soviet and Chinese communist policies. In their view, however, both the Soviets and Chinese had allowed elements of the old society to creep back into the new, revolutionary system. The Khmer Rouge sought to surmount this problem by the immediate, lightning-like collectivization of all aspects of Khmer society. The creation of the Khmer utopia required the destruction of both the power of the urban elites and the traditional ways of life of the largely peasant population. For Serb nationalists, utopia would be a state cleansed of any "foreign" elements. Only in a nationally pure Greater Serbia could the Serbian people flourish. In this case, like the German one, the old elite was not destroyed. The irony here is that the old elite was a communist one with bases of power in the party-state and the army, which transformed itself as it sought to remake the composition of Serbian society.

These four regimes were certainly not the only ones to perpetrate atrocities in the modern era. Liberal states have committed genocides against indigenous and colonial populations. But the four cases discussed in this book were responsible for some of the worst events of the twentieth century. If these movements and regimes envisaged distinctive utopias, they shared a common orientation in their determination to remake fundamentally the societies and states they had either conquered or inherited. Moreover, their goals entailed much more than the establishment of new political elites or the creation of state-run industries and collectivized farms. In their overarching drive to found utopia, these four regimes sought to create the "new man" and the "new woman." To do so required a refashioning of individual consciousness, a disciplining and self-disciplining even of the honored members of the population. It also meant the implementation of collective population politics on a vast scale, the purging of substantial segments of the existing society, sometimes classified by their social class background and political orientation, but always involving the forced deportations and killings of people categorized by race and nation. The effort to transform the very composition of the population required a powerful state that could unleash its security forces and mobilize populations to do the work of exclusions and genocides. By remaking the nature of state and society so thoroughly, by so utterly transforming the conditions of life for so many people, all four regimes were revolutionary in character.[1]

In acting upon the ideologies of race and nation, they drew upon Enlightenment conceptions of human progress and nineteenth-century scientific advances that posited the possibility, indeed, the desirability, of improving society by shaping its very composition.[2] By the turn into the twentieth century, there were increasingly loud claims that some categories of the population were incapable of improvement and constituted a drag on the well-being of the population as a whole. Depending on who was speaking and where, the lower classes generally, promiscuous women, African-descended peoples, Jews, criminals, the mentally ill, or some combination of all of these might be identified as the threatening group. The future progress of society, in this view, depended upon the protection of enterprising, productive people from the negative influences of dissolute and degenerate ones. When such ideas were linked to racial and national identities, as they so often were, then entire populations could be categorized as dangers to the well-being of the dominant group. Genocide in the twentieth century was the ultimate expression of this perspective, a policy of working on the population to shape its literal character by the forced, violent elimination of groups defined as "alien" and threatening.

In accordance with its particular utopian vision, each of the regimes lauded some groups and despised others. But defining what constituted the criteria of election or dishonor, and who fit into each category, was a complex political process. The regimes sought to impose uniformity, to "fix" identities, yet the social realities they faced were invariably messier than their own categories. To be sure, it was relatively easy to identify a proletarian in Magnitogorsk or a Jew in Breslau, to distinguish a Vietnamese trader from a Khmer peasant or a Muslim from a Serb in Banja Luka. But what of the myriad cases of intermarriage or of generational mobility, the people who had perhaps one Jewish grandparent and were well assimilated into Christian German society, the son or daughter of a bourgeois who worked in a factory in Petrograd, the children of Khmer and Vietnamese, Muslim and Serb marriages? Moreover, the lines between class, religious, national, and racial identities were often highly permeable. The Soviet Union and Cambodia rhetorically honored workers and peasants. But even in communist societies class was never the sole operative criterion. At distinct moments in their revolutions, the Soviet Union lauded Great Russians, and Democratic Kampuchea elevated Khmers above all other ethnic groups. Communist regimes might have pursued people primarily because of their class functions or perceived risks to military security. Koreans in the Soviet Union, for example, had cross-border ties to their counterparts in Japanese-controlled Manchuria, while ethnic Chinese and Vietnamese in Cambodia very often played important commercial roles in the economy prior to the Khmer Rouge victory. But once the Soviet state defined every single Korean as a security risk, once the Khmer Rouge began to treat all Chinese and Vietnamese in Cambodia as, ipso facto, enemies of the state, then those regimes had "racialized" identities that initially were "merely" class or ethnic in origin.[3]

Invariably the regimes in question employed the powerful metaphors of "cleanness" and "purity," as well as "productivity," in relation to the honored groups. Both Soviet and Nazi rhetoric was replete with images of strong, virile, healthy men and (from the mid-1930s in the Soviet case) maternal women. The Nazis claimed that only Aryans were a "culture-producing" and economically productive people, who, therefore, were entitled to dominate others. Like the Nazis, the Soviets linked health and productivity, honoring proletarians and peasants both for producing the wealth of the nation and for leading wholesome lives. Serb nationalists, possessed of less grandiose ambitions than the Nazis, their sights set on the Balkans rather than the entire European continent, claimed that they alone among South Slav peoples were productive and healthy. Serbs were the "historic" people of the South Slav lands, who in the nineteenth and twentieth centuries had led courageous struggles for democracy and national independence.[4] Typically, Pol Pot lauded the *"clean"* victory of the Khmer Rouge.[5] Radio Phnom Penh reported that "a clean social system is flourishing throughout new Cambodia."[6]

Cleanliness and purity are terms that, necessarily, invoke their binary opposites, the unclean and the impure. Those who were considered unclean were an active source of pollution that threatened to contaminate the clean and the pure. Hence they had to be at least quarantined and, in the most extreme cases, eradicated altogether. From the very beginning, the rhetoric of the Russian Revolution was infused with the biologically charged language of "cleaning out," "social prophylaxis," and "purge" itself.[7] In relation to the ethnic and national groups deported from the late 1930s into the early 1950s, the Soviets spoke of "cleansing actions" against "suspect" or "enemy" nations, against social parasites or "vermin" (*parazity, vrediteli*). These "vermin" could not repent and join the socialist fold; their very being placed them outside the collective body. As sources of pollution (*zasorenost'*) or filth (*griaz*), they endangered the "health" of the social body.[8] Nazi propaganda, as is well known, was replete with images of Jewish uncleanliness and filth, most viciously in the propaganda film *Jud Süss*. The entire rhetoric of Nazi antisemitism was bound up with the purported dangers of pollution from "Jewish blood." The Khmer Rouge claimed that city people were impure and unclean, as were politically suspect "base people."[9] Peasants, they claimed, "have rid the areas of all vestiges of the old regime, cleaning up the village, wiping out old habits, and taking up the new revolutionary morals."[10] Serb nationalists popularized the very term "ethnic cleansing," though it had precedents under both the Nazi and Soviet regimes. Even Orthodox priests called for cleansings to be carried out by "the entire Serb population."[11]

For some of the powerful revolutionary systems of the twentieth century, the dirt that the anthropologist Mary Douglas famously described as "matter out of place" was, in fact, human matter, and it had to be eradicated through political action. In excluding "dirt," these systems were "positively reordering [the] environment, making it conform to an idea."[12]

In carrying out vast purges of their populations, these four regimes (and the late Ottoman one as well) drew upon prior political models, which they then radicalized. Both the Russian and Ottoman Empires had moved entire populations around, usually for security or economic development purposes. The Young Turks and the Bolsheviks were well aware of those precedents and acted in many ways like their imperial predecessors. But never had the sultans attempted to annihilate physically an entire population, nor had the czars ever tried to track down every single member of targeted populations and deport them in conditions of such complete deprivation. In what was probably the first genocide of the twentieth century, Imperial Germany almost completely annihilated the Herero of Southwest Africa. It is striking that the first German *Rassenschande* (racial defilement) laws were decreed in Southwest Africa, banning marriages between German settlers and African women, even retroactively, and depriving German males in these relationships of all rights and privileges accorded German citizens. These laws bear close similarities to aspects of the Nuremberg Laws. In 1940 — to close the circle — draft amendments to the Nuremberg Laws were discussed within the Nazi government. Specifically related to the colonial empire the Nazis fully expected to recapture, these amendments would have extended the ban on sexual relations between so-called Aryans and Jews to relations between Africans and Germans. It is again striking that a few individuals who would play important roles in the SS or in the academic and planning institutions with close ties to the SS had had direct experience in the colonies and functioned as mentors — literary, scientific, professional — to the younger generation of Nazi officials.[13]

Adolf Hitler was well aware of another precedent — the genocide of the Armenians. In an oft-quoted statement, he reportedly said, "Who, after all, speaks today about the annihilation of the Armenians?" His remarks were made not in regard to the Holocaust but in relation to the upcoming invasion of Poland.[14] To his officers he laid out a policy of ruthless repression and exploitation of Poles, including the uprooting of tens of thousands of people from their traditional areas of settlement in regions Germany claimed as its own. If not yet rationalizing a genocide, Hitler certainly used the Armenian example to allay the concerns of his officers about the brutalities expected of them toward a civilian population that he considered racially inferior. "Our war aim," he stated, "is not to attain a particular line, but the physical destruction of the enemy."[15]

The Soviet and Nazi regimes emerged directly out of World War I. The profound discontents and dislocations engendered by the war enabled both movements to seize power. But the lines of influence ran still more deeply. Because the industrial-scale killing of World War I inspired not just revulsion but also hope, fascination, and desire, World War I provided a new imagination of power and violence — and a new model for conducting politics.[16] The powerful states that sent millions of men to their deaths would be replicated, even strengthened, by the succeeding revolutionary regimes, which had few if any compunctions about engaging in massive political violence to restructure their populations. The two regimes transferred the culture of the battlefield to politics, advocating brutality and violence, including mass population purges, as the path to a higher order of existence. Through the militarization of the Russian Revolution, the Left also came to celebrate political violence as the means of progress. World War I created not only a culture of death but also a culture of killing — one that was often tied to the ideology of race and nation. It is no accident that one of the first modern campaigns of genocide, the late Ottoman Empire's slaughter of Armenians, occurred in the context of the war.

The two later regimes, Democratic Kampuchea and Serbia, were also linked back to World War I and the revolutions that ensued. The Khmer Rouge formed the last communist movement to seize power in the twentieth century, and they exercised it in the most radical conceivable manner. For all the apparently unique elements of their revolution — the immediate, complete evacuation of the cities, the belief that efforts of will could double and triple the rice harvest — their actions sit firmly in the lineage of communist politics established first in the Soviet Union. Yugoslavia was a creation of both world wars, an effort, in the postimperial, national age, to create some kind of blend of nation-state and multinationality. In destroying Yugoslavia, Slobodan Milošević and his allies used some of the techniques of communist rule, which they harnessed to the brutalities of population purges that both Nazis and Croatian fascists had pioneered in World War II. By constantly invoking the memory of Jasenovac, the Ustaša concentration and extermination camp, Serb nationalists sought to destroy the very idea of multinationality. By the viciousness of their actions, they destroyed multinationality in fact.

The systematic nature of the twentieth-century genocides discussed in this book required the organizing capacities of the modern state, its bureaucracies that slotted people into defined categories and its security forces that imprisoned, deported, and killed members of the targeted populations. Because these regimes asserted total claims over society, obliterating, at least theoretically, the distinction between public and private realms that is a defining feature of liberalism, they recognized no inherent limits to their intention to remake society. They were "project states" or, in the words of James C. Scott, authoritarian "high modernist" regimes.[17] The possession of state power and the ideological conviction of utopia gave them license to launch all sorts of huge projects, from the construction of dams through the massive deployment of human labor to reshaping the very composition of society by granting the honored members privileged access to resources and by interning, deporting, and, ultimately, killing the dishonored ones.[18] However, in carrying out genocides as well as other aspects of their policies, the regimes never relied solely on the employees of the state, whether soldiers or bureaucrats. They also mobilized their populations. As the historian Alf Lüdtke writes specifically about the Third Reich, but with words that can be generalized to the other cases: "The gruesome attraction of complicity [*Mitmachen*] operates in relation to exclusions and suppressions — and ultimately to murder actions. Participation [*Mit-Täterschaft*] in tormenting other human beings became an integral part of the 'work of domination,' such that the boundary between the guilt of a few and the innocence of many blended away."[19] The reverberations of World War I are clearly evident here as well: the corollary of total war, with its model of complete state organization of society and mobilization for military victory, was found in the revolutionary regimes of the twentieth century, which sought an even greater level of societal organization and mobilization to purify the population. Mobilization for extreme population politics joined people to the revolutionary cause, imbued them with its ideology and rituals — even if this meant a virtual civil war against their fellow citizens — in the effort to create a homogeneous society. Such efforts went far beyond the capabilities of states prior to the twentieth century and far beyond the claims of liberal states that, by definition, leave realms of society to private, autonomous self-organization.

As a critical element in the unfolding of genocides, the regimes mobilized people to do the work of population politics. They organized people to serve as the brigade leaders, social workers, and pioneers, but also the jailers, guards, torturers, and killers, of the revolution. Each of the regimes had large and powerful paramilitary and security forces that mobilized tens and hundreds of thousands of men whose major tasks entailed population purges — the Interior Ministry troops in the Soviet Union, the Nazi SS, the Khmer Rouge army, and Serbian paramilitaries like Arkan's Tigers, who operated in conjunction with Interior Ministry and regular army troops. In the more highly developed states of the Soviet Union and Nazi Germany, the regimes established separate bureaucracies that ran the extensive concentration camp systems, which employed thousands of people. They were complemented by those who worked in the "normal" state and party agencies, who cooperated in the ventures of deportations and killings by compiling lists of those to be removed, organizing transports, and supplying the security forces with war matériel. In all the cases, the circle of complicity extended still further to the population at large, to include those, for example, who watched gleefully as the Nazis or their auxiliaries killed Jews in market squares and synagogues or as Serbian forces killed Muslims. In all of the cases, neighbors and bystanders seized the properties of Jews, Crimean Tatars, Vietnamese, or Bosnian Muslims forced out of their homes. Genocides on the scale discussed in this book were possible only with the participation of these many thousands, some of whom were active agents in mass killings, others of whom reaped the benefits, material and otherwise, of the removal of their neighbors.[20]

The reasons why people allowed themselves to become mobilized in the service of the respective regimes, and of their genocidal policies in particular, were quite varied.[21] Some people were ideologically and politically committed to the new regimes. The heady enthusiasms inspired by these ideologies should never be underestimated. The communist vision of an egalitarian and prosperous future had enormous appeal to people around the globe, a basic fact sometimes forgotten in the postcommunist world. The Nazi ideal of a racially pure society that would dominate all of Europe also exercised an enormous attraction, as did the Serbian vision of the South Slav lands controlled by a nationally pure Serbian state. Many of those most committed to their respective ideologies had been hardened by years spent in tough organizational work when the prospects for imminent success appeared quite dim. All the Soviet leaders had spent time in prison and exile; many of the Khmer Rouge had moved around in the jungle, often just one step ahead of their very powerful enemies. Nazi leaders had rarely endured prison terms, but they were battle-hardened from street brawls with Communists and Social Democratic–led police forces. Almost alone, Serbian leaders had enjoyed the prestige and comforts of high office, but the movement they initiated also drew in many "new men," including gangsters, who had suffered criminal and political repression in Tito's Yugoslavia. For all of these people, the seizure of power represented the fulfillment of their grandest hopes, and they were intent now on implementing their ideas. Thousands more joined them after the victory, determined to be on the side of the winners.

Along with ideological convictions, many of these people were motivated by an inner, psychological drive for acceptance and by the thrill of belonging to the victorious side. As the partisans of the new order, these people — the old fighters and the newcomers — were the immediate beneficiaries and the most explicit practitioners of the new politics that the regimes fostered. The Red Army soldier and Cheka operative, the Nazi *Gauleiter* and SS officer, the Khmer Rouge commander, the Serb paramilitary soldier — all were imbued with a sense of grand self-confidence, even arrogance. They moved around with the swagger of power, clothed in the uniform of the revolution, and partook of the material benefits afforded those on the winning side, from better food to access to resources and power.

For the broad population, outward conformity and mass participation sometimes masked inner doubts and opposition. In societies ruled by party-states that exerted claims of total control and demanded total conformity, the outer and inner faces of authority relations were often in stark contrast with one another.[22] Schizophrenia became a social phenomenon. Many people attended rallies, mouthed slogans, and even worked in the bureaucracy because they sought the resources they needed, from basic items of food and shelter to opportunities for professional advancement and social mobility. Over time, many of them came to accept the ideological goals of the regime; they internalized the new structures of authority.[23] Still, the inner face might have been entirely different. Some people marched in demonstrations and were still hostile to the new order. Or they tried to retreat into a private world. The borders between inner and outer were never fixed, nor were the two realms ever completely separate.

The exercise of power and the mobilization of the population were never, then, solely matters of command. They were ongoing processes of negotiation, marked by conformity, compliance, distance, and withdrawal; by conviction and compromise; by fluid movement between inner and outer faces. Many people willingly complied with the new regimes and aided in the establishment of new authority relations — perhaps least so in Democratic Kampuchea, perhaps most powerfully in Nazi Germany. Yet at the same time, the reality of compulsion, of the exercise of naked force and violence, was ever present in these revolutions. Many people wore the outer face of compliance because of fear — of the loss of a job, of blocked opportunities for one's children, and, most egregiously, of bodily harm, and not just at the moment of beatings and torture. To quote Alf Lüdtke again:

> Violence does not only mean physical injury or the threat of physical injury, which at the specific moment can be felt as pain. In the foreground is *memory*, which is formed into *experience* — of further suffering, the symbolically transmitted presence of "older" suffering, and the fear bound up with it of the possibility of renewed suffering. Pain and fear, caused by the thorns that lie buried within the inner being, are at least as hard and durable in causing torment and, above all, degradation as the means of compulsion and violence that are felt at the moment the blows rain down upon the body.[24]

The four regimes that carried out genocides developed rituals as a means of binding the population to the new order and thereby securing legitimacy.[25] But two critical developments also altered the character of rituals in the twentieth century. First, the elaboration of rituals was designed to incorporate vast elements of the population, not just in the symbolic representation of power, but also in its implementation. More and more people become active agents, helping to formulate and execute policies, even, perhaps especially so, in dictatorial systems. The scale of politics became greatly enhanced in the twentieth century.[26] Second, the technical means emerged to reach ever larger segments of the population through print, radio, and film and the rapid movement of people and ideas via rail, road, and air. The technology of twentieth-century communications, from the rapidly reproducible leaflet to radio and smuggled cassette recordings, drew ever larger numbers into the world of politics, if as passively complicit as much as actively participant.[27] To be involved in revolutionary ritual, one no longer had to be in the physical space in which the performance was carried out. One could watch party rallies or newsreels in film theaters and then on television, or listen to them on radio. An individual might know that killings were being carried out in the name of Aryan Germany or Greater Serbia and become involved, not necessarily in the direct act of violence, but through actions of support — demonstrations, rallies, denunciations — for the regime that had initiated the killings.

Revolutionary regimes were quick to recognize the possibilities of such technologies, and both the Soviets and the Nazis were adept at using radio and film. They also orchestrated grand events, May Day or torchlight marches, huge party rallies, that were broadcast to the entire nation. Such events were artfully planned—the movement of the crowds immersed in a sea of flags, the arc of the lights, the immense height of the review stand and podium that the leaders mounted.[28] These were made possible by electrification and other new technologies, and by a new aesthetics of monumentality that also came out of World War I memorials. For those not physically present, the events were broadcast on radio and replayed on film in movie theaters. The Khmer Rouge used radio to reach the most remote parts of the country, broadcasting revolutionary songs and speeches. The very secrecy of the communist leadership inspired awe and fear, a sense conveyed even by the abstract name, "the Organization," given to the party. The Serb nationalists used radio broadcasts and the very palpable, immediate physical presence of armed soldiers to convey their drive to power, to inspire followers and cow opponents. All these rituals displayed the power of revolution and endowed the supporters with the fascination of belonging, while enhancing the sense of fear and domination among those targeted as the enemies.

The incorporation of the population through rituals involved also the most extreme aspect of regime politics, namely, genocide. Killing is a brute, physical act. It entails, most obviously, the exercise of complete domination, of ultimate power, over the victim. But the way people are killed is a ritual that carries layers of symbolic meaning, just as human sacrifice does in premodern societies. In genocides, the meanings of the act are conveyed to the thousands, even millions, of people involved, the perpetrators, bystanders, victims, and survivors, through the treatment of the body. As two scholars have written about the mass killings in Indonesia in 1965, when paramilitary gangs killed people by hacking them apart, dumping most of the body parts somewhere else, but leaving the organs in front of the victims' houses, "the body becomes not simply the means of death but a vehicle for effecting more traumatic symbolic and ritual violence."[29]

With a few exceptions, the phenomena associated with the genocides discussed in this book—roundups, deportations, killings—were notably similar across the specific cases.[30] Mass execution in gas chambers was a Nazi specialty, torture as a part of ritual confession was perfected by communists, and systematic sexual violence against women was a particular practice of Serb nationalists. But Nazis drove people out in deportations and death marches, and probably 40 percent of Jews were killed not at Auschwitz and the other death camps but in mass shootings and by the deprivations of transport and confinement.[31] Nazis, too, at times extracted confessions as acts of public humiliation from their Jewish victims and routinely tortured all sorts of other people.[32] Despite some limitations imposed by the *Rassenschande* laws, which made sexual relations between Germans and Jews a criminal act, the German army and the SS established brothels of Slavic women all around eastern Europe, and incidents of sexual exploitation appear in all the cases.

The immense brutalities depicted here were made possible by the complete powers granted to the perpetrators by the regimes they served. The new forms of political power created by the revolutionary regimes meant that those who carried out purges and killings had complete license, not only to murder, but also to humiliate and brutalize those under their domination. The perpetrators were also enormously inventive in the exercise of brutalities. They created their own rituals of violence, a sign of the centrality of popular participation in genocides. The Nazi guards who ran over children's bodies or deployed Zyklon B gas at Auschwitz, the Khmer Rouge cadres who selected ethnic Chinese or "new people" and tortured prisoners, the NKVD troops who deported Tatars, and the Serbs who beat Muslims at Srebenica — they all invented the brutalities they inflicted upon the targeted populations. And these were always social acts, carried out by groups of perpetrators acting in concert and witnessed by many others, victims, bystanders, and additional or future perpetrators. Indeed, the SS commandant of Dachau, Theodor Eicke, issued explicit regulations that beatings of prisoners were never to be carried out by an individual guard but always with others and with witnesses.

The brutalities they enacted were initiated and carried through under the immense pressure of conformity and often under the formal command structure of an army or security force. The individual perpetrators had, no doubt, a range of reactions, from inner revulsion to begrudging compliance to intense enthusiasm — the ever shifting boundaries of the inner and outer faces of authority relations.[33] Small, everyday gestures — common laughter, a slap on the shoulder, shared drinks — bound the perpetrators together in the enterprise of mass murder. Like other, less brutal forms, rituals of genocidal killings create emotional bonds among the perpetrators, joining them together in a structure of feeling and a community of action.[34]

And they were bound together by gender. Few were the women directly involved in such actions, even in Cambodia where the regime went to great lengths to mobilize them for the revolution. Women of the dominant group were, though, often complicit as bystanders who enjoyed the spectacles of violence, and as plunderers who seized the homes and other property of those who were removed. But the direct acts of violence in genocides and ethnic cleansings were overwhelmingly the work of men. These men were sometimes worn down by the killing; many times they killed simply because they were following orders. But many also derived thrills from the common devotion to a higher cause, from their immense power over other human beings, from the freedom to transgress wildly the normal boundaries of human interaction. They reveled in the killing, in the display of power and brutality. Others simply became numb.[35]

The perpetrators came as agents of the state. They carried the epaulets of power on their bodies: uniforms, fearsome insignia, jackboots, weapons of various kinds—these were the trappings of the NKVD troops who deported the Crimean Tatars, the Nazi concentration camp guards, Khmer Rouge soldiers, and Serbian paramilitaries. They arrived rapidly, often in screeching trucks or running in formation, with weapons displayed. Or they stood guard over their victims, beating or shooting them at will, or even trampling over their bodies, as was the case of the Roma and Sinti children. They spread fear, deliberately, by their display of power and by the fact, which quickly became apparent to the victims, that the perpetrators could take life at any moment.

The killers took control of a defined space, whether a building, camp, neighborhood, train car, or field. They surrounded the area with security forces, making escape nearly impossible. In guard towers or on the hills above an area, they attained visual domination over the victims. While individuals might be rendered inhuman by the blank look on a guard's face, as a mass the victims were subject to sweeping visual control.[36] The total power over space is fear-inspiring because it means control over the individual body: where it can move, where it cannot. This is the meaning of the concentration camp, pioneered by the Americans in the Philippines and the British in the Boer War, which then became one of the key features of the twentieth century. It is also the meaning of the places of roundup and selection, often the market square in a village or the meeting in open air or in a large hall, as when the Khmer Rouge separated out ethnic Chinese. The concentration camp, the marketplace, and the meeting hall, secured by troops, marked the ultimate control over humans-in-space. In the confined space of the camps, the guards were given license to brutalize and kill, and death became a routine, daily occurrence.[37] In these confined spaces, they were even free to shoot randomly, killing and maiming at will.

The killers also took control of that other dimension of human existence, time. They did not kill everyone immediately, not even at Auschwitz nor at Omarska, the concentration camp for Bosnian Muslims. They dragged out the process, for hours, days, months on end. Sometimes they knew that they would kill their victims; sometimes they just demonstrated a complete disregard for human life that, over time, led to death from deliberate deprivation and brutality. In face-to-face killings, they changed the rhythm of the process—going for long breaks, for example, while the victims waited in fear. They took their time, made a sport out of the terror they inspired. Such was the fate of many Jews and Roma and Sinti confined to concentration camps, and also of the victims in Tuol Sleng, the infamous Khmer Rouge prison.[38]

It is particularly difficult to make sense of the matter of confession when both the torturer and victim knew that the victim would in any case be killed. Clearly, torture is a form of total domination in which some people revel at the complete physical and psychological destruction they deliver to the individual. But the infliction of pain is always associated with the interrogation, the physical and verbal acts running together.[39] Torture rarely involves the eliciting of substantive information; it is about "deconstructing" and destroying the individual prisoner and, by extension, the groups he or she is said to represent.[40] Torture is "world-destroying," as Elaine Scarry says, and the rings of destruction radiate outward from the individual to family, friends, nation, the cause, all of which are inevitably betrayed in the confession extracted by torturers.[41] When prisoners were then forced to torture one another—a pattern that seems not to have been the case in the Soviet Union but was definitely practiced in Nazi Germany, Democratic Kampuchea, and, especially, Serbian concentration camps—the destruction of life-worlds was so enormous as to be almost indescribable.[42] The intent in these cases was to so utterly humiliate people, to so completely destroy the self and all the ties of family and community that make life possible, that all that was left to survivors—if there were survivors—was mere existence and unending pain and sorrow. The effects extended beyond the victims to the witnesses as well—and there were always, deliberately, other inmates who were forced to watch the transaction of torture. Even when the torture took place within a room, the confined space closing in ever more tightly around the victim, the torturers allowed the screams to be heard, and others could hear or see the victim as he or she was returned to the cell.[43]

As with killings, the torturers' actions were licensed by the murderous policies of the regimes they served. The revolutionary regimes of the twentieth century all revived and expanded the practice of torture, which had begun to wane from the Enlightenment and especially in the course of the nineteenth century.[44] Ironically, the immensely powerful revolutionary states of the twentieth century imagined enemies everywhere. Those who seek total power and are completely convinced of the rightness of their cause can explain failures only by treachery and sabotage, which leads to a continual, paranoiac search for enemies. Rule by terror has a way of folding in on itself, becoming an endless cycle that ultimately consumes its very perpetrators. As Hannah Arendt wrote, "Totalitarian domination based on terror . . . turns not only against its enemies but against its friends and supporters as well, being afraid of all power, even the power of its friends. The climax of terror is reached when the police state begins to devour its own children, when yesterday's executioner becomes today's victim."[45]

Yet this pattern of "devouring" the children of the revolution, of extracting ritualized confessions, seems typical not just of any police state but of communist ones in particular. Perhaps here we see a perverse transformation of the communist ideal of a harmonious society. The Nazis and Serb nationalists defined their enemies in overtly racialist or nationalist terms, by descent. Communist ideology, rooted in Enlightenment universalism, presumed that all human beings, regardless of descent, would come to see the light of communism. Hence the enemies had to be forced to confess their sins to find the path to the cause, even while their transgressions were so great that they had also to be killed. Torture demonstrated the power of the regime on the body of the victims; it was a "spectacle of absolute power."[46] On a more basic level, the torturers seem also to have enjoyed their complete domination, their ability to reduce the victim to a body in pain, closed in on itself so that all it knows is the hurt.[47] At Tuol Sleng their final power lay in the arbitrary decision of when finally to kill the individual whose fate had been sealed the moment he or she was arrested.

In the end, even the corpses of victims were denied dignity, thrown from freight cars, shoved around by bulldozers, left to rot or to be devoured by animals. The notion of the "body as a symbol of society . . . the powers and dangers credited to social structure reproduced in small on the human body" relates even to the dead body of those considered beyond the pale.[48] Like the body of a Crimean Tatar thrown from a train taking its passenger-load to the place of exile, the bodies of the Kolyma laborers were the final mark, real and symbolic, of the violent population politics of modern states. The corpses of the ensnared individuals—thrown, deposed, shoved, slashed—were denied the barest shred of respect, like the bodies of Jews burned in crematoria or those of Cambodians left to rot in the killing fields. The dead bodies were, indeed, like the logs the great Soviet author and Gulag prisoner Varlam Shalamov first took them to be. Violated in life, the bodies were degraded in death. And the degradation occurred not anonymously but at the hands of a guard on a transport leading a population into exile or of a fellow inmate who wielded the controls of a tractor.

Genocide is, then, a dual process. The perpetrators never acted solely on their own; they operated within a structure of action defined by regime goals. But they also created rituals of their own—running over children's bodies, delivering blows to particular body parts, shooting wildly into rooms, throwing corpses from trains—that gave meaning, chilling meaning, to the killings.

The genocides discussed in this book were not anarchic eruptions of age-old hatreds, nor the result of individuals and groups acting solely of their own accord. The killings took place within the larger frame of revolutionary politics centered on the reshaping of the composition of society. However random some of the killings, however arbitrary the fate of an individual as victim or survivor, the actions always involved some level of planning and unfolded within a larger regime context of domination and exclusion.

The genocides occurred at moments of extreme societal crisis, often generated by the very policies of the regimes. Although total wars, revolutionary politics, and ideologies of race and nation all provide critical historical context illuminating the depth and frequency of twentieth-century genocides, in the end such massive violations of human rights were the results of political decisions. There was nothing inevitable about any of the cases discussed in this book. Other revolutionary regimes in the past century exercised political repression but promoted multiracial ideologies that prevented the unfolding of the most extreme forms of population politics. There is, then, a very substantial element of contingency to the emergence of genocides related to very specific historical conjunctures.

The connection between genocides and extreme societal crisis is so critical because both war and revolution break standard codes of human interaction. Revolutions by definition overthrow the legal norms of a polity and, in the process, undermine existing legal and cultural constraints on human behavior. In wartime states typically impose emergency conditions that give officials the freedom to act in ways they would not dare venture in peacetime. The upheavals of revolution and war heighten the sense of insecurity, leading to calls for swift and forceful actions to remove those who are seen as dangers to the national cause or to the creation of the new society. At the same time, wars open up vistas of pleasure in the future and present great opportunities for vast restructurings of societies and populations. Wars and revolutions are by definition also violent acts; they create cultures of violence and killing. This was especially the case in the twentieth century because total war required the mobilization of entire societies in the enterprise of violence. The battlefields of World War I set standards of violence that revolutionary states sought to replicate in their deliberate purges of defined population groups.

Hence it was not accidental that the Armenian genocide occurred in the crisis setting of World War I; that the Soviet purge of nationalities began during the decade of the "great transformation," when the immense upheavals of crash industrialization and forced collectivization created social havoc, and then became still more extensive amid the cataclysm of the German invasion in World War II; that the systematic discrimination against Jews in the Third Reich escalated into genocide only in the context of total war; that in Democratic Kampuchea the purge of city dwellers and then mass killings of minority populations and anyone deemed hostile to the new society occurred amid the immense disruptions of traditional Cambodian society caused by the American bombings and the flush enthusiasms of revolutionary victory; and that the ethnic cleansings and genocides of Muslims in Bosnia and Kosovo occurred within a state order that had become extremely unstable, and in which wars of separation quickly escalated into violent purges of populations.

Genocides are deadly to the victims; they are also events whose corrupting character travels deep into the population. The successors to the societies that have been consumed by mass violence cannot escape the legacy; they remain overburdened by the past, precisely because of the participatory nature of genocides in the modern era.[49]

Is it possible, then, to move beyond the brutal and corrupting nature of these events, to envisage a world without genocide? Among the many factors that I have tried to lay out as causes for genocides, the ideologies of race and nation have been fundamental. Race thinking emerged around 1500 with the European explorations. It developed in tandem with New

World slavery and, especially, with eighteenth-century scientific, social, and political developments. It has nothing to offer as the basis for building a more humane, less violent world. The nation-state is more problematic. It has been the vital locus of popular sovereignty and political rights in the modern world. But along with racial models, the belief that the state should be the representative of one single people, and that only those people should live within its bounded territory, has also been the source of many of the tragedies discussed in this book. It took 130 years, from the French Revolution in 1789 to the Versailles Treaty in 1919, for the nation-state to become the dominant form of political organization in the West, another 40 years or so, to the end of colonial empires, for the nation-state to become universal. In a vastly accelerated world, it should be possible to envisage the waning of the nation-state over, say, the next 50 years.

The United Nations Security Council convened in the 1990s two international tribunals, one in the Hague for the former Yugoslavia, the other in Arusha for Rwanda. The Genocide Convention formed the legal basis of their writ, along with the Universal Declaration of Human Rights (adopted by the UN General Assembly on 10 December 1948, one day after the adoption of the Genocide Convention) and the precedents of the Nuremberg and Tokyo War Crimes Tribunals.[50] Both the Hague and the Arusha Tribunals have indicted and convicted officials of both states, Serbia and Rwanda, on charges of genocide, and they have also convicted some of the major perpetrators of the "lesser" counts of war crimes and crimes against humanity. These events are major advances in international human rights and direct responses to the issues and cases discussed in this book. We are moving, slowly and hesitantly to be sure, toward a new international order in which the world community seems more willing to intervene in cases of massive violations of human rights. Those rushing to commit genocide might think twice because of the courtrooms and verdicts that might await them. Scholars can discuss endlessly the weak points of the Genocide Convention, but its increasing centrality to international affairs and international human rights — after it lay in virtual abeyance for some 40 years — suggests that some caution is warranted before it is intellectually dismantled and reconfigured.[51]

The Czech president and human rights advocate Václav Havel has spoken of a future devolution of power from the nation-state to the levels above and below, to transnational and global organizations and to the manifold institutions of civil society. States should become "far simpler and more civilized entities," he argues, and not the objects of emotional attachment. The global community, not the nation-state, should be the locus of sovereignty and the source and protector of basic human rights.[52] Havel's position might seem hopelessly idealistic. But the modern state, when linked to the ideologies of nation and race, has been the source of the genocides discussed in this book and many other cases of massive human rights violations around the globe. Havel's suspicion of the state, especially when populations invest in it so much hope and desire, is well founded. He has not proclaimed a future utopia but has articulated a long-term political project that, in some ways, began in the late 1940s with the UN's Universal Declaration of Human Rights and Genocide Convention—the assertion and protection of political liberties and human rights at the level not only of individual states but of the international community as well. Coupled with the notable advances in human rights enforcement over the last few years, that political vision holds the best chance for making genocides a part of our history, not our present.

notes

Unless otherwise noted, all translations throughout the text are mine.

An Armenian Prelude

1. Johannes Lepsius, *Bericht über die Lage des Armenischen Volkes in der Türkei* (Potsdam: Tempelverlag, 1916), v.

2. Jackson to Morgenthau, 3 August 1915, U.S. State Department Record Group 59, 867.4016/126, in *United States Official Documents on the Armenian Genocide*, vol. 1, *The Lower Euphrates*, ed. Ara Sarafian (Watertown, MA: Armenian Review, 1993), 39–41, quotation 39. See also *The Treatment of Armenians in the Ottoman Empire: Documents Presented to Viscount Grey of Fallodon, Secretary of State for Foreign Affairs by Viscount Bryce* (London: Hodder and Stoughton, 1916); reprint, ed. Ara Sarafian (Princeton, NJ: Gomidas Institute, 2000).

3. Ibid., 41

4. The unfortunate distinction for the first genocide of the century probably belongs to the Herero of German Southwest Africa, followed soon thereafter by the Armenians.

5. Lepsius, *Bericht über die Lage des Armenischen Volkes*, 21–23.

6. For effective syntheses and analyses, see Richard G. Hovannisian, "The Historical Dimensions of the Armenian Question, 1878–1923," and Robert Melson, "Provocation or Nationalism: A Critical Inquiry into the Armenian Genocide of 1915," both in *The Armenian Genocide in Perspective*, ed. Richard G. Hovannisian (New Brunswick, NJ: Transaction, 1986), 19–41, 61–84. For a variety of perspectives, see Ronald Grigor Suny, "Empire and Nation: Armenians, Turks, and the End of the Ottoman Empire," *Armenian Forum* 1:2 (1998): 17–51, with critical responses by Engin Deniz Akarli, Selim Deringil, and Vahakn N. Dadrian and a final rejoinder by Suny, 53–136. For the most thorough history of the genocide, see Vahakn N. Dadrian, *The History of the Armenian Genocide: Ethnic Conflict from the Balkans to Anatolia to the Caucasus*, 3d ed. (Providence: Berghahn, 1997), though I disagree with his argument for long-term continuity in Ottoman policies in relation to the Armenians. See

also Taner Akçam, *Armenien und der Völkermord: Die Istanbuler Prozesse und die türkische Nationalbewegung* (Hamburg: Hamburger Edition, 1996).

7. Reports from Cilicia and eastern Anatolia in Lepsius, *Bericht über die Lage des Armenischen Volkes*, 13–14, 24–26, and passim.

8. I am relying on Melson's conclusions in "Provocation or Nationalism," 64–67. As in every case of genocide, much uncertainty exists about the exact numbers. Estimates for the number of Armenian victims range from a few hundred thousand to 1.5 million.

9. Lepsius, *Bericht über die Lage des Armenischen Volkes*, 155.

10. See Dadrian, *History of the Armenian Genocide*, and Melson, "Provocation or Nationalism." The Turkish government continues to deny this conclusion and has significant support from some scholars.

11. Henry Morgenthau, *Ambassador Morgenthau's Story* (Garden City, NY: Doubleday, 1918), 351–52.

12. For some reports of Turkish efforts to aid Armenians, see Lepsius, *Bericht über die Lage des Armenischen Volkes*, 156–57.

INTRODUCTION
Genocides in the Twentieth Century

1. Lemkin's major work is still very much worth reading: *Axis Rule in Occupied Europe* (Washington, DC: Carnegie Endowment for International Peace, 1944). The text of the Genocide Convention is widely available, including *http://www1.umn.edu/humanrts/instree/xlcppcg.htm* [27 August 2002]. The count of 142 countries as party to the Convention as of 18 March 1996 comes from *http://serendipity.magnet.ch/more/con_geno.html* [23 October 2002].

2. For good reviews of the scholarly debates, see Eric Markusen, "The Meaning of Genocide as Expressed in the Jurisprudence of the International Criminal Tribunals for the Former Yugoslavia and Rwanda: A Non-Legal Scholar's Perspective" (paper presented at the Association of Genocide Scholars conference, Minneapolis, MN, June 2001); Frank Chalk and Kurt Jonassohn, *The History and Sociology of Genocide: Analyses and Case Studies* (New Haven: Yale University Press, 1990); and Helen Fein, "Genocide: A Sociological Perspective," *Current Sociology* 38:1 (1990): 1–126. For the ongoing discussion, see especially the *Journal of Genocide Research*.

3. Chalk and Jonassohn, *History and Sociology of Genocide*, 8–10, and Lemkin, *Axis Rule*.

4. For a strong argument in favor of abiding by the UN Convention in scholarly research, see Ben Kiernan, "Sur la notion de génocide," *Le Débat*, March–April 1999, 179–92. For various other perspectives, see Uwe Makino, "Final Solutions, Crimes against Mankind: On the Genesis and Criticism of the Concept of Genocide," *Journal of Genocide Research* 3:1 (2001): 49–73; Mihran

Dabag and Kristin Platt, eds., *Genozid und Moderne: Strukturen kollektiver Gewalt im 20. Jahrhundert* (Opladen: Leske und Budrich, 1998); Chalk and Jonassohn, *History and Sociology of Genocide*; and Leo Kuper, *Genocide: Its Political Use in the Twentieth Century* (New Haven: Yale University Press, 1981).

5. To cite just a few examples: Alex Alvarez, *Governments, Citizens, and Genocide: A Comparative and Interdisciplinary Approach* (Bloomington: Indiana University Press, 2001); Chalk and Jonassohn, *History and Sociology of Genocide*; Fein, "Genocide"; and Kuper, *Genocide*.

6. For another example of a "middle-ground" comparison, see Norman M. Naimark, *Fires of Hatred: Ethnic Cleansing in Twentieth-Century Europe* (Cambridge: Harvard University Press, 2001).

7. This is the highly tendentious argument of historians and ideologues who strive to diminish the crimes of National Socialism, notably Ernst Nolte, who argues that the Nazi regime simply adopted practices pioneered by the Soviets. Among other works, see Nolte, *Der europäische Bürgerkrieg 1917–1945: Nationalsozialismus und Bolschewismus* (Berlin: Propyläen, 1987), and his contributions to the *Historikerstreit*, in *Forever in the Shadow of Hitler? Original Documents of the Historikerstreit, the Controversy concerning the Singularity of the Holocaust*, ed. and trans. James Knowlton and Truett Cates (Atlantic Highlands, NJ: Humanities Press, 1993). But more careful historians, too, sometimes slip into assuming that a causal link existed between the policies of the Soviet Union under Stalin and the Third Reich, as did the eminent French historian François Furet in *The Passing of an Illusion: The Idea of Communism in the Twentieth Century*, trans. Deborah Furet (Chicago: University of Chicago Press, 1999; French original 1995), and in his correspondence with Nolte, published first in the French journal *Commentaire*, then gathered together in François Furet and Ernst Nolte, *Fascisme et communisme* (Paris: Plon, 1998).

8. For the most extensive defense of the uniqueness position, see Steven T. Katz, *The Holocaust in Historical Context*, vol. 1, *The Holocaust and Mass Death before the Modern Age* (New York: Oxford University Press, 1994). See also Avishai Margalit and Gabriel Motzkin, "The Uniqueness of the Holocaust," *Philosophy and Public Affairs* 25:1 (1996): 65–83, whose argument that only Jews were subject to deliberate humiliation before being killed I find completely untenable. For various positions, see Alan S. Rosenbaum, ed., *Is the Holocaust Unique? Perspectives on Comparative Genocide* (Boulder: Westview, 1996).

9. The term "social project" is Tim Mason's, and he applied it to fascist states in particular. But it certainly is relevant to communist states as well. See *Nazism, Fascism and the Working Class: Essays by Tim Mason*, ed. Jane Caplan (Cambridge: Cambridge University Press, 1995). See also Charles Maier, *Dissolution: The Crisis of Communism and the End of East Germany* (Princeton: Princeton University Press, 1997), 53, 57.

CHAPTER ONE
Race and Nation: An Intellectual History

1. "Universal Declaration of Human Rights," General Assembly res. 217A (III), U.N. Doc A/810 at 71 (1948). Text available at *http://www1.umn.edu/humanrts/instree/b1udhr.htm* [27 August 2002].

2. The major discussions were over whether the word "color" should be added to the document in addition to "race," and whether "national," "nationality," or "national origin" was the appropriate term. See Johannes Morsink, *The Universal Declaration of Human Rights: Origins, Drafting, and Intent* (Philadelphia: University of Pennsylvania Press, 1999), 102–5

3. Edward Steichen, *The Family of Man* (1955; New York: Museum of Modern Art, 1997). Information on the exhibition from *http://www.moma.org/research/archives/highlights/1955.html* [29 August 2002] and *http://www.clervaux-city.lu/index1.htm* [29 August 2002]. *The Family of Man* is now on permanent exhibit at the Château de Clervaux, Luxemburg.

4. See Werner Conze, "Rasse," in *Geschichtliche Grundbegriffe: Historisches Lexikon zur politisch-sozialen Sprache in Deutschland*, ed. Otto Brunner, Werner Conze, and Reinhard Koselleck (Stuttgart: Ernst Klett, 1984), 5:135–78, and Léon Poliakov, *The Aryan Myth: A History of Racist and Nationalist Ideas in Europe*, trans. Edmund Howard (New York: Basic Books, 1971), 136–37. Poliakov claims that the term "race" derives from the Arabic *ras*, but the etymology seems much disputed. In any case, it is clear that aside from some scattered and isolated uses in the medieval period, the word "race" became prevalent in the Romance and Germanic languages beginning in the sixteenth century.

5. See the very interesting, older article by Guido Zernatto, "Nation: The History of a Word," *Review of Politics* 6:3 (1944): 351–66.

6. See François Hartog, *The Mirror of Herodotus: The Representation of the Other in the Writing of History*, trans. Janet Lloyd (Berkeley and Los Angeles: University of California Press, 1988).

7. Herodotus, *The Histories*, trans. Aubrey de Sélincourt, rev. ed. John Marincola (1954; London: Penguin, 1996), 4.16–29 (pp. 222–26), 4.64 (p. 235).

8. Josh. 6:21–24.

9. For example, ibid., 8:24, 10:38, 11:20.

10. Ibid., 8:29, 10:26–27.

11. "And the Lord said to Samuel: 'Listen to the voice of the people in all that they say to you; for they have not rejected you but they have rejected me from being king over them.'" 1 Sam. 8:7.

12. Ps. 87:4–6.

13. Frank M. Snowden, Jr., *Before Color Prejudice: The Ancient View of Blacks* (Cambridge: Harvard University Press, 1983), 44–46.

14. Col. 3:11.

15. See Snowden, *Before Color Prejudice*, 82–87; Herodotus, *Histories* 9.122 (p. 543).

16. Herodotus, *Histories* 4.76–80 (pp. 239–41).

17. Ibid. 2.30 (pp. 96–97).

18. The Greeks, writes the classicist Frank Snowden, "developed no special theory concerning the inferiority of blacks" (*Before Color Prejudice*, 87, generally 85–87). And if that was the case, then there could be no special theory of "whiteness," the one being logically dependent upon the other.

19. See the section on Henry of Le Mans in Walter L. Wakefield and Austin P. Evans, eds. and trans., *Heresies of the High Middle Ages: Selected Sources* (New York: Columbia University Press, 1969), 108–9, 112–13, 122, 124. Some of these comments are by anonymous sources, others by the famed Bernard of Clairvaux.

20. On the latter point, see, for example, James H. Sweet, "The Iberian Roots of American Racist Thought," *William and Mary Quarterly* 54:1 (1997): 143–66.

21. For a review of the literature and critique of this thesis, see David Nirenberg, *Communities of Violence: Persecution of Minorities in the Middle Ages* (Princeton: Princeton University Press, 1996).

22. For a recent important and learned discussion along these lines, which emphasizes the instability and fluidity of premodern ethnic categorizations and depictions of blackness, see Benjamin Braude, "The Sons of Noah and the Construction of Ethnic and Geographical Identities in the Medieval and Early Modern Periods," *William and Mary Quarterly* 54:1 (1997): 103–41. See also Nicholas Hudson, "From 'Nation' to 'Race': The Origin of Racial Classification in Eighteenth-Century Thought," *Eighteenth-Century Studies* 29:3 (1996): 247–64. I find Braude's contribution more convincing than Sweet, "Iberian Roots," both published in the same thematic issue of the *William and Mary Quarterly* devoted to the construction of race.

23. Rogers Brubaker and David D. Laitin, "Ethnic and Nationalist Violence," *American Review of Sociology* 24 (1998): 428 n. 1, contend that the term "ethnic" encompasses "nationalist," but this position seems misplaced to me.

24. On the definitions of ethnicity and nationality, see some of the excellent collections that have appeared in recent years, such as Montserrat Guibernau and John Rex, eds., *The Ethnicity Reader: Nationalism, Multiculturalism, and Migration* (Cambridge: Polity, 1997); Geoff Eley and Ronald Grigor Suny, eds., *Becoming National: A Reader* (New York: Oxford University Press, 1996); Omar Dahbour and Micheline R. Ishay, *The Nationalism Reader* (Atlantic Highlands, NJ: Humanities Press International, 1995); and John Hutchinson and Anthony D. Smith, eds., *Nationalism* (Oxford: Oxford University Press, 1994).

25. I am drawing here on the recent theoretical and historical literature on race, e.g., George M. Fredrickson, *Racism: A Short History* (Princeton: Princeton University Press, 2002); idem, *The Comparative Imagination: On the History of Racism, Nationalism, and Social Movements* (Berkeley and Los Angeles: University of California Press, 1997); Ronald Aminzade, "The Politics of Race and Nation: Citizenship and Africanization in Tanganyika," *Political Power and Social Theory* 12 (2000): 51–88; Stephen Cornell and Douglas Hartmann, *Ethnicity and Race: Making Identities in a Changing World* (Thousand Oaks, CA: Pine Forge Press, 1998); Eduardo Bonilla-Silva, "Rethinking Racism: Toward a Structural Interpretation," *American Sociological Review* 62:3 (1997): 465–80; Michael Omi and Howard Winant, *Racial Formation in the United States: From the 1960s to the 1990s*, 2d ed. (New York: Routledge, 1994); Étienne Balibar and Immanuel Wallerstein, *Race, Nation, Class: Ambiguous Identities* (London: Verso, 1991); and David R. Roediger, *The Wages of Whiteness: Race and the Making of the American Working Class* (London: Verso, 1991). I leave aside some differences on particular issues among these authors and stress the common features of their interpretations.

26. See Fredrickson, *Racism*, who writes that it is "when differences that might otherwise be considered ethnocultural are regarded as innate, indelible, and unchangeable that a racist attitude or ideology can be said to exist" (5).

27. Notably, one strand in the development of racial ideology originated as a defense of aristocratic class privilege in eighteenth-century France. See the discussion of the comte de Boulainvillier's writing in Hannah Arendt, "Race-Thinking before Racism," *Review of Politics* 6:1 (1944): 36–73, here 42–47, and in Ivan Hannaford, *Race: The History of an Idea in the West* (Washington, DC: The Woodrow Wilson Center Press, 1996), 188, 195–96.

28. See especially Cornell and Hartmann, *Ethnicity and Race*, 15–38, and Omi and Winant, *Racial Formation*.

29. Balibar, "Is There a 'Neo-Racism?'" in idem and Wallerstein, *Race, Nation, Class*, 22, emphases in original. See also the similar formulation in George M. Fredrickson, "Understanding Racism: Reflections of a Comparative Historian," in idem, *Comparative Imagination*, 84–85.

30. For a very forceful argument about the modernity of New World slavery, see Robin Blackburn, *The Making of New World Slavery: From the Baroque to the Modern, 1492–1800* (London: Verso, 1997).

31. There is, of course, an immense literature on the connection of race and slavery, which goes back at least to Eric Williams: "Slavery was not born of racism: rather, racism was the consequence of slavery," which is the general approach I follow. See Williams, *Capitalism and Slavery* (Chapel Hill: University of North Carolina Press, 1944), 7. For the recent economic argument, see William D. Phillips, Jr., *Slavery from Roman Times to the Early Transatlantic Trade* (Minneapolis: University of Minnesota Press, 1985), 173–84. For a counterposition, see David Eltis, "Europeans and the Rise and Fall of African Slavery in the

Americas: An Interpretation," *American Historical Review* 98:5 (1993): 1399–1423. For the differences in European attitudes toward Native Americans and Africans, on which there is also an immense literature, the classic works of Winthrop D. Jordan, *White over Black: American Attitudes Toward the Negro, 1550–1812* (Chapel Hill: University of North Carolina Press, 1968), and David Brion Davis, *The Problem of Slavery in Western Culture* (Ithaca: Cornell University Press, 1966), are still a good entry point into the discussion. For recent considerations, see David Brion Davis, "Looking at Slavery from Broader Perspectives," *American Historical Review* 105:2 (2000): 452–66, and idem, "Constructing Race: A Reflection," *William and Mary Quarterly* 54:1 (1997): 7–18. Ira Berlin, *Many Thousands Gone: The First Two Centuries of Slavery in North America* (Cambridge: Harvard University Press, Belknap Press, 1998), emphasizes the changing forms of race and sees its full-blown character emerging first in the nineteenth century.

32. For this issue in a later colonial context, see Ann Laura Stoler, *Race and the Education of Desire: Foucault's "History of Sexuality" and the Colonial Order of Things* (Durham: Duke University Press, 1995).

33. See Kirsten Fischer, *Suspect Relations: Sex, Race, and Resistance in Colonial North Carolina* (Ithaca: Cornell University Press, 2002).

34. Ibid., 55–97.

35. Ibid., 86.

36. Ibid.

37. See Nancy Shoemaker, "How Indians Got to Be Red," *American Historical Review* 102:3 (1997): 625–44.

38. See Hudson, "From 'Nation' to 'Race.'"

39. Fischer, *Suspect Relations*, 129–30.

40. See Jordan, *White over Black*, 136–78.

41. Fischer, *Suspect Relations*, 160–61.

42. Davis, *Problem of Slavery*, 47. See also M. I. Finley, "Slavery," in the *International Encyclopedia of the Social Sciences*, ed. David L. Sills, vol. 14 (New York: Crowell, Collier and Macmillan, 1968), 307–13, here 308, 309, and the excerpts from Emperor Constantine's regulations in Phillips, *Slavery*, 27. Despite the quotation, generally Davis, *Problem of Slavery*, and Orlando Patterson, *Slavery and Social Death: A Comparative Study* (Cambridge: Harvard University Press, 1982), emphasize, at times implicitly, the continuities between premodern and New World slavery. Two factors seem different to me: the congruence of slavery and blackness, as argued above, and the integration of slavery into the dynamic, commercial, and capitalist world economy of the early modern era.

43. See Hannah Arendt, *The Origins of Totalitarianism* (1951; Cleveland: Meridian Books, 1958), 139–43, and Hannaford, *Race*, 191–94.

44. See the classic article by Eric Voegelin, "The Growth of the Race Idea," *Review of Politics* 2:3 (1940): 283–317.

45. Ibid., 293, 294.

46. See Hannaford, *Race*, 155–58.

47. See ibid., 197–202, quotation 199.

48. As Davis writes: "Insofar as the Enlightenment divorced anthropology and comparative anatomy from theological assumptions, it opened the way for theories of racial inferiority." *Problem of Slavery*, 446.

49. See Hannaford, *Race*, 204.

50. Arendt, "Race-Thinking before Racism," 42–47.

51. See Voegelin, "Growth of the Race Idea," 295–302.

52. Peter Gay, *The Cultivation of Hatred*, vol. 3 of *The Bourgeois Experience: Victoria to Freud* (New York: Norton, 1993), 72.

53. See Stephen Jay Gould, *The Mismeasure of Man*, rev. ed. (New York: Norton, 1996).

54. Eric Hobsbawm, *Nations and Nationalism since 1780: Programme, Myth, Reality*, 2d ed. (Cambridge: Cambridge University Press, 1990), 18–19. Among the major writers, only Elie Kedourie, *Nationalism*, 4th ed. (Oxford: Blackwell, 1993), seems resistant to the almost universally positive view of the nationalism of the French Revolution.

55. Joan Landes, *Women and the Public Sphere in the Age of the French Revolution* (Ithaca: Cornell University Press, 1988).

56. Hannah Arendt argued quite differently, that race thinking undermined the principle of nationality. See "Race-Thinking before Racism," the ideas of which were reworked into her classic *Origins of Totalitarianism*.

57. See Peter S. Onuf, *Jefferson's Empire: The Language of American Nationhood* (Charlottesville: University Press of Virginia, 2000), esp. 147–88.

58. Quoted in Walker Connor, "Man Is a National Animal," in idem, *Ethnonationalism: The Quest for Understanding* (Princeton: Princeton University Press, 1994), 201.

59. Amid a huge literature on the interplay of race and nation in U.S. history, see, for example, Gary Gerstle, *American Crucible: Race and Nation in the Twentieth Century* (Princeton: Princeton University Press, 2001); Roediger, *Wages of Whiteness*; and Reginald Horsman, *Race and Manifest Destiny: The Origins of American Racial Anglo-Saxonism* (Cambridge: Harvard University Press, 1986). Gerstle shows the swings back and forth in the twentieth century between racial and political definitions of the nation.

60. On the issue of race in the French Revolution, see Carolyn E. Fick, "The French Revolution in Saint Domingue: A Triumph or Failure?" in *A Turbulent Time: The French Revolution and the Greater Caribbean*, ed. David Barry Gaspar and David Patrick Geggus (Bloomington: Indiana University Press, 1997), 51–75; Lynn Hunt, ed., *The French Revolution and Human Rights* (Boston: Bedford Books, 1996), 51–59, 101–18; Shanti Marie Singham, " 'Betwixt Cattle and Men': Jews, Blacks, and Women and the Declaration of the Rights of Man," in *The French Idea of Freedom: The Old Regime and the Declaration of*

Rights of 1789, ed. Dale Van Kley (Stanford: Stanford University Press, 1994), 114–53; David Geggus, "Racial Equality, Slavery, and Colonial Secession during the Constituent Assembly," *American Historical Review* 94:5 (1989): 1290–1308; and Jacques Thibau, ed., *Le Temps de Saint-Domingue: L'esclavage et la révolution française* (Paris: Éditions Jean-Claude Lattès, 1989). On the earlier debates in eighteenth-century France, see Sue Peabody, *"There Are No Slaves in France": The Political Culture of Race and Slavery in the Ancien Régime* (New York: Oxford University Press, 1996).

61. William H. Sewell, Jr., *A Rhetoric of Bourgeois Revolution: The Abbé Sieyes and "What Is the Third Estate?"* (Durham: Duke University Press, 1994).

62. Sieyes quoted in ibid., 58.

63. Sieyes quoted in ibid., 59.

64. Sieyes quoted in ibid., 62. Emphasis in original.

65. On Kant as a philosopher of nationalism, see Kedourie's forceful, though controversial, argument in *Nationalism*.

66. Though Kant did argue in *The Different Races of Humankind* (1775) that within the unity of the species, there are distinct races, which are based on geography but then acquire a certain immutability.

67. Quoted in Arendt (in German), in "Race-Thinking before Racism," 49 n. 26.

68. The cult of the body as the marker for inner being had already been formulated by Enlightenment scientists and *philosophes* like the Dutch anatomist Peter Camper and his German counterpart Johann Kaspar Lavater. See George L. Mosse, *Toward the Final Solution: A History of European Racism* (Madison: University of Wisconsin Press, 1985), 17–34. See also Suzanne L. Marchand, *Down from Olympus: Archaeology and Philhellenism in Germany, 1750–1970* (Princeton: Princeton University Press, 1996).

69. See Hannaford, *Race*, 235–76.

70. Ibid., 258.

71. Arthur comte de Gobineau, "Essay on the Inequality of the Human Races," in *Gobineau: Selected Political Writings*, ed. Michael D. Biddiss (New York: Harper and Row, 1970), 41.

72. Ibid., 164.

73. Ibid., 135–37.

74. Ibid., 113.

75. Ibid.

76. Ibid.

77. Ibid., 173.

78. Gobineau was not alone, only particularly effective as a propagandizer. The Scottish anatomist Robert Knox, in a much quoted line, said: "Race is everything in human history." And: "Race, or hereditary descent, is everything; it stamps the man." Quoted in Gay, *Cultivation*, 73, from Robert Knox, *The Races of Man* (1850; 1862 ed.), 8, 6.

79. This is an immense area of controversy within scholarship on Darwin and the theory of evolution. For one recent study that firmly links Darwin's intellectual system and personal beliefs to Social Darwinism, see Mike Hawkins, *Social Darwinism in European and American Thought, 1860–1945* (Cambridge: Cambridge University Press, 1997). For the contrary view, even more forcefully stated, see Ernst Mayr, *The Growth of Biological Thought: Diversity, Evolution, and Inheritance* (Cambridge: Harvard University Press, Belknap Press, 1982), 385–86, 493–94.

80. Quoted in Gay, *Cultivation*, 41. As he does throughout the multivolume *Bourgeois Experience*, Gay qualifies the received views, in this case, of Spencer as a heartless misanthrope. Gay shows his more humane side as well. For a more extended analysis that firmly places Spencer in the Social Darwinist camp, see Hawkins, *Social Darwinism*, 82–103.

81. For a succinct discussion, see Mosse, *Toward the Final Solution*, 105–8.

82. Houston Stewart Chamberlain, *Foundations of the Nineteenth Century* (New York: John Lane, 1910), 1:lxv.

83. Ibid., lxvi.

84. Ibid., lxvii–lxviii.

85. Ibid., 257.

86. Ibid., 269.

87. Ibid., lxxvii–lxxix, 329–493.

88. Ibid., 330–31.

89. Ibid., 334.

90. Ibid., 253–55.

91. These paragraphs draw on Paul Weindling, *Health, Race and German Politics between National Unification and Nazism, 1870–1945* (Cambridge: Cambridge University Press, 1989). See also Daniel J. Kevles, *In the Name of Eugenics: Genetics and the Uses of Human Heredity* (Berkeley and Los Angeles: University of California Press, 1985).

92. Robert Koch isolated the anthrax bacillus in 1876 and the tubercular bacillus in 1882, and other scientists soon identified the bacterial causes of diphtheria and typhoid.

93. See Paul Weindling, "Theories of the Cell State in Imperial Germany," in *Biology, Medicine and Society, 1840–1940*, ed. Charles Webster (Cambridge: Cambridge University Press, 1981), 99–155, and idem, *Health, Race and German Politics*, 19, 39.

94. Karl Pearson, *The Scope and Importance to the State of the Science of National Eugenics*, University of London, Galton Laboratory for National Eugenics, Eugenics Laboratory Section no. 1 (London: Dulau and Co., 1909), 38.

95. Pearson, *Scope and Importance to the State*, 12. See also idem, *National Life from the Standpoint of Science*, University of London, Galton Laboratory for National Eugenics, Eugenics Lecture Series no. 11 (Cambridge: Cambridge University Press, n.d.).

96. Pearson, *National Life*, 21. See also idem, "The Bearing of Our Present Knowledge of Heredity upon Conduct" (1904), in *National Life*, 102–3; and idem, *The Problem of Practical Eugenics*, University of London, Galton Laboratory for National Eugenics, Eugenics Laboratory Lecture Series no. 5 (London: Dulau and Co., 1912), 31–34.

97. Pearson, *Scope and Importance to the State*, 40.

98. Pearson, *Practical Eugenics*, 36. Also 38 for the term "race suicide."

99. See Weindling, *Health, Race and German Politics*, 120–33.

100. Alfred Ploetz, "Die Begriffe Rasse und Gesellschaft und die davon abgeleiteten Disziplinen," *Archiv für Rassen- und Gesellschafts-Biologie* (hereafter *AfRGB*) 1 (1904): 1–26, quotations 3.

101. Ibid., 7, 8.

102. See, for example, Karl Munn, "Tatsachen zur Frage der ungenügenden Fortpflanzung der Intellektuellen und ihrer Ursachen," *AfRGB* 13 (1918–21): 171–75.

103. Weindling, *Health, Race and German Politics*, 100–101, 185–86. German eugenicists followed with great interest American legislation that allowed the compulsory sterilization of the mentally and physically handicapped. See, for example, G. von Hoffmann, "Das Sterilisierungsprogramm in den Vereinigten Staaten von Nordamerika," *AfRGB* 11 (1914–16): 184–92.

104. Ploetz, "Begriffe," 11.

105. Alfred Ploetz, "Neomalthusianismus und Rassenhygiene," *AfRGB* 10 (1913): 166–72; Albert Reibmayr, "Zur Entwicklungsgeschichte der wichtigsten Charaktere und Anlagen der indogermanischen Rasse," *AfRGB* 7 (1910): 328–53; and Weindling, *Health, Race and German Politics*, 153.

106. See Alfred Ploetz, "Ableitung einer Gesellschafts-Hygiene und ihrer Beziehungen zur Ethik," *AfRGB* 3 (1906): 253–59, and Gustav Ratzenhofer, "Die Rassenfrage vom ethischen Standpunkte," *AfRGB* 1 (1904): 737–48.

107. Ploetz, "Ableitung einer Gesellschafts-Hygiene," 256. Emphases in original.

108. Ibid., 255.

109. Weindling, *Health, Race and German Politics*, 131, provides a somewhat more cautious interpretation of Ploetz's position before World War I. "Yet the most altruistic and humane method was to control reproduction. Ploetz concluded that if no more weaklings were bred, then they need not be exterminated" (131). In one of the passages to which Weindling refers, Ploetz writes, "If no more defective traits [*Schwachen*] are reproduced, then they do not need again to be expurgated [*ausgemerzt zu werden*]" ("Begriffe," 26). But what if the traits are not expurgated? And some of Ploetz's other writings were not even this tentative.

110. *The Mountain Wreath of P. P. Nyegosh*, trans. James W. Wiles (London: George Allen and Unwin, 1930), lines 3–6, 18–19.

111. Giuseppe Mazzini, "Duties towards Your Country," in *Introduction to*

Contemporary Civilization in the West, 3d ed., vol. 2 (New York: Columbia University Press, 1961), 540–43, quotation 541.

112. Quoted in Raymond F. Betts, *The False Dawn: European Imperialism in the Nineteenth Century* (Minneapolis: University of Minnesota Press, 1975), 33.

113. For one recent, extraordinary discussion, see Sven Lindqvist, *"Exterminate All the Brutes": One Man's Odyssey into the Heart of Darkness and the Origins of European Genocide*, trans. Joan Tate (New York: New Press, 1996).

114. Depiction of the Ashanti king and his mother crawling to the British in ibid., 54–57.

115. Quoted in ibid., 53–54.

116. I follow here Arendt's argument in *Origins of Totalitarianism* rather than some newer studies that claim to see an unbroken line of antisemitic sentiment in Germany. The more recent arguments revive the approach of some of the studies of the 1940s and 1950s that were far less sophisticated than Arendt's. For the older argument redux, see Daniel Jonah Goldhagen, *Hitler's Willing Executioners: Ordinary Germans and the Holocaust* (New York: Knopf, 1996), who seems unaware of the lineage of his own views.

117. The phrase "overtly racist regimes" is from Fredrickson, *Racism*.

118. Quotation from Davis, *Problem of Slavery*, 4.

119. Not until the late 1930s and the "new synthesis" of population ecology and genetics did Darwin again become the central figure for scientists. See Mayr, *Growth of Biological Thought*.

120. Some of the classic studies of race thinking in general and antisemitism in particular picture them more as the ideologies of the "mob" or the "rabble," as in Arendt, *Origins of Totalitarianism*. Older intellectual surveys, like George L. Mosse, *The Crisis of German Ideology: Intellectual Origins of the Third Reich* (New York: Grosset and Dunlap, 1964), also implied that race thinking became operative when it descended from intellectuals like Fichte and Jahn to the popular classes. I follow more recent studies that stress the biomedical dimensions of race thinking and its deadly application by highly trained professionals and bureaucrats.

121. Darwin and his followers had great difficulties with the issue of "evolutionary progress." For a careful consideration of the problem, see Mayr, *Growth of Biological Thought*, 631–34. Mayr's conclusion is that Darwin resisted the notion of any finality to evolution but of course recognized that species progressed by becoming more diverse and more complex (though complexity is not always a mark of greater adaptability to the environment). This would mark a difference between his views and those of race theorists, who did believe in perfectability.

122. Thomas Huxley, *Evolution and Ethics* (London: Macmillan, 1893).

123. George L. Mosse, *Fallen Soldiers: Reshaping the Memory of the World Wars* (New York: Oxford University Press, 1990), 173–74.

124. See, for example, many of the propaganda posters reproduced in Peter

Paret, Beth Irwin Lewis, and Paul Paret, *Persuasive Images: Posters of War and Revolution from the Hoover Institution Archives* (Princeton: Princeton University Press, 1992).

125. See William W. Hagen, "Before the 'Final Solution': Toward a Comparative Analysis of Political Anti-Semitism in Interwar Germany and Poland," *Journal of Modern History* 68:2 (1996): 351–81.

126. See the still valuable work by Stephen Ladas, *The Exchange of Minorities* (New York: Macmillan, 1932). Most thoroughly on Armenia, see Richard G. Hovannisian, *The Republic of Armenia*, 4 vols. (Berkeley and Los Angeles: University of California Press, 1971–96).

127. There is a huge literature on the cultural impact of the war. Among the most important works are Omer Bartov, *Murder in Our Midst: The Holocaust, Industrial Killing, and Representation* (New York: Oxford University Press, 1996); Modris Eksteins, *Rites of Spring: The Great War and the Birth of the Modern Age* (Boston: Houghton Mifflin, 1989); Eric J. Leed, *No Man's Land: Combat and Identity in World War I* (Cambridge: Cambridge University Press, 1979); and Paul Fussell, *The Great War and Modern Memory* (London: Oxford University Press, 1975).

128. Ernst Jünger, *Copse 125: A Chronicle from the Trench Warfare of 1918*, trans. Basil Creighton (London: Chatto and Windus, 1930).

CHAPTER TWO
Nation, Race, and State Socialism:
The Soviet Union under Lenin and Stalin

1. The troikas were composed of the first secretary of the district party committee, the president of the executive committee of the district soviet, and the local secret police official.

2. Document in Nicolas Werth, "Un État contre son peuple: Violences, répressions, terreurs en Union sovietique," in *Le Livre noir du communisme: Crimes, terreur et répression*, ed. Stéphane Courtois (Paris: Robert Laffont, 1997), 218–19.

3. See, for example, the primary sources in James von Geldern and Richard Stites, eds., *Mass Culture in Soviet Russia* (Bloomington: Indiana University Press, 1995), and William G. Rosenberg, ed., *Bolshevik Visions: First Phase of the Cultural Revolution in Soviet Russia* (Ann Arbor: Ardis, 1984). See also Richard Stites, *Revolutionary Dreams: Utopian Vision and Experimental Life in the Russian Revolution* (New York: Oxford University Press, 1989), and Sheila Fitzpatrick, ed., *Cultural Revolution in Russia, 1928–1931* (Bloomington: Indiana University Press, 1978). See also the early work by René Fueloep-Miller, *The Mind and Face of Bolshevism: An Examination of Cultural Life in Soviet Russia* (1927; New York: Harper and Row, 1965).

4. See, for example, P. I. Lebedev-Polyansky, "Revolution and the Cultural

Tasks of the Proletariat," and L. Trotsky, "The Struggle for Cultured Speech," in Rosenberg, *Bolshevik Visions*, 62–70, 185–88.

5. N. Krupskaya, "What a Communist Ought to Be Like," in Rosenberg, *Bolshevik Visions*, 38.

6. A. A. Solts, "Communist Ethics," in Rosenberg, *Bolshevik Visions*, 49–50.

7. For various sides to this argument, see Solts, "Communist Ethics"; A. Kollontai, "Make Way for the Winged Eros"; and P. Vinogradskaya, "The 'Winged Eros' of Comrade Kollantai," all in Rosenberg, *Bolshevik Visions*, 51–52, 96–106, 217–38. See also Wendy Z. Goldman, *Women, the State, and Revolution: Soviet Family Policy and Social Life, 1917–1936* (Cambridge: Cambridge University Press, 1993).

8. Kollontai, "The Family and the Communist State," in Rosenberg, *Bolshevik Visions*, 79–88, quotation 84.

9. Stalin quoted in Stephen Kotkin, *Magnetic Mountain: Stalinism as a Civilization* (Berkeley and Los Angeles: University of California Press, 1995), 29.

10. Ibid., 30.

11. Stalin, "The Task of Business Executives," 4 February 1931, in idem, *Problems of Leninism* (Moscow: Foreign Languages Publishing House, 1947), 356.

12. Ibid.

13. Ibid., 357–58.

14. Quoted in Kotkin, *Magnetic Mountain*, 92.

15. Quoted in Mikhail Heller and Aleksandr Nekrich, *Utopia in Power: The History of the Soviet Union from 1917 to the Present*, trans. Phyllis B. Carlos (New York: Summit Books, 1986), 224.

16. Kotkin, *Magnetic Mountain*, 16.

17. Krupskaya, "What a Communist Ought to Be Like."

18. Stalin, "Report on the Work of the Central Committee to the Seventeenth Congress of the C.P.S.U.(b.), 26 January 1934, in *Problems of Leninism*, 501.

19. Stalin, "Speech at the First All-Union Conference of Stakhanovites," 17 November 1935, in *Problems of Leninism*, 531.

20. See Kotkin, *Magnetic Mountain*, 73–85, and Lynn Viola, *The Best Sons of the Fatherland: Workers in the Vanguard of Soviet Collectivization* (New York: Oxford University Press, 1987).

21. Quoted in Kotkin, *Magnetic Mountain*, 73, from one of the pamphlets extolling the construction of Magnitogorsk. See also Stalin, "Speech at the First All-Union Conference of Stakhanovites."

22. See Lewis H. Siegelbaum and Ronald Grigor Suny, eds., *Making Workers Soviet: Power, Class, and Identity* (Ithaca: Cornell University Press, 1994).

23. On social mobility, see Sheila Fitzpatrick, *The Russian Revolution* (New York: Oxford University Press, 1982), and idem, *Education and Social Mobility in the Soviet Union, 1921–1934* (New York: Cambridge University Press, 1979).

24. See, for example, Martin E. Malia, *The Soviet Tragedy: A History of Socialism in Russia, 1917–1991* (New York: Free Press, 1994); Richard Pipes, *The Bolshevik Revolution* (New York: Knopf, 1990); and Heller and Nekrich, *Utopia in Power*. In contrast, Ronald Grigor Suny, *The Soviet Experiment: Russia, the USSR, and the Successor States* (New York: Oxford University Press, 1998), emphasizes the historical context in which the Soviet leaders made their political decisions, but downplays the aspects of Bolshevik ideology that encouraged the formation of a dictatorship.

25. Quoted in Werth, "État contre son peuple," 58.

26. See Israel Getzler's convincing argument, "Lenin's Conception of Revolution as Civil War," *Slavonic and East European Review* 74:3 (1996): 464–72.

27. Lenin at the Third Congress of Soviets, 11 January 1918, quoted in ibid., 465.

28. Quoted in ibid., 466.

29. Quoted in Werth, "État contre son peuple," 69.

30. I am elaborating a bit on Werth, "État contre son peuple," 70–71, whose statement in this instance refers to the summer of 1917. On a Europe-wide basis, a white terror lasted from 1917 to 1945, and it was no less systematic and perhaps even more gruesome than the Soviet one. Werth, 94–96, downplays too greatly the nature of the white terror. In contrast, Arno Mayer places too much emphasis on counterrevolutionary violence as the motivation for the Bolsheviks' use of terror and ignores the Bolsheviks' ideological commitment to political violence. See Arno J. Mayer, *The Furies: Violence and Terror in the French and Russian Revolutions* (Princeton: Princeton University Press, 2000).

31. Quoted in Werth, "État contre son peuple," 84. Emphasis in original.

32. Quoted in Heller and Nekrich, *Utopia in Power*, 80.

33. Quoted in Aleksandr I. Solzhenitsyn, *The Gulag Archipelago, 1918–1956: An Experiment in Literary Investigation*, trans. Thomas P. Whitney (New York: Harper and Row, 1973), 1–2: 27.

34. On the use of military metaphors, see Jeffrey Brooks, *"Thank You, Comrade Stalin!" Soviet Public Culture from Revolution to Cold War* (Princeton: Princeton University Press, 2000), 21–27.

35. See especially Nicolas Werth's contributions in Henry Ruosso, ed., *Stalinisme et nazisme: Histoire et mémoire comparées* (Brussels: Éditions Complexe, 1999), and the documents and commentary in Lewis Siegelbaum and Andrei Sokolov, *Stalinism as a Way of Life: A Narrative in Documents* (New Haven: Yale University Press, 2000).

36. For one example, see Stalin, "The Results of the First Five-Year Plan," 7 January 1933, in *Problems of Leninism*, 423–24.

37. Stalin, "Reply to Collective Farm Comrades," 3 April 1930, in *Problems of Leninism*, 347. Though Stalin here quotes Lenin, who also wrote of "bloodsuckers . . . spiders . . . leeches."

38. Quoted in Erik van Ree, "Stalin's Organic Theory of the Party," *Russian Review* 52:1 (1993): 43–57, quotation 56.

39. Quoted in ibid., 56–57.

40. See Diane P. Koenker, William G. Rosenberg, and Ronald Grigor Suny, eds., *Party, State, and Society in the Russian Civil War: Explorations in Social History* (Bloomington: Indiana University Press, 1989).

41. For some recent works that concentrate on the disciplining of individuals, see Peter Holquist, "State Violence as Technique: The Logic of Violence in Soviet Totalitarianism," in *The Making and Management of Societies: Twentieth-Century Population Politics in a Comparative Framework*, ed. Amir Weiner (Stanford: Stanford University Press, 2003); Amir Weiner, *Making Sense of War: The Second World War and the Fate of the Bolshevik Revolution* (Princeton: Princeton University Press, 2001); Sheila Fitzpatrick, *Everyday Stalinism: Ordinary Life in Extraordinary Times. Soviet Russia in the 1930s* (New York: Oxford University Press, 1999); Jochen Hellbeck, "Fashioning the Stalinist Soul: The Diary of Stepan Podlubnyi (1931–1939)," *Jahrbücher für Geschichte Osteuropas* 44:3 (1996): 344–73; Stefan Plaggenborg, *Revolutionskultur: Menschenbilder und kulturelle Praxis in Sowjetrußland zwischen Oktoberrevolution und Stalinismus* (Cologne: Böhlau, 1996); and Kotkin, *Magnetic Mountain*.

42. See James C. Scott, *Seeing Like a State: How Certain Schemes to Improve the Human Condition Have Failed* (New Haven: Yale University Press, 1998).

43. See Sheila Fitzpatrick, "Ascribing Class: The Construction of Social Identity in Soviet Russia," *Journal of Modern History* 65:4 (1993): 745–70.

44. See Moshe Lewin, *Russian Peasants and Soviet Power: A Study of Collectivization* (London: Allen and Unwin, 1968); Teodor Shanin, *The Awkward Class: Political Sociology of the Peasantry in a Developing Society. Russia 1910–1925* (Oxford: Clarendon, 1972); and Sheila Fitzpatrick, *Stalin's Peasants: Resistance and Survival in the Russian Village after Collectivization* (New York: Oxford University Press, 1994).

45. See especially Golfo Alexopoulos, "Rights and Passages: Making Outcasts and Making Citizens in Soviet Russia" (Ph.D. diss., University of Chicago, 1996). According to Nicolas Werth and Gaël Moullec, eds., *Rapport secrets soviétiques: La société russe dans les documents confidentiels, 1921–1991* (Paris: Gallimard, 1994), 116 n. 1, the *lishentsy* constituted 3 to 4 percent of the population at the end of the 1920s.

46. See the secret police documents, 7 July 1925 and 10 July 1933, in Werth and Moullec, *Rapport secrets soviétiques*, 33, 43–44. Work is just beginning to appear on the topic of social marginals. See Alexopoulos, "Rights and Passages"; Lynn Viola, "The Second Coming: Class Enemies in the Soviet Countryside, 1927–1935," in *Stalinist Terror: New Perspectives*, ed. J. Arch Getty and Roberta T. Manning (Cambridge: Cambridge University Press, 1993), 65–98; and Fitzpatrick, "Ascribing Class."

47. Fitzpatrick, *Stalin's Peasants*, 201–3.

48. Solzhenitsyn, *Gulag Archipelago*, 1–2:96.

49. See Francine Hirsch, "Empire of Nations: Colonial Technologies and the Making of the Soviet Union, 1917–1939" (Ph.D. diss., Princeton University,

1998); idem, "The Soviet Union as a Work-in-Progress: Ethnographers and the Category *Nationality* in the 1926, 1937, and 1939 Censuses," *Slavic Review* 56:2 (1997): 251–78; Yuri Slezkine, "N. Ia. Marr and the National Origins of Soviet Ethnogenetics," *Slavic Review* 55:4 (1996): 826–62; and idem, "The USSR as a Communal Apartment, or How a Socialist State Promoted Ethnic Particularism," *Slavic Review* 52:2 (1994): 414–52.

50. J. V. Stalin, *Marxism and the National Question* (1913), in idem, *Works*, vol. 2, *1907–1913* (Moscow: Foreign Languages Publishing House, 1953), 300–381.

51. Ibid., 307.

52. Ibid. Stalin went much further than Lenin, whose concessions on the national issue were always strategic and tactical. See Hélène Carrère d'Encausse, *The Great Challenge: Nationalities and the Bolshevik State, 1917–1930*, trans. Nancy Festinger (New York: Holmes and Meier, 1992), 35–39.

53. Stalin, "Deviations on the National Question" (1930), in idem, *Marxism and the National Question: Selected Writings and Speeches* (New York: International Publishers, 1942), 208–9.

54. Ibid., 212.

55. On the dilemmas inherent in the multinational character of the empire, see Geoffrey Hosking, *Russia: People and Empire, 1552–1917* (Cambridge: Harvard University Press, 1997), and Andreas Kappeler, *Rußland als Vielvölkerreich: Entstehung, Geschichte, Zerfall* (Munich: Beck, 1993). Their divergent emphases can be read in tandem.

56. See Werth, "État contre son peuple," 112–17, and Peter Holquist, "A Russian Vendée: The Practice of Revolutionary Politics in the Don Countryside" (Ph.D. diss., Columbia University, 1995).

57. Holquist, "Russian Vendée," 381.

58. Werth, "État contre son peuple," 116–17, and Holquist, "Russian Vendée," 420, 431–32.

59. Technically the Bolsheviks in 1917 turned over ownership of the land to the village soviets.

60. Stalin, "Problems of Agrarian Policy in the U.S.S.R.," 27 December 1929, in *Problems of Leninism*, 316.

61. Ibid., 313. See also his comments on rural women, who, he says, can become emancipated only on the basis of collective farming: "Speech Delivered at the First All-Union Congress of Collective-Farm Shock Workers," 10 February 1933, in *Problems of Leninism*, 450–51.

62. Werth, "État contre son peuple," 164–77, quotation 164.

63. See Stalin, "Problems of Agrarian Policy in the U.S.S.R.," 317, and "The Policy of Eliminating the Kulaks as a Class," 21 January 1930, also in *Problems of Leninism*, 322–25.

64. Stalin, "The Policy of Eliminating the Kulaks as a Class," 325. Emphases in original.

65. Werth, "État contre son peuple," 164, 174, 178–88. Werth, along with

Robert Conquest, *The Harvest of Sorrow: Soviet Collectivization and the Terror-Famine* (New York: Oxford University Press, 1986), argues that the regime deliberately created the famine, a highly debatable contention.

66. See Viola, "Second Coming."

67. The first quotation is from Werth, "État contre son peuple," 206, the second from Robert Conquest, *The Great Terror: A Reassessment* (New York: Oxford University Press, 1990), 258. For the American "revisionist" views, see Getty and Manning, *Stalinist Terror*.

68. Werth, "État contre son peuple," 210. The point he makes here is somewhat in contradiction with his statement on 206.

69. See ibid., 214, 216–17, and the contributions in Getty and Manning, *Stalinist Terror*.

70. J. Arch Getty and William Chase, "Patterns of Repression among the Soviet Elite in the Late 1930s: A Biographical Approach," in Getty and Manning, *Stalinist Terror*, 243–44.

71. See Brooks, *"Thank You, Comrade Stalin!"*, 126–58.

72. Both quotations in Conquest, *Great Terror*, 320.

73. This is the argument of the American "revisionists," which I accept in modified form. See Getty and Manning, *Stalinist Terror*. For Werth's criticism, see "État contre son peuple," 208. For a good critique of the literature in general, written before Werth's contribution, see Kotkin, *Magnetic Mountain*, 282–86. The early, especially vociferous dispute can be followed in *Russian Review* 45:4 (October 1986) and 46:4 (October 1987).

74. See Roberta T. Manning, "The Soviet Economic Crisis of 1936–1940 and the Great Purges," Robert Thurston, "The Stakhanovite Movement: Background to the Great Terror in the Factories, 1935–1938," and David L. Hoffmann, "The Great Terror on the Local Level: Purges in Moscow Factories, 1936–1938," in Getty and Manning, *Stalinist Terror*, 116–67. See also Siegelbaum and Sokolov, *Stalinism as a Way of Life*.

75. My own inclination is to accept the more moderate estimates offered by predominantly U.S., British, and Australian researchers, mostly because they rest on archival research and more astute demographic knowledge. See many of the contributions in Getty and Manning, *Stalinist Terror*, and J. Arch Getty, Gabor T. Rittersporn, and Viktor N. Zemskov, "Victims of the Soviet Penal System in the Pre-war Years: A First Approach on the Basis of Archival Evidence," *American Historical Review* 98:4 (1993): 1017–49. Werth's estimates run to the moderately high side. See "État contre son peuple," 213, 229–30, 260, 264. For the traditional interpretations with estimates ranging from twenty to even forty million victims of Stalinism, see Conquest, *Great Terror*; Roy Medvedev, *Let History Judge: The Origins and Consequences of Stalinism*, trans. George Shriver, rev. and expanded ed. (New York: Columbia University Press, 1989); and Solzhenitsyn, *Gulag Archipelago*.

76. I am adapting the term "euphoria of victory" from Christopher Brown-

ing's explanation for the radicalization of Nazi policies toward the Jews, in *The Path to Genocide: Essays on Launching the Final Solution* (Cambridge: Cambridge University Press, 1992), 121.

77. The term "quicksand society" is Moshe Lewin's. See *The Making of the Soviet System* (New York: Pantheon, 1985).

78. Slezkine, "USSR as a Communal Apartment," 432.

79. Terry D. Martin, "An Affirmative Action Empire: Ethnicity and the Soviet State, 1923–1938" (Ph.D. diss., University of Chicago, 1996).

80. For some figures, see ibid., 511, and Slezkine, "USSR as a Communal Apartment," 430.

81. Carrère d'Encausse, *Great Challenge*, 179–88.

82. "Speaking Bolshevik" is the title of chap. 5. Kotkin, *Magnetic Mountain*, 198–237.

83. See Yuri Slezkine, "From Savages to Citizens: The Cultural Revolution in the Soviet Far North, 1928–1938" *Slavic Review* 51:1 (1992): 52–76, and idem, *Arctic Mirrors: Russia and the Small Peoples of the North* (Ithaca: Cornell University Press, 1994).

84. Hirsch, "Soviet Union as a Work-in-Progress."

85. Martin, "Affirmative Action Empire," 562.

86. Weiner, *Making Sense of War*.

87. Amir Weiner, "Nature, Nurture, and Memory in a Socialist Utopia: Delineating the Soviet Socio-Ethnic Body in the Age of Socialism," *American Historical Review* 104:4 (1999): 1114–55, quotation 1122. See also Martin, "Affirmative Action Empire," 956–60.

88. Hirsch, "Soviet Union as a Work-in-Progress," 276–77.

89. J. V. Stalin, "The National Question and the Soviet Constitution" (1936), in *Marxism and the National Question: Selected Writings and Speeches*, 218.

90. All these examples from Martin, "Affirmative Action Empire," 944–47, 964–65.

91. Norman M. Naimark, *Fires of Hatred: Ethnic Cleansing in Twentieth-Century Europe* (Cambridge: Harvard University Press, 2001), 89–92.

92. Slezkine, "N. Ia. Marr," 852–53.

93. For summaries of the various deportations, see Naimark, *Fires of Hatred*, 85–107; J. Otto Pohl, *Ethnic Cleansing in the USSR, 1937–1949* (Westport, CT: Greenwood Press, 1999); Weiner, "Nature, Nurture, and Memory"; and N. F. Bugai, "K voprosu o deportatsii narodov SSSR v 30–40-kh godakh," *Istoriia SSSR* 6 (1989): 135–144. Summaries can also be gleaned from some of the documents published by N. F. Bugai, e.g., "'Pogruzheny v eshelony i otprveleny k mestam poselenii . . .': L. Beriia-I. Stalinu," *Istoriia SSSR* 1 (1991): 143–60, and "20–40-e gody: Tragediia narodov," *Vostok* 2 (1992): 122–39. See also Jean-Jacques Marie, *Les Peuples déportés d'Union soviétique* (Brussels: Éditions Complexe, 1995), and the older but still useful work by Aleksandr M. Nekrich, *The Punished Peoples: The Deportation and Fate of Soviet Minorities at the*

End of the Second World War, trans. George Saunders (New York: Norton, 1978).

94. Terry D. Martin, "The Origins of Soviet Ethnic Cleansing," *Journal of Modern History* 70:4 (1998): 813–61, here 839.

95. Martin, "Affirmative Action Empire," 753–54.

96. Martin, "Origins of Soviet Ethnic Cleansing," 847. Other historians would date the beginning of this transition a bit later, in 1937.

97. Ibid., 815.

98. See Michael Gelb, "An Early Soviet Ethnic Deportation: The Far-Eastern Koreans," *Russian Review* 54:3 (1995): 389–412, and N. F. Bugai, "Vyselenie sovetskikh koreitsev s dal'nego vostoka," *Voprosy Istorii* 5 (1994): 141–48.

99. Germans were expelled from the Red Army even earlier, by a decree of 8 September 1941, the others somewhat later. As late as March 1949, some 63,000 ex–Red Army soldiers from targeted nationalities were counted in the special settlements, including 33,615 ethnic Germans, 8,995 Crimean Tatars, 6,184 Kalmyks, 4,248 Chechens, 2,543 Karachai, and 946 Ingush. See Weiner, "Nature, Nurture, and Memory," 1134, and Nekrich, *Punished Peoples*, 83.

100. Gelb, "Early Soviet Ethnic Deportation," 401.

101. Martin, "Origins of Soviet Ethnic Cleansing," 855, 858.

102. Werth, "État contre son peuple," 241, 242.

103. Quoted in ibid., 241.

104. See Bugai, " 'Pogruzheny v eshelony i otprveleny k mestam poselenii . . . ,' " and in English, Pohl, *Ethnic Cleansing*, and Nekrich, *Punished Peoples*.

105. Nekrich, *Punished Peoples*, 88.

106. Bugai, "K voprosu o deportatsii," 135, 137; idem, "20–40-e gody," 122.

107. Nicolas Werth, "Logiques de violence dans l'URSS stalinienne," in Ruosso, *Stalinisme et nazisme*, 122.

108. Nekrich, *Punished Peoples*, 42–48.

109. For a very effective general description of how these operations work, see Jacques Semelin, "Analysis of a Mass Crime: Ethnic Cleansing in the Former Yugoslavia, 1991–1999," in *The Specter of Genocide*, ed. Robert Gellately and Ben Kiernan (Cambridge: Cambridge University Press, 2003). Semelin emphasizes three elements: "a hierarchy in the structure of command, a sealed up theater of operations, [and] a culture of impunity" (12–13).

110. The organized nature of the operations comes through in the documents, e.g., Bugai, "20–40-e gody."

111. Quoted in Nikolai Fedorovich Bugai, "The Truth about the Deportation of the Chechen and Ingush Peoples," *Soviet Studies in History* 30:2 (1991): 78.

112. Naimark, *Fires of Hatred*, 96–99. 101–4, and Nekrich, *Punished Peoples*, 34–35, 59–60.

113. As was the case with Balkarians. See Bugai, "K voprosu o deportatsii," 140.

114. Norman M. Naimark, "Ethnic Cleansing in Twentieth Century Eu-

rope," in Donald W. Treadgold Papers No. 19, The Henry M. Jackson School of International Studies (Seattle: University of Washington, 1998), 22–24.

115. Nekrich, *Punished Peoples*, 114.

116. Bugai, "Truth about the Deportation," 67.

117. Werth, "Logiques," 121–22.

118. Werth, "État contre son peuple," 261–62, and Terry D. Martin, "Terror gegen Nationen in der Sowjetunion," *Osteuropa* 50:6 (2000): 608.

119. Werth, "État contre son peuple," 260–64.

120. Conquest, *Great Terror*, 234.

121. Bugai, "K voprosu o deportatsii," 141–42.

122. See Werth, "État contre son peuple," 269–76.

123. Weiner, *Making Sense of War*, 198; Werth, "État contre son peuple," 276; and Suny, *Soviet Experiment*, 374.

124. This point is cogently made by Rogers Brubaker, "Nationhood and the National Question in the Soviet Union and Its Successor States," in idem, *Nationalism Reframed: Nationhood and the National Question in the New Europe* (Cambridge: Cambridge University Press, 1996), 23–54.

125. See Slezkine, "N. Ia. Marr," 858.

126. Vasily Grossman, *Forever Flowing*, trans. Thomas P. Whitney (New York: Harper and Row, 1972), 64.

127. Ibid., 34. Grossman is referring to Nikolai Andreyevich here.

128. Ibid., 71.

129. Ibid., 74–75.

130. Primo Levi, *The Drowned and the Saved*, trans. Raymond Rosenthal (New York: Summit Books, 1988), 36–69.

131. Anna Akhmatova, *Requiem*, in *Requiem and Poem without a Hero*, trans. D. M. Thomas (Athens: Ohio University Press, 1976), 25.

132. Solzhenitsyn, *Gulag Archipelago*, 1–2:4.

133. Ibid.

134. Ibid., 5.

135. Varlam Shalamov, "The Lawyers' Plot," in *Kolyma Tales*, trans. John Glad (New York: Norton, 1980), 151–70.

136. Akhmatova, *Requiem*, 32.

137. Quoted in Boris A. Starkov, "Narkom Ezhov," in Getty and Manning, *Stalinist Terror*, 33.

138. Ibid., 34. At least some evidence indicates that the NKVD were able to protect their own during the worst period of the Terror.

139. Aleksandr I. Solzhenitsyn, *The Gulag Archipelago, 1918–1956: An Experiment in Literary Investigation*, vols. 5–7, trans. Harry Willetts (New York: Harper and Row, 1976), 388–89. See also Nekrich, *Punished Peoples*, 109–11.

140. X. Arapiev, party head of the North-Ossetian Oblast Committee KPSS, quoted in Bugai, "K voprosu o deportatsii," 140.

141. Nekrich, *Punished Peoples*, 108–9.

142. On the problem of returned *kulaks*, see Fitzpatrick, *Stalin's Peasants*, 233–61.

143. See ibid.

144. See Lewis H. Siegelbaum, *Stakhanovism and the Politics of Productivity in the USSR, 1935–1941* (Cambridge: Cambridge University Press, 1988), and Kotkin, *Magnetic Mountain*, esp. 201–25.

145. Quoted in Kotkin, *Magnetic Mountain*, 212.

146. See Fitzpatrick, *Stalin's Peasants*, 16–18, 262–85.

147. Grossman, *Forever Flowing*, 68–69.

148. For the Third Reich, see especially Robert Gellately, *The Gestapo and German Society: Enforcing Racial Policy, 1933–1945* (Oxford: Clarendon, 1990). For the Soviet case, see Sheila Fitzpatrick, "Signals from Below: Soviet Letters of Denunciation in the 1930s," *Journal of Modern History* 68:4 (1996): 831–66, and Vladimir A. Kozlov, "Denunciation and Its Functions in Soviet Governance: A Study of Denunciations and Their Bureaucratic Handling from Soviet Police Archives, 1944–1953," *Journal of Modern History* 68:4 (1996): 867–98. See also Jan T. Gross, *Revolution from Abroad: The Soviet Conquest of Poland's Western Ukraine and Western Belorussia* (Princeton: Princeton University Press, 1988), 114–22, for a very interesting discussion about how the Soviet regime "privatized the public realm" by using personal feuds to political ends and incorporating entire families into the administrative apparatus.

149. Conquest, *Great Terror*, 253.

150. Kotkin, *Magnetic Mountain*, 196.

151. This paragraph is drawn from Conquest, *Great Terror*, 121–30, 277–82, and Solzhenitsyn, *Gulag Archipelago*, 1–2:93–143.

152. Werth, "État contre son peuple," 215. He is quoting here Annie Kriegel.

153. Quoted in Conquest, *Great Terror*, 390.

154. Quoted in ibid., 390, 391.

155. See Anna Larina, *This I Cannot Forget: The Memoirs of Nikolai Bukharin's Widow*, trans. Gary Kern (New York: Norton, 1993).

156. All these cases from Conquest, *Great Terror*, 395–96.

157. Testimony of Tenzila Ibraimova in Nekrich, *Punished Peoples*, 116–17.

158. Conquest, *Great Terror*, 327, 338–39.

159. Ibid., 338.

160. Shalamov, "Lend-Lease," in *Kolyma Tales*, 179–80.

161. The first quotation is from Kotkin, *Magnetic Mountain*, 364, the second from Weiner, "Nature, Nurture, and Memory," 1114. Generally on the "high modernism" of social engineering schemes, see Scott's trenchant analysis in *Seeing Like a State*.

162. Getty, Rittersporn, and Zemskov, "Victims of the Soviet Penal System," and Weiner, *Making Sense of War*, 201–9.

163. See Victor Klemperer, *I Will Bear Witness: A Diary of the Nazi Years*, trans. Martin Chalmers, 2 vols. (New York: Random House, 1998–99); Nathan

Stoltzfus, *Resistance of the Heart: Intermarriage and the Rosenstrasse Protest in Nazi Germany* (New York: Norton, 1996); and George H. Stein, *The Waffen SS: Hitler's Elite Guard at War* (Ithaca: Cornell University Press, 1966), 179–85.

164. See Werth, "État contre son peuple."

165. See Victoria E. Bonnell, *Iconography of Power: Soviet Political Posters under Lenin and Stalin* (Berkeley and Los Angeles: University of California Press, 1997).

166. See Omer Bartov, "Defining Enemies, Making Victims: Germans, Jews, and the Holocaust," *American Historical Review* 103:3 (1998): 771–816, on the mutually constitutive process of making victims and perpetrators. On the nature of complicity under Soviet rule, see Gross's concluding remarks in *Revolution from Abroad*, 232–40.

167. See the text of the Genocide Convention, *http://www1.umn.edu/humanrts/instree/xlcppcg.htm* [27 August 2002].

168. Naimark, *Fires of Hatred*, 98.

169. On the supplying of provisions and establishment of institutions for some of the purged groups, see, for example, resolutions of the State Defense Committee, May 1944 and July 1944, and communiqué from the Kazakh Communist Party to the National Commissariat of the Interior, 10 January 1945, all in Bugai, "20–40e gody," 132–36.

CHAPTER THREE
The Primacy of Race: Nazi Germany

1. Quotations from the diary of SS Dr. Kremer, in *"The Good Old Days": The Holocaust as Seen by Its Perpetrators and Bystanders*, ed. Ernst Klee, Willi Dressen, and Volker Riess, trans. Deborah Burnstone (New York: Free Press, 1991), 256–68. Further biographical information in ibid., 296. At the end of the war the British detained Kremer and found the diary in his apartment, then extradited him to Poland. He was sentenced to death in December 1947, a judgment commuted to life imprisonment. He was released in January 1958, then tried in a West German court that sentenced him to ten years as an accessory to murder. His Polish prison time was counted against the sentence, and the court released him.

2. Hitler, "Appeal to the German People," 31 January 1933, in Jeremy Noakes and Geoffrey Pridham, eds. *Nazism 1919–1945: A Documentary Reader*, vol. 1, *The Rise to Power, 1919–1934* (Exeter: University of Exeter Press, 1983), 131–34.

3. Goebbels diary, 20 January 1933, in Wolfgang Michalka, ed., *Das Dritte Reich: Dokumente zur Innen- und Außenpolitik*, vol. 1, *"Volksgemeinschaft" und Großmachtpolitik 1933–1939* (Munich: DTV, 1985), 14–15.

4. Earlier analyses tended to ignore Hitler's ideology and to see him only as

power-driven, as in Alan Bullock, *Hitler: A Study in Tyranny* (London: Odhams, 1952). Bullock later revised his views in subsequent editions of his biography, and in *Hitler and Stalin: Parallel Lives* (London: HarperCollins, 1991) gives an accounting of his ideology. For a thorough examination of the origins and development of Hitler's views, see Eberhard Jäckel, *Hitler's World View: A Blueprint for Power*, trans. Herbert Arnold (Cambridge: Harvard University Press, 1981).

5. A view Hitler expressed in 1919 in his earliest surviving writing, an oft-quoted letter to Adolf Gemlich, one of the participants in his army propaganda course: "[T]he final aim [of antisemitism] . . . must be the uncompromising removal of the Jews altogether." Quoted in Noakes and Pridham, *Nazism*, 1:13.

6. Adolf Hitler, *Mein Kampf*, trans. Ralph Manheim (Boston: Houghton Mifflin, 1943), 56. Hereafter cited as *MK*.

7. *MK*, 57.

8. See the thorough vetting of the various sources in Ian Kershaw, *Hitler, 1889–1936: Hubris* (New York: Norton, 1999), 62–67.

9. *MK*, 123.

10. Kershaw, *Hitler, 1889–1936*, 66–67.

11. Jäckel, *Hitler's World View*, 58–59, provides an even larger catalog of such expressions found in *MK*.

12. *MK*, 325.

13. Robert N. Proctor, *The Nazi War on Cancer* (Princeton: Princeton University Press, 1999), 46.

14. Quoted in Jäckel, *Hitler's World View*, 65.

15. *MK*, 290.

16. *MK*, 299.

17. Himmler in a lecture to a Wehrmacht class, "Wesen und Aufgabe der SS und der Polizei," January 1937, in Michalka, *Drittes Reich*, 1:161–62.

18. There is a third group, the "culture bearers," in Hitler's conception. *MK*, 290–96.

19. Quoted in Jäckel, *Hitler's World View*, 92.

20. *MK*, 65.

21. See, for example, Hitler memorandum on the Four-Year Plan, 1936, in Jeremy Noakes and Geoffrey Pridham, eds., *Nazism, 1919–1945: A Documentary Reader*, vol. 2, *State, Economy and Society, 1933–1939* (Exeter: University of Exeter Press, 1984), 282.

22. *MK*, 300.

23. *Hitlers Zweites Buch: Ein Dokument aus dem Jahr 1928*, ed. Gerhard L. Weinberg (Stuttgart: Deutsche Verlags-Anstalt, 1961), 223.

24. Hitler's secret memorandum on the Four-Year Plan, August 1936, in Michalka, *Drittes Reich*, 1:189. Emphases in original.

25. Hitler, 30 March 1941, in Wolfgang Michalka, ed., *Das Dritte Reich*, vol. 2, *Weltmachtanspruch und nationaler Zusammenbruch 1939–1945* (Munich: DTV, 1985), 51–53, quotation 52.

26. Quoted in Michael Burleigh and Wolfgang Wippermann, *The Racial*

State: Germany 1933–1945 (Cambridge: Cambridge University Press, 1991), 107.

27. Quoted in Noakes and Pridham, *Nazism*, 2:439.

28. See especially the chapter "Nation and Race" in *MK*, 284–329.

29. *MK*, 65, 288, 290.

30. *MK*, 286.

31. "Germanhood and the Aryan world were on the path to perdition if the struggle against the Jews was not joined; this was to be a struggle to the death. Redemption would come as liberation from the Jews — as their expulsion, possibly their annihilation." Saul Friedländer, *Nazi Germany and the Jews*, vol. 1, *The Years of Persecution, 1933–1939* (New York: HarperCollins, 1997), 87. But by then locating the origins of this trend "in that meeting point of German Christianity, neoromanticism, the mystical cult of sacred Aryan blood, and ultraconservative nationalism" (ibid.), Friedländer slights the specifically revolutionary, modernist, twentieth-century character of redemptive antisemitism.

32. On the theme of health and Nazism, see Proctor, *Nazi War on Cancer*, and the multivolume series from the Hamburg Institut für Sozialforschung, *Beiträge zur nationalsozialistischen Gesundheits- und Sozialpolitik*.

33. For a synthesis of a vast literature, see Burleigh and Wippermann, *Racial State*. See also Detlev Peukert, *Inside Nazi Germany: Conformity, Opposition, and Racism in Everyday Life*, trans. Richard Deveson (New Haven: Yale University Press, 1987). Peukert's book, though immensely interesting and significant, drastically underestimates the successes of the Nazi *Volksgemeinschaft*.

34. Doc. 35 referring to Strength through Joy, in Noakes and Pridham, *Nazism*, 2:351.

35. Ibid.

36. Hitler speech on 1 May 1934, in ibid., 2:354.

37. Hitler in a speech to the opening of the House of German Art in Munich, 19 July 1937, in ibid., 2:399. The comment is similar to Stalin's in relation to collectivization and industrialization: "Life has improved, comrades. Life is getting more joyous." Stalin, "Speech at the First All-Union Conference of Stakhanovites," 17 November 1935, in idem, *Problems of Leninism* (Moscow: Foreign Languages Publishing House, 1947), 531.

38. Proctor, *Nazi War on Cancer*, 77.

39. Hitler at the Nuremberg Party Rally, 14 September 1935, in Noakes and Pridham, *Nazism*, 2:416.

40. *MK*, 356. Hitler used this phrase often, sometimes altering it slightly. See, for example, Hitler at the Nuremberg Party Rally, 14 September 1935, in Noakes and Pridham, *Nazism*, 2:416–17.

41. This applied even to scientific and technical language. See Proctor, *Nazi War on Cancer*, 46–50.

42. Hitler memorandum on the Four-Year Plan, 1936, in Noakes and Pridham, *Nazism*, 2:281.

43. For the state as an instrument of the race, see *MK*, 391–94.

44. Quoted in Martin Broszat, "The Concentration Camps 1933–45," in Helmut Krausnick and Martin Broszat, *Anatomy of the SS State*, trans. Richard Barry, Marian Jackson, Dorothy Long (New York: Walker, 1968), 171. I have reworked the translation a bit. See also Ulrich Herbert, *Best: Biographische Studien über Radikalismus, Weltanschauung und Vernunft 1903–1989* (Bonn: J.H.W. Dietz, 1996).

45. Jäckel, *Hitler's World View*, 82.

46. See Ian Kershaw's works, especially *Hitler, 1889–1936*, and *Hitler: Profiles in Power* (London: Longman, 1991).

47. Sebastian Haffner, *The Meaning of Hitler*, trans. Ewald Osers (New York: Macmillan, 1979), 19.

48. See, for example, Goebbels speech to the press, 15 March 1933, in Michalka, *Drittes Reich*, 1:119–20.

49. Goebbels on the role of art in the revolution, 8 May 1933, in Michalka, *Drittes Reich*, 1:124–25.

50. Ibid.

51. On the importance of this concept, see Kershaw, *Hitler, 1889–1936*, xxix, 527–91, and idem, "'Working towards the Führer': Reflections on the Nature of the Hitler Dictatorship," in *Stalinism and Nazism: Dictatorships in Comparison*, ed. idem and Moshe Lewin (Cambridge: Cambridge University Press, 1997), 88–106.

52. Hitler's antisemitism, writes Eberhard Jäckel, "presupposes war, it demands the methods of warfare, and it is therefore not surprising that it should have reached its bloody climax during the next war, which was a part of Hitler's program from the start." Jäckel, *Hitler's World View*, 60–61.

53. Proctor, *Nazi War on Cancer*, 7–8.

54. Quotations from ibid., 120, 124.

55. Ibid., 47–48.

56. Noakes and Pridham, *Nazism*, 2:224. Under pressure from President von Hindenburg, the law excluded those non-Aryans who were already in service before 1914, had fought in World War I, or had sons or fathers killed during the war.

57. See Jeremy Noakes and Geoffrey Pridham, *Nazism 1919–1945: A Documentary Reader*, vol. 3, *Foreign Policy, War and Racial Extermination* (Exeter: University of Exeter Press, 1988), 1005–9.

58. A process first defined by Raul Hilberg. See *The Destruction of the European Jews*, rev. ed., 3 vols. (1961; New York: Holmes and Meier, 1985).

59. Noakes and Pridham, *Nazism*, 2:224, including n. 8.

60. Text of the laws in ibid., 535–37.

61. Text of decree in ibid., 538–39.

62. Friedländer, *Nazi Germany and the Jews*, 158.

63. See Robert Gellately, *The Gestapo and German Society: Enforcing Racial Policy, 1933–1945* (Oxford: Clarendon, 1990).

64. On these matters, see especially David Martin Luebke and Sybil Milton, "Locating the Victim: An Overview of Census-Taking, Tabulation Technology, and Persecution in Nazi Germany," *IEEE Annals of the History of Computing* 16:3 (1994): 25–39, and Friedländer, *Nazi Germany and the Jews,* esp. 177–210. Similar materials were gathered in the occupied countries during World War II, generally with the active compliance of statisticians and other officials.

65. Friedländer, *Nazi Germany and the Jews,* 326–28.

66. Luebke and Milton, "Locating the Victim," 33.

67. Quoted in Burleigh and Wippermann, *Racial State,* 49–50. See also Henry Friedlander, *The Origins of Nazi Genocide: From Euthanasia to the Final Solution* (Chapel Hill: University of North Carolina Press, 1995), 24–25.

68. On Nazi policies, see especially Michael Zimmermann, *Rassenutopie und Genozid: Die nationalsozialistische "Lösung der Zigeunerfrage"* (Hamburg: Hans Christians, 1996), and Sybil Milton, "Vorstufe zur Vernichtung: Die Zigeunerlage nach 1933," *Vierteljahrshefte für Zeitgeschichte* 43:1 (1995): 115–30. Before the Third Reich, the most comprehensive law relating to Gypsies was passed by Bavaria in 1926. See the commentary and text in Ludwig Eiber, *"Ich wußte, es wird schlimm": Die Verfolgung der Sinti und Roma in München 1933–1945* (Munich: Buchendorfer, 1993), 40–45.

69. The term is from Zimmermann, *Rassenutopie und Genozid,* 147–55. For the following, see ibid., passim; Burleigh and Wippermann, *Racial State,* 114, 118–21; and Eiber, *"Ich wußte, es wird schlimm",* 47–49.

70. Eiber, *"Ich wußte, es wird schlimm",* 58.

71. Ibid., 58–62, quotation 62.

72. Quoted in Milton, "Vorstufe zur Vernichtung," 128 n. 46.

73. Quoted in Burleigh and Wippermann, *Racial State,* 137.

74. See Gisela Bock, *Zwangssterilisation im Nationalsozialismus: Studien zur Rassenpolitik und Frauenpolitik* (Opladen: Westdeutscher Verlag, 1986), and Friedlander, *Origins of Nazi Genocide.*

75. See Jeremy Noakes, "Social Outcasts in the Third Reich," in *Life in the Third Reich,* ed. Richard Bessel (Oxford: Oxford University Press, 1987), 92. See also Robert Gellately and Nathan Stoltzfus, eds., *Social Outsiders in Nazi Germany* (Princeton: Princeton University Press, 2001).

76. Circular, Reich Ministry of Interior, 18 July 1940, in Burleigh and Wippermann, *Racial State,* 182.

77. "Himmler über Bekämpfung jugendlicher Cliquen," 25 October 1944, in Michalka, *Drittes Reich,* 2:374–76, quotation 375.

78. Victor Klemperer, *I Will Bear Witness: A Diary of the Nazi Years, 1933–1941,* trans. Martin Chalmers, 2 vols. (New York: Random House, 1998–99), 1:34.

79. Ibid., 52.

80. Ibid., 64.

81. Text of the decree in Noakes and Pridham, *Nazism,* 2:553.

82. Quoted in Burleigh and Wippermann, *Racial State*, 94–95.

83. See especially Marion Kaplan, *Between Dignity and Despair: Jewish Life in Nazi Germany* (New York: Oxford University Press, 1998).

84. Ibid., 38, 45.

85. See ibid., 94–118, quotation 117.

86. Quoted in ibid., 131.

87. For a synthesis of the various discriminatory measures, see Friedländer, *Nazi Germany and the Jews*. For a valuable collection of documents, see Joseph Walk, ed., *Das Sonderrecht für die Juden im NS-Staat* (Heidelberg: Müller Juristischer Verlag, 1981).

88. Testimony of Wanda Michaelis in Peter Sandner, *Frankfurt. Auschwitz. Die nationalsozialistische Verfolgung der Sinti und Roma in Frankfurt am Main* (Frankfurt am Main: Brandes and Apsel, 1998), 258–62.

89. On the Frankfurt camp, see Sandner, *Frankfurt. Auschwitz.*, 121–73, quotations 150, 152.

90. For one testimony from Bavaria, see Eiber, *"Ich wußte, es wird schlimm"*, 107.

91. Yet for one case, where local health officials blocked the efforts to sterilize a Sinta who wanted to marry an Aryan, see Sandner, *Frankfurt. Auschwitz.*, 212–21. The physician and official who sought to carry out the procedure was none other that Otmar Freiherr von Verschuer, Josef Mengele's mentor. In his campaign against other officials, he obtained strong support from Robert Ritter.

92. "Bericht des Reichsjustizministers Thierack über eine Besprechung mit Himmler," 18 September 1942, in Michalka, *Drittes Reich*, 2:250.

93. For the following, see Friedlander, *Origins of Nazi Genocide*, as well as the documentation in Noakes and Pridham, *Nazism*, 3:1005–48.

94. Henry Friedlander calls the killing center "the unprecedented institution that would symbolize Nazi Germany and the early twentieth century." *Origins of Nazi Genocide*, 86.

95. Ibid., 78.

96. Quoted in Noakes and Pridham, *Nazism*, 3:1027.

97. Quoted in Wolfgang U. Eckart, " 'Euthanasia Project T4' and Medical Science in Germany, 1933–1945" (manuscript), *http://www.uni-heidelberg.de/institute/fak5/igm/g47/eck—euta.htm* [29 August 2002], quotation 5.

98. Ibid.

99. Friedlander, *Origins of Nazi Genocide*, 127–35.

100. Hitler decree, "[Zur] Festigung deutschen Volkstums," 7 October 1939, in Michalka, *Drittes Reich*, 2:118.

101. Himmler, "Einige Gedanken über die Behandlung der Fremdvölkischen im Osten," 15 May 1940, in Michalka, *Drittes Reich*, 2:163–66. Hitler said much the same thing in his musings, 17/18 September 1941, in Michalka, *Drittes Reich*, 2:185–87.

102. "Befehl des Armeeoberkommandos 6 über das Verhalten der Truppen

im Ostraum," 10 October 1941, in Michalka, *Drittes Reich*, 2:189–90. Emphasis in original.

103. See especially Götz Aly and Susanne Heim, *Vordenker der Vernichtung: Auschwitz und die deutschen Pläne für eine neue europäische Ordnung* (1991; Frankfurt am Main: Fischer, 1993).

104. Excerpts and comments in Michalka, *Drittes Reich*, 2:198–207. The plan was first drafted in July 1941. See also Helmut Heiber, "Der Generalplan Ost," *Vierteljahrshefte für Zeitgeschichte* 6:3 (1958): 281–325. For similar plans, see Reichsleiter Martin Bormann to Reichsleiter Alfred Rosenberg, communicating Hitler's recommendations for the treatment of the non-German population in the East, 23 July 1942, in Michalka, *Drittes Reich*, 2:208–10.

105. Figure from Götz Aly, "'Judenumsiedlung': Überlegungen zur politischen Vorgeschichte des Holocaust," in *Nationalsozialistische Vernichtungspolitik 1939–1945: Neue Forschungen und Kontroversen*, ed. Ulrich Herbert (Frankfurt am Main: Fischer, 1998), 67.

106. Ibid., 85.

107. Dieter Pohl, "Die Ermordung der Juden im Generalgouvernement," in Herbert, *Nationalsozialistische Vernichtungspolitik*, 101.

108. Christopher R. Browning, "Nazi Resettlement Policy and the Search for a Solution to the Jewish Question, 1939–1941," in idem, *The Path to Genocide: Essays on Launching the Final Solution* (Cambridge: Cambridge University Press, 1992), passim, 20–21 for figures.

109. Aly, "'Judenumsiedlung,'" 76.

110. Ibid., 87–88.

111. Issued by Heydrich on 2 July 1941. Excerpt in Noakes and Pridham, *Nazism*, 3:1091–92. On the Einsatzgruppen, see especially Helmut Krausnick and Hans-Heinrich Wilhelm, *Die Truppe des Weltanschauungskrieges: Die Einsatzgruppen der Sicherheitspolizei und des SD, 1938–1942* (Stuttgart: Deutsche Verlags-Anstalt, 1981).

112. Testimony of SS Commander Otto Ohlendorf, quoted in Krausnick, "Persecution of the Jews," in Broszat and Krausnick, *Anatomy of the SS State*, 79.

113. Christopher R. Browning, "Beyond 'Intentionalism' and 'Functionalism': The Decision for the Final Solution Reconsidered," in idem, *Path to Genocide*, 104–11.

114. Ulrich Herbert, "Vernichtungspolitik: Neue Antworten und Fragen zur Geschichte des 'Holocaust,'" in idem, *Nationalsozialistische Vernichtungspolitik*, 48–49.

115. Quoted in Krausnick, "Persecution of the Jews," 80–81.

116. See Walter Manoschek, "Die Vernichtung der Juden in Serbien," in Herbert, *Nationalsozialistische Vernichtungspolitik*, 209–34, quotation 232. See also Christopher R. Browning, "Bureaucracy and Mass Murder: The German Administrator's Comprehension of the Final Solution," in idem, *Path to Genocide*, 125–44.

117. Thomas Sandkühler, "Judenpolitik und Judenmord im Distrikt Galizien, 1941–1942," in Herbert, *Nationalsozialistische Vernichtungspolitik*, 128.

118. Ibid., 114.

119. See the account in Noakes and Pridham, *Nazism*, 3:1138–43. Chelmno was in operation from December 1941 to early 1943 but then was revived from 23 June to mid-July 1944. In January 1944 the few remaining Jews were shot.

120. Herbert, "Vernichtungspolitik," 50, argues that the turning point came once the prospects for a quick victory had dimmed, that is, by the late summer. Michael Zimmermann, "Die nationalsozialistische 'Lösung der Zigeunerfrage,'" in Herbert, *Nationalsozialistische Vernichtungspolitik*, 250, argues more in accord with Browning: the Nazi leadership believed at the end of July and early August 1941 that victory over the Soviet Union was imminent; hence Himmler radicalized the tasks of the Einsatzgruppen with orders "to murder completely the Jewish population of the occupied Soviet Union. At the same time the murder command was extended to cover the Gypsies." Nonetheless, the Nazis did not systematically search out the Roma and Sinti, as they did the Jews. Christian Gerlach, "Deutsche Wirtschaftsinteressen, Besatzungpolitik und der Mord an den Juden in Weißrußland, 1941–1943," in Herbert, *Nationalsozialistische Vernichtungspolitik*, 263–91, states that with the grinding down of the German invasion plans in the autumn of 1941, the result was "the *move from utopian plans for the murder of a people [Völkermordplänen] to the actual implementation of a mass murder program* (283, emphasis in original).

121. See Gerlach, "Wirtschaftsinteressen," 289–91, for a similar argument. And for the most effective reviews of the literature, see Herbert, "Vernichtungspolitik," and Dieter Pohl, "Die Holocaust-Forschung und Goldhagens Thesen," *Vierteljahrshefte für Zeitgeschichte* 45:1 (1997): 12–48.

122. Tobias Jersak, "Die Interaktion von Kriegsverlauf und Judenvernichtung: Ein Blick auf Hitlers Strategie im Spätsommer 1941," *Historische Zeitschrift* 268 (1999): 311–74, here 327–28, and Browning, *Path to Genocide*, 106–11, though Browning suggests that these developments did signify mass killings, not just deportations.

123. Quoted in Aly, "'Judenumsiedlung,'" 92.

124. Ibid., 73–74.

125. Pohl, "Ermordung der Juden," 114. See also Herbert, "Vernichtungspolitik," 45.

126. This comment goes to the heart of debates about the exercise of power in the Third Reich. I follow here especially Ian Kershaw, who has in numerous instances cited the catchphrase "working toward the Führer," which captures the essence of Nazi functionaries acting more or less on their own according to what they thought were the Führer's wishes. For a concise statement, see Kershaw, "'Working towards the Führer.'"

127. The following draws on Jersak, "Interaktion von Kriegsverlauf und Judenvernichtung."

128. Ibid., 321–25.

129. Ibid., 370–71. Jersak's views are parallel to those of Christian Gerlach in "Die Wannsee Konferenz, das Schicksal der deutschen Juden und Hitlers politische Grundsatzentscheidung, alle Juden Europas zu ermorden," *Werkstatt-Geschichte* 6:18 (1997): 7–44, though Gerlach does not recognize a first order in August 1941. While both Jersak and Gerlach provide insightful and highly plausible interpretations, their identification of a Hitler order or orders remains based on circumstantial evidence.

130. Most recently and thoroughly on Wannsee, see Gerlach, "Wannsee-Konferenz,"

131. See Noakes and Pridham, *Nazism*, 3:1143–56, for the construction and operation of the "Reinhard Action" death camps, Belzec, Sobibor, and Treblinka. On Auschwitz, see ibid., 1173–90.

132. Pohl, "Ermordung der Juden," 104–7.

133. About 60 percent of the six million Jewish victims were killed in the extermination camps. Herbert, "Vernichtungspolitik," 57.

134. Sometimes the connection between the two groups was quite immediate and physical. One official document read, "In relation to the deportation of Gypsies it is communicated that on Friday, 20 October 1939, the first Jewish transport departed from Vienna. To this transport three to four cars of Gypsies can be attached." Quoted in Milton, "Vorstufe zur Vernichtung," 127.

135. Michaelis in Sandner, *Frankfurt. Auschwitz*, 262.

136. On these conditions, See Burleigh and Wippermann, *Racial State*, 121–27, and Eiber, *"Ich wußte, es wird schlimm"*, 75–78, 85, 92–94.

137. Pohl, "Ermordung der Juden," 114.

138. Hans Mommsen, "The Realization of the Unthinkable: The 'Final Solution of the Jewish Question' in the Third Reich," in idem, *From Weimar to Auschwitz*, trans. Philip O'Connor (Princeton: Princeton University Press, 1991), 224–53.

139. The primacy of race thinking in Nazi policies may seem so self-evident that it is hardly worth belaboring. Yet, in fact, in case after case, scholars have made race a secondary factor derivative of other social processes. To give just a few more or less recent examples: Arno Mayer, *Why Did the Heavens Not Darken? The "Final Solution" in History* (New York: Pantheon, 1988), sought to make Nazi antisemitism derivative of the Nazis' anticommunism. Hans Mommsen and Martin Broszat, with their notion of "cumulative radicalization," were so focused on the internal workings of the Nazi system that one loses any sense of the role of ideology, in particular racial antisemitism, in causing the Holocaust. See Mommsen, "Realization of the Unthinkable," and Broszat, *The Hitler State: The Foundation and Development of the Internal Structure of the Third Reich*, trans. John W. Hiden (London: Longman, 1981). Some feminist writings on the Third Reich have sought to depict women as a category as victims, a position that blends out the distinctions between race and

gender. See Bock, *Zwangssterilisation*, and, especially, "Gleichheit und Differenz in der nationalsozialistischen Rassenpolitik," *Geschichte und Gesellschaft* 19:3 (1993): 277–310. Even Christopher R. Browning's very important book, *Ordinary Men: Reserve Police Battalion 101 and the Final Solution in Poland* (New York: HarperCollins, 1992), tends to de-emphasize the role of ideology. In his self-described "moderate functionalist" view, aspects of group psychology— peer pressure, the desire to belong, but not antisemitism—are the main factors that explain how "ordinary men" became perpetrators of genocide. Finally, the recent, pathbreaking work of Aly and Heim on the planners, *Vordenker der Vernichtung*, devotes a good deal of attention to Nazi antisemitism. But the authors then argue that the planners' real motivation was economic rationalization. The Holocaust then becomes a by-product of the modernizing impulse of a technical class.

140. The term is from Michael Omi and Howard Winant, *Racial Formation in the United States: From the 1960s to the 1990s*, 2d ed. (New York: Routledge, 1994).

141. Quoted in Noakes and Pridham, *Nazism*, 3:1044–45.

142. Quoted in Friedländer, *Nazi Germany and the Jews*, 29.

143. Testimony of Lili G., Fortunoff Video Collection for Holocaust Testimonies, T-691. Sterling Memorial Library, Yale University. Hereafter FVC.

144. Generally on the meaning of violence, see Wolfgang Sofsky, *Traktat über die Gewalt* (Frankfurt am Main: Fischer, 1996); Alf Lüdtke, "Einleitung: Herrschaft als soziale Praxis," in *Herrschaft als soziale Praxis: Historische und sozial-anthroplogische Studien*, ed. idem (Göttingen: Vandenhoeck and Ruprecht, 1991), 9–63; Thomas Lindenberger and Alf Lüdtke, eds., *Physische Gewalt: Studien zur Geschichte der Neuzeit* (Frankfurt am Main: Suhrkamp, 1995); and Michael Wildt, "Gewalt gegen Juden in Deutschland 1933 bis 1939," *WerkstattGeschichte* 6:18 (1997): 59–80.

145. Zimmermann, *Rassenutopie und Genozid*, 121–24.

146. "Mass Murder in Kovno": report of a colonel, in Klee, Dressen, and Riess, *"The Good Old Days"*, 28–29.

147. "Thin crust" from Hugh Trevor-Roper's forward to *"The Good Old Days"*, x. See also the story of Polish villagers who killed the Jewish inhabitants in Jan Gross, *Neighbors: The Destruction of the Jewish Community in Jedwabne, Poland* (Princeton: Princeton University Press, 2002).

148. "Mass Murder in Kovno": reports of a photographer and a sergeant-major, in *"The Good Old Days"*, 31–32, 33.

149. Affidavit of Otto Ohlendorf, in *"The Good Old Days"*, 60.

150. Member of Sonderkommando 4a, in *"The Good Old Days"*, 118.

151. Major Rösler to Infantry General Schniewindt, 3 January 1942, in *"The Good Old Days"*, 118.

152. The Jäger Report; Statement of Kurt Werner, member of Sonderkom-

mando 4a; and SS-Gruppenführer Friedrich Katzmann, 30 June 1943, all in *"The Good Old Days"*, 55, 67, 106.

153. Testimonies of a war correspondent and of Erich Bauer, the "gas Master" of Sobibor, in *"The Good Old Days"*, 129, 232.

154. Testimony on the Babi Yar massacre, in *"The Good Old Days"*, 63–68, quotation 65–66.

155. Testimony of Irving R. on the mass killings in Latvia, FVC T-1100.

156. Testimony of Loni K., FVC T-691.

157. Testimony of Lili G., FVC T-1779.

158. Testimony of Prof. Wilhelm Pfannenstiel, Waffen-SS hygienist, in *"The Good Old Days"*, 244.

159. Testimony of Rudolf Höss, commandant of Auschwitz, in *"The Good Old Days"*, 269–74, quotation 270.

160. Ibid., 273–74.

161. Kaplan, *Between Dignity and Despair*, 71–72, 131–35.

162. SS-Obersturmführer Karl Kretschmer (Sonderkommando 4a), 27 September–19 October 1942, in *"The Good Old Days"*, 164, 165–66, 167, 169.

163. Testimony of Loni K., FVC T-691.

164. Ibid.

165. Ibid.

166. Proctor, *Nazi War on Cancer*, 40.

167. Kaplan, *Between Dignity and Despair*, 229.

168. Michael Geyer, "The Nazi State Reconsidered," in Bessel, *Life in the Third Reich*, 62.

169. Robert Gellately, *Backing Hitler: Consent and Coercion in Nazi Germany* (Oxford: Oxford University Press, 2001), 257.

170. Michael Geyer, "Restorative Elites, German Society and the Nazi Pursuit of War," in *Fascist Italy and Nazi Germany: Comparisons and Contrasts*, ed. Richard Bessel (Cambridge: Cambridge University Press, 1996), 134–64, here 154.

171. Herbert, "Vernichtungspolitik," 42–43.

172. On Fischer, see Wolfgang U. Eckart, *Medizin und Kolonialimperialismus: Deutschland 1884–1945* (Paderborn: Ferdinand Schöningh, 1997), 257, 270–71; Paul Weindling, *Health, Race and German Politics between National Unification and Nazism, 1870–1945* (Cambridge: Cambridge University Press, 1989), passim; and Robert N. Proctor, "From *Anthropologie* to *Rassenkunde* in the German Anthropological Tradition," in *Bones, Bodies, Behavior: Essays on Biological Anthropology*, ed. George W. Stocking, Jr. (Madison: University of Wisconsin Press, 1988), 138–79.

173. Proctor, "From *Anthropologie* to *Rassenkunde*," 160–61.

174. Ibid., 147.

175. Hannah Arendt, *Eichmann in Jerusalem: A Report on the Banality of Evil*, rev. ed. (New York: Viking, 1964).

CHAPTER FOUR
Racial Communism: Cambodia under the Khmer Rouge

1. Quoted in *Cambodian Witness: The Autobiography of Someth May*, ed. James Fenton (London: Faber and Faber, 1986), 117.

2. As Jean-Louis Margolin writes: "Pol Pot clearly believed that his renowned predecessors — Marx, Lenin, Stalin and Mao Zeodong — could be surpassed. The revolution of the twenty-first century would speak Khmer, just as that of the twentieth century had spoken Russian and Chinese." "Cambodge: Au pays du crime déconcertant," in *Le Livre noir du communisme: Crimes, terreur et répression*, ed. Stéphane Courtois (Paris: Robert Laffont, 1997), 631.

3. I am drawing here from David P. Chandler, *The Tragedy of Cambodian History: Politics, War, and Revolution since 1945* (New Haven: Yale University Press, 1991).

4. See David P. Chandler, *Brother Number One: A Political Biography of Pol Pot*, 2d ed. (Boulder: Westview, 1999), 12–40.

5. Serge Thion, "The Cambodian Idea of Revolution," in *Revolution and Its Aftermath in Kampuchea: Eight Essays*, ed. David P. Chandler and Ben Kiernan, Yale University Southeast Asia Studies no. 25 (New Haven: Yale University Southeast Asia Studies, 1983), 10–33, here 14–15. Thion taught in a lycée in Phnom Penh in the 1960s.

6. See Penny Edwards, "Imaging the Other in Cambodian Nationalist Discourse before and during the UNTAC Period," in *Propaganda, Politics, and Violence in Cambodia: Democratic Transition under United Nations Peacekeeping*, ed. Steve Heder and Judy Ledgerwood (Armonk, NY: M. E. Sharpe, 1996), 50–72.

7. The figure of "almost one-quarter" comes from a personal communication from David Chandler.

8. Chandler, *Brother Number One*, 31–40.

9. Ben Kiernan, *How Pol Pot Came to Power: A History of Communism in Kampuchea, 1930–1975* (London: Verso, 1985), 120.

10. Chandler, *Brother Number One*, 38–39.

11. Quoted in Margolin, "Cambodge," 684.

12. Ben Kiernan, *The Pol Pot Regime: Race, Power, and Genocide in Cambodia under the Khmer Rouge, 1975–79* (New Haven: Yale University Press, 1996), 11.

13. For biographic information on Nuon Chea and Ta Mok, see Yale University Cambodia Genocide Program, Biographic Database: *http://www.yale.edu/cgp/*, records Y01062 and Y04151 [30 August 2002], respectively.

14. Chandler, *Tragedy*, 109–11, 336 n. 72.

15. David P. Chandler, *Voices from S-21: Terror and History in Pol Pot's Secret Prison* (Berkeley and Los Angeles: University of California Press, 1999), 14–40.

16. "Their [the Khmer Rouge's] victory in 1975, given their resources and history, was unexpected." Chandler, *Brother Number One*, 66. See also Chandler's comments in *Tragedy*, 107–8, as well as Kate G. Frieson, "Revolution and Rural Response in Cambodia: 1970–1975," in *Genocide and Democracy in Cambodia: The Khmer Rouge, the United Nations and the International Community*, ed. Ben Kiernan, Yale University Southeast Asia Studies no. 41 (New Haven: Yale University Southeast Asia Studies, 1993), 33–50.

17. Quoted in Chandler, *Tragedy*, 240. For biographical information on Ieng Sary, see Yale University Cambodia Genocide Program, Biographic Database: *http://www.yale.edu/cgp/*, record Y06688 [30 August 2002].

18. Quoted in Chandler, *Brother Number One*, 140. See also Karl D. Jackson, "The Ideology of Total Revolution," in *Cambodia 1975–1978: Rendezvous with Death*, ed. idem (Princeton: Princeton University Press, 1989), 37–78. For biographical information on Pol Pot, see Chandler, *Brother Number One*, and Yale University Cambodia Genocide Program, Biographic Database: *http:www.yale.edu/cgp/*, record Y00999 [30 August 2002].

19. For a different view that emphasizes the racial elements of Khmer Rouge policies, see Kiernan, *Pol Pot Regime*, and, in an earlier formulation focused more on chauvinism, idem, "Kampuchea and Stalinism," in *Marxism in Asia*, ed. Colin Mackerras and Nick Knight (London: Croom Helm, 1985), 232–49. For strong critiques of Kiernan's interpretation, see Steve Heder, "Racism, Marxism, Labelling, and Genocide in Ben Kiernan's *The Pol Pot Regime*," *South East Asia Research* 5:2 (1997): 101–53, and David Chandler's review of *Pol Pot Regime*, in *Journal of Asian Studies* 55:4 (1996): 1063–64.

20. Quoted in Kiernan, *Pol Pot Regime*, 204. For biographic information, see Yale University Cambodia Genocide Program, Biographic Database: *http://www.yale.edu/cgp/*, record Y00196 [30 August 2002].

21. Quoted in Jackson, "Ideology of Total Revolution," 77.

22. Ibid., 59. For a contrary view of Democratic Kampuchea as a peasant revolution, see Michael Vickery, *Cambodia 1975–1982* (Boston: South End Press, 1983), 286; for a view of the regime as a return to feudal times, see Wilfred Burchett, "Preface," in *Peasants and Politics in Kampuchea, 1942–1981*, ed. Ben Kiernan and Chanthou Boua (London: Zed, 1982), ii. See also the running exchange between Vickery and Ben Kiernan in *Bulletin of Concerned Asian Scholars* 20–22 (1988–90).

23. See Charles H. Twining, "The Economy," in Jackson, *Cambodia 1975–1978*, 109–50.

24. Chandler, *Brother Number One*, 114–22.

25. Kiernan, *Pol Pot Regime*, 222–23.

26. Quoted in Jackson, "Ideology of Total Revolution," 59.

27. "Excerpted Report on the Leading Views of the Comrade Representing the Party Organization at a Zone Assembly," June 1976, in *Pol Pot Plans the Future: Confidential Leadership Documents from Democratic Kampuchea,*

1976–1977, trans. and ed. David P. Chandler, Ben Kiernan, and Chanthou Boua, Yale University Southeast Asia Studies no. 33 (New Haven: Yale University Southeast Asia Studies, 1988), 24.

28. See, for example, the slogan "With Angkar, there is a great leap forward, a prodigious leap forward," in Henri Locard, *Le "Petit livre rouge" de Pol Pot ou Les Paroles de l'Angkar* (Paris: L'Harmattan, 1996), 49. See also Chandler, *Brother Number One*, 3.

29. Kiernan, *Pol Pot Regime*, 78.

30. CPK Party Center, "The Party's Four-Year Plan to Build Socialism in All Fields, 1977–1980," July–August 1976, in *Pol Pot Plans the Future*, 107.

31. Kalyanee E. Mam, "An Oral History of Family Life under the Khmer Rouge," Yale Center for International and Area Studies, Genocide Studies Program, Working Paper GS 10, 9.

32. But see memoirs for signs of resistance to this ideology, for example, Loung Ung, *First They Killed My Father: A Daughter of Cambodia Remembers* (New York: HarperCollins, 2000), and Dith Pran and Kim DePaul, eds., *Children of Cambodia's Killing Fields: Memoirs by Survivors* (New Haven: Yale University Press, 1997).

33. CPK Party Center, "Preliminary Explanation before Reading the Plan, by the Party Secretary," 21 August 1976, in *Pol Pot Plans the Future*, 158.

34. Mam, "An Oral History of Family Life," 17–19.

35. CPK Party Center, "Summary of the Results of the 1976 Study Session," undated, in *Pol Pot Plans the Future*, 176.

36. Locard, *Le "Petit livre rouge" de Pol Pot*, 116.

37. "Excerpted Report on the Leading Views of the Comrade Representing the Party Organization at a Zone Assembly," June 1976, in *Pol Pot Plans the Future*, 27.

38. Quoted in Chandler, *Brother Number One*, 115.

39. Quoted in François Ponchaud, "Social Change in the Vortex of Revolution," in Jackson, *Cambodia 1975–1978*, 151–77, here 167.

40. "Excerpted Report on the Leading Views of the Comrade," 16, 20.

41. Locard, *Le "Petit livre rouge" de Pol Pot*, 73.

42. CPK Party Center, "Preliminary Explanation before Reading the Plan," 160.

43. Kiernan, *Pol Pot Regime*, 97.

44. CPK Party Center, "Party's Four-Year Plan," 45–46.

45. Quotations in Kiernan, *Pol Pot Regime*, 148, 153.

46. "Sharpen the Consciousness of the Proletarian Class to Be As Keen and Strong As Possible," *Revolutionary Flags* Special Issue, September–October 1976, trans. Kem Sos and Timothey Carney, in Jackson, *Cambodia 1975–1978*, 269–91, here 279.

47. Ibid., 281.

48. Ibid., 269.

49. Quoted in Chandler, *Brother Number One*, 117, and Jackson, "Ideology of Total Revolution," 59, 60.

50. Timothy Carney, "The Organization of Power," in Jackson, *Cambodia 1975–1978*, 79–107, here 85.

51. Ibid., 86, and Kiernan, *Pol Pot Regime*, 246.

52. See Carney, "Organization of Power," titles 88–89, 92, 100–107; Yale University Cambodia Genocide Program, Biographic Database: *http://www.yale.edu/cgp/*, records Y03100 (Son Sen) and Y00999 (Pol Pot) [30 August 2002]; and Chandler, *Voices from S-21*, 18–20.

53. CPK Eastern Region Military Political Service, "Summary of Annotated Party History," in Jackson, *Cambodia 1975–1978*, 251–68, quotations 251, 253, 260, 262, 268.

54. Quoted in Locard, *Le "Petit livre rouge" de Pol Pot*, 34.

55. "Sharpen the Consciousness of the Proletarian Class," 270.

56. Quotations from ibid., 273, 277, 278.

57. Quoted in Jackson, "Ideology of Total Revolution," 44. See also Pol Pot quotation in Kiernan, *Pol Pot Regime*, 94.

58. Both quotations from Jackson, "Ideology of Total Revolution," 67.

59. Quotations from "Sharpen the Consciousness of the Proletarian Class," 295, 297, and 282.

60. CPK Party Center, "Preliminary Explanation before Reading the Plan," 126.

61. CPK Party Center, "Report of Activities of the Party Center according to the General Political Tasks of 1976," 20 December 1976, in *Pol Pot Plans the Future*, 183, 207.

62. Ibid., 183–84, 189, 190.

63. Quoted in Kenneth M. Quinn, "The Pattern and Scope of Violence," in Jackson, *Cambodia 1975–1978*, 179–208, here 185.

64. Quoted in Kiernan, *Pol Pot Regime*, 246.

65. Ponchaud, "Social Change," 161. For a similar point, see Alexander Laban Hinton, "Why Did You Kill? The Cambodian Genocide and the Dark Side of Face and Honor," *Journal of Asian Studies* 57:1 (1998): 93–122.

66. See Chandler's scattered comments in *Brother Number One*, 6, 10–11, 76–77, and generally on Pol Pot's early life, ibid., 7–21. Though he also notes: "To many Cambodians, forests were also places of illness, danger, and fearsome spiritual powers" (76). See also Ponchaud, "Social Change," esp. 160–61.

67. Chandler, *Tragedy*, 218, drawing on contemporary accounts.

68. See also the interesting collection and analysis of Locard, *Le "Petit livre rouge" de Pol Pot*, and also John Marston, "Metaphors of the Khmer Rouge," in *Cambodian Culture since 1975: Homeland and Exile*, ed. May M. Ebihara, Carol A. Mortland, and Judy Ledgerwood (Ithaca: Cornell University Press, 1994), 105–18.

69. Quoted in Ponchaud, "Social Change," 157.

70. Kiernan, *Pol Pot Regime*, 172.

71. See Heder, "Racism, Marxism, Labelling, and Genocide," on the Marxist inclination to blend class and national categories.

72. Margolin, "Cambodge," 638.

73. Ibid., 640. See also Carney, "Organization of Power."

74. Kiernan, *Pol Pot Regime*, 178–79.

75. Ibid., 176–77. See also Carney, "Organization of Power," 84, and CPK, "Pay Attention to Pushing the Work of Building Party and People's Collective Strength Even Stronger," *Revolutionary Flags* 3 (March 1978): 37–53, trans. Kem Sos and Timothey Carney, in Jackson, *Cambodia 1975–1978*, 298.

76. Kiernan, *Pol Pot Regime*, 184–86, 191.

77. Twining, "Economy," 127–29.

78. See "Sharpen the Consciousness of the Proletarian Class," 275–76, and Carney, "Organization of Power," 83, 99–100.

79. See James C. Scott, *Seeing Like a State: How Certain Schemes to Improve the Human Condition Have Failed* (New Haven: Yale University Press, 1998).

80. Quoted in Chandler, *Tragedy*, 208.

81. Kiernan, *Pol Pot Regime*, 251.

82. Quoted in ibid., 269.

83. Quoted in ibid., 271.

84. Quoted in ibid., 283.

85. Ponchaud, "Social Change," 153–54.

86. See Heder, "Racism, Marxism, Labelling, and Genocide," 101–17.

87. Quotations from Ponchaud, "Social Change," 163, 164.

88. Ibid., 162–69.

89. Ibid., 164–65.

90. Locard, *Le "Petit livre rouge" de Pol Pot*, 82–84.

91. Ibid., 82.

92. Quoted in Jackson, "Ideology of Total Revolution," 56.

93. See Ponchaud, "Social Change," 164–66, and some of the photographs that accompany David Hawk, "The Photographic Record," in Jackson, *Cambodia 1975–1978*, 209–13.

94. See Edwards, "Imaging the Other," 50–72.

95. Ibid., 54.

96. See Chandler, *Tragedy*, 6–7.

97. This paragraph draws on Edwards, "Imaging the Other."

98. Quoted in Quinn, "Pattern and Scope of Violence," 204.

99. See Chandler, *Tragedy*, 246–55.

100. See Margolin, "Cambodge," 637, and Kiernan, *Pol Pot Regime*, 39–49.

101. For some of these reports, see Kiernan, *Pol Pot Regime*, 39–54.

102. See, for example, Ung, *First They Killed My Father*; Pran and Paul, *Children of Cambodia's Killing Fields*; and May, *Cambodian Witness*.

103. Kiernan, *Pol Pot Regime*, 216–17.

104. Ibid., 170–71.

105. See May Ebihara, "A Cambodian Village under the Khmer Rouge, 1975–1979," in Kiernan, *Genocide and Democracy in Cambodia*, 51–63, here 54.

106. Personal communication from David Chandler.

107. Kiernan, *Pol Pot Regime*, 147–56, quotation 156.

108. Quoted in ibid., 62. See also Quinn, "Pattern and Scope of Violence."

109. See Jackson, "Ideology of Total Revolution," 60–61.

110. *Kampuchea: Decade of the Genocide. Report of a Finnish Inquiry Commission*, ed. Kimmo Kiljunen (London: Zed, 1984), 15.

111. See the very effective use of interviews of nearly five hundred survivors in Kiernan, *Pol Pot Regime*.

112. For one harrowing account, see Ung, *First They Killed My Father*.

113. Quoted in Kiernan, *Pol Pot Regime*, 165.

114. Quoted in Margolin, "Cambodge," 654.

115. Quoted in ibid., 666.

116. Ibid., 668.

117. See especially Michael Vickery, "Democratic Kampuchea: Themes and Variations," and Ben Kiernan, "Wild Chickens, Farm Chickens and Cormorants: Kampuchea's Eastern Zone under Pol Pot," both in Chandler and Kiernan, *Revolution and Its Aftermath*, 99–135, 136–211, and Kiernan, *Pol Pot Regime*. This interpretation of strict regional differences is disputed by Heder, "Racism, Marxism, Labelling, and Genocide."

118. See Chandler, *Voices from S-21*, 20–23. For additional biographic information, see Yale University Cambodia Genocide Program, Biographic Database: *http://www.yale.edu/cgp/*, record Y00153 [30 August 2002].

119. Quotations from Kiernan, *Pol Pot Regime*, 336.

120. See ibid., 386–439.

121. Chandler, *Brother Number One*, 108.

122. Kiernan, *Pol Pot Regime*, 198–99.

123. Quoted in ibid., 226.

124. Pin Yathay, quoted in Margolin, "Cambodge," 640.

125. See especially Chandler, *Voices from S-21*.

126. Quoted in Margolin, "Cambodge," 649.

127. Ibid., 648–50.

128. See Chandler, *Brother Number One*, 76.

129. Chandler, *Tragedy*, 203.

130. Kiernan, *Pol Pot Regime*, 75.

131. Ibid., 82–83, 111, and Margolin, "Cambodge," 649.

132. Ponchaud, "Social Change," 153; Kiernan, *Pol Pot Regime*, 64.

133. See Kiernan, *Pol Pot Regime*, 252–88, and Margolin, "Cambodge," 650.

134. Quoted in David R. Hawk, "International Human Rights Law and Democratic Kampuchea," in *The Cambodian Agony*, ed. David A. Ablin and Marlowe Hood (Armonk, NY: M. E. Sharpe, 1990), 127–28.

135. Hawk, "International Human Rights Law," 129. Cambodian population statistics are inexact. See the exchange on this issue (and others) between Michael Vickery and Ben Kiernan in *Bulletin of Concerned Asian Scholars* 20–22 (1988–90).

136. Chandler, *Tragedy*, 209–10, 216–17, and idem, *Voices from S-21*, 21–22.

137. Kiernan, *Pol Pot Regime*, 107.

138. Ibid., 107–9.

139. Quoted in ibid., 366.

140. Locard, *Le "Petit livre rouge" de Pol Pot*, 139.

141. Quoted in Kiernan, *Pol Pot Regime*, 386.

142. Quoted in ibid., 387.

143. Quoted in ibid., 387–88.

144. Quoted in ibid., 365.

145. Ibid., 111, 386–90.

146. As David Chandler argues, "many Cambodian Communists shared racially based ideas about Vietnam with their countrymen who had executed Vietnamese civilians in May 1970." Chandler, *Tragedy*, 216.

147. Kiernan, *Pol Pot Regime*, 296–98.

148. See also Margolin, "Cambodge," 694, and Heder, "Racism, Marxism, Labelling, and Genocide."

149. Kiernan, *Pol Pot Regime*, 298–308.

150. Figures from Margolin, "Cambodge," 648–50. Again, Cambodian population statistics are not completely reliable, which explains the fairly wide range given for all estimates.

151. Edwards, "Imaging the Other," 60.

152. For a searing critique of the tendency to displace responsibility for atrocities in Cambodia onto conspiracies and outside powers, thereby reproducing the colonialist tropes of Cambodians as passive, gentle, and powerless, see ibid., 60–62.

153. Quoted in Kiernan, *Pol Pot Regime*, 170.

154. Quoted in ibid., 169–70.

155. Ibid., 175.

156. See ibid., 205–10.

157. Quoted in ibid., 414–15.

158. Testimony of Denise Affonço before the People's Revolutionary Tribunal in Phnom Penh, 1979, quoted in Alexander Laban Hinton, "Genocidal Bricolage: A Reading of Human Liver-Eating in Cambodia," Yale Center for International and Area Studies, Genocide Studies Program, Working Paper GS 06, 20–21.

159. I draw here on Hinton, "Genocidal Bricolage."

160. Someth May, *Cambodian Witness*, 203, and Sarom Prak, "The Unfortunate Cambodia," in Pran and DePaul, *Children of Cambodia's Killing Fields*, 67–71. Chandler interviewed Affonço in 1987. See his comments in *Tragedy*, 277–78.

161. Ung, *First They Killed My Father*.

162. See Margolin, "Cambodge," 663–74, and May, *Cambodian Witness*.

163. Testimony of Peang Sophi, "The Early Phases of Liberation," in Kiernan and Boua, *Peasants and Politics*, 318–26, quotation 323.

164. Youkimny Chan, "One Spoon of Rice," in Pran and DePaul, *Children of Cambodia's Killing Fields*, 19–25, quotation 22.

165. See Toni Samantha Phim, "Terror and Aesthetics," Yale Center for International and Area Studies, Genocide Studies Program, Working Paper GS 06, 1998. Of Cambodia's professional artists, 80 to 90 percent died under the Khmer Rouge according to the post-DK government. Ibid., 9–10.

166. Mam, "An Oral History of Family Life," 20–21.

167. For biographical information, see Chandler, *Voices from S-21*, 64.

168. "Planning the Past: The Forced Confessions of Hu Nim," in *Pol Pot Plans the Future*, 227–317, quotations 234, 235, 240, 241, 244, 317.

169. Chandler, *Tragedy*, 253.

170. Quoted in ibid., 284.

171. Ibid.

172. Kiernan, *Pol Pot Regime*, 249.

173. Locard, *Le "Petit livre rouge" de Pol Pot*, 69–71.

174. Ebihara, "Cambodian Village," 55, 61 n. 14.

175. Locard, *Le "Petit livre rouge" de Pol Pot*, 104–6.

176. Figures from Kiernan, *Pol Pot Regime*, 335.

177. Margolin, "Cambodge," 670–74.

178. Christopher R. Browning, *Ordinary Men: Reserve Police Battalion 101 and the Final Solution in Poland* (New York: HarperCollins, 1992). See also Chandler's comments in *Voices from S-21*, 143–55.

179. For this paragraph, I draw on Chandler, *Voices of S-21*, esp. 49–51, 110–27, 143–55.

180. Ung, *First They Killed My Father*, 92.

181. Quoted in Sophiline Cheam Shapiro, "Songs My Enemies Taught Me," in Pran and DePaul, *Children of Cambodia's Killing Fields*, 2–3.

182. Quoted in Jackson, "Ideology of Total Revolution," 73.

183. Testimony of Peang Sophi, in Kiernan and Boua, *Peasants and Politics*, 326.

184. Quoted in Ebihara, "Cambodian Village," 54.

185. Ibid.

186. Margolin, "Cambodge," 643–46, summarizes the different evaluations. See also Kiernan, *Pol Pot Regime*, 456–60, table 458, and Chandler, *Brother*

Number One, 160. See also Judith Banister and Paige Johnson, "After the Nightmare: The Population of Cambodia," in Kiernan, *Genocide and Democracy in Cambodia*, 65-139, statistics 65-67. Chandler seems to accept the higher figure of 1.7 million in *Voices from S-21*, vii, a more recent work.

187. Patrick Heuveline, "'Between One and Three Million': Towards the Demographic Reconstruction of a Decade of Cambodian History (1970-79)," *Population Studies* 52 (1998): 49-65.

188. Kiernan, *Pol Pot Regime*, 456-60, table 458.

189. Ebihara, "Cambodian Village," 58.

190. Margolin, "Cambodge," 645.

191. See Ebihara, Mortland, and Ledgerwood, *Cambodian Culture since 1975*.

192. Chandler, *Tragedy*, 242.

193. See Anthony Barnett, "Democratic Kampuchea: A Highly Centralized Dictatorship," in Chandler and Kiernan, *Revolution and Its Aftermath*, 212-29, who provides an effective critique of Vickery's overemphasis on decentralization.

194. On this period, see Chandler, *Brother Number One*, 178-88.

195. Chandler, introduction to the CPK document "Preliminary Explanation before Reading the Plan," 123.

196. For forceful arguments in support of the appropriateness of the term "genocide" to Democratic Kampuchea, see Kiernan, *Pol Pot Regime*, 460-65; Hawk, "International Human Rights Law"; and Gregory H. Stanton, "The Cambodian Genocide and International Law," in Kiernan, *Genocide and Democracy in Cambodia*, 141-61. For a contrary view, see Serge Thion, "Genocide as a Political Commodity," in Kiernan, *Genocide and Democracy in Cambodia*, 163-90.

197. Although I generally agree with Kiernan's argument about race, he goes too far, in my view, by arguing that "Khmer Rouge notions of race overshadowed those of class" (*Pol Pot Regime*, 26). This position neglects the diverse character of mass killings in Democratic Kampuchea, which were about class *and* race within the overarching goal of creating homogeneity. At the same time, Vickery, *Cambodia*, argues too narrowly that DK represented a peasant rather than a communist revolution.

198. On their role as teachers, see Kiernan, *How Pol Pot Came to Power*, 176-77.

199. The phrase "true reactionaries" is Kiernan's, in ibid., 27.

CHAPTER FIVE
National Communism: Serbia and the Bosnian War

1. Biographical information from International Criminal Tribunal for the Former Yugoslavia (hereafter, ICTY), Opinion and Judgment in Prosecutor v.

Dusko Tadic a/k/a/ "Dule," 7 May 1997, ¶180–82, *http://www.un.org/icty/ tadic/trialc2/judgement/index.htm* [29 August 2002]. Verdict in ICTY, "Tadic Case: The Verdict," Press Release CC/PIO/190-E, 7 May 1997, *http:// www.un.org/icty/pressreal/p190-e.htm* [29 August 2002]. I use diacritical marks for Serbo-Croatian names except when those marks are absent in primary sources, as is the case with the documents produced by the ICTY.

2. The descriptor "unthinkable" comes from Robert M. Hayden, "Imagined Communities and Real Victims: Self-Determination and Ethnic Cleansing in Yugoslavia," *American Ethnologist* 23:4 (1996): 783–801, quotation 783.

3. Ian Fisher, "Power Drove Milosevic to Crime, Prosecutors Say As Trial Opens," *New York Times*, 13 February 2002, A1.

4. Quoted in Laura Silber and Allan Little, *Yugoslavia: Death of a Nation*, rev. ed. (New York: Penguin, 1997), 37–38.

5. On the cultivation of the Kosovo myth, see Olga Zirojević, "Kosovo in the Collective Memory," in *The Road to War in Serbia: Trauma and Catharsis*, ed. Nebojša Popov (1996; Budapest: Central European University Press, 2000), 188–211, and Wayne S. Vucinich and Thomas A. Emmert, eds., *Kosovo: Legacy of a Medieval Battle*, Minnesota Mediterranean and East European Monographs (Minneapolis: Modern Greek Studies at the University of Minnesota, 1991).

6. *The Mountain Wreath of P. P. Nyegosh*, trans. James W. Wiles (London: George Allen and Unwin, 1930), lines 2599–2613.

7. Among many sources on the development of nationalism in the South Slav lands in the nineteenth and twentieth centuries, see Andrew Baruch Wachtel, *Making a Nation, Breaking a Nation: Literature and Cultural Politics in Yugoslavia* (Stanford: Stanford University Press, 1998); Aleksa Djilas, *The Contested Country: Yugoslav Unity and Communist Revolution, 1919–1953* (Cambridge: Harvard University Press, 1991), 29–30; and Ivo Banac, *The National Question in Yugoslavia: Origins, History, Politics* (Ithaca: Cornell University Press, 1984). Banac's contention that, in contrast to Serbian nationalism, Croatian articulations were more open and "embraced the wider Slavic world" (75) seems rather one-sided.

8. See the excerpts from "Memorandum of the Serbian Academy of Sciences and Arts" (1986) in Peter F. Sugar, ed., *Eastern European Nationalism in the Twentieth Century* (Washington, DC: American University Press, 1995), 332–46, and more extensively in "Le Mémorandum de l'Académie serbe," in *Le Nettoyage ethnique: Documents historiques sur une idéologie serbe*, ed. Mirko Grmek, Marc Gjidara, and Neven Šimac (Paris: Fayard, 1993), 231–69. In the English-language excerpt alone, the claim of genocide appears five times, on 333, 336, 338, 344, and 345. For an analysis, see Olivera Milosavilević, "The Abuse of the Authority of Science," in Popov, *Road to War*, 274–302.

9. "Memorandum," 342.

10. Ibid., 341.

11. Vojislav K. Stojanović, president of the Association of University

Teachers and Scientists of Serbia, open letter to "International Association of University Professors and Assistants, and to Public Opinion in the World of Science, Culture, and Politics," February 1990, in Grmek, Gjidara, and Šimac, *Nettoyage ethnique*, 285–87. Albanian nationalists did exercise pressure and sometimes violence against Serbs in Kosovo; Albanians were also victims of Serbian nationalism. For an effort at a balanced analysis, see Marina Blagojević, "The Migration of Serbs from Kosovo during the 1970s and 1980s: Trauma and/or Catharsis," in Popov, *Road to War*, 212–43.

12. See also the discussion about the importance of Lazar's bones as relics in the earlier period, in Tim Judah, *The Serbs: History, Myth and the Destruction of Yugoslavia* (New Haven: Yale University Press, 1997), 29–47.

13. Quoted in Zirojević, "Kosovo in Collective Memory," 207.

14. Quoted in Silber and Little, *Yugoslavia*, 72.

15. Quoted in ibid., 61.

16. See Judah, *Serbs*, 1–47.

17. Patriarch Paul, "Le message pascal de 1991," in Grmek, Gjidara, and Šimac, *Nettoyage ethnique*, 276–78, quotations 277 and 278.

18. On the Orthodox Church and Serbian nationalism, see Radmila Radić, "The Church and the 'Serbian Question,'" in Popov, *Road to War*, 247–73.

19. Quoted in Judah, *Serbs*, 47.

20. Quoted in Grmek, Gjidara, and Šimac, *Nettoyage ethnique*, 295.

21. See James Gow, "Serbian Nationalism and the Hissssing Ssssnake in the International Order: Whose Sovereignty? Whose Nation?" *Slavonic and East European Review* 72:3 (1994): 456–76, here 457–58.

22. See, for example, statements by Milošević and Monseignor Lukijan, quoted in Grmek, Gjidara, and Šimac, *Nettoyage ethnique*, 272 and 281.

23. Quoted in Grmek, Gjidara, and Šimac, *Nettoyage ethnique*, 294. See also the discussion in Wachtel, *Making a Nation, Breaking a Nation*, 198–203.

24. See Lenard J. Cohen, *Broken Bonds: The Disintegration of Yugoslavia* (Boulder: Westview, 1993), 53–54.

25. Quoted in ibid., 187–88.

26. See Marija Obradović, "The Ruling Party," and Miroslav Hadžić, "The Army's Use of Trauma," both in Popov, *Road to War*, 425–48 and 509–34, and Cohen, *Broken Bonds*, 181–92.

27. Quoted in Obradović, "Ruling Party," 426.

28. Ibid., 432–435, quotation 435.

29. See Sreten Vujović, "An Uneasy View of the City," in Popov, *Road to War*, 123–45, esp. 132, 135, 137.

30. For example, Milan Paroški, a deputy and one of the leaders of the Serbian rebellion in Slavonia, quoted in Grmek, Gjidara, and Šimac, *Nettoyage ethnique*, 319.

31. General Ratko Mladić, quoted in Vujović, "Uneasy View of the City," 138.

32. See Susan L. Woodward's trenchant comments in "Violence-Prone Area or International Transition? Adding the Role of Outsiders in Balkan Violence," in *Violence and Subjectivity*, ed. Veena Das et al. (Berkeley and Los Angeles: University of California Press, 2000), 19–45, esp. 29.

33. For background, see John R. Lampe, *Yugoslavia as History: Twice There Was a Country*, 2d ed. (Cambridge: Cambridge University Press, 2000); Mark Pinson, ed., *The Muslims of Bosnia-Herzegovina: Their Historic Development from the Middle Ages to the Dissolution of Yugoslavia*, Harvard Middle Eastern Monographs 28 (Cambridge: Harvard University Press, 1993); Robert J. Donia and John V. A. Fine, Jr., *The Muslims of Bosnia and Hercegovina: A Tradition Betrayed* (New York: Columbia University Press, 1994); Fred Singleton, *A Short History of the Yugoslav Peoples* (Cambridge: Cambridge University Press, 1985); and Banac, *National Question*.

34. Banac, *National Question*, argues strongly that national consciousness prevailed among Croats, Serbs, and Bulgars well before the modern era and in contrast to the outlook of the Slovenes, Montenegrins, Macedonians, and Bosnian Muslims.

35. Ivo Banac, "Bosnian Muslims: From Religious Community to Socialist Nationhood and Postcommunist Statehood, 1918–1992," in Pinson, *Muslims of Bosnia-Herzegovina*, 132.

36. For a concise, masterful treatment of this process, see Mark Mazower, *The Balkans: A Short History* (New York: Modern Library, 2000).

37. See the comments by John V. A. Fine, "The Medieval and Ottoman Roots of Modern Bosnian Society," in Pinson, *Muslims of Bosnia-Herzegovina*, 20, and Banac, "Bosnian Muslims," 134. See also Francine Friedman, *The Bosnian Muslims: Denial of a Nation* (Boulder: Westview, 1996), and for an especially nuanced discussion about the meaning of religious identity in the Bosnian context, Tone Bringa, *Being Muslim the Bosnian Way: Identity and Community in a Central Bosnian Village* (Princeton: Princeton University Press, 1995).

38. Bringa, *Being Muslim the Bosnian Way*, 30–32.

39. Ibid., 29–36.

40. Statistics from Steven L. Burg and Paul S. Shoup, *The War in Bosnia-Herzegovina: Ethnic Conflict and International Intervention* (Armonk, NY: M. E. Sharpe, 1999), 29, 32, 42.

41. Bringa, *Being Muslim the Bosnian Way*, 19–20.

42. Slobodanka Konstantinović-Vilić, "Psychological Violence and Fear in War, and Their Consequences for the Psychological Health of Women," in *Women, Violence and War: Wartime Victimization of Refugees in the Balkans*, ed. Vesna Nikolić-Ristanović, trans. Borislav Radović (1995; Budapest: Central European University Press, 2000), 99–133.

43. See also Bringa, *Being Muslim the Bosnian Way*, 39.

44. ICTY, Opinion and Judgment in Prosecutor v. Dusko Tadic a/k/a/ "Dule," 7 May 1997, ¶151.

45. Lampe, *Yugoslavia as History*, 322–23, 333.

46. I draw the following analysis especially from Woodward, "Violence-Prone Area or International Transition?" and idem, *Balkan Tragedy: Chaos and Dissolution after the Cold War* (Washington, DC: Brookings Institution, 1995).

47. See Rogers Brubaker, "Nationhood and the National Question in the Soviet Union and Its Successor States," in idem, *Nationalism Reframed: Nationhood and the National Question in the New Europe* (Cambridge: Cambridge University Press, 1996), 23–54. See also Gow's trenchant analysis in "Serbian Nationalism," and Ronald Grigor Suny, *The Revenge of the Past: Nationalism, Revolution, and the Collapse of the Soviet Union* (Stanford: Stanford University Press, 1993). Generally on the role of federalism in the Yugoslav collapse, see Valerie Bunce, *Subversive Institutions: The Design and the Destruction of Socialism and the State* (Cambridge: Cambridge University Press, 1999).

48. In general on the structure of the Yugoslav state, see Djilas, *Contested Country*, 150–80; Vesna Pešić, "The War for Ethnic States," in Popov, *Road to War*, 9–49; and Veljko Marko Vujacic, "Communism and Nationalism in Russia and Serbia" (Ph.D. diss., University of California at Berkeley, 1995), 106–22.

49. See V. P. Gagnon, Jr., "Ethnic Nationalism and International Conflict," *International Security* 19:3 (1994/95): 130–66.

50. On the critical role the JNA played in the Yugoslav system, see Hadžić, "Army's Use of Trauma," and James Gow, *Legitimacy and the Military: The Yugoslav Crisis* (New York: St. Martin's Press, 1992).

51. Lampe, *Yugoslavia as History*, 312.

52. Vojin Dimitrijević, "The 1974 Constitution as a Factor in the Collapse of Yugoslavia, or as a Sign of Decaying Totalitarianism," in Popov, *Road to War*, 399–424, quotation 405.

53. Sabrina P. Ramet, *Balkan Babel: The Disintegration of Yugoslavia from the Death of Tito to the War for Kosovo*, 3d ed. (Boulder: Westview, 1999), tracks these developments very well.

54. This is the major argument of Ramet, *Balkan Babel*, and a key element in the more theoretically inclined argument of Bunce, *Subversive Institutions*.

55. Pešić, "War for Ethnic States," 27.

56. Quoted in Cohen, *Broken Bonds*, 208.

57. Silber and Little, *Yugoslavia*, 26. For a similar point, see Ramet, *Balkan Babel*, 6.

58. See the account in Silber and Little, *Yugoslavia*, 37–47, and Ramet, *Balkan Babel*, 25–47.

59. Ramet, *Balkan Babel*, 112–13.

60. On the role of the Western powers, see Woodward, "Violence-Prone Area or International Transition?" 33–37, and Silber and Little, *Yugoslavia*, 198–201.

61. Silber and Little, *Yugoslavia*, 131–32.

62. Ibid., 103.

63. See ibid., 92–104.

64. Quoted in ibid., 128.

65. Quoted in ibid., 129.

66. Judah, *Serbs*, 170–71, 186–89.

67. The impact of the German position is much debated among analysts. See the discussion in Burg and Shoup, *War in Bosnia-Herzegovina*, 92–102, 120–27.

68. Silber and Little, *Yugoslavia*, 169.

69. See Hadžič, "Army's Use of Trauma," 517–28.

70. Silber and Little, *Yugoslavia*, 179–80.

71. Ibid., 198.

72. Ibid., 210, and Burg and Shoup, *War in Bosnia-Herzegovina*, 46–56.

73. For details on the transformation of the JNA, see Silber and Little, *Yugoslavia*, 217–18, 242; Burg and Shoup, *War in Bosnia-Herzegovina*, 74; and ICTY, Opinion and Judgment in Prosecutor v. Dusko Tadic a/k/a/ "Dule," 7 May 1997, ¶106–26.

74. Burg and Shoup, *War in Bosnia-Herzegovina*, 74–75.

75. Quoted in ibid., 78.

76. For these events, see ICTY, Opinion and Judgment in Prosecutor v. Dusko Tadic a/k/a/ "Dule," 7 May 1997, ¶148–50, and, generally, Roy Gutman, *A Witness to Genocide* (New York: Macmillan, 1993).

77. See Judah, *Serbs*, 226–29, who derives his information from the Final Report of the United Nations Investigative Committee, Annexes, 48–49.

78. Burg and Shoup, *War in Bosnia-Herzegovina*, 119.

79. Ibid., 129.

80. Ibid., 129–30, and Bringa, *Being Muslim the Bosnian Way*.

81. Quoted in Silber and Little, *Yugoslavia*, 233.

82. Ibid., 233.

83. Burg and Shoup, *War in Bosnia-Herzegovina*, 132–33.

84. Reports were circulating in governments and the UN in spring 1992 about Serbian atrocities, but these became public only through the diligence of reporters who exposed the concentration camps toward the end of July. See Silber and Little, *Yugoslavia*, 250–53, and on Srebenica, 265–75, and Burg and Shoup, *War in Bosnia-Herzegovina*, 202, 402.

85. On conditions in Omarska and the other northern Bosnian camps, see Gutman, *Witness to Genocide*, and ICTY, Opinion and Judgment in Prosecutor v. Dusko Tadic a/k/a/ "Dule," 7 May 1997, ¶154–78.

86. "Radislav Krstic Becomes the First Person to Be Convicted of Genocide at the ICTY," ICTY Press Release OF/P.I.S./609e, 2 August 2001, *http://www.un.org/icty/pressreal/p609-e.htm* [29 August 2002].

87. For details, see ibid., and the very important book by Jan Willem Honig and Norbert Both, *Srebenica: Record of a War Crime* (London: Penguin, 1996).

88. See Burg and Shoup, *War in Bosnia-Herzegovina*, 208.

89. Quoted in Silber and Little, *Yugoslavia*, 247.

90. See Burg and Shoup, *War in Bosnia-Herzegovina*, 128–88, 324–27, and Honig and Both, *Srebenica*, 163.

91. Silber and Little, *Yugoslavia*, 350, and especially, Honig and Both, *Srebenica*.

92. Burg and Shoup, *War in Bosnia-Herzegovina*, 307–9, 338–40.

93. I am drawing here on the thorough and careful account of Burg and Shoup, *War in Bosnia-Herzegovina*, and also Silber and Little, *Yugoslavia*. On U.S. policy in particular, see also Samantha Power, *"A Problem from Hell": America and the Age of Genocide* (New York: Basic Books, 2002), 247–327, 391–441, and David Halberstam, *War in a Time of Peace: Bush, Clinton, and the Generals* (New York: Scribner, 2001).

94. Burg and Shoup, *War in Bosnia-Herzegovina*, 368. Other aspects of the Dayton Agreement were perhaps less favorable to nationalists. Refugees were granted the right of return, all citizens freedom of movement. The signatories pledged cooperation with the International Criminal Tribunal in the Hague. A 60,000-strong NATO-led Implementation Force (IFOR) moved in over the next weeks to secure the peace. The United States provided 20,000 of the troops. In December 1996 the force strength was reduced to 31,000 and renamed the Stabilization Force (SFOR). For a strong defense of the agreement by the major American negotiator, see Richard Holbrooke, *To End a War*, rev. ed. (New York: Modern Library, 1999).

95. See Nikolić-Ristanović, *Women, Violence and War*, and Alexandra Stiglmayer, ed., *Mass Rape: The War against Women in Bosnia-Herzegovina*, trans. Marion Faber (Lincoln: University of Nebraska Press, 1994).

96. Figure in Silber and Little, *Yugoslavia*, 252.

97. See Bringa's discussion in *Being Muslim the Bosnian Way*, 85–118.

98. See the summary account in Lampe, *Yugoslavia as History*, 406–15.

99. "Radislav Krstic Becomes the First Person to Be Convicted of Genocide at the ICTY," ICTY Press Release OF/P.I.S./609e, 2 August 2001.

100. ICTY, Judgement, Prosecutor v. Radislav Krstic, ¶56, *http://www.un. org/icty/krstic/TrialC1/judgement/index.htm* [29 August 2002].

101. ICTY, Opinion and Judgment in Prosecutor v. Dusko Tadic a/k/a/ "Dule," 7 May 1997, ¶201.

102. Ibid., ¶206.

103. Quoted in Judah, *Serbs*, 234.

104. ICTY, Judgement, Prosecutor v. Radislav Krstic, ¶68.

105. Ibid., ¶70.

106. Ibid., ¶151–53.

107. Ibid., ¶207.

108. The witness, Dražen Erdemović, was, oddly enough, a Croat who had been conscripted into the Bosnian Serb Army. The interview with him was pub-

lished in *Le Figaro*. I have used Judah's rendering of the interview in *Serbs*, 240–41.

109. ICTY, Judgement, Prosecutor v. Radislav Krstic, ¶226–28.

110. Ibid.

111. ICTY, "Judgement of Trial Chamber II in the Kunarac, Kovac and Vukovic Case," Press Release JL/P.I.S./566-e, 22 February 2001, *http://www.un.org/icty/foca/TrialC2/judgement/index.htm* [29 August 2002].

112. Ibid.

113. Ibid.

114. See, for example, ICTY, testimony of Witness 75 in Transcripts Gagovic and Others (IT-96–23), 000330ed, 30 March 2000, *http://www.un.org/icty/ind-e.htm* [29 August 2002]. For some specific examples of the verbal taunts, see pp. 1416, 1449, 1450, 1460.

115. ICTY, "Judgement of Trial Chamber II in the Kunarac, Kovac and Vukovic Case," 22 February 2001.

116. ICTY, Judgement, Prosecutor v. Radislav Krstic, ¶92, 93.

117. Burg and Shoup, *War in Bosnia-Herzegovina*, 169–70.

118. Lampe, *Yugoslavia as History*, 373.

119. Figure and quotation from Burg and Shoup, *War in Bosnia-Herzegovina*, 170.

120. Figures in ibid., 171–72.

121. Lampe, *Yugoslavia as History*, 399.

122. Ibid., 404. Whether this was the worst ever is disputed. Judah cites still more drastic numbers but says that Weimar Germany in 1923, Greece in November 1944, and Hungary in April 1946 had even worse hyperinflations, Hungary's the absolute worst. See Judah, *Serbs*, 267–68.

123. See Burg and Shoup, *War in Bosnia-Herzegovina*, 63; Woodward, "Violence-Prone Area or International Transition?" 28; and Bunce, *Subversive Institutions*, 152–56, all of whom label as a revolution the events in Yugoslavia (and, in Bunce's case, all over Eastern Europe).

124. Cohen, *Broken Bonds*, 164–72.

125. See Judah, *Serbs*, 242–58, for many interesting vignettes on criminals and wartime commerce.

126. See Ivan Ćolović, "Football, Hooligans and War," in Popov, *Road to War*, 373–96.

127. The example about church and mosque construction comes from Bringa, *Being Muslim the Bosnian Way*, 75. Even this village could not stave off the national tides around it. According to Bringa, local Muslims were most distressed that even their neighbors eventually turned on them.

128. For a contrary interpretation, see Vesna Nikolić-Ristanović, "Sexual Violence," in idem, *Women, Violence and War*, 41–77: "The idea of rape as a method of ethnic cleansing contains a very deep patriarchal construction; women are seen as objects, 'recipients' that passively accept male seed without

adding anything original, anything personal. Within that context, the identity of the child, a human being, depends only on the man. Thus, the children of the women impregnated through enemy rape will be of the rapist's nationality" (67).

129. For very effective analyses that strongly situate the Yugoslav collapse within the international order, moderating or relativizing the usual emphasis on ethnic conflict, see Bunce, *Subversive Institutions*, and Woodward, *Balkan Tragedy*.

130. "Radislav Krstic Becomes the First Person to Be Convicted of Genocide at the ICTY," ICTY Press Release OF/P.I.S./609e, 2 August 2001.

131. Mazower, *Balkans*, 148.

Conclusion

1. I am contesting here the overwhelming emphasis on structural matters and the concomitant inclination to think of revolutions as solely left-wing affairs, both of which are tendencies that prevail in the vast scholarly literature on revolutions. See, for example, the definition of revolutions in Peter Calvert, *Revolution and Counter-Revolution* (Minneapolis: University of Minnesota Press, 1990), 17–18; Anthony Giddens, *Sociology* (Oxford: Polity Press, 1989), 604–5; Theda Skocpol, *States and Social Revolutions: A Comparative Analysis of France, Russia, and China* (Cambridge: Cambridge University Press, 1979); Charles Tilly, *From Mobilization to Revolution* (Reading, MA: Addison-Wesley, 1978); and Hannah Arendt, *On Revolution* (New York: Viking, 1963). Typical for this approach is Tilly's rather frail definition: "A revolutionary outcome is the displacement of one set of power holders by another." Tilly, *From Mobilization to Revolution*, 193.

2. Amid a large literature, see Amir Weiner, ed., *Landscaping the Human Garden: Twentieth-Century Population Management in a Comparative Framework* (Stanford: Stanford University Press, 2003).

3. Generally on the mobility of racial categorizations, see Stephen Cornell and Douglas Hartmann, *Ethnicity and Race: Making Identities in a Changing World* (Thousand Oaks, CA: Pine Forge Press, 1998), and Michael Omi and Howard Winant, *Racial Formation in the United States: From the 1960s to the 1990s*, 2d ed. (New York: Routledge, 1994).

4. See "Le Mémorandum de l'Académie serbe," in *Le Nettoyage ethnique: Documents historiques sur une idéologie serbe*, ed. Mirko Grmek, Marc Gjidara, and Neven Šimac (Paris: Fayard, 1993), 231–69, here 260–61.

5. Quoted in Ben Kiernan, *The Pol Pot Regime: Race, Power, and Genocide in Cambodia under the Khmer Rouge, 1975–79* (New Haven: Yale University Press, 1996), 94.

6. Quoted in Karl D. Jackson, "The Ideology of Total Revolution," in *Cam-*

bodia 1975–1978: Rendezvous with Death, ed. idem (Princeton: Princeton University Press, 1989), 67.

7. See Aleksandr I. Solzhenitsyn, *The Gulag Archipelago, 1918–1956: An Experiment in Literary Investigation*, vols. 1–2, trans. Thomas P. Whitney (New York: Harper and Row, 1973), 35, 42, 77.

8. Amir Weiner, *Making Sense of War: The Second World War and the Fate of the Bolshevik Revolution* (Princeton: Princeton University Press, 2001), 35.

9. Kiernan, *Pol Pot Regime*, 62, 216–17.

10. Quoted in Jackson, "Ideology of Total Revolution," 67.

11. Monsignor Lukijan, Orthodox Archbishop of Slavonia, quoted in Grmek, Gjidara, and Šimac, *Nettoyage ethnique*, 281.

12. Mary Douglas, *Purity and Danger: An Analysis of the Concepts of Pollution and Taboo* (1966; London: Routledge, 1996), quotations 2, 36.

13. See Wolfgang Eckart, *Medizin und Kolonialimperialismus: Deutschland 1884–1945* (Paderborn: Ferdinand Schöningh, 1997).

14. Quoted in Norman M. Naimark, *Fires of Hatred: Ethnic Cleansing in Twentieth-Century Europe* (Cambridge: Harvard University Press, 2001), 57. There is some dispute about whether he even made the remarks, but at least some authorities—like Gerhard L. Weinberg and Richard Breitman, as well as Vahakn N. Dadrian—take the statement as fact. In any case, the genocide of the Armenians was widely known in Europe (the term, of course, came later), and Hitler and his top aides certainly knew about it. For a thorough vetting of the source, see Richard Breitman, *The Architect of Genocide: Himmler and the Final Solution* (London: Bodley Head, 1991), 43 and 258 n. 47; Naimark, *Fires of Hatred*, 57–58; and Gerhard L. Weinberg, *A World at Arms: A Global History of World War II* (Cambridge: Cambridge University Press, 1994), 59. See also Vahakn N. Dadrian, *The History of the Armenian Genocide: Ethnic Conflict from the Balkans to Anatolia to the Caucasus*, 3d ed. (Providence: Berghahn, 1997), 403–9.

15. Quoted in Naimark, *Fires of Hatred*, 58.

16. "Industrial killing" is Omer Bartov's term in *Murder in Our Midst: The Holocaust, Industrial Killing, and Representation* (New York: Oxford University Press, 1996).

17. See James C. Scott, *Seeing Like a State: How Certain Schemes to Improve the Human Condition Have Failed* (New Haven: Yale University Press, 1998).

18. "Honor" and "dishonor" are terms George M. Fredrickson adopts from Max Weber's writings on ethnicity. See Fredrickson, *Racism: A Short History* (Princeton: Princeton University Press, 2002), and idem, *The Comparative Imagination: On the History of Racism, Nationalism, and Social Movements* (Berkeley and Los Angeles: University of California Press, 1997).

19. Alf Lüdtke, "Einleitung: Herrschaft als soziale Praxis," in *Herrschaft als soziale Praxis: Historische und sozial-anthropologische Studien*, ed. idem (Göttingen: Vandenhoeck and Ruprecht, 1991), 44.

20. "Perpetrators and witnesses stimulate one another," writes Wolfgang Sofsky, *Traktat über die Gewalt* (Frankfurt am Main: Fischer, 1996), 116. On denunciation as a social practice, see the *Journal of Modern History* 68:4 (1997), edited by Sheila Fitzpatrick and Robert Gellately. See also Robert Gellately, *Backing Hitler: Consent and Coercion in Nazi Germany* (Oxford: Oxford University Press, 2001).

21. Studies of ethnic cleansings and genocides also tend to focus almost exclusively on the regimes and not the ways that they mobilized supporters. See, for example, Naimark's important study, *Fires of Hatred*, and Ben Kiernan's general statement, "Sur la notion de génocide," *Le Débat*, March–April 1999, 179–92.

22. For the analysis here and in the following paragraphs, I am drawing especially from Lüdtke, "Herrschaft," and Thomas Lindenberger, "Die Diktatur der Grenzen. Zur Einleitung," in *Herrschaft und Eigen-Sinn in der Diktatur: Studien zur Gesellschaftsgeschichte der DDR*, ed. idem (Cologne: Böhlau, 1999), 13–44. See also James C. Scott, *Domination and the Arts of Resistance: Hidden Transcripts* (New Haven: Yale University Press, 1990), and for a less metaphorical treatment of "face," Alexander Laban Hinton, "Why Did You Kill? The Cambodian Genocide and the Dark Side of Face and Honor," *Journal of Asian Studies* 57:1 (1998): 93–122.

23. For both Max Weber and Antonio Gramsci, the ultimate success of power emerges when subordinate groups have internalized its workings.

24. Lüdtke, "Herrschaft," 49. See also Sofsky, *Traktat über die Gewalt*, 65–82.

25. I am drawing here on Lüdtke, "Herrschaft," 15–18, 27–29, and the classic studies of Victor Turner, *The Forest of Symbols: Aspects of Ndembu Ritual* (Ithaca: Cornell University Press, 1973), and idem, *Dramas, Fields, and Metaphors: Symbolic Action in Human Society* (Ithaca: Cornell University Press, 1974), and of Douglas, *Purity and Danger*, as well as Sally F. Moore and Barbara G. Myerhoff, "Secular Ritual: Forms and Meanings," in *Secular Ritual*, ed. idem (Amsterdam: Van Gorcum, 1977), 3–24, quotation 4. See also Edward Muir, *Rituals in Early Modern Europe* (Cambridge: Cambridge University Press, 1997), and David I. Kertzer, *Ritual, Politics, and Power* (New Haven: Yale University Press, 1988).

26. On the importance of scale, see John Agnew, "Representing Space: Space, Scale and Culture in Social Science," in *Place/Culture/Representation*, ed. J. Duncan and D. Ley (London: Routledge, 1993), 251–79.

27. I am drawing from and somewhat revising the classic formulation of the "aestheticization of politics," developed in scattered, numerous writings by Siegfried Kracauer, Walter Benjamin, and many others. Peter Reichel, *Der schöne Schein des Dritten Reiches: Faszination und Gewalt des Faschismus* (Frankfurt am Main: Fischer, 1993), provides many apt quotations. See also the classic essays of Kracauer, "The Mass Ornament," in *The Mass Ornament:*

Weimar Essays, trans. Thomas Y. Levin (Cambridge: Harvard University Press, 1995), 75–86, and of Benjamin, "The Work of Art in the Age of Mechanical Reproduction," in *Illuminations*, trans. Harry Zohn (New York: Harcourt, Brace and World, 1968), 243–44. However, by placing the emphasis so heavily on the ornament and manipulation, Kracauer and Benjamin undervalued the participatory nature of fascism, turning the masses into mere spectators and the essence of the entire movement into spectacle.

28. For the example of the Third Reich, see Gitta Sereny, *Albert Speer: His Battle with Truth* (New York: Vintage, 1995), as well as his own memoir, *Inside the Third Reich: Memoirs*, trans. Richard and Clara Winston (New York: Macmillan, 1970).

29. Leslie Dwyer and Degung Santikarma, "'When the World Turned to Chaos': 1965 and Its Aftermath in Bali, Indonesia," in *The Specter of Genocide*, ed. Robert Gellately and Ben Kiernan (Cambridge: Cambridge University Press, 2003).

30. Amid a substantial literature, I draw here especially from Wolfgang Sofsky, *The Order of Terror: The Concentration Camp*, trans. William Templer (Princeton: Princeton University Press, 1997); idem, *Traktat über die Gewalt*; and idem, "Gesetz des Gemetzels," *Die Zeit* 15 (2 April 1998): 53. See also Naimark, *Fires of Hatred*, for a careful discussion of similarities and differences in various ethnic cleansings.

31. See Ulrich Herbert, ed., *Nationalsozialistische Vernichtungspolitik 1939–1945: Neue Forschungen und Kontroversen* (Frankfurt am Main: Fischer, 1998), and Christopher Browning, *Ordinary Men: Reserve Police Battalion 101 and the Final Solution in Poland* (New York: HarperCollins, 1992). The classic work about the anonymous, bureaucratic nature of the killings is, of course, Hannah Arendt, *Eichmann in Jerusalem: A Report on the Banality of Evil*, rev. ed. (New York: Viking, 1964), who based much of her evaluation on Raul Hilberg, *The Destruction of the European Jews* (Chicago: Quadrangle Books, 1961). The "neatness" of Nazi exterminations, a supposedly anonymous, bureaucratic process, has been hugely exaggerated.

32. Heinrich Himmler issued an order in 1942 that officially sanctioned torture to gain "useful information," but these kinds of activities had been going on since the moment the Nazis seized power in 1933. See also Edward Peters, *Torture*, expanded ed. (Philadelphia: University of Pennsylvania Press, 1996), 105, 124–25.

33. See Browning, *Ordinary Men*, for the range of reactions at the outset of the killing operation.

34. "Structure of feeling" comes from Raymond Williams, *Keywords: A Vocabulary of Culture and Society* (New York: Oxford University Press, 1976). See also Sofsky, *Traktat über die Gewalt*.

35. See Sofsky, *Traktat über die Gewalt*, 56–57. Daniel Jonah Goldhagen, *Hitler's Willing Executioners: Ordinary Germans and the Holocaust* (New

York: Knopf, 1996), offers a highly simplistic and misplaced interpretation of the Holocaust. Its one virtue is that it reveals some of the enthusiasm of the perpetrators. That some of the torturers at the notorious Tuol Seng prison in Cambodia had to be restrained from excessive brutality is clear from the "Interrogator's Manual." The point is also bizarre, since the system itself promoted nearly unfathomable brutalities. See the text in Peters, *Torture*, 270–72, and the more extended analysis in David Chandler, *Voices from S-21: Terror and History in Pol Pot's Secret Prison* (Berkeley and Los Angeles: University of California Press, 1999), 134–37, 143–55.

36. Compare Omer Bartov, *Mirrors of Destruction: War, Genocide, and Modern Identity* (New York: Oxford University Press, 2000), 3–4 and 232 n. 1, with Allen Feldman, "Violence and Vision: The Prosthetics and Aesthetics of Terror," in *Violence and Subjectivity*, ed. Veena Das et al. (Berkeley and Los Angeles: University of California Press, 2000), 46–78.

37. Note the guidelines given to SS concentration camp guards at Dachau in the early 1930s, which demanded an extreme level of brutality. See the text in Jeremy Noakes and Geoffrey Pridham, eds., *Nazism, 1919–1945: A Documentary Reader*, vol. 2, *State, Economy and Society, 1933–1939* (Exeter: University of Exeter Press, 1984), 502–4.

38. See Chandler, *Voices from S-21*.

39. See Elaine Scarry, *The Body in Pain: The Making and Unmaking of the World* (New York: Oxford University Press, 1985), 27–59.

40. Ibid., 19–20.

41. Ibid., 29.

42. See, for example, the extensive testimony in ICTY, Opinion and Judgement: Prosecutor v. Dusko Tadic a/k/a/ "Dule," 7 May 1997, *http://www.un.org/icty/tadic/trialc2/judgement/index.htm* [29 August 2002].

43. See Scarry's interesting and searing discussion of space and of the inversion of objects, in *Body in Pain*, 38–45. But she neglects here the social aspects of torture, the deliberate extension of the knowledge of torture beyond the victim.

44. Peters, *Torture*, 74–140.

45. Hannah Arendt, *On Violence* (New York: Harcourt, Brace and World, 1969), 55.

46. Sofsky, *Traktat über die Gewalt*, 83–100, quotation 88. Allen Feldman goes further: "The performance of torture does not apply power; rather, it manufactures it from the 'raw' ingredient of the captive's body. The surface of the body is the stage where the state is made to appear as an effective material force." *Formations of Violence: The Narrative of the Body and Political Terror in Northern Ireland* (Chicago: University of Chicago Press, 1991), 115.

47. "[Beauty] opens out to the world, inviting further signs, objects, and interpretants to partake of its bounty, of its essence. Pain, by contrast, when embodied, closes in on itself. Where beauty extends itself, pain finds affirmation in its intensification. Beauty repressed can be painful; pain expressed is susceptible

to incredulity." E. Valentine Daniel, *Charred Lullabies: Chapters in an Anthropography of Violence* (Princeton: Princeton University Press, 1996), 139.

48. The quotation is from Douglas, *Purity and Danger*, 116. See also Feldman, *Formations of Violence*.

49. I have adapted this point from E. Valentine Daniel's comment that "the Sri Lankan experience is overburdened with the present, a present 'under (traumatic) erasure.'" See *Charred Lullabies*, 107.

50. See ICTY, Opinion and Judgement, Prosecutor v. Dusko Tadic a/k/a/ "Dule," 7 May 1997, ¶618–23, and ICTY Press Release OF/P.I.S./609e, "Radislav Krstic Becomes the First Person to Be Convicted of Genocide at the ICTY," 2 August 2001, section II, *http://www.un.org/icty/pressreal/p609-e.htm* [29 August 2002].

51. For a strong argument in favor of abiding by the UN Convention, see Kiernan, "Sur la notion de génocide."

52. Václav Havel, "Kosovo and the End of the Nation-State" (speech given to the Canadian Senate and the House of Commons on 29 April 1999), in *New York Review of Books* 46:10 (10 June 1999): 4–6, quotation 4.

bibliography

Agnew, John. "Representing Space: Space, Scale and Culture in Social Science." In *Place/Culture/Representation*, ed. J. Duncan and D. Ley, 251–79. London: Routledge, 1993.

Akçam, Taner. *Armenien und der Völkermord: Die Istanbuler Prozesse und die türkische Nationalbewegung*. Hamburg: Hamburger Edition, 1996.

Akhmatova, Anna. *Requiem and Poem without a Hero*. Trans. D. M. Thomas. Athens: Ohio University Press, 1976.

Albin, David A., and Marlowe Hood, eds. *The Cambodian Agony*. Armonk, NY: M. E. Sharpe, 1990.

Alexopoulos, Golfo. "Rights and Passages: Making Outcasts and Making Citizens in Soviet Russia." Ph.D. diss., University of Chicago, 1996.

Allen, Naomi, ed. *The Challenge of the Left Opposition (1923–25)*. New York: Pathfinder Press, 1975.

Alvarez, Alex. *Governments, Citizens, and Genocide: A Comparative and Interdisciplinary Approach*. Bloomington: Indiana University Press, 2001.

Aly, Götz. " 'Judenumsiedlung': Überlegungen zur politischen Vorgeschichte des Holocaust." In *Nationalsozialistische Vernichtungspolitik 1939–1945: Neue Forschungen und Kontroversen*, ed. Ulrich Herbert, 69–97. Frankfurt am Main: Fischer, 1998.

Aly, Götz, and Susanne Heim. *Vordenker der Vernichtung: Auschwitz und die deutschen Pläne für eine neue europäische Ordnung*. 1991; Frankfurt am Main: Fischer, 1993.

Aminzade, Ronald. "The Politics of Race and Nation: Citizenship and Africanization in Tanganyika." *Political Power and Social Theory* 12 (2000): 51–88.

Arendt, Hannah. *Eichmann in Jerusalem: A Report on the Banality of Evil*. Rev. ed. New York: Viking, 1964.

———. *The Origins of Totalitarianism*. 1951; Cleveland: Meridian Books, 1958.

———. *On Revolution*. New York: Viking, 1963.

———. *On Violence*. New York: Harcourt, Brace and World, 1969.

———. "Race-Thinking before Racism." *Review of Politics* 6:1 (1944): 36–73.

Balibar, Étienne, and Immanuel Wallerstein. *Race, Nation, Class: Ambiguous Identities*. London: Verso, 1991.

Banac, Ivo. "The Fearful Asymmetry of War: The Causes and Consequences of Yugoslavia's Demise." *Daedalus* 121:2 (1992): 141–74.

———. *The National Question in Yugoslavia: Origins, History, Politics*. Ithaca: Cornell University Press, 1984.

Banister, Judith, and Paige Johnson. "After the Nightmare: The Population of Cambodia." In *Genocide and Democracy in Cambodia: The Khmer Rouge, the United Nations and the International Community*, ed. Ben Kiernan, 65–139. Yale University Southeast Asia Studies no. 41. New Haven: Yale University Southeast Asia Studies, 1993.

Barnett, Anthony. "Democratic Kampuchea: A Highly Centralized Dictatorship." In *Revolution and Its Aftermath in Kampuchea: Eight Essays*, ed. David Chandler and Ben Kiernan, 212–29. Yale University Southeast Asia Studies no. 25. New Haven: Yale University Southeast Asia Studies, 1983.

Bartov, Omer. "Defining Enemies, Making Victims: Germans, Jews, and the Holocaust." *American Historical Review* 103:3 (1998): 771–816.

———. *Mirrors of Destruction: War, Genocide, and Modern Identity*. New York: Oxford University Press, 2000.

———. *Murder in Our Midst: The Holocaust, Industrial Killing, and Representation*. New York: Oxford University Press, 1996.

Bauman, Zygmunt. *Modernity and the Holocaust*. Ithaca: Cornell University Press, 1989.

Becker, Elizabeth. *When the War Was Over: The Voices of Cambodia's Revolution and Its People*. New York: Simon and Schuster, 1986.

Benjamin, Walter. "The Work of Art in the Age of Mechanical Reproduction." In idem, *Illuminations*, trans. Harry Zohn, 217–52. New York: Harcourt, Brace and World, 1968.

Berezin, Mabel. *Making the Fascist Self: The Political Culture of Interwar Italy*. Ithaca: Cornell University Press, 1997.

Berlin, Ira. *Many Thousands Gone: The First Two Centuries of Slavery in North America*. Cambridge: Harvard University Press, Belknap Press, 1998.

Bessel, Richard, ed. *Fascist Italy and Nazi Germany: Comparisons and Contrasts*. Cambridge: Cambridge University Press, 1996.

———, ed. *Life in the Third Reich*. Oxford: Oxford University Press, 1987.

Betts, Raymond F. *The False Dawn: European Imperialism in the Nineteenth Century*. Minneapolis: University of Minnesota Press, 1975.

Biddiss, Michael D., ed. *Gobineau: Selected Political Writing*. New York: Harper and Row, 1970.

Blackburn, Robin. *The Making of New World Slavery: From the Baroque to the Modern, 1492–1800*. London: Verso, 1997.

Blagojević, Marina. "The Migration of Serbs from Kosovo during the 1970s and 1980s: Trauma and/or Catharsis." In *The Road to War in Serbia:*

Trauma and Catharsis, ed. Nebojša Popov, 212–43. Budapest: Central European University Press, 2000.

Bock, Gisela. "Gleichheit und Differenz in der nationalsozialistischen Rassenpolitik." *Geschichte und Gesellschaft* 19:3 (1993): 277–310.

———. *Zwangssterilisation im Nationalsozialismus: Studien zur Rassenpolitik und Frauenpolitik*. Opladen: Westdeutscher, 1986.

Bonilla-Silva, Eduardo. "Rethinking Racism: Toward a Structural Interpretation." *American Sociological Review* 62:3 (1997): 465–80.

Bonnell, Victoria E. *Iconography of Power: Soviet Political Posters under Lenin and Stalin*. Berkeley and Los Angeles: University of California Press, 1997.

Braude, Benjamin. "The Sons of Noah and the Construction of Ethnic and Geographical Identities in the Medieval and Early Modern Periods." *William and Mary Quarterly* 54:1 (1997): 103–41.

Breitman, Richard. *The Architect of Genocide: Himmler and the Final Solution*. London: Bodley Head, 1991.

Bringa, Tone. *Being Muslim the Bosnian Way: Identity and Community in a Central Bosnian Village*. Princeton: Princeton University Press, 1995.

Brooks, Jeffrey. *"Thank You, Comrade Stalin!" Soviet Public Culture from Revolution to Cold War*. Princeton: Princeton University Press, 2000.

Broszat, Martin. "The Concentration Camps 1933–45." In Helmut Krausnick and Martin Broszat, *Anatomy of the SS State*, trans. Richard Barry, Marian Jackson, and Dorothy Long, 141–249. New York: Walker, 1968.

———. *The Hitler State: The Foundation and Development of the Internal Structure of the Third Reich*. Trans. John W. Hiden. London: Longman, 1981.

Browning, Christopher R. *Ordinary Men: Reserve Police Battalion 101 and the Final Solution in Poland*. New York: HarperCollins, 1992.

———. *The Path to Genocide: Essays on Launching the Final Solution*. Cambridge: Cambridge University Press, 1992.

Brubaker, Rogers. *Nationalism Reframed: Nationhood and the National Question in the New Europe*. Cambridge: Cambridge University Press, 1996.

Brubaker, Rogers, and David D. Laitin. "Ethnic and Nationalist Violence." *American Review of Sociology* 24 (1998): 423–52.

Bugai, N. F. "K voprosu o deportatsii narodov SSSR v 30–40-kh godakh." *Istoriia SSSR* 6 (1989): 135–144.

———. " 'Pogruzheny v eshelony i otprveleny k mestam poselenii . . .': L. Beriia-I. Stalinu." *Istoriia SSSR* 1 (1991): 143–60.

———. "The Truth about the Deportation of the Chechen and Ingush Peoples." *Soviet Studies in History* 30:2 (1991): 66–82.

———. "20–40-e gody: Tragediia narodov." *Vostok* 2 (1992): 122–39.

———. "Vyselenie sovetskikh koreitsev s dal'nego vostoka." *Voprosy Istorii* 5 (1994): 141–48.

Bullock, Alan. *Hitler: A Study in Tyranny*. London: Odhams, 1952.

————. *Hitler and Stalin: Parallel Lives*. London: HarperCollins, 1991.

Bunce, Valerie. *Subversive Institutions: The Design and the Destruction of Socialism and the State*. Cambridge: Cambridge University Press, 1999.

Burchett, Wilfred. "Preface." In *Peasants and Politics in Kampuchea, 1942–1981*, ed. Ben Kiernan and Chanthou Boua. London: Zed, 1982.

Burg, Steven L. and Paul S. Shoup. *The War in Bosnia-Herzegovina: Ethnic Conflict and International Intervention*. Armonk, NY: M. E. Sharpe, 1999.

Burleigh, Michael, and Wolfgang Wippermann. *The Racial State: Germany 1933–1945*. Cambridge: Cambridge University Press, 1991.

Calvert, Peter. *Revolution and Counter-Revolution*. Minneapolis: University of Minnesota Press, 1990.

Cambodia Genocide Program, Yale University, Biographic Database: *http://www.yale.edu/cgp/* [29 August 2002].

Caplan, Jane, ed. *Nazism, Fascism and the Working Class: Essays by Tim Mason*. Cambridge: Cambridge University Press, 1995.

Carroll, David. *French Literary Fascism: Nationalism, Anti-Semitism, and the Ideology of Culture*. Princeton: Princeton University Press, 1995.

Carrère d'Encausse, Hélène. *The Great Challenge: Nationalities and the Bolshevik State, 1917–1930*. Trans. Nancy Festinger. New York: Holmes and Meier, 1992.

Chalk, Frank, and Kurt Jonassohn. *The History and Sociology of Genocide: Analyses and Case Studies*. New Haven: Yale University Press, 1990.

Chamberlain, Houston Stewart. *Foundations of the Nineteenth Century*. New York: John Lane, 1910.

Chan, Youkimny. "One Spoon of Rice." In *Children of Cambodia's Killing Fields: Memoirs by Survivors*, ed. Dith Pran and Kim DePaul, 19–25. New Haven: Yale University Press, 1997.

Chandler, David P. *Brother Number One: A Political Biography of Pol Pot*. 2n ed. Boulder: Westview, 1999.

————. *The Tragedy of Cambodian History: Politics, War, and Revolution since 1945*. New Haven: Yale University Press, 1991.

————. *Voices from S-21: Terror and History in Pol Pot's Secret Prison*. Berkeley and Los Angeles: University of California Press, 1999.

Chandler, David, and Ben Kiernan, eds. *Revolution and Its Aftermath in Kampuchea: Eight Essays*. Yale University Southeast Asia Studies no. 25. New Haven: Yale University Southeast Asia Studies, 1983.

Chandler, David, Ben Kiernan, and Chanthou Boua, eds. *Pol Pot Plans the Future: Confidential Leadership Documents from Democratic Kampuchea, 1976–77*. Trans. David Chandler, Ben Kiernan, and Chanthou Boua. Yale Southeast Asia Studies no. 33. New Haven: Yale University, Southeast Asia Studies, 1988.

Clendinnen, Inga. *The Aztecs: An Interpretation*. New York: Cambridge University Press, 1997.

Cocker, Mark. *Rivers of Blood, Rivers of Gold: Europe's Conquest of Indigenous Peoples.* New York: Grove Press, 1998.

Cohen, Lenard J. *Broken Bonds: The Disintegration of Yugoslavia.* Boulder: Westview, 1993.

Ćolović, Ivan. "Football, Hooligans and War." In *The Road to War in Serbia: Trauma and Catharsis,* ed. Nebojša Popov, 373–96. Budapest: Central European University Press, 2000.

Connor, Walker. *Ethnonationalism: The Quest for Understanding.* Princeton: Princeton University Press, 1994.

Conquest, Robert. *The Great Terror: A Reassessment.* New York: Oxford University Press, 1990.

———. *The Harvest of Sorrow: Soviet Collectivization and the Terror-Famine.* New York: Oxford University Press, 1986.

Conze, Werner. "Rasse." In *Geschichtliche Grundbegriffe: Historisches Lexikon zur politisch-sozialen Sprache in Deutschland,* ed. Otto Brunner, Werner Conze, and Reinhard Koselleck, 5:135–78. Stuttgart: Ernst Klett, 1984.

Cornell, Stephen, and Douglas Hartmann. *Ethnicity and Race: Making Identities in a Changing World.* Thousand Oaks, CA: Pine Forge Press, 1998.

Dabag, Mihran, and Kristin Platt, eds. *Genozid und Moderne: Strukturen kollektiver Gewalt im 20. Jahrhundert.* Opladen: Leske und Budrich, 1998.

Dadrian, Vahakn N. *The History of the Armenian Genocide: Ethnic Conflict from the Balkans to Anatolia to the Caucasus.* 3d ed. Providence: Berghahn, 1997.

Daniel, E. Valentine. *Charred Lullabies: Chapters in an Anthropography of Violence.* Princeton: Princeton University Press, 1996.

D'Annunzio, Gabriele. *Nocturne and Five Tales of Love and Death.* Trans. Raymond Rosenthal. Marlboro, VT: Marlboro Press, 1988.

———. *The Rally.* Milan: Casa Editrice, n.d.

———. *Scritti politici di Gabriele D'Annunzio.* Ed. Paolo Alatri. Milan: Feltrinelli, 1980.

Dahbour, Omar and Micheline R. Ishay, eds. *The Nationalism Reader.* Atlantic Highlands, NJ: Humanities Press International, 1995.

Das, Veena, et al., eds. *Violence and Subjectivity.* Berkeley and Los Angeles: University of California Press, 2000.

Davis, David Brion. "Constructing Race: A Reflection." *William and Mary Quarterly* 54:1 (1997): 7–18.

———. "Looking at Slavery from Broader Perspectives." *American Historical Review* 105:2 (2000): 452–66.

———. *The Problem of Slavery in Western Culture.* Ithaca: Cornell University Press, 1966.

Denitch, Bogdan. *Ethnic Nationalism: The Tragic Death of Yugoslavia.* Minneapolis: University of Minnesota Press, 1994.

Dimitrijević, Vojin. "The 1974 Constitution as a Factor in the Collapse of

Yugoslavia, or as a Sign of Decaying Totalitarianism." In *The Road to War in Serbia: Trauma and Catharsis*, ed. Nebojša Popov, 399–424. Budapest: Central European University Press, 2000.

Djilas, Aleksa. *The Contested Country: Yugoslav Unity and Communist Revolution, 1919–1953*. Cambridge: Harvard University Press, 1991.

Domansky, Elisabeth. "The Transformation of State and Society in World War I Germany." In *Landscaping the Human Garden: Twentieth-Century Population Management in a Comparative Framework*, ed. Amir Weiner. Stanford: Stanford University Press, 2003.

Donia, Robert J., and John V. A. Fine, Jr. *The Muslims of Bosnia and Hercegovina: A Tradition Betrayed*. New York: Columbia University Press, 1994.

Douglas, Mary. *Purity and Danger: An Analysis of the Concepts of Pollution and Taboo*. 1966; London: Routledge, 1996.

Duncan, J., and D. Ley, eds. *Place/Culture/Representation*. London: Routledge, 1993.

Dwyer, Leslie, and Degung Santikarma. " 'When the World Turned to Chaos': 1965 and Its Aftermath in Bali, Indonesia." In *The Specter of Genocide*, ed. Robert Gellately and Ben Kiernan. Cambridge: Cambridge University Press, 2003.

Ebihara, May. "A Cambodian Village under the Khmer Rouge, 1975–1979." In *Genocide and Democracy in Cambodia: The Khmer Rouge, the United Nations and the International Community*, ed. Ben Kiernan, 51–63. Yale University Southeast Asia Studies no. 41. New Haven: Yale University Southeast Asia Studies, 1993.

Ebihara, May, Carol A. Mortland, and Judy Ledgerwood, eds. *Cambodian Culture since 1975: Homeland and Exile*. Ithaca: Cornell University Press, 1994.

Eckart, Wolfgang U. " 'Euthanasia Project T4' and Medical Science in Germany, 1933–1945." Manuscript. *http://www.uni-heidelberg.de/institute/fak5/igm/g47/eck—euta.htm* [29 August 2002].

———. *Medizin und Kolonialimperialismus: Deutschland 1884–1945*. Paderborn: Ferdinand Schöningh, 1997.

Edwards, Penny. "Imaging the Other in Cambodian Nationalist Discourse before and During the UNTAC Period." In *Propaganda, Politics, and Violence in Cambodia: Democratic Transition under United Nations Peacekeeping*, ed. Steve Heder and Judy Ledgerwood, 50–72. Armonk, NY: M. E. Sharpe, 1996.

Eiber, Ludwig. *"Ich wußte, es wird schlimm": Die Verfolgung der Sinti und Roma in München 1933–1945*. Munich: Buchendorfer, 1993.

Eksteins, Modris. *Rites of Spring: The Great War and the Birth of the Modern Age*. Boston: Houghton Mifflin, 1989.

Eley, Geoff, and Ronald Grigor Suny, eds. *Becoming National: A Reader*. New York: Oxford University Press, 1996.

Eltis, David. "Europeans and the Rise and Fall of African Slavery in the Americas: An Interpretation." *American Historical Review* 98:5 (1993): 1399–1423.

Fein, Helen. "Genocide: A Sociological Perspective." *Current Sociology* 38:1 (1990): 1–126.

———. "Revolutionary and Antirevolutionary Genocides: A Comparison of State Murders in Democratic Kampuchea, 1975 to 1979, and in Indonesia, 1965 to 1966." *Comparative Studies in Society and History* 33:4 (1993): 796–823.

Feldman, Allen. *Formations of Violence: The Narrative of the Body and Political Terror in Northern Ireland.* Chicago: University of Chicago Press, 1991.

———. "Violence and Vision: The Prosthetics and Aesthetics of Terror." In *Violence and Subjectivity*, ed. Veena Das et al., 46–78. Berkeley and Los Angeles: University of California Press, 2000.

Fick, Carolyn E. "The French Revolution in Saint Domingue: A Triumph or Failure?" In *A Turbulent Time: The French Revolution and the Greater Caribbean*, ed. David Barry Gaspar and David Patrick Geggus, 51–75. Bloomington: Indiana University Press, 1997.

Finley, M. I. "Slavery." In *International Encyclopedia of the Social Sciences*, ed. David L. Sills, 14:307–13. New York: Crowell, Collier and Macmillan, 1968.

Fisher, Ian. "Power Drove Milošević to Crime, Prosecutors Say As Trial Opens." *New York Times*, 13 February 2002, A1.

Fischer, Kirsten. *Suspect Relations: Sex, Race, and Resistance in Colonial North Carolina.* Ithaca: Cornell University Press, 2002.

Fitzpatrick, Sheila. "Ascribing Class: The Construction of Social Identity in Soviet Russia." *Journal of Modern History* 65:4 (1993): 745–70.

———. *Education and Social Mobility in the Soviet Union, 1921–1934.* New York: Cambridge University Press, 1979.

———. *Everyday Stalinism: Ordinary Life in Extraordinary Times. Soviet Russia in the 1930s.* New York: Oxford University Press, 1999.

———. *The Russian Revolution.* New York: Oxford University Press, 1982.

———. "Signals from Below: Soviet Letters of Denunciation in the 1930s." *Journal of Modern History* 68:4 (1996): 831–66.

———. *Stalin's Peasants: Resistance and Survival in the Russian Village after Collectivization.* New York: Oxford University Press, 1994.

———, ed. *Cultural Revolution in Russia, 1928–1931.* Bloomington: Indiana University Press, 1978.

Fitzpatrick, Sheila, and Robert Gellately, eds. "Special Issue on Denunciation." *Journal of Modern History* 68:4 (1997).

Fortunoff Video Collection for Holocaust Testimonies. Sterling Memorial Library, Yale University.

Foucault, Michel. "Leben machen und Sterben lassen: Die Geburt des

Rassismus." In Sebastian Reinfeldt, Richard Schwarz, and Michel Foucault, *Bio-Macht DISS-Texte*, Nr. 25, 27–50. Duisburg: Duisburger Institut für Sprach und Sozialforschung, 1992. Original in *Les Temps modernes 535* (February 1992): 51–58.

———. "Vom Licht des Krieges zur Geburt der Geschichte." Lecture given at the Collège de France, 21 January 1976. Ed. Walter Seitter. Berlin: Merve Verlag, 1986.

Fredrickson, George M. *The Comparative Imagination: On the History of Racism, Nationalism, and Social Movements*. Berkeley and Los Angeles: University of California Press, 1997.

———. *Racism: A Short History*. Princeton: Princeton University Press, 2002.

Friedlander, Henry. *The Origins of Nazi Genocide: From Euthanasia to the Final Solution*. Chapel Hill: University of North Carolina Press, 1995.

Friedländer, Saul. *Nazi Germany and the Jews*. Vol. 1, *The Years of Persecution, 1933–1939*. New York: HarperCollins, 1997.

Friedman, Francine. *The Bosnian Muslims: Denial of a Nation*. Boulder: Westview, 1996.

Frieson, Kate G. "Revolution and Rural Response in Cambodia: 1970–1975." In *Genocide and Democracy in Cambodia: The Khmer Rouge, the United Nations and the International Community*, ed. Ben Kiernan, 33–50. Yale University Southeast Asia Studies no. 41. New Haven: Yale University Southeast Asia Studies, 1993.

Fueloep-Miller, René. *The Mind and Face of Bolshevism: An Examination of Cultural Life in Soviet Russia*. 1927; New York: Harper and Row, 1965.

Furet, François. *The Passing of an Illusion: The Idea of Communism in the Twentieth Century*. Trans. Deborah Furet. Chicago: University of Chicago Press, 1999.

Furet, François, and Ernst Nolte. *Fascisme et communisme*. Paris: Plon, 1998.

Fussell, Paul. *The Great War and Modern Memory*. London: Oxford University Press, 1975.

Gagnon, V. P., Jr. "Ethnic Nationalism and International Conflict." *International Security* 19:3 (1994/95): 130–66.

Gaspar, David Barry, and David Patrick Geggus, eds. *A Turbulent Time: The French Revolution and the Greater Caribbean*. Bloomington: Indiana University Press, 1997.

Gay, Peter. *The Cultivation of Hatred*. Vol. 3 of *The Bourgeois Experience: Victoria to Freud*. New York: Norton, 1993.

Geggus, David. "Racial Equality, Slavery, and Colonial Secession during the Constituent Assembly." *American Historical Review* 94:5 (1989): 1290–1308.

Gelb, Michael. "An Early Soviet Ethnic Deportation: The Far-Eastern Koreans." *Russian Review* 54:3 (1995): 389–412.

Geldern, James von, and Richard Stites, eds. *Mass Culture in Soviet Russia*. Bloomington: Indiana University Press, 1995.

Gellately, Robert. *Backing Hitler: Consent and Coercion in Nazi Germany*. Oxford: Oxford University Press, 2001.

———. *The Gestapo and German Society: Enforcing Racial Policy, 1933–1945*. Oxford: Clarendon, 1990.

Gellately, Robert, and Nathan Stoltzfus, eds. *Social Outsiders in Nazi Germany*. Princeton: Princeton University Press, 2001.

Gerlach, Christian. "Deutsche Wirtschaftsinteressen, Besatzungpolitik und der Mord an den Juden in Weißrußland, 1941–1943." In *Nationalsozialistische Vernichtungspolitik 1939–1945: Neue Forschungen und Kontroversen*, ed. Ulrich Herbert, 263–91. Frankfurt am Main: Fischer, 1998.

———. "Die Wannsee Konferenz, das Schicksal der deutschen Juden und Hitlers politische Grundsatzentscheidung, alle Juden Europas zu ermorden." *WerkstattGeschichte* 6:18 (1997): 7–44.

Gerstle, Gary. *American Crucible: Race and Nation in the Twentieth Century*. Princeton: Princeton University Press, 2001.

Getty, J. Arch, and William Chase. "Patterns of Repression among the Soviet Elite in the Late 1930s: A Biographical Approach." In *Stalinist Terror: New Perspectives*, ed. J. Arch Getty and Roberta T. Manning, 225–46. Cambridge: Cambridge University Press, 1993.

Getty, J. Arch, and Roberta T. Manning, eds. *Stalinist Terror: New Perspectives*. Cambridge: Cambridge University Press, 1993.

Getty, J. Arch, Gabor T. Rittersporn, and Viktor N. Zemskov. "Victims of the Soviet Penal System in the Pre-war Years: A First Approach on the Basis of Archival Evidence." *American Historical Review* 98:4 (1993): 1017–49.

Getzler, Israel. "Lenin's Conception of Revolution as Civil War." *Slavonic and East European Review* 74:3 (1996): 464–72.

Geyer, Michael. "Restorative Elites, German Society and the Nazi Pursuit of War." In *Fascist Italy and Nazi Germany: Comparisons and Contrasts*, ed. Richard Bessel, 134–64. Cambridge: Cambridge University Press, 1996.

———. "The Stigma of Violence, Nationalism, and War in Twentieth-Century Germany." *German Studies Review*, Special Issue (Winter 1992): 75–110.

Giddens, Anthony. *Sociology*. Oxford: Polity Press, 1989.

Gladkov, Fyodor Vasilievich. *Cement*. Trans. A. S. Arthur and C. Ashleigh. New York: Frederick Ungar, 1974.

Glenny, Misha. *The Balkans: Nationalism, War and the Great Powers, 1804–1899*. New York: Viking, 2000.

———. *The Fall of Yugoslavia: The Third Balkan War*. 3d rev. ed. London: Penguin, 1996.

Gobineau, Arthur comte de. "Essay on the Inequality of the Human Races." In *Gobineau: Selected Political Writing*, ed. Michael D. Biddiss, 37–176. New York: Harper and Row, 1970.

Goldhagen, Daniel Jonah. *Hitler's Willing Executioners: Ordinary Germans and the Holocaust*. New York: Knopf, 1996.

Goldman, Wendy Z. *Women, the State, and Revolution: Soviet Family Policy and Social Life, 1917–1936*. Cambridge: Cambridge University Press, 1993.

Gould, Stephen Jay. *The Mismeasure of Man*. Rev. ed. New York: Norton, 1996.

Gow, James. *Legitimacy and the Military: The Yugoslav Crisis*. New York: St. Martin's Press, 1992.

———. "Serbian Nationalism and the Hissssing Ssssnake in the International Order: Whose Sovereignty? Whose Nation?" *Slavonic and East European Review* 72:3 (1994): 456–76.

Grmek, Mirko, Marc Gjidara, and Neven Šimac, eds. *Le Nettoyage ethnique: Documents historiques sur une idéologie serbe*. Paris: Fayard, 1993.

Gross, Jan T. *Neighbors: The Destruction of the Jewish Community in Jedwabne, Poland*. Princeton: Princeton University Press, 2001.

———. *Revolution from Abroad: The Soviet Conquest of Poland's Western Ukraine and Western Belorussia*. Princeton: Princeton University Press, 1988.

Grossman, Vasily. *Forever Flowing*. Trans. Thomas P. Whitney. New York: Harper and Row, 1972.

Guibernau, Montserrat, and John Rex, eds. *The Ethnicity Reader: Nationalism, Multiculturalism, and Migration*. Cambridge: Polity, 1997.

Gurr, Ted Robert, and Barbara Harff. *Ethnic Conflict in World Politics*. Boulder: Westview, 1994.

Gutman, Roy. *A Witness to Genocide*. New York: Macmillan, 1993.

Hadžić, Miroslav. "The Army's Use of Trauma." In *The Road to War in Serbia: Trauma and Catharsis*, ed. Nebojša Popov, 509–34. Budapest: Central European University Press, 2000.

Haffner, Sebastian. *The Meaning of Hitler*. Trans. Ewald Osers. New York: Macmillan, 1979.

Hagen, William W. "Before the 'Final Solution': Toward a Comparative Analysis of Political Anti-Semitism in Interwar Germany and Poland." *Journal of Modern History* 68:2 (1996): 351–81.

Halberstam, David. *War in a Time of Peace: Bush, Clinton, and the Generals*. New York: Scribner, 2001.

Halpern, Joel M., and David A. Kideckel, eds. *Neighbors at War: Anthropological Perspectives on Yugoslav Ethnicity, Culture, and History*. University Park: Pennsylvania State University Press, 2000.

Hannaford, Ivan. *Race: The History of an Idea in the West*. Washington, DC: The Woodrow Wilson Center Press, 1996.

Hartog, François. *The Mirror of Herodotus: The Representation of the Other in the Writing of History*. Trans. Janet Lloyd. Berkeley and Los Angeles: University of California Press, 1988.

Hawk, David R. "International Human Rights Law and Democratic Kampuchea." In *The Cambodian Agony*, ed. David A. Albin and Marlowe Hood, 118–45. Armonk, NY: M. E. Sharpe, 1990.

———. "The Photographic Record." In *Cambodia 1975–1978: Rendezvous with Death*, ed. Karl D. Jackson, 209–13. Princeton: Princeton University Press, 1989.

Hawkins, Mike. *Social Darwinism in European and American Thought, 1860–1945*. Cambridge: Cambridge University Press, 1997.

Hayden, Robert M. "Imagined Communities and Real Victims: Self-Determination and Ethnic Cleansing in Yugoslavia." *American Ethnologist* 23:4 (1996): 783–801.

Heder, Steve. "Racism, Marxism, Labelling, and Genocide in Ben Kiernan's *The Pol Pot Regime*." *South East Asia Research* 5:2 (1997): 101–53.

Heder, Steve, and Judy Ledgerwood, eds. *Propaganda, Politics, and Violence in Cambodia: Democratic Transition under United Nations Peace-keeping*. Armonk, NY: M. E. Sharpe, 1996.

Heiber, Helmut. "Der Generalplan Ost." *Vierteljahrshefte für Zeitgeschichte* 6:3 (1958): 281–325.

Hellbeck, Jochen. "Fashioning the Stalinist Soul: The Diary of Stepan Podlubnyi (1931–1939)." *Jahrbücher für Geschichte Osteuropas* 44:3 (1996): 344–73.

Heller, Mikhail, and Aleksandr Nekrich. *Utopia in Power: The History of the Soviet Union from 1917 to the Present*. Trans. Phyllis B. Carlos. New York: Summit Books, 1986.

Herbert, Ulrich. *Best: Biographische Studien über Radikalismus, Weltanschauung und Vernunft, 1903–1989*. Bonn: J.H.W. Dietz, 1996.

———. "Vernichtungspolitik: Neue Antworten und Fragen zur Geschichte des 'Holocaust.'" In *Nationalsozialistische Vernichtungspolitik 1939–1945: Neue Forschungen und Kontroversen*, ed. idem, 9–66. Frankfurt am Main: Fischer, 1998.

———, ed. *Nationalsozialistische Vernichtungspolitik 1939–1945: Neue Forschungen und Kontroversen*. Frankfurt am Main: Fischer, 1998.

Herodotus. *The Histories*. Trans. Aubrey de Sélincourt. Rev. ed. John Maricola. 1954; London: Penguin, 1996.

Heuveline, Patrick. "'Between One and Three Million': Towards the Demographic Reconstruction of a Decade of Cambodian History (1970–79)." *Population Studies* 52:1 (1998): 49–65.

Hilberg, Raul. *The Destruction of the European Jews*. Rev. ed. 3 vols. 1961; New York: Holmes and Meier, 1985.

Hinton, Alexander Laban. "Genocidal Bricolage: A Reading of Human Liver-Eating in Cambodia," Yale Center for International and Area Studies, Genocide Studies Program, Working Paper GS 06.

———. "Why Did You Kill? The Cambodian Genocide and the Dark Side of Face and Honor." *Journal of Asian Studies* 57:1 (1998): 93–122.

Hirsch, Francine. "Empire of Nations: Colonial Technologies and the Making of the Soviet Union, 1917–1939." Ph.D. diss., Princeton University, 1998.

———. "The Soviet Union as a Work-in-Progress: Ethnographers and the Category *Nationality* in the 1926, 1937, and 1939 Censuses." *Slavic Review* 56:2 (1997): 251–78.

Hitler, Adolf. *Mein Kampf*. Trans. Ralph Manheim. Boston: Houghton Mifflin, 1943.

Hobsbawm, Eric. *Nations and Nationalism since 1780: Programme, Myth, Reality*. 2d ed. Cambridge: Cambridge University Press, 1990.

Hochschild, Adam. *King Leopold's Ghost: A Story of Greed, Terror, and Heroism in Colonial Africa*. Boston: Houghton Mifflin, 1998.

Hoffmann, David L. "The Great Terror on the Local Level: Purges in Moscow Factories, 1936–1938." In *Stalinist Terror: New Perspectives*, ed. J. Arch Getty and Roberta T. Manning, 163–67. Cambridge: Cambridge University Press, 1993.

Hoffmann, G. von. "Das Sterilisierungsprogramm in den Vereinigten Staaten von Nordamerika." *Archiv für Rassen- und Gesellschafts-Biologie* 11 (1914–16): 184–92.

Holbrooke, Richard. *To End a War*. Rev. ed. New York: Modern Library, 1999.

Holquist, Peter. "A Russian Vendée: The Practice of Revolutionary Politics in the Don Countryside." Ph.D. diss., Columbia University, 1995.

———. "State Violence as Technique: The Logic of Violence in Soviet Totalitarianism." In *The Making and Management of Societies: Twentieth-Century Population Politics in a Comparative Framework*, ed. Amir Weiner. Stanford: Stanford University Press, 2003.

Honig, Jan Willem, and Norbert Both. *Srebenica: Record of a War Crime*. London: Penguin, 1996.

Horkheimer, Max, and Theodor W. Adorno. *Dialectic of Enlightenment*. Trans. John Chumming. 1947; New York: Herder and Herder, 1972.

Horsman, Reginald. *Race and Manifest Destiny: The Origins of American Racial Anglo-Saxonism*. Cambridge: Harvard University Press, 1986.

Hosking, Geoffrey. *Russia: People and Empire, 1552–1917*. Cambridge: Harvard University Press, 1997.

Hovannisian, Richard G. "The Historical Dimensions of the Armenian Question, 1878–1923." In *The Armenian Genocide in Perspective*, ed. idem, 19–41. New Brunswick, NJ: Transaction, 1986.

———. *The Republic of Armenia*. 4 vols. Berkeley and Los Angeles: University of California Press, 1971–96.

———, ed. *The Armenian Genocide in Perspective*. New Brunswick, NJ: Transaction, 1986.

Hudson, Nicholas. "From 'Nation' to 'Race': The Origin of Racial Classification in Eighteenth-Century Thought." *Eighteenth-Century Studies* 29:3 (1996): 247–64.

Hunt, Lynn, ed. *The French Revolution and Human Rights*. Boston: Bedford Books, 1996.

Hutchinson, John, and Anthony D. Smith, eds. *Nationalism*. Oxford: Oxford University Press, 1994.

Huxley, Thomas. *Evolution and Ethics*. London: Macmillan, 1893.

Jäckel, Eberhard. *Hitler's World View: A Blueprint for Power*. Trans. Herbert Arnold. Cambridge: Harvard University Press, 1981.

Jackson, Karl D. "The Ideology of Total Revolution." In *Cambodia 1975–1978: Rendezvous with Death*, ed. idem, 37–78. Princeton: Princeton University Press, 1989.

———, ed. *Cambodia 1975–1978: Rendezvous with Death*. Princeton: Princeton University Press, 1989.

Jersak, Tobias. "Die Interaktion von Kriegsverlauf und Judenvernichtung: Ein Blick auf Hitlers Strategie im Spätsommer 1941." *Historische Zeitschrift* 268 (1999): 311–74.

Jordan, Winthrop D. *White over Black: American Attitudes Toward the Negro, 1550–1812*. Chapel Hill: University of North Carolina Press, 1968.

Judah, Tim. *The Serbs: History, Myth and the Destruction of Yugoslavia*. New Haven: Yale University Press, 1997.

Jünger, Ernst. *Copse 125: A Chronicle from the Trench Warfare of 1918*. Trans. Basil Creighton. London: Chatto and Windus, 1930.

Kaplan, Marion. *Between Dignity and Despair: Jewish Life in Nazi Germany*. New York: Oxford University Press, 1998.

Kaplan, Robert D. *Balkan Ghosts: A Journey through History*. New York: St. Martin's, 1993.

Kappeler, Andreas. *Rußland als Vielvölkerreich: Entstehung, Geschichte, Zerfall*. Munich: Beck, 1993.

Katz, Steven T. *The Holocaust in Historical Context*. Vol. 1, *The Holocaust and Mass Death before the Modern Age*. New York: Oxford University Press, 1994.

Kedourie, Elie. *Nationalism*. 4th ed. Oxford: Blackwell, 1993.

Keegan, John. *A History of Warfare*. New York: Vintage, 1993.

Kershaw, Ian. *Hitler, 1889–1936: Hubris*. New York: Norton, 1999.

———. *Hitler: Profiles in Power*. London: Longman, 1991.

———. "'Working towards the Führer': Reflections on the Nature of the Hitler Dictatorship." In *Stalinism and Nazism: Dictatorships in Comparison*, ed. idem and Moshe Lewin, 88–106. Cambridge: Cambridge University Press, 1997.

Kershaw, Ian, and Moshe Lewin, eds. *Stalinism and Nazism: Dictatorships in Comparison*. Cambridge: Cambridge University Press, 1997.

Kertzer, David I. *Ritual, Politics, and Power*. New Haven: Yale University Press, 1988.

Kevles, Daniel J. *In the Name of Eugenics: Genetics and the Uses of Human Heredity*. Berkeley and Los Angeles: University of California Press, 1985.

Kiernan, Ben. "Kampuchea and Stalinism." In *Marxism in Asia*, ed. Colin Mackerras and Nick Knight, 232–49. London: Croom Helm, 1985.

———. *How Pol Pot Came to Power: A History of Communism in Kampuchea, 1930–1975*. London: Verso, 1985.

———. *The Pol Pot Regime: Race, Power, and Genocide in Cambodia under the Khmer Rouge, 1975–79*. New Haven: Yale University Press, 1996.

———. "Sur la notion de génocide." *Le Débat*, March–April 1999, 179–92.

———. "Wild Chickens, Farm Chickens and Cormorants: Kampuchea's Eastern Zone under Pol Pot." In *Revolution and Its Aftermath in Kampuchea: Eight Essays*, ed. David P. Chandler and Ben Kiernan, 136–211. Yale University Southeast Asia Studies no. 25. New Haven: Yale University Southeast Asia Studies, 1983.

Kiernan, Ben, ed. *Genocide and Democracy in Cambodia: The Khmer Rouge, the United Nations and the International Community*. Yale University Southeast Asia Studies no. 41. New Haven: Yale University Southeast Asia Studies, 1993.

Kiernan, Ben, and Chanthou Boua, eds. *Peasants and Politics in Kampuchea, 1942–1981*. London: Zed, 1982.

Kiljunen, Kimmo, ed. *Kampuchea: Decade of the Genocide. Report of a Finnish Inquiry Commission*. London: Zed, 1984.

Klee, Ernst, Willi Dressen, and Volker Riess, eds. *"The Good Old Days": The Holocaust as Seen by Its Perpetrators and Bystanders*. Trans. Deborah Burnstone. New York: Free Press, 1991.

Klemperer, Victor. *I Will Bear Witness: A Diary of the Nazi Years*. Trans. Martin Chalmers. 2 vols. New York: Random House, 1998–99.

Knowlton, James, and Truett Cates, eds. and trans. *Forever in the Shadow of Hitler? Original Documents of the Historikerstreit, the Controversy concerning the Singularity of the Holocaust*. Atlantic Highlands, NJ: Humanities Press, 1993.

Koenker, Diane P., William G. Rosenberg, and Ronald Grigor Suny, eds. *Party, State, and Society in the Russian Civil War: Explorations in Social History*. Bloomington: Indiana University Press, 1989.

Kollontai, A. "The Family and the Communist State." In *Bolshevik Visions: First Phase of the Cultural Revolution in Soviet Russia*, ed. William G. Rosenberg, 79–88. Ann Arbor: Ardis, 1984.

———. "Make Way for the Winged Eros." In *Bolshevik Visions: First Phase of the Cultural Revolution in Soviet Russia*, ed. William G. Rosenberg, 96–106. Ann Arbor: Ardis, 1984.

Konstantinović-Vilić, Slobodanka. "Psychological Violence and Fear in War, and Their Consequences for the Psychological Health of Women." In *Women, Violence and War: Wartime Victimization of Refugees in the Balkans*, ed. Vesna Nikolić-Ristanović, trans. Borislav Radović, 99–133. 1995; Budapest: Central European University Press, 2000.

Kotkin, Stephen. *Magnetic Mountain: Stalinism as a Civilization*. Berkeley and Los Angeles: University of California Press, 1995.

Kozlov, Vladimir A. "Denunciation and Its Functions in Soviet Governance: A Study of Denunciations and Their Bureaucratic Handling from Soviet Police Archives, 1944–1953," *Journal of Modern History* 68:4 (1996): 867–98.

Kracauer, Siegfried. *The Mass Ornament: Weimar Essays*. Trans. Thomas Y. Levin. Cambridge: Harvard University Press, 1995.

Krausnick, Helmut. "The Persecution of the Jews." In idem and Martin Broszat, *Anatomy of the SS State*, trans. Richard Barry, Marian Jackson, and Dorothy Long, 17–139. New York: Walker, 1968.

Krausnick, Helmut, and Martin Broszat. *Anatomy of the SS State*. Trans. Richard Barry, Marian Jackson, Dorothy Long. New York: Walker, 1968.

Krausnick, Helmut, and Hans-Heinrich Wilhelm. *Die Truppe des Weltanschauungskrieges: Die Einsatzgruppen der Sicherheitspolizei und des SD, 1938–1942*. Stuttgart: Deutsche Verlags-Anstalt, 1981.

Krupskaya, N. "What a Communist Ought to Be Like." In *Bolshevik Visions: First Phase of the Cultural Revolution in Soviet Russia*, ed. William G. Rosenberg, 38–41. Ann Arbor: Ardis, 1984.

Kuper, Leo. *Genocide: Its Political Use in the Twentieth Century*. New Haven: Yale University Press, 1981.

Ladas, Stephen. *The Exchange of Minorities*. New York: Macmillan, 1932.

Lampe, John R. *Yugoslavia as History: Twice There Was a Country*. 2d ed. Cambridge: Cambridge University Press, 2000.

Landes, Joan. *Women and the Public Sphere in the Age of the French Revolution*. Ithaca: Cornell University Press, 1988.

Larina, Anna. *This I Cannot Forget: The Memoirs of Nikolai Bukharin's Widow*. Trans. Gary Kern. New York: Norton, 1993.

Lebedev-Polyansky, P.I. "Revolution and the Cultural Tasks of the Proletariat." In *Bolshevik Visions: First Phase of the Cultural Revolution in Soviet Russia*, ed. William G. Rosenberg, 62–70. Ann Arbor: Ardis, 1984.

Leed, Eric J. *No Man's Land: Combat and Identity in World War I*. Cambridge: Cambridge University Press, 1979.

Lemkin, Raphael. *Axis Rule in Occupied Europe*. Washington, DC: Carnegie Endowment for International Peace, 1944.

Lepsius, Johannes. *Bericht über die Lage des Armenischen Volkes in der Türkei*. Potsdam: Tempelverlag, 1916.

Levi, Primo. *The Drowned and the Saved*. Trans. Raymond Rosenthal. New York: Summit Books, 1988.

Lewin, Moshe. *The Making of the Soviet System*. New York: Pantheon, 1985.

———. *Russian Peasants and Soviet Power: A Study of Collectivization*. London: Allen and Unwin, 1968.

Lindenberger, Thomas. "Die Diktatur der Grenzen. Zur Einleitung." In *Herr-*

schaft und Eigen-Sinn in der Diktatur: Studien zur Gesellschaftsgeschichte der DDR, ed. idem, 13–44. Cologne: Böhlau, 1999.

——, ed. *Herrschaft und Eigen-Sinn in der Diktatur: Studien zur Gesellschaftsgeschichte der DDR*. Cologne: Böhlau, 1999.

Lindenberger, Thomas, and Alf Lüdtke, eds. *Physische Gewalt: Studien zur Geschichte der Neuzeit*. Frankfurt am Main: Suhrkamp, 1995.

Lindqvist, Sven. *"Exterminate All the Brutes": One Man's Odyssey into the Heart of Darkness and the Origins of European Genocide*. Trans. Joan Tate. New York: New Press, 1996.

Locard, Henri. *Le "Petit livre rouge" de Pol Pot ou Les Paroles de l'Angkar*. Paris: L'Harmattan, 1996.

Lüdtke, Alf. "Einleitung: Herrschaft als soziale Praxis." In *Herrschaft als soziale Praxis: Historische und sozial-anthropologische Studien*, ed. idem, 9–66. Göttingen: Vandenhoeck and Ruprecht, 1991.

——, ed. *Herrschaft als soziale Praxis: Historische und sozial-anthropologische Studien*. Göttingen: Vandenhoeck and Ruprecht, 1991.

Luebke, David Martin, and Sybil Milton. "Locating the Victim: An Overview of Census-Taking, Tabulation Technology, and Persecution in Nazi Germany." *IEEE Annals of the History of Computing* 16:3 (1994): 25–39.

Luxemburg, Rosa. *Gesammelte Briefe*. Vol. 5. Ed. Institut für Marxismus-Leninismus beim ZK der SED. Berlin: Dietz Verlag, 1984.

Mackerras, Colin, and Nick Knight, eds. *Marxism in Asia*. London: Croom Helm, 1985.

Maier, Charles. *Dissolution: The Crisis of Communism and the End of East Germany*. Princeton: Princeton University Press, 1997.

Makino, Uwe. "Final Solutions, Crimes against Mankind: On the Genesis and Criticism of the Concept of Genocide." *Journal of Genocide Research* 3:1 (2001): 49–73.

Malia, Martin E. *The Soviet Tragedy: A History of Socialism in Russia, 1917–1991*. New York: Free Press, 1994.

Mam, Kalyanee E. "An Oral History of Family Life under the Khmer Rouge." Yale Center for International and Area Studies, Genocide Studies Program, Working Paper GS 10.

Manning, Roberta T. "The Soviet Economic Crisis of 1936–1940 and the Great Purges." In *Stalinist Terror: New Perspectives*, ed. J. Arch Getty and Roberta T. Manning, 116–41. Cambridge: Cambridge University Press, 1993.

Manoschek, Walter. "Die Vernichtung der Juden in Serbien." In *Nationalsozialistische Vernichtungspolitik 1939–1945: Neue Forschungen und Kontroversen*, ed. Ulrich Herbert, 209–34. Frankfurt am Main: Fischer, 1998.

Marchand, Suzanne L. *Down from Olympus: Archaeology and Philhellenism in Germany, 1750–1970*. Princeton: Princeton University Press, 1996.

Margalit, Avishai, and Gabriel Motzkin. "The Uniqueness of the Holocaust." *Philosophy and Public Affairs* 25:1 (1996): 65–83.

Margolin, Jean-Louis. "Cambodge: Au pays du crime déconcertant." In *Le Livre noir du communisme: Crimes, terreur et répression*, ed. Stéphane Courtois, 630–95. Paris: Robert Laffont, 1997.

Marie, Jean-Jacques. *Les Peuples déportés d'Union soviétique*. Brussels: Éditions Complexe, 1995.

Markusen, Eric. "The Meaning of Genocide as Expressed in the Jurisprudence of the International Criminal Tribunals for the Former Yugoslavia and Rwanda: A Non-Legal Scholar's Perspective." Paper presented at the Association of Genocide Scholars conference, Minneapolis, MN, June 2001.

Marston, John. "Metaphors of the Khmer Rouge." In *Cambodian Culture since 1975: Homeland and Exile*, ed. May M. Ebihara, Carol A. Mortland, and Judy Ledgerwood, 105–18. Ithaca: Cornell University Press, 1994.

Martin, Terry D. "An Affirmative Action Empire: Ethnicity and the Soviet State, 1923–1938." Ph.D. diss., University of Chicago, 1996.

———. "The Origins of Soviet Ethnic Cleansing." *Journal of Modern History* 70:4 (1998): 813–61.

———. "Terror gegen Nationen in der Sowjetunion." *Osteuropa* 50:6 (2000): 606–16.

May, Someth. *Cambodian Witness: The Autobiography of Someth May*. Ed. James Fenton. London: Faber and Faber, 1986.

Mayer, Arno. *The Furies: Violence and Terror in the French and Russian Revolutions*. Princeton: Princeton University Press, 2000.

———. *Why Did the Heavans Not Darken? The "Final Solution" in History*. New York: Pantheon, 1988.

Mayr, Ernst. *The Growth of Biological Thought: Diversity, Evolution, and Inheritance*. Cambridge: Harvard University Press, Belknap Press, 1982.

Mazower, Mark. *The Balkans: A Short History*. New York: Modern Library, 2000.

Mazzini, Giuseppe. "Duties towards Your Country." In *Introduction to Contemporary Civilization in the West*, 2:540–43, 3d ed. New York: Columbia University Press, 1961.

Medvedev, Roy. *Let History Judge: The Origins and Consequences of Stalinism*. Trans. George Shriver. Rev. and expanded ed. New York: Columbia University Press, 1989.

Melson, Robert. "Provocation or Nationalism: A Critical Inquiry into the Armenian Genocide of 1915." In *The Armenian Genocide in Perspective*, ed. Richard G. Hovannisian, 61–84. New Brunswick, NJ: Transaction, 1986.

———. *Revolution and Genocide: On the Origins of the Armenian Genocide and the Holocaust*. Chicago: University of Chicago Press, 1992.

"Le Mémorandum de l'Académie serbe." In *Le Nettoyage ethnique: Documents historiques sur une idéologie serbe*, ed. Mirko Grmek, Marc Gjidara, and Neven Šimac, 231–69. Paris: Fayard, 1993.

Michalka, Wolfgang, ed. *Das Dritte Reich: Dokumente zur Innen- und Außen-politik*. 2 vols. Munich: DTV, 1985.

Milosavilević, Olivera. "The Abuse of the Authority of Science." In *The Road to War in Serbia: Trauma and Catharsis*, ed. Nebojša Popov, 274–302. Budapest: Central European University Press, 2000.

Milton, Sybil. "Holocaust: The Gypsies." In *Genocide in the Twentieth Century: Critical Essays and Eyewitness Accounts*, ed. Samuel Totten, William S. Parsons, and Israel W. Charny, 209–64. New York: Garland, 1995.

———. "Vorstufe zur Vernichtung: Die Zigeunerlage nach 1933." *Viertel-jahrshefte für Zeitgeschichte* 43:1 (1995): 115–30.

Mommsen, Hans. "The Realization of the Unthinkable: The 'Final Solution of the Jewish Question' in the Third Reich." In idem, *From Weimar to Ausch-witz*, trans. Philip O'Connor, 224–53. Princeton: Princeton University Press, 1991.

Moore, Sally F., and Barbara G. Myerhoff. "Secular Ritual: Forms and Mean-ings." In *Secular Ritual*, ed. idem, 3–24. Amsterdam: Van Gorcum, 1977.

———, eds. *Secular Ritual*. Amsterdam: Van Gorcum, 1977.

Morgenthau, Henry. *Ambassador Morgenthau's Story*. Garden City, NY: Dou-bleday, 1918.

Morsink, Johannes. *The Universal Declaration of Human Rights: Origins, Drafting, and Intent*. Philadelphia: University of Pennsylvania Press, 1999.

Moses, A. Dirk. "An Antipodean Genocide? The Origins of the Genocidal Mo-ment in the Colonization of Australia." *Journal of Genocide Research* 2:1 (2000): 89–106.

Mosse, George L. *The Crisis of German Ideology: Intellectual Origins of the Third Reich*. New York: Grosset and Dunlap, 1964.

———. *Fallen Soldiers: Reshaping the Memory of the World Wars*. New York: Oxford University Press, 1990.

———. *Toward the Final Solution: A History of European Racism*. Madison: University of Wisconsin Press, 1985.

The Mountain Wreath of P. P. Nyegosh. Trans. James W. Wiles. London: George Allen and Unwin, 1930.

Muir, Edward. *Rituals in Early Modern Europe*. Cambridge: Cambridge Univer-sity Press, 1997.

Munn, Karl. "Tatsachen zur Frage der ungenügenden Fortpflanzung der Intellek-tuellen und ihrer Ursachen." *Archiv für Rassen- und Gesellschafts-Biologie* 13 (1918–21): 171–75.

Naimark, Norman M. "Ethnic Cleansing in Twentieth Century Europe." In Donald W. Treadgold Papers no. 19, The Henry M. Jackson School of In-ternational Studies. Seattle: University of Washington, 1998.

———. *Fires of Hatred: Ethnic Cleansing in Twentieth-Century Europe*. Cam-bridge: Harvard University Press, 2001.

Nekrich, Aleksandr M. *The Punished Peoples: The Deportation and Fate of Soviet Minorities at the End of the Second World War.* Trans. George Saunders. New York: Norton, 1978.

Niewyk, Donald L. "Holocaust: The Genocide of the Jews." In *Genocide in the Twentieth Century: Critical Essays and Eyewitness Accounts*, ed. Samuel Totten, William S. Parsons, and Israel W. Charny, 167–207. New York: Garland, 1995.

Nikolić-Ristanović, Vesna. "Sexual Violence." In *Women, Violence and War: Wartime Victimization of Refugees in the Balkans*, ed. idem, trans. Borislay Radovic, 41–77. Budapest: Central European University, 2000.

———, ed. *Women, Violence and War: Wartime Victimization of Refugees in the Balkans.* Trans. Borislay Radovic. Budapest: Central European University, 2000.

Nirenberg, David. *Communities of Violence: Persecution of Minorities in the Middle Ages.* Princeton: Princeton University Press, 1996.

Noakes, Jeremy. "Social Outcasts in the Third Reich." In *Life in the Third Reich*, ed. Richard Bessel, 83–96. Oxford: Oxford University Press, 1987.

Noakes, Jeremy, and Geoffrey Pridham, eds. *Nazism 1919–1945: A Documentary Reader.* Vol. 1, *The Rise To Power, 1919–1934.* Exeter: University of Exeter Press, 1983.

———, eds. *Nazism, 1919–1945: A Documentary Reader.* Vol. 2, *State, Economy and Society, 1933–1939.* Exeter: University of Exeter Press, 1984.

———, eds. *Nazism 1919–1945: A Documentary Reader.* Vol. 3, *Foreign Policy, War and Racial Extermination.* Exeter: Exeter University Publications, 1988.

Nolte, Ernst. *Der europäische Bürgerkrieg 1917–1945: Nationalsozialismus und Bolschewismus.* Berlin: Propyläen, 1987.

Obradović, Marija. "The Ruling Party." In *The Road to War in Serbia: Trauma and Catharsis*, ed. Nebojša Popov, 425–48. Budapest: Central European University Press, 2000.

Omi, Michael, and Howard Winant. *Racial Formation in the United States from the 1960s to the 1990s.* 2d ed. New York: Routledge, 1994.

Onuf, Peter S. *Jefferson's Empire: The Language of American Nationhood.* Charlottesville: University Press of Virginia, 2000.

Ostrovsky, Nikolai. *How the Steel Was Tempered.* Moscow: Progress, n.d.

Paret, Peter, Beth Irwin Lewis, and Paul Paret. *Persuasive Images: Posters of War and Revolution from the Hoover Institution Archives.* Princeton: Princeton University Press, 1992.

Patterson, Orlando. *Slavery and Social Death: A Comparative Study.* Cambridge: Harvard University Press, 1982.

Peabody, Sue. *"There Are No Slaves in France": The Political Culture of Race and Slavery in the Ancien Régime.* New York: Oxford University Press, 1996.

Pearson, Karl. *National Life from the Standpoint of Science*. University of London, Galton Laboratory for National Eugenics, Eugenics Lecture Series no. 11. Cambridge: Cambridge University Press, n.d.

———. *The Problem of Practical Eugenics*. University of London, Galton Laboratory for National Eugenics, Eugenics Laboratory Lecture Series no. 5. London: Dulau and Co., 1912.

———. *The Scope and Importance to the State of the Science of National Eugenics*. University of London, Galton Laboratory for National Eugenics, Eugenics Laboratory Section no. 1. London: Dulau and Co., 1909.

Pešić, Vesna. "The War for Ethnic States." In *The Road to War in Serbia: Trauma and Catharsis*, ed. Nebojša Popov, 9–49. Budapest: Central European University Press, 2000.

Peters, Edward. *Torture*. Expanded ed. Philadelphia: University of Pennsylvania Press, 1996.

Peukert, Detlev. *Inside Nazi Germany: Conformity, Opposition, and Racism in Everyday Life*. Trans. Richard Deveson. New Haven: Yale University Press, 1987.

Phillips, Jr., William D. *Slavery from Roman Times to the Early Transatlantic Trade*. Minneapolis: University of Minnesota Press, 1985.

Phim, Toni Samantha. "Terror and Aesthetics." Yale Center for International and Area Studies, Genocide Studies Program, Working Paper GS 06, 1998.

Pin, Yathay with John Man. *Stay Alive, My Son*. Rev. ed. Ithaca: Cornell University Press, 2000.

Pinson, Mark, ed. *The Muslims of Bosnia-Herzegovina: Their Historic Development from the Middle Ages to the Dissolution of Yugoslavia*. Harvard Middle Eastern Monographs 28. Cambridge: Harvard University Press, 1993.

Pipes, Richard. *The Bolshevik Revolution*. New York: Knopf, 1990.

Plaggenborg, Stefan. *Revolutionskultur: Menschenbilder und kulturelle Praxis in Sowjetrußland zwischen Oktoberrevolution und Stalinismus*. Cologne: Böhlau, 1996.

Ploetz, Alfred. "Ableitung einer Gesellschafts-Hygiene und ihrer Beziehungen zur Ethik." *Archiv für Rassen- und Gesellschafts-Biologie* 3 (1906): 253–59.

———. "Die Begriffe Rasse und Gesellschaft und die davon abgeleiteten Disziplinen." *Archiv für Rassen- und Gesellschafts-Biologie* 1 (1904): 1–26.

———. "Neomalthusianismus und Rassenhygiene." *Archiv für Rassen- und Gesellschafts-Biologie* 10 (1913): 166–72.

———. "Zu Darwins Gedächtnis." *Archiv für Rassen- und Gesellschafts-Biologie* 5 (1909): 145.

Pohl, Dieter. "Die Ermordung der Juden im Generalgouvernement." In *Nationalsozialistische Vernichtungspolitik 1939–1945: Neue Forschungen und Kontroversen*, ed. Ulrich Herbert, 98–121. Frankfurt am Main: Fischer, 1998.

————. "Die Holocaust-Forschung und Goldhagens Thesen." *Vierteljahrshefte für Zeitgeschichte* 45:1 (1997): 12–48.

Pohl, J. Otto. *Ethnic Cleansing in the USSR, 1937–1949.* Westport, CT: Greenwood Press, 1999.

Poliakov, Léon. *The Aryan Myth: A History of Racist and Nationalist Ideas in Europe.* Trans. Edmund Howard. New York: Basic Books, 1971.

Ponchaud, François. "Social Change in the Vortex of Revolution." In *Cambodia 1975–1978: Rendezvous with Death,* ed. Karl D. Jackson, 151–77. Princeton: Princeton University Press, 1989.

Popov, Nebojša, ed. *The Road to War in Serbia: Trauma and Catharsis.* 1996; Budapest: Central European University Press, 2000.

Power, Samantha. *"A Problem from Hell": America and the Age of Genocide.* New York: Basic Books, 2002.

Prak, Sarom. "The Unfortunate Cambodia." In *Children of Cambodia's Killing Fields: Memoirs by Survivors,* ed. Dith Pran and Kim DePaul, 67–71. New Haven: Yale University Press, 1997.

Pran, Dith, and Kim DePaul, eds. *Children of Cambodia's Killing Fields: Memoirs by Survivors.* New Haven: Yale University Press, 1997.

Proctor, Robert N. "From *Anthropologie* to *Rassenkunde* in the German Anthropological Tradition." In *Bones, Bodies, Behavior: Essays on Biological Anthropology,* ed. George W. Stocking, Jr., 138–79. Madison: University of Wisconsin Press, 1988.

————. *The Nazi War on Cancer.* Princeton: Princeton University Press, 1999.

Quinn, Kenneth M. "The Pattern and Scope of Violence." In *Cambodia 1975–1978: Rendezvous with Death,* ed. Karl D. Jackson, 179–208. Princeton: Princeton University Press, 1989.

Radić, Radmila. "The Church and the 'Serbian Question.'" In *The Road to War in Serbia: Trauma and Catharsis,* ed. Nebojša Popov, 247–73. Budapest: Central European University Press, 2000.

Ramet, Sabrina P. *Balkan Babel: The Disintegration of Yugoslavia from the Death of Tito to the War for Kosovo.* 3d ed. Boulder: Westview, 1999.

Ratzenhofer, Gustav. "Die Rassenfrage vom ethischen Standpunkte." *Archiv für Rassen- und Gesellschafts-Biologie* 1 (1904): 737–48.

Ree, Erik van. "Stalin's Organic Theory of the Party." *Russian Review* 52:1 (1993): 43–57.

Reibmayr, Albert. "Zur Entwicklungsgeschichte der wichtigsten Charaktere und Anlagen der indogermanischen Rasse." *Archiv für Rassen- und Gesellschafts-Biologie* 7 (1910): 328–53.

Reichel, Peter. *Der schöne Schein des Dritten Reiches: Faszination und Gewalt des Faschismus.* Frankfurt am Main: Fischer, 1993.

Reinfeldt, Sebastian, and Richard Schwarz, eds. *Bio-Macht DISS-Texte.* Nr. 25. Duisburg: Duisburger Institut für Sprach und Sozialforschung, 1992.

Riches, David. "The Phenomenon of Violence." In *The Anthropology of Violence*, ed. idem, 1–27. Oxford: Basil Blackwell, 1986.

Roediger, David R. *The Wages of Whiteness: Race and the Making of the American Working Class*. London: Verso, 1991.

Rosenbaum, Alan S., ed. *Is the Holocaust Unique? Perspectives on Comparative Genocide*. Boulder: Westview, 1996.

Rosenberg, William G., ed. *Bolshevik Visions: First Phase of the Cultural Revolution in Soviet Russia*. Ann Arbor: Ardis, 1984.

Ruosso, Henry, ed. *Stalinisme et nazisme: Histoire et mémoire comparées*. Brussels: Éditions Complexe, 1999.

Sandkühler, Thomas. "Judenpolitik und Judenmord im Distrikt Galizien, 1941–1942." In *Nationalsozialistische Vernichtungspolitik 1939–1945: Neue Forschungen und Kontroversen*, ed. Ulrich Herbert, 122–47. Frankfurt am Main: Fischer, 1998.

Sandner, Peter. *Frankfurt. Auschwitz. Die nationalsozialistische Verfolgung der Sinti und Roma in Frankfurt am Main*. Frankfurt am Main: Brandes and Apsel, 1998.

Sarafian, Ara, ed. *The Treatment of Armenians in the Ottoman Empire: Documents Presented to Viscount Grey of Fallodon, Secretary of State for Foreign Affairs by Viscount Bryce*. London: Hodder and Stoughton, 1916. Reprint, Princeton, NJ: Gomidas Institute, 2000.

Scarry, Elaine. *The Body in Pain: The Making and Unmaking of the World*. New York: Oxford University Press, 1985.

Scott, James C. *Domination and the Arts of Resistance: Hidden Transcripts*. New Haven: Yale University Press, 1990.

———. *Seeing Like a State: How Certain Schemes to Improve the Human Condition Have Failed*. New Haven: Yale University Press, 1998.

Semelin, Jacques. "Analysis of a Mass Crime: Ethnic Cleansing in the Former Yugoslavia, 1991–1999." In *The Specter of Genocide*, ed. Robert Gellately and Ben Kiernan. Cambridge: Cambridge University Press, 2003.

Sereny, Gitta. *Albert Speer: His Battle with Truth*. New York: Vintage, 1995.

Service, Robert. *A History of Twentieth-Century Russia*. Cambridge: Harvard University Press, 1998.

Sewell, Jr., William H. *A Rhetoric of Bourgeois Revolution: The Abbé Sieyes and "What Is the Third Estate?"* Durham: Duke University Press, 1994.

Shalamov, Varlam. *Kolyma Tales*. Trans. John Glad. New York: Norton, 1980.

Shanin, Teodor. *The Awkward Class: Political Sociology of Peasantry in a Developing Society. Russia 1910–1925*. Oxford: Clarendon, 1972.

Shoemaker, Nancy. "How Indians Got to Be Red." *American Historical Review* 102:3 (1997): 625–44.

Sholokhov, Mikhail Aleksandrovich. *The Silent Don*. Vols. 1 and 2, *And Quiet Flows the Don* and *The Don Flows Home to the Sea*. Trans. Stephen Garry. New York: Knopf, 1942.

Siegelbaum, Lewis H. *Stakhanovism and the Politics of Productivity in the USSR, 1935–1941*. Cambridge: Cambridge University Press, 1988.

Siegelbaum, Lewis H., and Andrei Sokolov. *Stalinism as a Way of Life: A Narrative in Documents*. New Haven: Yale University Press, 2000.

Siegelbaum, Lewis H., and Ronald Grigor Suny, eds. *Making Workers Soviet: Power, Class, and Identity*. Ithaca: Cornell University Press, 1994.

Silber, Laura, and Allan Little. *Yugoslavia: Death of a Nation*. Rev. ed. New York: Penguin, 1997.

Singham, Shanti Marie. "'Betwixt Cattle and Men': Jews, Blacks, and Women and the Declaration of the Rights of Man." In *The French Idea of Freedom: The Old Regime and the Declaration of Rights of 1789*, ed. Dale Van Kley, 114–53. Stanford: Stanford University Press, 1994.

Singleton, Fred. *A Short History of the Yugoslav Peoples*. Cambridge: Cambridge University Press, 1985.

Skocpol, Theda. *States and Social Revolutions: A Comparative Analysis of France, Russia, and China*. Cambridge: Cambridge University Press, 1979.

Slezkine, Yuri. *Arctic Mirrors: Russia and the Small Peoples of the North*. Ithaca: Cornell University Press, 1994.

———. "From Savages to Citizens: The Cultural Revolution in the Soviet Far North, 1928–1938." *Slavic Review* 51:1 (1992): 52–76.

———. "N. Ia. Marr and the National Origins of Soviet Ethnogenetics." *Slavic Review* 55:4 (1996): 826–62.

———. "The USSR as a Communal Apartment, or How a Socialist State Promoted Ethnic Particularism." *Slavic Review* 52:2 (1994): 414–52.

Snowden, Jr., Frank M. *Before Color Prejudice: The Ancient View of Blacks*. Cambridge: Harvard University Press, 1983.

Sofsky, Wolfgang. "Gesetz des Gemetzels." *Die Zeit* 15 (2 April 1998): 53.

———. *The Order of Terror: The Concentration Camp*. Trans. William Templar. Princeton: Princeton University Press, 1997.

———. *Traktat über die Gewalt*. Frankfurt am Main: Fischer, 1996.

Solts, A. A. "Communist Ethics." In *Bolshevik Visions: First Phase of the Cultural Revolution in Soviet Russia*, ed. William G. Rosenberg, 42–54. Ann Arbor: Ardis, 1984.

Solzhenitsyn, Aleksandr I. *The Gulag Archipelago, 1918–1956: An Experiment in Literary Investigation*. Vols. 1–2. Trans. Thomas P. Whitney. New York: Harper and Row, 1974.

———. *The Gulag Archipelago, 1918–1956: An Experiment in Literary Investigation*. Vols. 5–7. Trans. Harry Willetts. New York: Harper and Row, 1976.

Speer, Albert. *Inside the Third Reich: Memoirs*. Trans. Richard and Clara Winston. New York: Macmillan, 1970.

Stalin, J. V. *Marxism and the National Question*. 1913. In idem, *Works*, vol. 2, *1907–1913*, 300–81. Moscow: Foreign Languages Publishing House, 1953.

———. *Marxism and the National Question: Selected Writings and Speeches.* New York: International Publishers, 1942.

———. *Problems of Leninism.* Moscow: Foreign Languages Publishing House, 1947.

Stanton, Gregory H. "The Cambodian Genocide and International Law." In *Genocide and Democracy in Cambodia: The Khmer Rouge, the United Nations and the International Community,* ed. Ben Kiernan, 141–61. Yale University Southeast Asia Studies no. 41. New Haven: Yale University Southeast Asia Studies, 1993.

Steichen, Edward. *The Family of Man.* 1955; New York: Museum of Modern Art, 1997.

Stein, George H. *The Waffen SS: Hitler's Elite Guard at War.* Ithaca: Cornell University Press, 1966.

Stiglmayer, Alexandra, ed. *Mass Rape: The War against Women in Bosnia-Herzegovina.* Trans. Marion Faber. Lincoln: University of Nebraska Press, 1994.

Stites, Richard. *Revolutionary Dreams: Utopian Vision and Experimental Life in the Russian Revolution.* New York: Oxford University Press, 1989.

Stokes, Gale. *The Walls Came Tumbling Down: The Collapse of Communism in Eastern Europe.* New York: Oxford University Press, 1993.

Stokes, Gale, John Lampe, and Dennison Rusinow, with Julie Mostov. "Instant History: Understanding the Wars of Yugoslav Succession." *Slavic Review* 55:1 (Spring 1996): 136–60.

Stoler, Ann Laura. *Race and the Education of Desire: Foucault's* History of Sexuality *and the Colonial Order of Things.* Durham: Duke University Press, 1995.

Stoltzfus, Nathan. *Resistance of the Heart: Intermarriage and the Rosenstrasse Protest in Nazi Germany.* New York: Norton, 1996.

Sugar, Peter F., ed. *Eastern European Nationalism in the Twentieth Century.* Washington, DC: American University Press, 1995.

Suny, Ronald Grigor. "Empire and Nation: Armenians, Turks, and the End of the Ottoman Empire." *Armenian Forum* 1:2 (1998): 17–51.

———. *The Revenge of the Past: Nationalism, Revolution, and the Collapse of the Soviet Union.* Stanford: Stanford University Press, 1993.

———. *The Soviet Experiment: Russia, the USSR, and the Successor States.* New York: Oxford University Press, 1998.

Sweet, James H. "The Iberian Roots of American Racist Thought." *William and Mary Quarterly* 54:1 (1997): 143–66.

Theweleit, Klaus. *Male Fantasies.* Trans. Stephan Conway in collaboration with Erica Carter and Chris Turner. 2 vols. Minneapolis: University of Minnesota Press, 1987–89.

Thibau, Jacques, ed. *Le Temps de Saint-Domingue: L'esclavage et la révolution française.* Paris: Éditions Jean-Claude Lattès, 1989.

Thion, Serge. "The Cambodian Idea of Revolution." In *Revolution and Its Aftermath in Kampuchea: Eight Essays*, ed. David Chandler and Ben Kiernan, 10–33. Yale University Southeast Asia Studies Monograph Series no. 25. New Haven: Yale University Southeast Asia Studies, 1983.

———. "Genocide as a Political Commodity." In *Genocide and Democracy in Cambodia: The Khmer Rouge, the United Nations and the International Community*, ed. Ben Kiernan, 163–90. Yale University Southeast Asia Studies no. 41. New Haven: Yale University Southeast Asia Studies, 1993.

Thurston, Robert. "The Stakhanovite Movement: Background to the Great Terror in the Factories, 1935–1938." In *Stalinist Terror: New Perspectives*, ed. J. Arch Getty and Roberta T. Manning, 142–62. Cambridge: Cambridge University Press, 1993.

Tilly, Charles. *From Mobilization to Revolution*. Reading, MA: Addison-Wesley, 1978.

Totten, Samuel, William S. Parsons, and Israel W. Charny, eds. *Genocide in the Twentieth Century: Critical Essays and Eyewitness Accounts*. New York: Garland, 1995.

Trotsky, Leon. "Lessons of October." In *The Challenge of the Left Opposition (1923–25)*, ed. Naomi Allen, 199–258. New York: Pathfinder Press, 1975.

———. "The Struggle for Cultured Speech." In *Bolshevik Visions: First Phase of the Cultural Revolution in Soviet Russia*, ed. William G. Rosenberg, 185–88. Ann Arbor: Ardis, 1984.

Turner, Victor. *Dramas, Fields, and Metaphors: Symbolic Action in Human Society*. Ithaca: Cornell University Press, 1974.

———. *The Forest of Symbols: Aspects of Ndembu Ritual*. Ithaca: Cornell University Press, 1973.

Ung, Loung. *First They Killed My Father: A Daughter of Cambodia Remembers*. New York: HarperCollins, 2000.

United Nations, International Criminal Tribunal for the Former Yugoslavia. "Judgement of Trial Chamber II in the Kunarac, Kovac and Vukovic Case," Press Release JL/P.I.S./566-e, 22 February 2001. *http://www.un.org/icty/foca/trialc2/judgement/index.htm* [29 August 2002].

———. "Judgement, Prosecutor v. Radislav Krstic," *http://www.un.org/icty/krstic/TrialC1/judgement/index.htm* [29 August 2002].

———. "Opinion and Judgement: Prosecutor v. Dusko Tadic a/k/a/ 'Dule.'" 7 May 1997. *http://www.un.org/icty/tadic/trialc2/judgement/index.htm* [29 Augut 2002].

———. "Radislav Krstic Becomes the First Person to Be Convicted of Genocide at the ICTY and Is Sentenced to 46 Years Imprisonment," Press Release OF/P.I.S./609e, 2 August 2001, section II. *http://www.un.org/icty/pressreal/p609-e.htm* [29 August 2002].

———. "Tadic Case: The Verdict," Press Release CC/PIO/190-E, 7 May 1997, *http://www.un.org/icty/pressreal/p190-e.htm* [29 August 2002].

————. Testimony of Witness 75 in Transcripts Gagovic and Others (IT-96–23), 000330ed, 30 March 2000. *http://www.un.org/icty/ind-e.htm* [29 August 2002].

United Nations General Assembly. "Convention on the Prevention and Punishment of the Crime of Genocide." 78 U.N.T.S. 277. *http://www1.umn.edu/humanrts/instree/x1cppcg.htm* [27 August 2002].

————. "Universal Declaration of Human Rights." General Assembly res. 217A (III), U.N. Doc A/810 at 71 (1948). *http://www1.umn.edu/humanrts/instree/b1udhr.htm* [27 August 2002].

United States Official Documents on the Armenian Genocide. Vol. 1, *The Lower Euphrates*, ed. Ara Sarafian. Watertown, MA: Armenian Review, 1993.

Van Kley, Dale, ed. *The French Idea of Freedom: The Old Regime and the Declaration of Rights of 1789*. Stanford: Stanford University Press, 1994.

Vickery, Michael. *Cambodia 1975–1982*. Boston: South End Press, 1983.

————. "Democratic Kampuchea: Themes and Variations." In *Revolution and Its Aftermath in Kampuchea: Eight Essays*, ed. David P. Chandler and Ben Kiernan, 99–135. Yale University Southeast Asia Studies no. 25. New Haven: Yale University Southeast Asia Studies, 1983.

Vinogradskaya, P. "The 'Winged Eros' of Comrade Kollantai." In *Bolshevik Visions: First Phase of the Cultural Revolution in Soviet Russia*, ed. William G. Rosenberg, 217–38. Ann Arbor: Ardis, 1984.

Viola, Lynn. *The Best Sons of the Fatherland: Workers in the Vanguard of Soviet Collectivization*. New York: Oxford University Press, 1987.

————. "The Second Coming: Class Enemies in the Soviet Countryside, 1927–1935." In *Stalinist Terror: New Perspectives*, ed. J. Arch Getty and Roberta T. Manning, 65–98. Cambridge: Cambridge University Press, 1993.

Voegelin, Eric. "The Growth of the Race Idea." *Review of Politics* 2:3 (1940): 283–317.

Vucinich, Wayne S., and Thomas A. Emmert, eds. *Kosovo: Legacy of a Medieval Battle*. Minnesota Mediterranean and East European Monographs. Minneapolis: Modern Greek Studies at the University of Minnesota, 1991.

Vujacic, Veljko Marko. "Communism and Nationalism in Russia and Serbia." Ph.D. diss., University of California at Berkeley, 1995.

Vujović, Sreten. "An Uneasy View of the City." In *The Road to War in Serbia: Trauma and Catharsis*, ed. Nebojša Popov, 123–45. Budapest: Central European University Press, 2000.

Wachtel, Andrew Baruch. *Making a Nation, Breaking a Nation: Literature and Cultural Politics in Yugoslavia*. Stanford: Stanford University Press, 1998.

Wakefield, Walter L., and Austin P. Evans, eds. and trans. *Heresies of the High Middle Ages: Selected Sources*. New York: Columbia University Press, 1969.

Walk, Joseph, ed. *Das Sonderrecht für die Juden im NS-Staat*. Heidelberg: Müller Juristischer Verlag, 1981.

Webster, Charles, ed. *Biology, Medicine and Society, 1840–1940*. Cambridge: Cambridge University Press, 1981.

Weinberg, Gerhard L. *A World at Arms: A Global History of World War II*. Cambridge: Cambridge University Press, 1994.

———, ed. *Hitlers Zweites Buch: Ein Dokument aus dem Jahr 1928*. Stuttgart: Deutsche Verlags-Anstalt, 1961.

Weindling, Paul. *Health, Race and German Politics between National Unification and Nazism, 1870–1945*. Cambridge: Cambridge University Press, 1989.

———. "Theories of the Cell State in Imperial Germany." In *Biology, Medicine and Society, 1840–1940*, ed. Charles Webster, 99–155. Cambridge: Cambridge University Press, 1981.

Weiner, Amir. *Making Sense of War: The Second World War and the Fate of the Bolshevik Revolution*. Princeton: Princeton University Press, 2001.

———. "Nature, Nurture, and Memory in a Socialist Utopia: Delineating the Soviet Socio-Ethnic Body in the Age of Socialism." *American Historical Review* 104:4 (1999): 1114–55.

Weiner, Amir, ed. *Landscaping the Human Garden: Twentieth-Century Population Management in a Comparative Framework*. Stanford: Stanford University Press, 2003.

Weitz, Eric D. *Creating German Communism, 1890–1990: From Popular Protests to Socialist State*. Princeton: Princeton University Press, 1997.

———. "Racial Politics without the Concept of Race: Reevaluating Soviet Ethnic and National Purges." *Slavic Review* 61:1 (Spring 2002): 1–29.

Werth, Nicolas. "Un État contre son peuple: Violences, répressions, terreurs en Union sovietique." In *Le Livre noir du communisme: Crimes, terreur et répression*, ed. Stéphane Courtois, 49–295. Paris: Robert Laffont, 1997.

Werth, Nicolas, and Gaël Moullec, eds. *Rapport secrets soviétiques: La société russe dans les documents confidentiels, 1921–1991*. Paris: Gallimard, 1994.

Wildt, Michael. "Gewalt gegen Juden in Deutschland 1933 bis 1939." *WerkstattGeschichte* 6:18 (1997): 59–80.

Williams, Eric. *Capitalism and Slavery*. Chapel Hill: University of North Carolina Press, 1944.

Williams, Raymond. *Keywords: A Vocabulary of Culture and Society*. New York: Oxford University Press, 1976.

Winter, Jay. *Sites of Memory, Sites of Mourning: The Great War in European Cultural History*. Cambridge: Cambridge University Press, 1995.

Winter, Jay, and Blaine Baggett. *The Great War and the Shaping of the Twentieth Century*. New York: Penguin Studio, 1996.

Wohl, Robert. *The Generation of 1914*. Cambridge: Harvard University Press, 1979.

Woodward, Susan L. *Balkan Tragedy: Chaos and Dissolution after the Cold War*. Washington, DC: Brookings Institution, 1995.

———. "Violence-Prone Area or International Transition? Adding the Role of Outsiders in Balkan Violence." In *Violence and Subjectivity*, ed. Veena Das et al., 19–45. Berkeley and Los Angeles: University of California Press, 2000.

Zernatto, Guido. "Nation: The History of a Word." *Review of Politics* 6:3 (1944): 351–66.

Zimmermann, Michael. "Die nationalsozialistische 'Lösung der Zigeunerfrage.'" In *Nationalsozialistische Vernichtungspolitik 1939–1945: Neue Forschungen und Kontroversen*, ed. Ulrich Herbert, 235–62. Frankfurt am Main: Fischer, 1998.

———. *Rassenutopie und Genozid: Die nationalsozialistische "Lösung der Zigeunerfrage"*. Hamburg: Hans Christians, 1996.

Zirojević, Olga. "Kosovo in the Collective Memory." In *The Road to War in Serbia: Trauma and Catharsis*, ed. Nebojša Popov, 188–211. Budapest: Central European University Press, 2000.

acknowledgments

One pleasurable act at the end of writing a book, especially one on so sad a topic as genocide, is the opportunity to thank many people and institutions for their critical help.

Carol, Lev, and Ben not only endured absences of various sorts while I was researching and writing this book. They also provided the joys of family life, which are a welcome respite from the book's subject matter.

A Century of Genocide began as a lecture that I was invited to give upon receiving the Carl A. Mellby Award at St. Olaf College, where I taught until 1999. I thank the Dean of the College at the time, James Pence, and the Faculty Development Committee for granting me the award. The initial research and writing of this book were supported by a sabbatical grant from St. Olaf College. A short-term research fellowship from the German Academic Exchange Service (DAAD) allowed me to spend three very productive months at the Zentrum für Zeithistorische Forschung in Potsdam, and I thank the two directors, Konrad Jarausch and Christoph Kleßmann, as well as Thomas Lindenberger, for their support. After I moved to the University of Minnesota, I received generous support from the College of Liberal Arts and the History Department in the form of start-up research funds and from the Office of the Vice President for Research and Dean of the Graduate School through a Faculty Summer Research Fellowship and a McKnight Summer Research Fellowship. I was fortunate to join the faculty at Minnesota shortly after the founding of the Center for German and European Studies, a consortium of the Universities of Minnesota and Wisconsin–Madison that is funded by the DAAD. The Center has also provided research support and has been an excellent venue in which to test many of my ideas, and I thank its director, Jack Zipes. At the final stages of the project I received generous research support through the Arsham and Charlotte Ohanessian Chair in the College of Liberal Arts at the University of Minnesota.

Funding from these various sources at the University of Minnesota enabled me to hire three excellent research assistants at different stages of the project: Sarah Danielsson, Angelo Georgakis, and Wendy Jo Gertjejanssen. At the very end, the Center for German and European Studies enabled me to employ two other excellent research assistants, Angelica Fenner and Roni Shapira, who helped in the final assemblage of the manuscript.

Aside from various conference papers I presented, the critical responses of the audiences were especially helpful at invited lectures at the Zentrum für Zeithistorische Forschung in Potsdam, the Max-Planck-Institut für Geschichte in Göttingen, the Columbia University Seminar on Twentieth-Century Politics and Culture, the Russian History Workshop and the Modern Europe Workshop at the University of Chicago, and the United States Holocaust Memorial Museum. The Comparative Genocides Conference, sponsored by the Harry Frank Guggenheim Foundation and held in Barcelona, Spain, in December 2000, was an especially fruitful opportunity for me. I would like to thank all the participants at these events, and especially Robert Gellately, Atina Grossman, Sheila Fitzpatrick, Ben Kiernan, Thomas Lindenberger, Alf Lüdtke, and Ron Suny.

In writing a book that included topics outside my usual areas of geographic and linguistic knowledge, I benefited enormously from many colleagues and friends who provided bibliographic advice and read various drafts. I would especially like to thank those who commented on particular chapters: David Barclay, Jan Behrends, David Chandler, Peter Holquist, Mario Kessler, Erika Lee, Thomas Lindenberger, Alf Lüdtke, Norman Naimark, J. B. Shank, Thomas Wolfe, and my colleagues in the History Department Colloquium at my former institution, St. Olaf College.

The University of Minnesota has been my institutional home for a good part of the writing of this book. The History Department and the College of Liberal Arts have provided wonderfully stimulating intellectual environments, and from many colleagues I have learned more than I can ever assess. At two long, intense sessions, one when I was just starting to write the book, one when I was just about finished, Barbara Laslett, Helga Leitner, M. J. Maynes, and Eric Sheppard, and then M. J. Maynes (again), J. B. Shank, Barbara Welke, and Tom Wolfe ventured the tough criticisms of which only true friends and colleagues are capable.

I am very grateful to David Chandler and Robert Gellately, who reviewed the manuscript for Princeton University Press. Their thorough and careful readings and constructive criticisms were very helpful to me in the final phase of writing. I also greatly appreciate the efforts of my friends and colleagues at Minnesota who managed, in the middle of the semester, to read the entire book in manuscript form. Whatever its present faults, it is a much better book because of the extensive and incisive comments of Ron Aminzade, Gary Cohen, Kirsten Fischer, M. J. Maynes, Eric Sheppard, and Barbara Welke.

It has been a pleasure to work with the production staff at Princeton University Press, who took the book in hand with enthusiasm, efficiency, and intelligence. My sharp-eyed and creative copyeditor, Lauren Lepow, provided the final polish that all manuscripts need but do not always receive.

I would especially like to thank my editor at Princeton, Brigitta van Rheinberg. Her keen comments on the argument, structure, and style of the book have been enormously helpful at every stage of the writing. Most important, she saw in a lecture the makings of a book before the idea had ever crossed my mind.

Whatever errors and shortcomings remain are, of course, my own.

30 August 2002
St. Paul, Minnesota

index

Adriatic, the, 201
Affonço, Denise, 179
Africa, 27; Southwest, 12, 46, 240; travel
    accounts from, 27
Africans, 22, 24, 26; intermarriage of with
    German settlers, 240; and race thinking,
    23, 25; and slavery, 22, 24, 45, 47–48.
    See also slavery
Akhmatova, Anna, 86; Requiem, 86
Albanians, ethnic, 192, 209; in Kosovo,
    195–97, 208, 221; nationalist, 196,
    298n.11
Aleppo, 5
Alexander the Great, 18
Allah, 19
Alsace-Lorraine, 126
America, 28; Declaration of Independence
    of, 28–29, 194; influence of over Cam-
    bodia, 145
Anacharsis, 19
Anatomical Institute (University of Mün-
    ster), 102
Angkar, 151, 154, 163, 170, 180, 183–
    84, 187
Angkor Wat, 164, 189
Annunzio, Gabriele D', 51
anthropology, 27; and Blumenbach, 37;
    and theories of racial inferiority,
    262n.48
antisemitism, 46–48, 266n.116; as deriva-
    tive of anticommunism, 285n.139;
    in Nazi Germany, 103–14, 124,
    132, 142, 239, 279n.31, 280n.52,
    286n.139; origin of term, 46; under
    Stalin, 82, 98

Archiv für Rassen-und Gesellschafts-
    Biologie (Journal for racial and social
    biology), 39, 41; as founded by Alfred
    Ploetz, 41
Arendt, Hannah, 25, 46, 142, 250; On
    the Origins of Totalitarianism, 25
aristocrats: Russian, 58; as victims of the
    Great Terror, 72
Arkan, 209, 214, 231; his paramilitary
    "Tigers," 214–15, 221, 231, 242
Armenia, 5
Armenians: as "anti-Soviet elements," 80,
    82; genocide of in Ottoman Empire, 1,
    3, 4, 5, 6, 8, 240–41, 252, 256n.8,
    305n.14; Hitler's reference to, 240; and
    Treaty of Lausanne, 51
Arndt, Ernst Moritz, 32
Arusha, 253
Aryan, the, 26, 40, 47, 99, 121, 133, 138;
    according to Chamberlain, 38; and ban
    on sexual relations with Jews, 240;
    blending concepts of race and nation,
    106, 108–9; classification of, 115; com-
    munism and Jews as ultimate enemy of,
    75, 107, 279n.313; gypsies as degener-
    ated Aryans, 118; and Hitler's prophecy,
    130; Jesus as, 38; and Jewish assimila-
    tion, 47, 114; Khmer as Aryan race
    among Asians, 164; as myth, 33–34;
    and utopia, 59
aryanization, 139
Asia Minor: Turkic peoples in, 3
asocials, the: as classification under Naz-
    ism, 119, 120, 161
assimilation, Jewish, 47, 114

Auschwitz, 74, 102–3, 131, 138, 140, 225, 246–47, 49. *See also* concentration camps; extermination camps
Australia: émigré Serbs in, 209
Austria, 195, 200, 220

Baden, 126
Baghdad, 5
Balibar, Étienne, 22
balijas, 190, 222. *See also* Muslims: in the former Yugoslavia
Balkan Wars, 4
Balkans, the, 44, 217, 219, 235, 238; communism in, 11
Balkars, 79–81
Banja Luka, 194, 204, 214, 220, 238
Bastille Day, 147
Bavarians, 126
Belgium: and imperialism, 45
Belgrade, 200, 203; Serb regime in, 190, 193, 200, 210–13, 222, 234
Belorussians, 78
Belzec, 131, 137. *See also* concentration camps; extermination camps
beredniak (poor peasants), 65
Bergen-Belsen, 140
Beria, L. P., 81
Berlin, 103, 117–18, 121, 129, 132, 134; University of, 142
Bessarabia, 126
Best, Werner, 111–12
Bible, the, 18. *See also* Hebrew Bible
Bihać, the region of, 215
Bijeljina, 215
Bildungsbürgertum, 142
Blumenbach, Johann Friedrich, 27–28, 32, 37; *On the Natural Variety of Mankind*, 27
Boas, Franz, 50
Bodin, Jean, 26
Boer War, 248
Bolshevism, 52, 54, 83, 97, 148, 158, 240, 271n.59; association of with Jews in Nazi ideology, 125; and civil war, 68–70; and denunciation of its leaders, 94; as encouraging dictatorship, 269nn. 24 and 30; and the Great Terror, 72;

and the Magnitogorsk Dam, 57; and national languages, 76; Nazi fight against, 108, 113; and proletarian revolution, 60–64, 104, 106, 194; and a "reclassed" society, 64, 66–67; and Trotsky's grandstanding, 104
Bormann, Martin, 131
Bosanksi Novi, 215
Bosnia, 200–204, 215, 217, 220–23, 225, 229–30, 234; Austro-Hungarian occupation of, 202; Croat nationals in, 213, 229–30; and Dayton Agreement, 211; 1990 elections in, 213; multinational character of, 208, 210; Muslim Army of, 217; Muslims in, 192, 202–4, 208, 210, 213–18, 222–23, 226–30, 234; and nationalism, 203, 211–13; recognized by EC, 214; Serbian destruction of mosques in, 220; Serbian nationals in, 207, 213, 218, 225, 229–31, 234; UN statistics on displaced people of, 230
Bosnia-Herzegovina, 210; Federation of, 220; Republic of, 220
Bosnian Serbs: army of, 190, 216–17, 221, 227; assembly of, 213; nationalist party of, 190, 234; republic of (Republika Srpska), 213–14, 218, 222
Boulainvilliers, comte de, 27
bourgeosie, the: in the NEP years, 57; in nineteenth-century Serbia, 199; in Russia during World War I, 60, 65; as victims of the Great Terror, 72, 77
Brandt, Karl, 114
Branković, Vuk, 193
Bratunac, 226
Breslau, 238
British Eugenics Education Society, 39
Browning, Christopher, 128, 184
Buchenwald, 134–35
Buddhism: destruction of Buddhist temples, 186; Khmer, 147, 156; Theravada, 156
Bugai, N. F., 80–81, 90
Bukharin, Nikolai, 70, 93–94
Bukovina, 126
Bulgaria, 44

Bulgarians, 80
Bulgars, 3
Burg, Steven L., 216, 220, 230
Burgenland, 135
Butler, Richard, 225
Byelorussia, 126, 129
Byron, George Gordon, Lord, 32

Cambodia, 1, 8, 9, 11, 12, 13, 14, 73, 94, 152, 177–79, 181, 183–89, 238–39, 294n.152; and communism, 145–89; and the Communist Party (CPK), 147, 151–58, 160–65, 167–69, 171–75, 177, 179–89; disruption of traditional society through American bombings of, 252; fate of its intellectuals, 166, 181; as a French creation, 164; under the Khmer Rouge, 145–89; mass killings in under Khmer Rouge, 144–45, 164–89, 251; and its modern leaders, 164; nationalities within, 144–45, 157–59, 162–64, 170–75, 186, 188–89. See also Kampuchea, Democratic; Khmer Rouge
Cambodians, 151, 163; burial rites of, 180; French perceptions of, 163; killing of, 165
cannibalism, 178–79
capitalism, 22, 152, 154; globalized, 205; and slavery, 22
capitalists: in old Russia, 58
castration, 25
categorization. See classification
Catholics, 203, 231
Caucasian race, 28
Caucasus, 58, 80–82
Celts, 33
Central Asia: Turkic peoples in, 3
Central Intelligence Agency, U.S. (CIA). See United States
Četniks, 190, 197, 233
Cham, the, 162, 165, 170–72, 175, 186, 188. See also Muslims
Chamberlain, Houston Stewart, 37–38, 48; Foundations of the Nineteenth Century, 37; and "German Christianity," 37; on Jews, 48; his notion of a "race-soul," 37; relationship of to Wagner, 37–38

Chandler, David, 171, 186–88
Charlemagne, 35
Chea, Nuon, 147, 173
Chechens, 12, 79–83, 86, 90, 98–100, 175
Cheka, 61, 244. See also Extraordinary Commission to Combat Counterrevolution and Sabotage
Chelmno, 128, 131. See also concentration camps; extermination camps
China, 152, 161, 171
Chinese, 144–45, 162, 164–65, 167, 170–73, 175, 184, 186, 188–89, 238; and Cultural Revolution, 153
Christ, Jesus, 19; body of, 26. See also Jesus
Christianity, 3, 19, 26; Enlightenment critique of, 27; iconography of in Petar Petrović Njegoš's The Mountain Wreath, 193; and Jewish assimilation, 47; and Judeophobia, 46; Latin and Orthodox, 202; and Manichaean thought, 26; and redemption, 43; among Russian peasants, 70; and sanctity of life, 124; theologians of, 20, 26; universalist teachings of, 46
Christians, 2, 3, 19, 25, 232; Ethiopian, 20; German, 114, 238, 279n.31
Christopher, Warren (U.S. secretary of state), 220
Church: Christian, 20; Evangelical, 117; Roman Catholic, 202
Churchill, Winston, 46
citizenship, 21, 29; definition of, 21; gendered, 29; Nazi ban on citizenship for Jews, 116; racial conditions on under Nazism, 116; and right to vote in Soviet Union, 64
class: consciousness of and the Khmer Rouge, 154, 175; and the Soviet system of classifying populations, 54
classification: under the Khmer Rouge, 159–64; under Nazism, 115–20; in the Soviet Union, 54, 64–66, 68, 83; systems of, 27, 32
"cleansing": of old Cambodian habits and consciousness, 154–55; and ideology of

"cleansing" (*cont.*)
 purity, 238–39; racial and ethnic, 113,
  125, 127, 248, 303n.128; by Serb na-
  tionalists, 191, 194, 209, 212, 215,
  221, 230–33, 235, 252; of Serbs by
  Croatians, 219; of suspect nations by
  Soviets, 239. *See also* purges
Clinton, Bill, 219
Cold War: and Yugoslavia, 205–7
collectivization, forced: under the Khmer
  Rouge, 150–52, 154, 236–37; in Soviet
  Union, 71, 73–76, 78, 90, 141, 175,
  237, 252, 271n.61
Collosians, the, 19
colonial empires, 2
colonies, British, 23–24
colonization, 23, 145–46
Columbus, Christopher, 48
Commissar Order, 127
Committee for Union and Progress, 2, 6
Committee of Public Safety, 61
communism, 10, 11, 99; abandonment of
  by Serbian nationalists, 230, 233; Chinese model of, 145; collapse of in Eastern Europe, 205–7, 233; final victory
  of, 74; and Jews as linked in Nazi ideology, 75, 105, 107–8; and Khmer
  Rouge, 145–89; Nazi opposition to,
  104; in the NEP years, 57; as rooted in
  Enlightenment universalism, 250;
  threats against, 54; as utopia, 55, 109;
  in the former Yugoslavia, 192, 205
communists: Cambodian, 144–89; Vietnamese, 145
complicity, of general populations in genocide: 129, 242–44, 247, 252–53,
  306n.21, 306n.27, 308n.35; and gender,
  247; as schizophrenia, 244
concentration camps, 120, 122, 124, 128,
  131, 140, 197–98, 216, 248. *See also*
  Auschwitz; Belzec; Bergen-Belsen;
  Buchenwald; Chelmno; Dachau; extermination camps; Jasenovac; Lodz; Manjača; Omarska; Ravensbrück;
  Sachsenhausen; Sobibor; Srebenica;
  Theresienstadt; Treblinka; Westerborg
confession, 182–83, 246, 249–50

Congo, the, 45
Constantinople. *See* Istanbul
Conti, Leonardo, 118
Convention on the Prevention and Punishment of the Crime of Genocide, 8–10,
  12, 170, 253
conversos, 46
Ćosić, Dobrica, 199
Cossacks, Don and Kuban, 69; biological
  categorization of, 69; deportation of,
  72, 85, 90, 99
Crimea, 80; Tatars of, 12, 79–81, 86, 90–
  91, 96, 98–100, 150, 175
Croatia, 192, 195, 198, 200, 202–3, 213,
  215, 231, 234; acknowledged by EC,
  213; eastern, 200; evasion of UN arms
  embargo by, 218; Greater, 209; and independence, 209–11; Independent State
  of, 195–97, 297n.7; Serbs in, 210–12,
  231, 234; in World War II, 1
Croats, 195–96, 198, 208–10, 231–32; in
  Bosnia, 208, 210, 217; brutality against,
  190, 212, 214–15, 219–20; fascist
  (Ustaše), 195, 198, 241; and nationalism, 191, 201–5, 232–33; and Serbian
  brutality against Serbs, 198, 219
Czechoslovakia, 208

Dachau, 132, 247
Darwin, Charles, 34–37, 46, 49,
  266n.119; *The Descent of Man,* 36;
  The Origin of Species, 34, 36; his the-
  ory of evolution, 36–37, 50, 264n.79,
  266n.121
Darwinians, 36
Darwinism, Social, 37, 39, 46, 49–50,
  107, 264n.79. *See also* Spencer, Herbert
David, 19
Davis, David Brion, 25
Dayton Agreement, 220–21, 302n.94
Declaration of Independence, American,
  28–29, 194
Declaration of the Rights of Man and Cit-
  izen, French 28, 194
Declaration of the Rights of Woman, 28
Delacroix, Eugène, 33
democracy, 51, 65, 146–47, 195

deportation, 237, 246; under Khmer Rouge, 145, 150, 165–67, 175, 177, 184, 188; under Nazism, 126–27, 130–32, 140–41; under Serbian nationalism in former Yugoslavia, 204, 212, 219–22, 230, 234; in Soviet Union on basis of ethnicity and nationality, 63, 71, 73–74, 78–85, 89–90, 98, 141, 179, 225, 240. See also purges

Dionysus, 19

Douglas, Mary, 239

Drina Wolves, 225, 233. See also Bosnian Serbs: Army of

Dubrovnik, 200

Dzerzhinsky, Feliks, 61

Ebihara, May, 186

Edwards, Penny, 164, 175

Egypt: British interest in, 45; troops of, 19

Eichmann, Adolf, 129, 142

Eicke, Theodor, 247

Einsatzgruppen, 127, 131, 139; "C," 128–29

Empire: British, 45; Habsburg, 202–3; Ottoman, 1–4, 7–8, 50, 202–3, 210, 239, 241; Russian, 4, 50, 63, 239

Endlösung. See Final Solution, the

Engels, Friedrich, 34; The Communist Manifesto, 34. See also Marx, Karl

England: and imperialism, 45

English, the, 26

Enlightenment, the, 27–28, 49, 237, 250; and anthropology, 27, 49; and Jewish assimilation, 47; and race science, 41, 49; thinkers of, 28; universalism of, 29

equality, 28; as gendered concept in French Revolution, 28

Estonia, 128

Estonians, 78

Ethiopia. See Kush

Ethiopians, 19, 28; in Psalms, 19

ethnicity, 22; defined in relation to race and nation, 21; and definition of genocide, 9; and groups that are racialized, 21; instability of premodern categories of, 259n.22; and minorities within Cambodia, 144–45, 157–59, 162–64,

170–75, 186, 188–89; Muslim as, 203; in Soviet Union, 63–64, 78, 140

ethnology, 33

eugenics, 38–39, 45–46, 49–50

Europe: antisemitism in, 106; émigré Serbs in, 209; Turkic peoples in, 3

European Community (EC), 213, 217; trade and political relations of with Yugoslavia, 206, 218

European hegemony, 2

Europeans: attitudes of toward Native Americans and Africans, 261n.31; and imperialism, 45–46, 49–50; medieval, 20; and race thinking, 23–25, 35, 49; and secularization, 26; during World War I, 148

euthanasia, 114, 118, 122–24, 128, 179

evolution, 36; according to Darwin, 36, 264n.79

extermination camps, 102, 128, 130–31, 135, 137–38. See also Auschwitz; Belzec; Bergen-Belsen; Buchenwald; Chelmno; concentration camps; Dachau; Jasenovac; Lodz; Manjača; Omarska; Ravensbrück; Sachsenhausen; Sobibor; Srebenica; Theresienstadt; Treblinka

Extraordinary Commission to Combat Counterrevolution and Sabotage, 61. See also Cheka

Family of Man, The, 16–17. See also Museum of Modern Art

Ferhadija (mosque), 194

Fichte, Johann Gottlieb, 31, 68; and the cultural concept of the nation, 31

Field of Blackbirds, 193, 196. See also Kosovo Polje

Final Solution, the, 114, 140

Finns, 78

Fischer, Eugen, 142–43

Fischer, Kirsten, 24–25

Fitzpatrick, Sheila, 64, 91

Fojnica, 215

France, 3, 27; education of Khmers in, 146, 161, 181, 188; Gobineau on the decline of, 34; and nobility, 27; and the

France (cont.)
  Third Estate, 27; Vichy, 126; and white European identity, 29
Frankfurt, 131
Franks, the, 27, 33
French, the, 26, 35, 176; colonial influence of over Cambodia, 145–46, 181, 188–89; and Communist Party, 146–47, 158, 189; their perceptions of Cambodians, 163; and revolutionary republicanism, 146, 189
French Declaration of the Rights of Man and Citizen, 28
Friedländer, Saul, 109
Führer, the, 111–12. See also Hitler, Adolf
Führerprinzip, 112
Führer's Chancellery, 122, 131

Galicia, eastern, 128–29
Galton, Francis, 38, 40; coinage of the term "eugenics" by, 38; and Laboratory for National Eugenics, 39
gas, extermination by, 102, 128, 130–31, 179, 246–47; and mobile vans, 127–28. See also Sonderaktion
Gauls, the, 27
Gay, Peter, 28
Gellately, Robert, 141
Generalplan Ost, 126
General Staff of the Revolutionary Armed Forces of Kampuchea, 154
genocide, 8, 10–16, 30, 51, 205, 236–37, 242, 248, 254, 256n.7, 306n.21; of Armenians, 1, 2, 3, 4, 5, 6, 8, 51, 232, 240–41, 252, 305n.14; of Bosnian Muslims, 215–16, 222, 231; in Cambodia under the Khmer Rouge, 8, 157–59, 165, 174, 184, 188, 296n.196; as defined by the Genocide Convention, 9–10, 100; of Herero in Southwest Africa, 12, 46, 240, 255n.4; as implemented by modern states, 6, 7; by Israelites in Canaan in Book of Joshua, 8; of Jews, 132–33, 234, 252; under Lenin and Stalin, 8, 222; in Nazi Germany, 8, 101, 132, 222; and Nazism, 140–42, 158; origin of the word, 8; as ritual, 246,

251–52; by Romans in Carthage, 8; in Rwanda, 253; of Serbs, 195, 198; of Serbs, Jews, and Roma and Sinti by Independent State of Croatia, 197–98; in former Yugoslavia, 8, 191–92, 209, 212, 215–16, 222, 230–35, 253
Genocide Convention. See Convention on the Prevention and Punishment of the Crime of Genocide
genos. See genocide
Géricault, Jean Louis André Théodore, 32
German Racial Hygiene Society, 39
Germans, the, 26, 32; and Chamberlain's notion of the "race-soul," 37; cultural achievements of, 106; ethnic Germans in Russia, 78–80, 83, 98; Germanic tribes, 26; their knowledge of Holocaust, 179; racial essence of, 112; resettlement of ethnic Germans (Reichs- und Volksdeutschen), 125–27, 129; in Southwest and East Africa, 46; and the Volksgemeinschaft, 111
Germany, 3, 4, 11, 44, 50–52; 102–43, 195, 200, 245; and the bureaucratic tradition, 3, 115, 242; and defeat in World War I, 105, 108; Hitler as chancellor of, 103–5; and the ideal of the Volksgemeinschaft, 110; Imperial, 51, 200; and invasion of Poland, 240; and invasion of Soviet Union, 81, 98; and military culture, 3, 12; as nation-state, 44; Soviet War against, 90; and support of nationalist parties in Croatia and Slovenia, 210–11; and world domination, 130; Yugoslavian migrant workers in, 206, 220. See also Nazi Germany; Third Reich
Germany, East, 207–8
Gestapo, 91, 120–22, 134
Geyer, Michael, 141
Gladkov: Cement, 99
Globocnik, Odilo, 131
Gobineau, Arthur de, 34–35, 37, 46, 48; Essay on the Inequality of the Human Races, 34–35, 37; on Jews, 48
Goebbels, Joseph, 104, 112–13, 117

Goering, Hermann, 143
Goethe, Johann Wolfgang von, 32
Goldhagen, Daniel Jonah, 266n.116
Gorky, Maxim, 93
Gouges, Olympia de, 28. *See also* Declaration of the Rights of Woman
Greece, 44, 126; and independence, 44
Greeks, 18, 19; ancient architecture of, 106; and city-states, 18; cleansing actions against in Soviet Union, 80, 82; as descendents of Helen, 21; and Treaty of Lausanne, 51; and understanding of difference, 24
Greiser, Artur, 128
Grossmann, Vasily: *Forever Flowing*, 84–86, 91–92
Gutman, Roy, 216
gypsies, 117–18, 122, 131, 281n.68, 284n.120. *See also* Roma; Sinti

Habsburg Empire, 50, 210
Haffner, Sebastian, 112
Hague Tribunal, the, 214, 216–17, 223, 225–29, 233, 253. *See also* International Criminal Tribunal for the Former Yugoslavia
Hallerworden, Julius, 123
handicapped, the, 114, 120, 122, 133
Hanoi, 171–72
Harambasic, Fikret, 224
Havel, Václav, 253
Hayden, Robert M., 197
Hebrew Bible, 18, 19
Hebrews, 24; and understanding of difference, 24
Hegel, Friedrich, 49
Herder, Johann Gottfried von, 31, 33, 68; and the cultural concept of the nation, 31; and rejection of the concept of race, 31, 78
Herero, the, 12, 46, 240
Herodotus, 18–19; *Histories*, 18–19
Heuveline, Patrick, 186
Heydrich, Reinhard, 111, 130
High Revolutionary Committee (of Khmer Rouge), 144
Himmler, Heinrich, 107–8, 118, 122, 125, 127–30, 138

Hindenburg, Paul von, 103
Hiroshima; bombing of, 9
history: Hitler's transcendent views of, 111; racial conception of, 126
Hitler, Adolf, 48, 112–13; 121, 124–25, 129–30, 143; appointment of as chancellor, 103–4, 191; on Jews and race thinking, 48, 104–6, 108–9, 114, 124, 277n.4, 278n.5, 280n.52; *Mein Kampf*, 104–6, 108–9; and resettlement of ethnic Germans, 125–27; 130; and visions of a Nazi utopia, 110, 13
Hobbes, Thomas, 25, 32
Hobsbawm, Eric, 28
Holbrooke, Richard (assistant U.S. secretary of state), 219
Holland, 140
Holocaust, 12, 13, 125, 128, 132, 135, 141–43, 167, 179; compared with Khmer Rouge killings, 184, 187; compared with Yugoslav crisis, 212, 214; contrasted with the Great Terror, 74; survivor of, 134; uniqueness of, 257n.8; as by-product of modernization, 286n.139
Holquist, Peter, 69
Hungary, 200
Hu Nim, 180–83
Huxley, Thomas, 50

Ieng Sary, 146–49, 182
imperialism, 45–46, 50; American, 152, 155, 181–82; czarist Russian, 68
India, 27; travel accounts from, 27
Indians. *See* Native Americans
indigenization, 76. See also *korenizatsiia*
Indochina: and anticolonial struggle, 188; and the Communist Party, 147, 158; and mass killings, 246; nationalism in, 145
Indo-European languages, 46
Indonesia: killing of Chinese Communists in, 9
industrialization: under the Khmer Rouge, 150, 167; in the Soviet Union, 56, 67, 74, 80–81, 90, 99, 175, 252
Ingush, 79–81, 90, 100

Institute for German Labor in the East (*Institut für Deutsche Ostarbeit*), 125

intermarriage, 238; and Jewish assimilation, 114; laws against, 24; in Nazi Germany, 119, 240; in Sarajevo, 210; in Southwest Africa, 240; in former Yugoslavia, 204–5, 231

International Criminal Tribunal for the Former Yugoslavia (ICTY), 190–91, 216–17, 222–25. *See also* Hague Tribunal

International Monetary Fund (IMF), 206

Iraq, 5

Islam, 19; supranational character of, 202–3

Israel, Kingdom of, 18

Israelites, the, 18, 19; in Canaan, 8; as descendents of Abraham, 21; status of as chosen people, 18

Istanbul, 5

Italy, 44, 195, 200; Ethiopian Christians in, 20

Izetbegović, Aliza, 213–14, 218–19, 231

Jackson, J. B., 1, 5

Japan: and colonial power over Cambodia, 145

Japan, Imperial, 9, 79

Japanese-Americans, 98

Jasenovac, 197–98.

Jay, John, 29; *The Federalist Papers,* 29

Jefferson, Thomas, 29

Jeremiah, 19

Jericho, 18

Jersak, Tobias, 130

Jesus, 19; as Aryan, 37

Jews, 2, 19, 237–38, 246, 249: according to Chamberlain, 38; as administrators within Soviet state, 83; daily discrimination toward, 119–24; depictions of by Nazis, 20; and diaspora, 107; as epitome of cosmopolitanism, 80; genocide against by Independent State of Croatia, 197; and intermarriage, 114, 116; Lazar Kaganovich, 98; linked to communism within Nazi ideology, 75, 105, 107–8, 125; Nazi atrocities against, 8, 12, 243, 251, 252; and Nazi classification of,

115–17, 119–20; Nazism and denunciation of, 117, 120; and Nuremberg Laws, 240; pogroms against in Russian Empire, 4; purge of Moscow intellectuals in 1940s, 84–85; as racial enemy of National Socialism, 104–5; and sexualized and biologized imagery, 106–8; and Spanish Inquisition, 46; Stalinist attack on, 82; systematized extermination of, 112–13, 121–43, 177; tracts against by the Church, 20; "the wandering Jew," 47

Jim Crow era, 48

Joshua, Book of, 8, 18

Jovan, Bishop, 198–99

Judaism, 139

Judas, 193

Judeophobia, 46, 47. *See also* antisemitism

Jud Süss, 239

jugoslovjenstvo (Yugoslavism), 195

Jünger, Ernst, 51, 143: *In Stahlgewittern* (Storm of steel), 52; *Das Wäldchen 125* (Copse 125), 51

Kadijević, Veljko, 199

Kaganovich, Lazar, 98

Kaing Khek Iev, 168

Kaiser Wilhelm Institute (KWI): for Anthropology, Heredity, and Eugenics, 142; for Brain Research, 123–24

Kalmyks, 79–80, 82

Kampuchea, Democratic (DK), 12, 146, 153–55, 158, 160–61, 164–65, 170, 238, 296n.197; and biological symbolism, 155–56; building socialism in, 149, 151–52; and the Communist Party (CPK), 147, 151–58, 160–65, 167–69, 171–75, 177, 179–89; and complicity, 243–44; and genocide, 296; and the Khmer language, 170; link of to World War I, 241; loss of original cabinet members of, 169; and national homogeneity, 164; as peasant revolution, 289n.22, 296n.197; and purges, 164–89, 252; and treatment of the Cham, 172. *See also* Cambodia; Khmer Rouge

Kant, Immanuel, 31–32; and the categorical imperative, 85; and the political form of the nation-state, 31, 263n.68; and the self-articulating individual, 32
Kaplan, Marion, 140
Karachi, 79, 81
Karadžić, Radovan, 214–17, 231
Kazakhstan, 76, 79
Keller, Helen, 139
Kershaw, Ian, 105, 112
Khemchines, 80
Khieu Ponnary, 147
Khieu Samphan, 146, 149
Khieu Thirith, 147
Khmer, the, 145–46, 146, 150, 152, 162–66, 169–70, 172–76, 185–86, 188–89, 238; and Buddhism, 147, 156; and family relations, 162–65, 185–86; traditions of, 156–57
Khmer, medieval kingdom of, 146
Khmer Rouge, 1, 8, 10, 14, 144–89, 191, 239, 242–43; attack on the family by, 151; and biological symbolism, 155–56; and classification madness, 159–64, 187; and collectivization, 236; and the discourse of cleansing, 239; as genocidal regime, 174, 183–84, 188; and genocide against national minorities, 9, 157–59, 247–48; as last communist movement of twentieth century, 241; leaders of, 146–47, 155–56, 243; mass killings under, 144–46, 167, 188; and population purges, 153, 155, 158, 162–89; and racialization of class and nationality, 174–75, 185, 188, 289n.19; and revolution, 145–46, 149, 152, 154–55, 162–65, 187; compared with Serbian nationalism, 204–5, 222; and use of radio, 246; and utopia, 151, 157–58, 173, 236. See also Cambodia; communism; Democratic Kampuchea
Kiernan, Ben, 157, 166, 177, 186, 296n.197, 306n.21
Kirgizstan, 76, 79–80
Kirov, Sergei, 93
Klemperer, Victor, 119–21
Koestler, Arthur: Darkness at Noon, 93

Kollontai, Alexandra, 55
Kolyma, 95, 250
Komsomol (Young Communists), 71, 76
Koran, the, 172
Korea, 152
Koreans, 238; as colonized by Japan, 79; forced removal of by Soviets, 79, 83, 98, 100
korenizatsiia, 76. See also indigenization
kosang, 183
Kosarac, 190
Kosovo, 192, 195–98, 203, 206–8, 210, 221, 230; as center of Serbian nationalism, 195–96, 213; Kosovar Muslims, 192, 232; Liberation Army of, 222; as medieval Serbian kingdom, 193
Kosovo Polje, 193, 196. See also Field of Blackbirds
Kostic, Jagos, 228
Kotkin, Stephen, 56–57
Kovač, Radomir, 228
Kovno, 135–36
Krajina, 200–201, 204, 210–11; Serb Republic of, 219; Serbs in, 211–14, 219, 221, 232
Kremer, Johannes Paul, 102
Kretschmer, Karl, 139
Kristallnacht, 121, 134, 139
Krstić, General Radislav, 222–23, 225–26, 233
Kućan, Milan, 208
kulaks (wealthy peasants), 54, 61–62, 65, 72, 92; collectivization and deportation of, 74, 77–79, 82, 98; liquidation of, 70–71. See also aristocrats
Kurds, 1, 6, 80
Kush, 19
Kushites. See Ethiopians; Kush

Lampe, John, 207
Landes, Joan, 29
Laotians, 162
Latsis, M. I., 66
Latvians, 78
Lausanne, Treaty of, 50
Law for the Restoration of the Professional Civil Service, 114–15

Law for the Protection of German Blood and German Honor, 116
Lazar, Prince, 42, 193, 196–97
League of Communists of Yugoslavia (LCY), 199–200, 207–9
Leistung, 110
Leistungsmedizin, 110
Lemberg, 128. See also Lvov
Lempkin, Raphael, 8, 10
Lenin, Nikolai, 93, 104, 153; and Bolshevik Revolution, 57, 60–62, 67, 194, 104; Imperialism, 146; and New Economic Policy (NEP), 70
Leningrad, 84
Lepsius, Johannes, 1, 5
Levi, Primo, 86
Lewin, Moshe, 75
Liberalism, 241
Linnaeus, Carolus, 27, 32, 37
lishentsy (the legally disenfranchised), 65–66, 76, 161; in the Great Terror, 72
Lithuania, 126–27
Lithuanians, 127, 135, 177
Little, Allan, 197, 211, 216
Locke, John, 26
Lodz, 131
Lombards, 33
London, Jack, 139
Long Van, 166
Lon Nol, 148, 159, 161, 164, 166–67, 171, 177, 184
Louis XIV, King, 35
Loung Ung, 165, 179, 184
Lublin, 129, 131. See also concentration camps; extermination camps
Lüdtke, Alf, 242, 245
Luther, Martin, 20
Lvov, 131. See also Lemberg
Lyell, Charles, 37

Macedonia, 200
Madagascar, 129
Magnitogorsk, 57–58, 92, 238
Malay, 28
Manchuria, 79, 238
Manjača, 216
Mann, Thomas, 139

Mans, Henry le, 20
Mao, 153, 161
Margolin, Jean-Louis, 159
Marr, N. I., 78
Marr, Wilhelm, 46
marriage: laws controlling, 24
Marx, Karl, 34–35, 49, 146; Capital, 146; The Communist Manifesto, 34. See also Engels, Friedrich
Marxism: and the Bolsheviks, 54; categorization under, 64; as linked to Judaism by Nazis, 107–8, 139; Stalin's contribution to, 62
Marxism-Leninism, 146, 154, 191, 200
Mason, Tim, 257n.9
Mauthausen, 135
Mazower, Mark, 235
Mazzini, Giuseppe, 43; "Duties towards Your Country" (1854), 43; on secular nationalism
Mengele, Josef, 137, 142
Meskhetians, 79; Turkish, 80
Michaelis, Wanda, 121, 131
Milošević, Slobodan: indictment of, 233; and political revolution, 230–32; and Serbian nationalism, 191–93, 195–200, 208–11, 218–19, 230–34; and war crimes, 191, 233
Ministry of Interior, 142; forces of, Serbian, 214, 221–22
Mischlinge, 131; Nazi definitions of, 116, 118
mitmachen, 242
Mittäterschaft, 242
mixed marriage. See intermarriage
Mladić, General Ratko, 214–17, 226
Molière (Jean-Baptiste Poquelin), 209
Molotov, V. M., 73
monarchies, 147
Mongolian race, 28
Montenegro, 200, 214
Montesquieu, 26
Morgenthau, Henry, 1, 6
Moscow, 84, 128
Moses, 19
mosques, 231; Serbian destruction of, 215, 220

Mosse, George L., 50
Muhammad, 19
mulatto, 23
Mumba, Judge Florence, 228
Murat, Sultan, 42
Museum of Modern Art (MOMA), 16–17
Muslimovic, Senad, 223–24
Muslims, 2, 3, 191, 195, 203, 238; Albanian, 196; and atrocities against Serbs, 198; Bosnian, 192, 202–4, 208, 210, 213, 217–18, 230, 232–33, 243, 249; Chams under the Khmer Rouge, 162, 165, 170–72; as ethnic category in Yugoslavia, 203; genocide of Bosnian and Kosovar Muslims, 192, 214–16, 222–23, 225, 252; migration of to Turkey, 202; and nationalism, 201–3; in the Ottoman Empire, 6; racialization by Serbian nationalists, 232; Serbian brutality against, 190, 194, 212–17, 219–20, 222–23, 226–29, 243; tracts against by the Church, 20; in the former Yugoslavia, 190; in Yugoslavia compared to Jews in Third Reich, 205, 243
muzhik, 56. See also peasants

Nagasaki, bombing of, 9
Naimark, Norman M., 257n.6, 306n.21
Napoleon, 35
naradnost' (people), 76
nation, the, 28–30, 44; and the concept of people, 28; as ethnic and racial community, 29–31, 45; Hitler's racialized definition of, 105; as political concept in France, 31, 45; Sieyes's definition of, 30; Stalin's definition of, 67; in terms of gendered citizenship, 29–31
National Assembly and Convention, the 30; French Revolution as model of, 146
nationalism, 44, 50; cultural, 49; democratic, 43; French version of, 146, 262n.54; and Hobbes, 26; and Khmer Rouge, 145–46; and indigenization, 76; Italian, 44; Khmer national struggle as class struggle, 174; N. Ia. Marr on language and culture as expression of national essence, 78; medieval attitudes

toward, 20; militant, 43; in nineteenth-century Europe, 203; racialized, 136, 232; secular, 43; Serbian, 43–44, 191–235; Turkish, 3
nationality, 22; as ambivalent vector of Soviet identity, 82–83; as basis of identity, 21; as basis for Soviet classifications, 54, 66; and categorization under the Khmer Rouge, 162, 164; and cultural Russification, 77; and definition of genocide, 9; diaspora nationalities in Soviet Union, 75–82; dual principle of nationality in Yugoslavia and Soviet Union, 207; and the establishment of Soviets, 76; Muslim as category of, 203; persecution in Soviet Union on basis of, 63–84, 89–90, 97–100; racialization of class and nationality by Khmer Rouge, 174–75; racially based understanding of in Soviet Union, 68, 83–84, 97–98; repression of ethnicities and nationalities by Khmer Rouge, 170–189; and Volkstum, 110; in the former Yugoslavia, 191–235
National Socialist German Workers Party (NSDAP), 105
nation-state, the, 2, 252; and democracy, 50; and ethnicity, 20–21; and Fichte and Herder, 31; Václav Havel's view on, 254; and Eric Hobsbawm, 28; and Mazzini, 44; its organizing capacities and genocide, 241
Native Americans, 9, 22–25; matrilineal culture among, 23
NATO: air strikes, 217, 219, 222
natsional'nost' (nationality), 76
natural selection, theory of, 36
nature: transcendent views of, 111
Nazi Germany, 1, 8, 10, 12, 13, 14, 48, 127; compared with CPK cadres of Khmer Rouge, 168, 183–84, 187; and complicity, 243–44; as genocidal regime, 12, 101, 132–33, 140–42; and population purges, 58–59, 103; and race thinking, 103, 132; as threat to Soviet Union, 77, 79, 97. See also Germany; Nazism

Nazism, 8, 12, 51–52, 63, 102, 112, 113, 148, 167, 174, 177, 243; as adoption of Soviet practices, 257n.7; and Aryanism, 34; and book burning, 139; and colonial empire, 240; compared and contrasted with Soviet system of classifying populations, 54, 65, 243; compared to Soviet utopia, 96, 99; compared with Soviet system of deportation and extermination, 86; comparison of with Serbian nationalism, 198, 200, 205, 213–14, 222, 232, 234, 243; comparison of with Soviet population purges, 140–41, 242–43; and comparison with Spanish Inquisition, 46; and definition of citizenship, 116; and the Führer State, 111–12; and *Gauleiter*, 244; and gender roles, 111; and the German body politic, 111, 113–14; hostility of to communism, 75; and invasion of Soviet Union, 124, 127–30; and invasion of Yugoslavia, 200; and Nuremberg Laws, 240; and population purges, 119–43, 246; and preoccupation with Jewish sexuality, 232; and propaganda about Jewish uncleanliness, 239; and race thinking, 104–11, 236; and a racialized social system, 132–33; and racial registries, 119–20; and racial utopia, 129, 135, 198, 243; as racial war, 113–15, 117, 250; and resettlement of ethnic Germans, 125–27; and social engineering, 126; and torture, 249; and use of radio and film, 245; and the vision of a society of domination and subordination, 109; and yellow Star of David, 120, 204
Nekrich, Aleksandr, 81, 90
neo-fascism, 11
New Economic Policy (NEP), 57, 65, 70, 158
Newton, Isaac, 43
New World, discoveries of, 20, 252
Nicholas II, Czar, 148
Njegoš, Petar Petrović, 42–44, 193–94; *The Mountain Wreath*, 42–43, 193–94
NKVD (Soviet secret police), 53, 66, 81, 86–88, 90, 248; comparison of to Gestapo, 91

nobles, Russian, 65
Nolte, Ernst, 11, 257n.7
Nordics, the, 26
Norodom Sihanouk, Prince, 146–48, 164, 181
North Carolina, 23; laws against intermarriage, 23
Nubians, the, 19
Nuon Chea, 183
Nuremberg Laws, 116–17, 240
Nuremberg War Crimes Tribunal, 253

Obilić, Miloš, 42
Ohlendorf, Otto, 136
Omarska, 190, 216, 223–24, 235, 249. *See also* concentration camps
Omdurman, Battle of, 46
Ong Thong Hoeung, 182
Ostrovsky, Nikolai: *How the Steel Was Tempered*, 99
Otto, King, 126
Ottomans, 3–5; and their army, 4, 6; and their defeat of Serbs, 42, 193; and their officials, 5–6; and their rulers, 6
Owen, Wilfrid, 51

Pale, 222, 234
Panić, Zivota, 212
parazity, 239
Paris: education of Khmer Rouge leaders in, 147; education of Serbian elite in, 194
Pasteur, Louis, 108
Pearl Harbor, 130
Pearson, Karl, 40–41, 49; "race culture," 40; "race suicide," 41
peasants, 56–57; and Cambodian communist abolition of private agriculture, 149–51; and categorization under the Khmer Rouge, 159–61; Khmer deportation of, 177; Khmer idealization of, 157; as obstacle to socialist future, 70, 236; purging of in Soviet Union, 70–72, 85, 90. See also *muzhik*
Persia, 27; travel accounts of, 27
Persians, 18

Peter the Great, 84
Petkovci School, 226–27
Petrograd, 148
phenotype, 21
Philippines, 248
Phnom Penh, 144, 148–50, 159–60, 165–66, 168–69, 171–72, 176–77, 179, 181, 184, 186, 191; Radio Phnom Penh, 149, 155, 174, 239
physiognomy, 26
Ploetz, Alfred, 41–42, 49
pogroms: against Armenians in Ottoman Empire, 6; against Jews in eastern Galicia, 128; against Jews in the Russian Empire, 4; against Vietnamese in Phnom Penh, 171; in the former Yugoslavia, 197
Poland, 125–26, 208, 240
Poles, 78, 83, 128, 240
Politburo, the, 73
Politika (Belgrade daily), 196
Pol Pot, 146–47, 149–50, 154–56, 161, 163–65, 168, 171, 173, 182–83, 185, 187, 239, 288n.2; "Brother Number One," 149, 163; "Monarchy or Democracy?" 147
Ponchaud, François, 156
Ponte, Carla del, 191
Potocari, 229
Prague, 139
Prijedor, 190, 204, 214
Proctor, Robert, 113
proletariat, the, 60–61, 238; and communist revolution, 104, 154; dictatorship of, 61, 153–54; and industrialization, 67; Soviet transformation of peasant into, 70
Psalms, 19
purges, of populations, 237, 239, 241–42, 252; under the Khmer Rouge, 153, 155, 158, 162–89; by Nazi Germany, 103, 108, 113, 115, 117–18, 121–43; in Soviet Union, 59, 62, 68–75, 78–79, 83–89, 94, 98, 101, 143, 252. See also deportation
purification: of populations, 238–39, 242. See also "cleansing"; purges

race, 9, 17, 24, 27, 35, 41, 46, 49; and anatomy, 41; and biology, 41; and Johann Friedrich Blumenbach, 28; as category of identity, 21; definition of and dangers of mixing, according to Alfred Ploetz, 41; and definition of genocide, 9; as entwined with land and language, 33, 49; etymology of word, 258n.4; and Arthur de Gobineau's theories of inequality, 34–35, 37–38; and Hitler's definition of the nation, 105, 108, 111, 243; and hygiene, 41, 238–39; ideology of in eighteenth-century France, 260n.27, 262n.60; and the ideology of race in the Soviet context, 97–98, 100; mixing as deterioration, according to Karl Pearson, 40; movements based on, 21–22; and naturalization of belonging, 22; and naturalization of conduct, 22; and Nazi policies, 103, 108, 111, 115, 117, 130, 132, 140–41, 236; as Nazi system of classification, 140; origins of the word, 17; and physiology, 41; racial registries under Nazism, 119–20; and racist regimes, 48; and science, 41; and sociology, 41; and Soviet rhetoric in World War II, 78; and Soviet system of classifying populations, 54, 63; as species, 49; theorists of, 49; and utopia under Nazism, 98–99, 109–10, 113, 129
race and nation: ideologies of, 15, 52, 237, 241, 251–54, 262n.59; as measure of human difference, 32; nationhood as racialized essence, 83, 98, 106, 115; under Nazism, 250; as primary categories of political and social organization in modern world, 2, 14, 16–17, 20, 21; in relation to ethnicity, 21–22; and Stalin's definitions of nationality, 67
race biology, 42, 50
race-culture, 40
race science, 41
race theorists, 36
race thinking, 38, 49, 50: according to Hannah Arendt, 266n.120; as advanced by secular society and Enlightenment thought, 47; under Khmer Rouge, 174;

race thinking (*cont.*)
in Nazi Germany, 103, 107–8, 114–15, 124, 132
race thinking, modern, 20, 22, 39, 252; emergence of with European explorations, 252; as hierarchical construction of difference, 21; and Hobbes, 26; and Montesquieu, 26
Racial-Hygienic and Heredity Research Center (RHA), 117–18, 131
racialization, 21, 23–24, 238; of Cossacks, 69; and the Khmer Rouge, 163, 174–75, 185, 188–89; of nationality by Serbs, 195, 232
rape: as degradation of the individual under Nazism, 179; of Muslim women, 220–22, 227–28, 232, 234; as signifying physical and psychological power of the master, 25; as social act, 228; and SS brothels of Slavic women, 247; as systematized part of Bosnian genocide, 232–35, 246, 303n.128; UN statistics on from Bosnian War, 230
Rassenschande (racial defilement), 138, 232, 240, 246
Ravensbrück, 132–34
Red Army, 61, 69, 71, 80, 90, 99, 225, 244, 274n.99
Reformation, the, 25
Reich Association of Non-Aryan Christians, 116
Reich Citizenship Law, 116
Reich Council for Productivity (*Reichskuratorium für Wirtschaftlichkeit*), 125
Reich Criminal Police Office, 118
Reich Health Office, 117, 122
Reich Ministry of the Interior, 122
Reich Office of Statistics, 117
religion: and definition of genocide, 9
Remarque, Erich Maria: *All Quiet on the Western Front,* 51
Revelations, 107
Revolution: American, 16, 28; Bolshevik, 57, 60–64, 194; Chinese Cultural, 147, 153, 182, 189; French, 16, 28–30, 36, 49, 61, 146–47, 252; Nazi, 155, 191; Russian, 57, 147, 191, 239, 241; Scientific, 49; Soviet, 155, 189; Yugoslav, 155
revolution: Bolsheviks and proletarian, 67, 104, 106; as civil war, 60–61, 90; democracy founded on, 146; and the discourse of cleansing, 239; and the Khmer Rouge, 145–46, 149, 152, 154–55, 162–65, 169–70, 177, 181–82, 187, 191; under Lenin, 62, 68; Nazism and racial, 106, 141; and political violence, 241, 251–52; revolutionary regimes, 242, 245, 247, 251; and Serbia, 191; under Stalin, 57, 62; theorization of, 304n.1; in post–World War I Europe, 63–64; World War I and glorification of, 110, 241
Rhodes, Cecil, 45
Ritter, Robert, 117–18
rituals: of confession, 250; of violence, 245–47, 251
Robespierre, 147
Rodrigues, Almiro, 222, 234
Roma, 65, 115, 117–18, 120–23, 128, 131–32, 134–35, 177, 197–98, 248–49. *See also* Sinti
Romanov dynasty, 75
romanticism, 32–33
Roosevelt, Eleanor, 16
Roosevelt, Theodore, 39; and "race suicide," 39
Rosenberg, Alfred, 117
Russia, 4; brutality of bureaucracy in, 83; and cultural Russification, 77; czarist, 70, 148; and defeat, 150; as ethnically defined, 207; Germans living in, 79; imperial, 58, 99; as modern nation, 55–56; as racialized nation, 77–78; reprisal of old estate system, 64. *See also* Soviet Union
Russian language, 57
Rwanda: genocide in, 13, 253
Rykov, A. I., 94

Saar, the, 126
Sachsenhausen, 122, 128. *See also* concentration camps; extermination camps
Saigon, 148

Saint Paul, 19
Salomon, Ernst von, 143
Santebel, 168
Sarajevo, 200, 210, 213, 217, 219; partitioning of, 215–16
Saxons, 33
Scandinavians, 26
Scarry, Elaine, 249
Schlegel, Friedrich, 33; *Concerning the Language and Wisdom of the Indians*, 33
Scott, James, 161, 241
Scythians, the, 18, 19
Selektionsmedizin, 110
Seng Horl, 176
Serbia, 44, 127–29, 190–92, 195–98, 207–14, 218, 220–21, 230–31, 235; break of with Bosnian and Krajinan Serbs, 219; evasion of UN arms embargo by, 218; Greater, 209, 211–12, 236, 245; and hyperinflation, 230; as nationally pure state, 243; leaders of, 243; as linked to revolutions ensuing after World War I, 241; and UN charges of genocide, 253; use of radio in, 246
Serbian Academy of Sciences, 195
Serbian Orthodox Church, 193, 197, 210
Serb Republic (Republika Serbska), 220
Serb Republic of Bosnia and Herzegovina, 213. *See also* Bosnian Serbs: republic of
Serbs, 3, 42–43, 174, 190–92, 196, 199–235, 238, 244, 246, 250; Bosnian, 207, 213, 218–19, 225, 229, 231; Croatian, 210, 213, 234; and discourse of ethnic cleansing, 239; and educational elite, 194; and nationalism, 191–236, 238, 241; population purges by, 59, 190–91, 194, 212–35, 243; subjected to ethnic cleansing by Croatians, 219; war strategies of compared to Nazis, 213–14, 232, 234; and use of torture in camps, 249
seredniak (middle peasants), 65
Seth Pich Chnay, 176
Sewall, Jr., William H., 30
Shakespeare, William, 209

Shalamov, Varlam, 87, 251; *Kolyma Tales*, 87
Shoup, Paul, S., 216, 220, 230
Siberia, 129
Sidorov, Vassili Klementovich, 53–54
Sieyes, Abbé, 30; *What Is the Third Estate?*, 30
Silber, Laura, 197, 211, 216
Silesia, 134
Sinti, 65, 115, 117–18, 120–23, 128, 131–32, 134–35, 177, 197–98, 248–49. *See also* Roma
Sisowath, Lycée, 181
slaveholders, North American, 20; and their depictions of Africans, 20
slavery, 20, 22, 29; and the American Constitution, 29; in colonial societies, 20, 22; in the Congo, 45; in the New World, 25, 32, 48, 252, 260n.31, 261n.27; racial, 22, 24–25; as social death, 25
Slavonia, 200, 212; deportation of Serbs from, 219
Sliwinski, Marek, 186
Slovenes, 191, 195–96, 209; and nationalism, 201–2, 208, 210
Slovenia, 192, 200–201, 204, 208; and independence, 209, 211; recognized by EC, 213
Sobibor, 131. *See also* concentration camps; extermination camps
social contract, the, 30
socialism: and Bolshevik utopia, 54–56, 60, 63, 80; and Democratic Kampuchea, 158; and the destiny of Yugoslavia, 196; final victory of, 74, 76; and ideology of nineteenth-century Europe, 157; and modernity, 56; and the nationalities principle, 77–78; policies of exclusion under, 83, 98; socialist culture, 67, 70; and state violence, 62. *See also* communism
Socialist Party of Serbia (SPS), 200
Solzhenitsyn, Aleksandr, 66, 90; *The Gulag Archipelago,* 89
Someth May, 144, 165
Sonderaktion, 102–3. *See also* gas, extermination by

Song of Roland, 20
Son Sen 147, 154, 183
South Africa, 48
Southeast Asia; communism in, 10; invasion of, 148; people of, 146–47
South Sea Islands, 27; travel accounts of, 27
South Slavs, 202, 238; and their lands, 232, 238, 243, 297n.7
South Tyrol, 126
Soviet Union, 1, 10–11, 63, 114, 141, 145, 151, 153, 167, 174–75, 199, 204–5, 238, 241–42, 249; and classification of nationalities, 54, 64–67, 115, 159, 243; compared with genocidal actions of Khmer Rouge, 183–84, 187; compared with population purges under Nazism, 140–41; compared with Serbian regime, 214, 220, 222, 225; Congress of Outstanding Kolkhozniks, 91; and cultural Russification, 77; and denunciation, 91–92; and destruction of private peasant agriculture, 70–72, 85, 90, 150; as federation of nationalities, 75–77, 82–83, 175, 207; and gender equality, 143; and the Great Terror, 59, 61, 72–75, 79, 82, 86, 92, 95, 163; and idealization of peasants, 237–38; as industrialized power, 74; invasion of by Germany, 124, 127–29, 136, 252; as "Jewish Empire," 108; leaders of, 243; under Lenin and Stalin, 8, 10, 14; and mass peasant deportations, 71, 179, 225; and party factionalism, 70; and population purges, 59, 62, 68–75, 78–79, 83–89, 94, 99–101, 126, 143, 158, 171, 243, 252, 272n.75; and racial politics, 97–101, 141; role of in Genocide Convention, 9; as utopia, 55–60, 96, 99; and Roma and Sinti, 131; and social engineering, 126; Stalinist purging of Bolshevik generation, 143; as supported by French Communist Party, 147; and transformation of the social structure, 236; and treatment of homeland of Chechens and Tatars, 220, 222; and use of radio and film, 245
Spanish Inquisition, 46

Spencer, Herbert, 36–37
Srebenica, 194, 216–18, 225–26, 229, 232, 234–35
Srebenica Syndrome, 229
SS, 102, 107, 111, 117, 122, 127–29, 134–36, 139, 141–42, 240, 242–43, 247
Stakhanovite, 91
Stalin, Joseph, 1, 62, 88, 91–92, 97, 99, 145–46, 150, 279n.37; attack of on Jews, 82; and Bolshevism, 62; and his control over the party, 70; and cultural Russification, 77; death of, 64; definition of the nation by, 67, 83; and establishment of criteria for nationality, 67; *Foundations of Leninism*, 146; and the Great Terror, 72–75; *Marxism and the National Question*, 67, 83, 147; as non-Russian, 98; and his penchant for biological metaphors, 62; purges under, 69, 101, 183–84; and show trials, 93, 182; and social engineering, 96; and socialist utopia, 56–58; and torture, 183; and transformation of peasant into proletarian, 70–71
Stambolić, Ivan, 192, 209
Standing Committee of the CPK Central Committee, 154
Stanislau, 128
Steichen, Edward, 16–17. *See also* Museum of Modern Art
sterilization, forced, 118, 122, 124, 126, 132, 140, 265n.103, 282n.91
Storm Troopers, 134, 191
Sudan, the: Winston Churchill in, 46
sultans, 2, 3, 193, 240
Suong Sikoeun, 147
"survival of the fittest," 36, 49. *See also* Spencer, Herbert
Svang Rieng, 177
Syclas, King, 19
Syria, 1, 5

Tabakdämmerung, 114
Ta Mok, 147
Tatars, Crimean, 79–81, 86, 90–91, 96, 98–100, 150, 175, 243, 248, 250

Terror, the Great, 59, 61, 72–75, 79, 82, 92, 95, 163, 269n.30
Teutons, 38; Italians of Renaissance as, 38; and revival of Hellenistic and Roman culture, 38
Thai, 162, 171
Theresienstadt, 140
Third Reich, 11, 101–3, 106, 110, 112–5, 119, 132–34, 141–43, 236, 252; compared with Khmer Rouge, 159; compared with Serbia under Milošević, 231; compared with Soviet regime, 91, 98; complicity with, 242. See also Nazi Germany
Thousand Year Reich, 109, 236. See also Third Reich
Tito, Josip Broz, 197, 207, 233, 243; and the founding of Yugoslavia, 191, 195
Tocqueville, Alexis de, 35
Tokyo War Crime Tribunal, 253
Tomsky, M. P., 94
torture, 246, 249–50, 308nn.43 and 46; and Khmer Rouge, 179–85, 247, 249–50, 308n.35; under Nazism, 249–50, 307n.32; by Serbian forces, 211, 223–24, 249–50
Treblinka, 131, 137. See also concentration camps; extermination camps
Trieste, 200–201
troika, 53
Trotsky, Lev, 61–62, 104
Trotskyites, 74
Tudjman, Franjo, 198, 208–10, 219, 231–33
Tuol Sleng, 163, 168–69, 181, 183–84, 249–50, 308n.35
Turkey, 3, 202; pan-Turkish state, 3–4
Turkic peoples, 3
Turkmenistan, 79
Turks, 6, 42, 209; Martin Luther's sermons about, 20; Ottoman defeat of Serbia, 193; Soviet deportation of, 82; under Treaty of Lausanne, 51. See also Young Turks
Turner, Harald, 127
Tuzla, 215

Ukraine, the, 58, 78–79, 82, 126, 128. See also Volga Republic
Ukrainians, 127
Umsiedler, 126. See also Germans
uniqueness, of Holocaust, 12
United Nations: and codification of the term "genocide," 8; General Assembly of, 16; and Genocide Convention, 8–10, 12, 170, 233; Human Rights Commission, 230; and as party to ethnic cleansing, 218; proclaimed "safe areas" in Bosnia, 217–18; Protection Force (UNPROFOR), 217–19; and sanctions imposed on Serbian economy, 218–19; Security Council, 190, 218, 253; and Universal Declaration of Human Rights, 16–17, 253–54
United States: ambivalent government knowledge of and military intervention in Yugoslavia, 210, 216–19; and bombing of Hiroshima and Nagasaki, 9; in Cambodia, 147–48, 166; Central Intelligence Agency (CIA), 229–30; émigré Serbs in, 209; German declaration of war on, 130; and imperialism, 45; in Southeast Asia, 146; and supposed designs on Yugoslav territory, 195; and trade relations with Yugoslavia, 206
Ustaše, 195–196, 210 See also Croatia: Independent State of
utopia, 254; and Bolshevism, 54–57, 60, 63, 80; communism as inclusive utopia, 109; as dependent upon mass deportation of alien groups, 59; and the Khmer Rouge, 151, 157–58, 173; and Nazism, 98–99, 109–10, 113, 129–30, 135; and revolutionary regimes, 14–15, 63, 237; and Serbian nationalism, 197–98, 230; socialist, 54–60, 96, 98–99, 109–10; under Stalinism, 57
Uzbekistan, 79, 81

Vareš, 215
Versailles, Treaty of, 253
Verschuer, Otmar von, 142
Vienna: education of Serbian elite in, 194; Hitler in, 104–5

Vietnam, 166, 171, 173–75, 187; and communism, 146, 152, 165; North, 148, 152, 171–72; South, 148, 152, 171; war in, 147, 171
Vietnamese, 144–45, 162–65, 170–75, 186, 188–89, 238, 243
violence: systematic, 63
Virginia, 23; and laws against intermarriage, 23
Vive Žene, 229
Vlasenica, 229
Vojvodina, 200, 207, 210
Volga Republic, 79
Volk, the, 33, 35; state as ultimate expression of, 33
Volksgemeinschaft, 110–11
Volkstum, 110
Vossische Zeitung, 134
vrediteli, 239
Vukovar, 200, 212
Vyshinsky, A. Ia., 73

Waffen-SS, 99, 102, 104, 106. See also SS
Wagner, Richard, 37
Wannsee Conference,131
Weber, Max, 22; and his definition of an ethnic group, 22
Wehrmacht, 113, 127, 130, 134, 136, 141
Weimar Republic, 103, 143
welfare state, the, 44; pioneered in Germany and Great Britain, 44
Werth, Nicholas, 61, 82, 99
Westerborg, 140
White Army, 61, 84
Wilson, Woodrow, 51
World Bank, 206, 230
World War I, 10, 50–52, 63; and the aesthetics of monumentality, 246; and a culture of death and killing, 241, 252; and emergence of Soviet regime, 240; and ensuing escalation of genocides, 51–52, 241; German veterans of, 114; Germany's defeat in, 105; and glorification of male combat and revolution, 110, 143; and Lenin, 60–61; Nazism as product of, 110, 240; and racialization of the enemy, 50; racism and antisemitism in Europe prior to, 106; status of Ottoman Empire in, 1–4; and state organization of society, 242
World War II: and antisemitism in Nazi Germany, 109; and the beginning of social engineering, 126; and decolonization, 145; and founding of Yugoslavia under Tito, 195; and internment of Japanese Americans, 98; as racial war between Slavs and Germans, 78
Wright-Patterson Air Force Base, 219

Yezhov, N. I., 88
Young Turks, 2–6, 240; and the Interior and War Ministries, 6
Yugoslav People's Army (JNA), 199–200, 207–14, 216–18, 221, 233–35
Yugoslavia, 8, 11–14, 190–91, 195, 199–205, 209, 211, 230–31, 233–34, 253; as blending nation-state and multinationality, 241; as creation of both world wars, 241; dissolution of, 209–12, 235; and dual principle of nationality, 207; as federation of republics, 206–8, 229; as model of prosperity in Eastern Europe, 206; and population purges, 58–59, 191; rump, 213, 219

Zadar, 200
Zagreb, 203, 211
Žepa, 217, 229
Zinovievites, 74
Zinoviev-Kamenev trial, 73